Abraham in History and Tradition

Abraham in History and Tradition

John Van Seters

Yale University Press
New Haven and London

Published with assistance from the foundation
established in memory of Rutherford Trowbridge.

Copyright © 1975 by Yale University.
All rights reserved.
This book may not be reproduced, in whole or in part,
in any form (beyond that copying permitted by Sections
107 and 108 of the U.S. Copyright Law and except by
reviewers for the public press), without written
permission from the publishers.

Library of Congress catalog card number: 74–20087
International standard book numbers: 0–300–01792–8 (cloth)
                                       0–300–04040–7 (pbk.)

Designed by John O. C. McCrillis
and set in Baskerville type.
Printed in the United States of America by
The Murray Printing Co., Westford, Massachusetts.

*The paper in this book meets the guidelines for
permanence and durability of the Committee on
Production Guidelines for Book Longevity of the
Council on Library Resources.*

10   9   8   7   6   5   4   3   2

To
Frederick Victor Winnett

Contents

Preface	ix
Abbreviations	xi
Introduction	1
PART I: Abraham in History	5
1. The Age of the Patriarchs	7
2. The Nomadism of the Patriarchs	13
3. Personal Names, Peoples, and Places	39
4. The Social Customs of the Patriarchs	65
5. Archaeology and the Patriarchs	104
PART II: Abraham in Tradition	123
6. Method I: A Critique	125
7. Method II: Some Guidelines	154
8. The Problem of the Beautiful Wife	167
9. The Birth of Ishmael and Isaac	192
10. The Lot-Sodom Tradition	209
11. Abraham and Isaac	227
12. The Covenant of Abraham: Genesis 15	249
13. The Priestly Traditions of Abraham	279
14. Victory over the Kings of the East	296
15. Conclusions	309
Appendix	313
Index	315

Preface

The subject of the patriarchs of ancient Israel has had a great deal of attention for many years, not only among scholars but also in the popular press. The continuous volume of archaeological discoveries from the ancient Near East has fostered many efforts to reconstruct the life and times of the forefather Abraham. In 1966 my colleague Professor Norman Wagner of Waterloo Lutheran University (now Wilfrid Laurier University), encouraged me to undertake a critical review of the "archaeological" evidence which was being used in such presentations. Two articles arising out of this study were subsequently published: "The Problem of Childlessness in Near Eastern Law and the Patriarchs of Israel," *JBL* 87 (1968): 401–8, and "Jacob's Marriages and Ancient Near Eastern Customs: A Reexamination," *HTR* 62 (1969): 377–95. These studies, pertaining to family customs in the patriarchal stories, were part of a much broader study then in preparation which was intended to deal with all the alleged parallels from the early- and mid-second millennium B.C. (see *JBL* 87:n.6).

But the promised review of this comparative data was delayed by another consideration already expressed in my first article (p. 408). This was the concern that any serious question about the antiquity of the tradition in terms of biblical chronology also had very important implications for elucidating the history of the tradition and for explaining its present form and function or intention in Israelite society. It is one thing to criticize the misuse of parallels in dating the patriarchal stories, but quite another to try to reconstruct their literary and ideological development. This latter question about the history of the tradition has long been the preoccupation of German biblical scholars, but their general assumption about the tradition's antiquity and basis in oral tradition caused me some misgivings about their approach as well. Consequently I made an investigation into both aspects of the Abraham tradition: the question of its antiquity, and the history of its formation.

During a half-term academic leave spent at Yale University in the winter and spring of 1973, I had the opportunity to write the present manuscript. I wish to thank the Department of Near Eastern Studies of the Yale Graduate School and members of the faculty of the Yale Divinity School for their warm hospitality. Special thanks are due to William W. Hallo, curator of the Babylonian Collection in the Sterling Library and to Stephen Peterson, Librarian, and his staff in the Yale Divinity School Library for their assistance during my work at Yale. I am also grateful to the Canada Council for a research grant to cover expenses during this period of leave.

Since the completion of this manuscript in July 1973 other articles and books related to the subject of this work have continued to appear, and I have made minor revisions to include some of them. However, there is one book which has just now appeared, Thomas L. Thompson's *The Historicity of the Patriarchal Narratives: The Quest for the Historical Abraham* (*BZAW* 133, 1974), which calls for special comment. This book represents a considerable overlap of the subject matter contained in Part One of my book and independently comes to many of the same conclusions regarding the antiquity of the patriarchal traditions. Since I myself have been publicly calling for such a reexamination since 1968 it is not surprising that one should finally appear, and I gladly welcome this support. Nevertheless, there are still so many differences in perspective and in details that I have not attempted to revise my own work to include any discussion of Thompson's. My own manuscript stands as an independent review of the data relevant to the question of the "historicity" of the Abraham tradition and then seeks, in Part Two, to carry forward the implications of this into a study of the tradition's formation.

I wish to express my appreciation to Yale University Press for their patience and interest in this work since it was first suggested to them several years ago. Jane Isay of the Press has been especially helpful in seeing it through the various stages of preparation. And a great deal of credit must go to my wife for the preparation of the typed manuscript and for assistance in many of the mundane tasks associated with publication.

This book is dedicated to Professor Frederick Victor Winnett, former teacher and now colleague and friend. In his presidential address to the Society of Biblical Literature in December 1964 he called for a "reexamining of the foundations" of pentateuchal criticism. The present volume is hereby offered, ten years later, as my response to that appeal.

June 1974   JOHN VAN SETERS

Abbreviations

AASOR	*Annual of the American Schools of Oriental Research.*
AHw	W. von Soden, *Akkadisches Handwörterbuch*, Wiesbaden, O. Harrassowitz, 1965–.
AJSL	*American Journal of Semitic Languages and Literatures.*
ANET	J. B. Pritchard, ed., *Ancient Near Eastern Texts Relating to the Old Testament*, 3rd. ed., Princeton, Princeton University Press, 1969.
AOAT	Alter Orient und Altes Testament.
AOTS	D. W. Thomas, ed., *Archaeology and Old Testament Study*, Oxford, Clarendon Press, 1967.
BA	*The Biblical Archaeologist.*
BAR	*The Biblical Archaeologist Reader*, vol. 2, D. N. Freedman and E. F. Campbell, eds., Garden City, Anchor Books, 1964.
BASOR	*Bulletin of the American Schools of Oriental Research.*
BBB	Bonner Biblische Beiträge.
BH	Biblia Hebraica Stuttgartensia.
Bi Or	*Bibliotheca Orientalis.*
BJRL	*Bulletin of the John Rylands Library.*
BR	*Biblical Research.*
BWANT	Beiträge zur Wissenschaft vom Alten und Neuen Testament.
BZ	*Biblische Zeitschrift.*
BZAW	*Beihefte zur Zeitschrift für die Alttestamentliche Wissenschaft.*
CA	*Current Anthropology.*
CAD	*The Assyrian Dictionary of the Oriental Institute of the University of Chicago*, ed. A. H. Oppenheim et al., Chicago, 1964—.
CAH	*The Cambridge Ancient History*, rev. ed., vols. 1 and 2, Cambridge, Cambridge University Press, issued in separate fascicles, 1961–70; 3rd. ed. 1973–.
CBQ	*Catholic Biblical Quarterly.*
CH	The Code of Hammurapi.

DBS	*Dictionnaire de la Bible, Supplément*, ed. I. Pirot, A. Robert, H. Cazelles, and A. Feuillet, Paris, Letouzey and Ané, 1928–.
DMAL	G. R. Driver and J. C. Miles, *The Assyrian Laws*, Oxford, Clarendon Press, 1935.
DMBL	G. R. Driver and J. C. Miles, *The Babylonian Laws*, 2 vols., Oxford, Clarendon Press, 1952–55.
EB	Early Bronze Age.
Encyc. Jud.	*Encyclopaedia Judaica*, ed. Cecil Roth, 16 vols., New York, Macmillan, 1971–72.
Ex. Times	*Expository Times.*
FRLANT	*Forschungen zur Religion und Literatur des Alten und Neuen Testament.*
HTR	*Harvard Theological Review.*
HUCA	*Hebrew Union College Annual.*
IDB	*The Interpreter's Dictionary of the Bible*, ed. G. A. Buttrick, 4 vols., New York, Abingdon Press, 1962.
IEJ	*Israel Exploration Journal.*
JAOS	*Journal of the American Oriental Society.*
JBL	*Journal of Biblical Literature.*
JCS	*Journal of Cuneiform Studies.*
JEA	*Journal of Egyptian Archaeology.*
JEOL	*Jaarbericht van het Vooraziatisch-Egyptisch Genootschap Ex Oriente Lux.*
JJP	*Journal of Juristic Papyrology.*
JNES	*Journal of Near Eastern Studies.*
JSOR	*Journal of the Society of Oriental Research.*
JSS	*Journal of Semitic Studies.*
LB	Late Bronze Age.
M-AL	Middle-Assyrian Laws.
MB	Middle Bronze Age.
MDIK	*Mitteilungen des deutschen Instituts für ägyptische Altertumskunde In Kairo.*
MDOG	*Mitteilungen des deutschen Orientgesellschaft.*
MVÄG	*Mitteilungen der Vorderasiatisch-Ägyptischen Gesellschaft.*
OB	Old Babylonian.
OTS	*Oudtestamentische Studiën.*
RA	*Revue d'Assyriologie et d'archéologie orientale.*
RB	*Revue biblique.*

SBS	Stuttgarter Bibelstudien.
SBT	Studies in Biblical Theology.
SG	*Studium Generale.*
SVT	*Supplements to Vetus Testamentum.*
TB	Theologische Bücherei.
TLA	*Theologische Literaturzeitung.*
TLZ	*Theologische Zeitschrift.*
VT	*Vetus Testamentum.*
YOS	Yale Oriental Series.
ZA	*Zeitschrift für Assyriologie und verwandte Gebiete.*
ZAW	*Zeitschrift für die Alttestamentliche Wissenschaft.*
ZDMG	*Zeitschrift der deutschen morgenländischen Gesellschaft.*
ZDPV	*Zeitschrift des deutschen Palästina-Vereins.*
ZKTh	*Zeitschrift für Katholische Theologie.*
ZTK	*Zeitschrift für Theologie und Kirche.*

Introduction

While the biblical tradition of Abraham is relatively short, comprising only a few chapters in Genesis (12–25) and brief allusions in only a few other places in the Old Testament, the discussion surrounding it has grown to very great proportions. This has now rendered it difficult to encompass in a single volume both a critical evaluation of the study of this tradition and a new detailed textual examination of the tradition itself. The present study is therefore offered as a prolegomenon to a history and exposition of the Abraham tradition.

The issues involved in such a task may be set out as a series of problems that will serve as a guide to the pursuit of our investigation. A basic problem is the antiquity of the tradition or any part of it. A great deal of attention has been given to this question in the interest of Hebrew origins, often to the exclusion of other considerations regarding the tradition's form and development. On the other hand, where the concern has been on the literary or preliterary history of the tradition, there is always a necessary presupposition about the tradition's antiquity or historical setting which plays a major role in the conclusions reached by such a work. Since any study of the biblical form and growth of the Abraham tradition cannot escape the prior question of dating the stories involved, a review of the arguments having to do with dating must be the first task of this book.

The problem of dating the tradition is complex, and a one-sided approach could be quite misleading. There is the matter, on the one hand, of dating the written form of the tradition and, on the other, of deciding on the antiquity of the tradition elements behind the written form. The fact that the question is put in this way means that two levels of data are regularly discussed: those which are regarded as the oldest and as reflecting the preliterary level of the tradition, and those which are related to the tradition's literary formation and to the concern of the writer or writers. Of course this cannot be reduced to an exercise in merely designating a number of late elements as anachronisms introduced into what is otherwise regarded as an ancient tradition. Literary judgments can help us discern the extent to which such late references are an integral part of the unit as a whole. So any effort at dating the tradition cannot be entirely independent from a close literary examination of the tradition as well.

The kinds of data relevant to the problem of dating the Abraham tradition are also complex. One type of evidence pertains to references in the stories to names of peoples and places, social customs, and economies, which may be set against the broader Near Eastern historical and cultural background of the second and first millennia B.C. It is this type of data which has attracted the most attention for dating the patriarchal traditions, and it can be dealt with, at least in a preliminary way, prior to any discussion about the literary formation of the tradition. I have endeavored to give an extensive review of the very numerous and detailed arguments related to this kind of data at the beginning of this study before I discuss the literary form of the tradition.

The results from this type of evidence for dating are not very conclusive in dealing with either the preliterary or literary levels of the Abraham tradition. However, this is not the only type of data used in fixing the tradition's historical background. Many scholars have put much weight on the question of the tradition's form. A distinction is made between the degree to which the tradition reflects an oral form originating in a preliterate stage of Israelite society with certain social functions in that setting, and the literate form of the later historical periods, representing the more special concerns of the author. In the latter case the data important for dating actually arise through a literary and form-critical analysis of the tradition itself and cannot, therefore, be dealt with prior to, or independent of, such a study. Consequently evidence for dating the tradition will be a by-product of literary criticism of the tradition, which is the major concern of the second part of this study.

Still a third type of data for dating the Abraham tradition is its reflection of particular stages in Israel's self-understanding as a people and the development of its social and religious consciousness and concerns. These data are probably the most elusive and can only be discussed after the antiquity or lateness of the various tradition elements has been established and after the general literary character of the tradition has become quite clear. Of primary importance here will be the comparison of the Abraham tradition with the perspectives of other biblical materials, such as the prophetic books and the Deuteronomic corpus, which have a greater degree of certainty as to their dating and their relationship to Israelite history.

It should not be assumed from these remarks that dating the Abraham tradition is the only, or even most important, concern of this study. The fact that so much attention must be given to it is a reflection of discussion on this part of the Bible in the last few decades. The dating of the tradition is only preliminary to an understanding of the nature and function or intention of the tradition, which is the real objective of this investigation. The most direct approach to this objective is a literary study with a scope broad enough to include the consideration of any possible preliterary form of the tradition as well. This will involve, first, an extensive review of literary method as it relates to the study of the Pentateuch in general and to the patriarchal narratives in particular. I do not entirely agree with the ways in which the methods of literary criticism, form criticism, and tradition history have been developed since the time of Wellhausen. Consequently, it cannot simply be a matter of applying given methods to a certain block of literature. The literary study is itself intended to be an attempt at developing a new methodology in the course of analyzing the material. Thus the two primary foci of this literary examination will be the form and development of the tradition, on the one hand, and the function or intention of the tradition in its historical and sociological context, on the other.

It is fair to ask whether, by limiting this study to the Abraham tradition, I can actually do what I have set out to do. It may be argued that these biblical chapters are not a completely self-contained unit of tradition and that many historical and literary questions go beyond these limits to include the other patriarchal narratives and even the rest of the Pentateuch. At some points I have felt the weight of this argument and made allowance for it. Thus, for instance, on the questions of dating I have considered arguments having to do with the patriarchal narratives as a whole. On the literary side I have also included the story of Isaac in Gen. 26, since it has so many close parallels with the Abraham tradition. But a further extension to include the Jacob stories in a literary analysis would make this study far too cumbersome.

There is also the opposite danger of selecting narrower limits, such as concentrating on a particular unit within the Abraham tradition. But this does not allow for any significant review of the literary method or comparison of variety of forms and sources within the tradition as a whole. This present study seeks to raise more basic questions about the present method of evaluating the traditions about early Israel. The Abraham tradition is a most suitable unit for this purpose. It contains, in a reasonably short compass, a variety of literary phenomena, such as the frequent presence of doublets, different types of literary genre and important thematic passages, all of which make it crucial for the development of any literary criticism for the Pentateuch as a whole.

To summarize: the study will review, in Part One, the nonliterary arguments for the dating of the patriarchal narratives. It will then proceed, in Part Two, to a literary analysis of the Abraham tradition in Genesis, giving particular attention to the question of the development of its literary form and, if any, its preliterary antecedents. It will also be concerned with the use of the Abraham tradition in various social and historical contexts corresponding to the evidence for dating and to its relationship to other parts of the biblical tradition.

PART I

Abraham in History

CHAPTER 1

The Age of the Patriarchs

The first question that must be dealt with in any study of the patriarchal traditions is that of the historical milieu out of which they arose. Now it may be disconcerting to many students of the Bible that this issue should be resurrected once again, for it was apparently settled by the last generation of Biblical scholars who dominated the field of Near Eastern studies.[1] In fact so broad had the general consensus about a patriarchal age in the second millennium B.C. become, that it is found in virtually every basic history and introduction in the Old Testament field. Reference to Mari or Nuzi hardly needs any explanation; their existence and significance are now common knowledge among Near Eastern scholars.

The securing of a historical background for the patriarchs in the second millennium B.C. was considered a hard-won gain against the older criticism such as that expressed by Wellhausen, who concluded that the patriarchal age only reflected the times of the later writers and not an older period in Israel's history.[2] This sentiment is very well expressed by W. F. Albright:

> Until recently it was the fashion among biblical historians to treat the patriarchal sagas of Genesis as though they were artificial creations of Israelite scribes of the Divided Monarchy or tales told by imaginative rhapsodists around Israelite campfires during the centuries following their occupation of the country. Eminent names among scholars can be cited for regarding every item of Gen. 11–50 as reflecting late invention, or at least retrojection of events and conditions under the Monarchy into the remote past, about which nothing was thought to have been really known to the writers of later days.

1. A bibliographical note appears at the end of this chapter.
2. J. Wellhausen, *Prolegomena to the History of Ancient Israel* (New York: World Publishing Co., Meridian Books, 1957), pp. 318–19.

The archaeological discoveries of the past generation have changed all this. Aside from a few die-hards among older scholars, there is scarcely a single biblical historian who has not been impressed by the rapid accumulation of data supporting the substantial historicity of patriarchal tradition.[3]

The archaeological discoveries, mentioned by Albright, have included not only the exploration of ancient sites in Palestine but also the opening up of the rich cities of Mesopotamia, North Syria and Anatolia: Ur, Babylon, Nuzi, Mari, Alalaḫ, Ugarit, and Hattusas (Bogazkoi). Their archives have yielded knowledge of second millennium history throughout the Levant as well as the names of persons, peoples, and places. Law codes were found, along with private legal and economic documents and personal and state correspondence, which gave a cross section of the social customs and mores of the times. Against this background, comparisons with the patriarchal narratives were made, and claims were established about the context of these stories in the second millennium B.C. The confidence inspired by these discoveries is very well reflected in a remark made by G. Ernest Wright:

> We shall probably never be able to prove that Abram really existed, that he did this or that, said thus and so, but what we can prove is that his life and times, as reflected in the stories about him, fit perfectly within the early second milliennium, but imperfectly within any later period. This is an exceedingly important conclusion, one of the most important contributions which archaeology has made to Old Testament study during the last four decades.[4]

However, cracks have begun to appear in this imposing edifice which indicate that the foundations may not be so secure after all. Firstly there has been little movement in the last fifty years towards agreement on when, within the second millennium, the patriarchs actually lived. Albright and Glueck have defended a date of MB I at the turn of the third to second millennium.[5] Many others, such

---

3. *The Biblical Period* (Pittsburgh: The Biblical Colloquium, 1950), p. 3.
4. *Biblical Archaeology*, p. 40.
5. W. F. Albright, "Abram the Hebrew: A New Archaeological Interpretation," *BASOR* 163 (October 1961): 36–54; N. Glueck, "The Age of Abraham in the Negeb," *BA* 18 (1955): 2–9; idem, *Rivers in the Desert*, ch. 3.

as Wright and Bright, prefer the MB II, or Old Babylonian period (around the nineteenth to seventeenth centuries B.C.).[6] Still others, such as Cyrus Gordon, have urged the Late Bronze-Amarna Age.[7] In Germany the tendency is to speak only in general terms of an early settlement period.[8] This range of opinion represents at least an eight-hundred-year spread, but if the dating of the patriarchal age cannot be fixed more precisely than this, then it has scarcely been established at all.

Secondly the approach to the patriarchal traditions which is most prominent in German scholarship is to emphasize the nomadic character of Israelite origins.[9] Parallels are drawn to nomadic customs and sociological phenomena, and all nomadic elements of Israelite culture are traced back to their nonsedentary beginnings. This approach actually represents much less of a break with older scholarship which always had a certain interest in nomadic origins.[10] Nevertheless, recent German scholarship places a substantial number of the patriarchal traditions in the prehistorical nomadic and early settlement phase of Israel's history because of its criterion of nomadism. In contrast to this approach, most of the comparisons made with the patriarchal stories by American scholars are largely based on sources which represent settled agricultural communities and city life. If such parallels from sedentary life are admissible, and German scholars appear to admit their validity,[11] then the nomadic criterion would seem to have little value for establishing what is primitive in Israelite life. If, on the other hand, one is convinced that Israel was originally nomadic, then the Genesis stories which reflect manners of the settled life must reflect this viewpoint after Israel itself became completely sedentary in spite of the dating of the parallels. But one cannot have it both ways. The contradiction of illustrating the patriarchal nomadic origins by non-nomadic parallels must be resolved. It is at this point that the two approaches of

6. Wright, *Biblical Archaeology*, pp. 40–52; Bright, *History of Israel*, pp. 69–78.
7. *Old Testament Times*, pp. 100–119.
8. Noth, *History of Israel*, pp. 121–27; Eissfeldt, *CAH*², pp. 10–17.
9. See esp. A. Alt, *Der Gott der Väter* BWANT 111/12 (1929), translated by R. A. Wilson as "The God of the Fathers," in *Essays on Old Testament History and Religion* (Oxford: Blackwell, 1966), pp. 1–77; see also G. Fohrer, *Introduction to the Old Testament* (New York and Nashville: Abingdon Press, 1968), pp. 121–26.
10. See W. Robertson Smith, Lectures on *the Religion of the Semites* (Edinburgh, 1889).
11. See Fohrer, *Introduction*, pp. 121–24.

American and German scholarship on the patriarchs have never really been resolved.[12]

Thirdly there is a weakness in the way in which the comparisons have been made. So strong is the prejudice for an early date that no serious consideration is given to material outside of this period. Sometimes it is even systematically excluded.[13] Only in a few instances have some of the parallels now begun to be questioned on the basis of materials dating to a later period. Ironically most of these latter materials have been available for a long time, yet it is more usual to find an appeal to a particular Nuzi, Mari, or Alalaḫ text as the all-important parallel without any perspective on the history of such customs over an extended period of time. How can the claim be repeatedly made that the customs in the patriarchal stories reflect *only* the "early or mid-second millennium" unless it is shown that they were no longer current at a late date? While there has been a great deal of interest in the social and legal history of the second millennium which has produced numerous studies on many different facets of society, nothing comparable exists for the first millennium. The obvious prejudice for the second millennium, created largely by the mood in biblical studies, has resulted in very meager treatment of the first millennium materials. This is also reflected in the standard reference work for Old Testament students, J. B. Pritchard's *Ancient Near Eastern Texts*,[14] in which there is scarcely anything at all in the area of social and legal documents from the later periods. Such a one-sided treatment of parallels by scholars dealing with the patriarchal stories does not inspire confidence in existing studies and more closely resembles an apologetic than a scholarly investigation.[15]

The task before us in this first part of the study is clear. It involves reviewing all the various kinds of arguments used to support the notion of a patriarchal age. In examining these arguments I will try

---

12. Some attempt at a mediating position is made by deVaux, *Histoire*, pp. 9, 172–79, who for this reason plays down the importance of social customs (see pp. 230–43).

13. Note the statement by J. M. Holt, *The Patriarchs of Israel* (Nashville: Vanderbilt University Press, 1964), pp. 25ff., on the limits of his investigation.

14. J. B. Pritchard, ed., *Ancient Near Eastern Texts Relating to the Old Testament*, 2nd ed. (Princeton: Princeton University Press, 1955); idem, *Supplementary Texts and Pictures Relating to the Old Testament* (Princeton: Princeton University Press, 1969).

15. A rather strong attack on this apologetic approach was made by Morton Smith, "The Present State of Old Testament Studies," *JBL* 88 (1969): 19–35.

to illustrate the abuses and weaknesses to which I have referred. But above all I want to consider anew the question of whether or not the patriarchal narratives do reflect a retrojection of conditions and perspectives of the monarchy or later into the remote past. To do this I will examine parallels from this late period alongside of those proposed from earlier times. In other words we must ascertain whether the notion of a "patriarchal age" is basically historical or idealistic and ideological. Let us now turn to the evidence to answer this question.

BIBLIOGRAPHICAL NOTE

1   In the last few decades, almost all the histories that deal with ancient Israel, the introductions to the literature of the Old Testament, and the commentaries on Genesis have adopted the position that a large part of the patriarchal traditions come from a period in the second millennium B.C. Some of the leading figures in biblical scholarship who have helped to shape this opinion or have given strong support to it are as follows: W. F. Albright in his early works, *The Archaeology of Palestine and the Bible* (New York: Revell, 1932; 2nd ed., 1933; 3rd ed., 1935); *From the Stone Age to Christianity: Monotheism and the Historical Process* (Baltimore: Johns Hopkins Press, 1940; 2nd ed., 1946); and in many subsequent works including one of his most recent, *Yahweh and the Gods of Canaan* (Garden City, N. Y.: Doubleday, 1968). His influence is also reflected in the works of his students G. Ernest Wright, *Biblical Archaeology* (Philadelphia: Westminster Press, 1957); and John Bright, *A History of Irsrael* (Philadelphia: Westminster Press, 1959; 2nd ed., 1972). Also influential were the writings of E. A. Speiser in numerous scholarly articles, now available in *Oriental and Biblical Studies: Collected Writings of E. A. Speiser*, ed. J. J. Finkelstein and M. Greenberg (Philadelphia: University of Pennsylvania Press, 1967); and his recent commentary, *Genesis, The Anchor Bible* (Garden City, N. Y.: Doubleday, 1964). Other works by leading scholars of the English-speaking world are: Cyrus H. Gordon, *Introduction to Old Testament Times* (Ventnor, N.J.: Ventnor Publishers, 1953), with later editions issued under new titles; Nelson Glueck, *Rivers in the Desert: A History of the Negeb* (New York: Farrar, Straus and Cudahy,

1959); T. J. Meek, *Hebrew Origins* (New York: Harper, 1936; 2nd ed., 1950); and H. H. Rowley, "Recent Discovery and the Patriarchal Age," *BJRL* 32 (1949–50):44–79. Among French-speaking scholars, see: Edouard Dhorme, "Abraham dans le cadre de l'histoire," *RB* 37 (1928):367–85, 481–511; 40 (1931):364–74, 503–18 (reprinted in *Recueil Edouard Dhorme; études biblique et orientales* [Paris: Imprimerie Nationale, 1951], pp. 191–272); Roland de Vaux, "Les patriarches hébreux et les découvertes modernes," *RB* 53 (1946):321–48; 55 (1948):321–47; 56 (1949):5–36 (cf. his more recent position in "Les patriarches hébreux et l'histoire," *RB* 72 [1965]; and *Histoire ancienne d'Israël, des origines à l'installation en Canaan* [Paris: Le coffre, 1971], pp. 157–273); Henri Cazelles, "Patriarches," *DBS* 7, cols. 82–156; André Parrot, *Abraham et son Temps*, Cahiers d'archéologie biblique 14 (Neuchâtel: Delachaux & Niestlé, 1962), translated by J. H. Farley as *Abraham and His Times* (Philadelphia: Fortress Press, 1968). German scholarship, however, has been more cautious. See M. Noth, *The History of Israel*, 2nd ed. (New York: Harper, 1960); cf. his later statement in *Die Ursprünge des alten Israel im Lichte neuer Quellen* (Arbeitsgemeinschaft für Forschung des Landes Nordrhein-Westfalen: Cologne, 1961); and Otto Eissfeldt, "Palestine in the Time of the Nineteenth Dynasty," *CAH*, rev. ed. (1965), fasc. 31.

CHAPTER 2

The Nomadism of the Patriarchs

The patriarchal traditions of Genesis are generally thought to reflect an age of nomadic existence by the forefathers of Israel prior to settlement.[1] In spite of the specific disagreement about dating the "age of the patriarchs" it is still strongly affirmed that the stories present a portrayal of a nomadic way of life which can be documented from the textual remains of the second millennium B.C. This general thesis is so basic to the current study of patriarchal tradition-history that it needs to be reviewed at the very beginning of this study.

The literature on the nature of nomadism has become quite extensive in recent years; however, its main features as it relates to the Near East seem clear enough.[2] Before the introduction of the camel as a basis of nomadic life, all nomads were breeders of small livestock, principally sheep but perhaps also goats. They also kept asses as a means of transportation and as beasts of burden. Such nomadism is frequently called "seminomadism" to distinguish it from the camel nomadism which represents a somewhat different way of life.[3] But the term "seminomad" is problematic in that it

1. DeVaux, *Histoire*, pp. 213–23, contains a good review of the subject with references to the current literature. See also Joseph Henninger, "Zum frühsemitischen Nomadentum," in *Viehwirtschaft und Hirtenkultur, Ethnographische Studien*, ed. L. Földes (Budapest: Akadémiai Kiadó, 1969), pp. 33–68, which contains an extensive bibliography. Henninger's work, however, is marred by the fact that he accepts uncritically the patriarchal narratives as primary data for second millennium nomadism, and it can only be used with great caution. A valuable collection of essays on the subject is contained in F. Gabrieli, ed., *L'antica società beduina*, Studi Semitici 2 (Rome: University of Rome, 1959). See also Manfred Weippert, *The Settlement of the Israelite Tribes in Palestine* (SBT 2/21, London: SCM. 1971), pp. 102–26.
2. For second millennium nomadism, see especially the studies of J.-R. Kupper, *Les nomades en Mésopotamie au temps des rois de Mari*, Bibliothèque de la Faculté de Philosophie et Lettres de l'Université de Liège 142 (Paris, 1957); D. O. Edzard, *Die 'zweite Zwischenzeit' Babyloniens* (Wiesbaden: O. Harrassowitz, 1957), pp. 30–43; idem, in E. Cassin, J. Bottéro, and J. Vercoutter, eds., *The Near East: The Early Civilizations* (London: Weidenfeld and Nicolson, 1967), pp. 180–86; see also works in n. 1 above.
3. On the problem of terminology see Henninger, "Nomadentum," pp. 53–57.

suggests, as well, a process of settling down, which is not necessarily the case for all sheep-breeding nomads. Another term used for second millennium nomadism is "ass-nomadism," used in contrast to camel-nomadism.[4] But this term is also a misnomer because asses were not herded or bred like the later camel herds and were secondary in importance to sheep. Large numbers of donkeys are only mentioned in connection with caravan activity, and such commercial enterprise is only carried on by settled, urban communities, or by certain seminomadic groups under the direct supervision of urban communities.[5] So donkey breeding can hardly be regarded as characteristic of the nomadic life itself. One may use the qualification "sheep-breeding" nomad if a distinction is needed to avoid confusion with the camel-nomads or bedouin of the first millennium B.C. and seminomads of pastoral tribes in the process of settling down, but other terms such as "ass-nomad" should be completely avoided.

One of the fundamental characteristics of nomads is their practice of transhumance. Nomads are primarily shepherds or herdsmen who must move their livestock from summer to winter pasture along with their whole families, and because of this seasonal movement they have no fixed abode. This must be qualified somewhat for the second millennium B.C., since the sources do speak of steppe-region settlements of a semipermanent nature that included sheep pens and living shelters.[6] It is a curious fact that tents are not mentioned in the Mari archives at all and only rarely in other second millennium sources.[7] This is in contrast to the tent encampments of the bedouin, which are a most distinctive feature by the mid-first millennium B.C. Nevertheless it is clear that the nomads did move with their total population at certain times of the year. It must be remembered that there was private and state ownership of flocks and herds in the settled community as well, and transhumance of animals with a

---

4. See Albright, "Abram the Hebrew," *BASOR* 163: 36–54.
5. For criticism of Albright, see deVaux, *Histoire*, pp. 217–20; Henninger, "Nomadentum," pp. 52–56; H. Klengel, "Zu einigen Problemen des altvorderasiatischen Nomadentums," *Ar. Or.* 30 (1962): 593; M. Weippert, "Abraham der Hebräer? Bemerkungen zu W. F. Albrights Deutung der Väter Israels," *Biblica* 52 (1971): 407–32.
6. On this terminology see A. Malamat, "Mari and the Bible: Some Patterns of Tribal Organization and Institutions," *JAOS* 82 (1962): 146–47; Weippert, *Settlement*, pp. 115–25.
7. See Kupper, *Nomades*, pp. 14–15; G. Dossin, "Les bédouins dans les textes de Mari," in *L'antica società bedouina*, p. 51 n. 36; Henninger, "Nomadentum," p. 56, who notes the rather late development of the black tents of the nomads.

shepherd was also necessary for these peoples.[8] In this case, however, the owner of the flocks and the families of the shepherds remained stationary while only the hired hands traveled with the animals.

The sheep-breeding nomads were limited in their movement to the steppe region of the desert within proximity to a water supply for their animals.[9] Only with the later domestication of the camel and its use as the principal animal of the nomads could the beduoin penetrate deep into the desert and fully utilize the oases of northern Arabia. In the second millennium the nomads were largely restricted to the outer edge of the Syrian desert adjacent to the settled lands of the fertile crescent with frequent incursions, both friendly and hostile, into the land of the Sown. Some of the nomads made the transition from pastoralists to farmers, while others were dependent upon trade or raiding for their agricultural products. It is also possible, even for full nomads such as the "Benjaminites" of Mari, that a little agriculture was carried on while they were quartered at their winter pastures.[10] But this does not reflect any great move to a sedentary life on the part of these nomads.

Another characteristic of nomads frequently mentioned in the sources of both the second and first millennia is their belligerence toward the settled regions. They are described as constantly raiding and plundering the towns and agricultural land, so that designations for nomadic groups often became synonyms for robbers and outlaws. Much of this belligerence may have been due simply to the struggle for survival, the necessity to obtain food when it was scarce. Conflict between the Desert and the Sown was often at its highest in times of general famine.[11] Furthermore not all nomads were warlike. Some entered into peaceful relations with the settled communities in

8. G. E. Mendenhall in "The Hebrew Conquest of Palestine," *BA* 25 (1962): p. 69 n. 7, has gone to the other extreme in denying nomadism altogether and regards it all as a case of "seasonal transhumance of sheep-herding villagers," but the distinction between such villagers and the nomads is quite clear in the texts. See the response to Mendenhall in Weippert, *Settlement*, p. 125.

9. See deVaux, *RB* 56:13 and the map indicating relative precipitation in the Near East; idem, *Histoire*, pp. 220–21; see also the map in L. H. Grollenberg, *Atlas of the Bible* (London and Edinburgh: Nelson, 1956), p. 29.

10. Kupper, in *Nomades*, p. 58, suggests that it was the state that provided the Benjaminites both seed and land from the royal estate to encourage their sedentarization. The nomads, however, did not take the decisive step of raising large cattle and were still primarily dedicated to the care of their sheep.

11. On this point see J. A. Brinkman, *A Political History of Post-Kassite Babylonia, 1158–722 B.C.* (Rome: Pontifical Biblical Institute, 1968), pp. 387–89.

exchange for certain seasonal pasturing rights and for purposes of commercial transactions. They may have become mercenaries or even have adopted temporary servitude for a livelihood. Nevertheless it is true that a certain antagonism frequently existed between the pastoral and the sedentary way of life.

From the above sketch it should be fairly obvious that there is very little in the patriarchal stories that reflects the nomadic life of the second millennium. The Abraham stories, more than any of the others, suggest that the patriarch was a "resident alien" (*gēr*),[12] a term not entirely appropriate as a general designation for nomad. Abraham also is considered to have had an original homeland in a settled region, whether Ur or Harran. It is true that he lived in tents and moved his livestock from place to place, but these movements do not clearly suggest transhumance. He moves about the land and thereby lays claim to what God has given him, which his offspring will *inherit*. The theme of land inheritance is utterly foreign to the nomadic way of life but a fundamental principle of the settled economy. In the Jacob story it is already assumed that the "land of Canaan" is Jacob's homeland, which he will give as an inheritance to his sons. Furthermore both Laban and later Jacob (in the Joseph story) represent landed gentry with large flocks as well as other wealth, which their sons and hired shepherds pasture. There is nothing nomadic about this. The one nomadic detail, that of the tents, is more suggestive of the first millennium than of the second.

The patriarchs' animals have also been a matter of considerable debate. They include sheep, goats, asses, cattle, and camels. While sheep and asses are known to have been used by the nomads of the Mari Age, the other animals are not. Furthermore, it is not possible to regard any one animal in the Abraham story as predominating since, apart from goats, they are given about equal weight in the biblical accounts. The attempt, for instance, to categorize Abraham as an ass-herdsman and caravaneer fails entirely to get any support from the tradition. Cattle are certainly animals of the settled land and not part of the nomadic culture. It should also be pointed out that asses, cattle, sheep, goats, and even camels were herded in Palestine in the period of the Judean monarchy, since Sennacherib

---

12. Gen. 23:4; cf. Gen. 15:13. See cognate terms in Gen. 12:10; 17:8; 19:9; 20:1; 21:23,34; 26:3; 28:4; 32:5; 35:27; 36:7; 37:1; 47:4,9.

indicates that he took large numbers of these animals as booty in his Judean campaign of 701 B.C.[13] The kinds of animals which Abraham possessed may not have been exceptional for many wealthy Judeans living in the time of the late monarchy.

A special comment is necessary on the mention of camels.[14] Most scholars, even those who argue for an early date for the patriarchal traditions, regard the mention of camels as an anachronism.[15] However, the attempt to view these references as glosses which replaced earlier mention of donkeys is entirely unconvincing.[16] The camels in such stories as Genesis 24 and 31 are quite integral to the accounts. There has been a great deal of debate over the question of the earliest domestication of the camel. Some evidence shows that a limited domestication was already practiced in Arabia in the third millennium B.C. But there is no evidence for any widespread domestication of camels, for camel-nomads in the Near East in contact with the Fertile Crescent, or for camels used by sheep-breeding nomads in the second millennium B.C. The occasional representation of a camel on a monument or the finding of camel bones in an early archaeological context in no way changes this picture. Only with the first millennium B.C. was the camel fully domesticated as a riding and burden-carrying animal,[17] and it was not until the eighth and seventh centuries that it became commonplace as a beast of burden within the region of arable land as well as the desert.

Some studies have been made of the social organization and institutions of nomads in the Mari Age.[18] What is revealing about these studies is how little these nomadic structures correspond to data in the Old Testament, especially in the patriarchal stories. For instance, the term $gōy$ in the patriarchal stories does not have the

13. *ANET*², p. 288.
14. See deVaux, *Histoire*, pp. 214–16 and the literature cited there.
15. The attempt by some to allow for the use of a few camels by the patriarchs in the second millennium B.C. seems to me a case of special pleading for apologetic reasons and not a judgment of historical probability. See J. A. Thompson, in *IDB* 1:490–19; K. A. Kitchen, *Ancient Orient and the Old Testament* (London: Tyndale Press, 1966), pp. 79–80.
16. So also deVaux, *Histoire*, p. 216.
17. This is the date suggested by W. Dostal, "The Evolution of Bedouin Life," *L'antica società bedouina*, p. 22. I do not accept the often repeated statement that the references to the camel-riding Midianites of Judges 6–8 is the earliest *historical* reference to camel domestication. This is still a *traditional* source contained in a late historical work that also needs critical evaluation.
18. Malamat, "Mari and the Bible," *JAOS* 82:143–50; deVaux, *Histoire*, pp. 221–23; Weippert, *Settlement*, pp. 112–25.

meaning of a tribal unit of families as the term *gāyum/gāwum* seems to have in the Mari texts. Instead it refers to the later nations and political states with which the ancestors are associated. This is especially true of the theme of patriarchal promises in which it is predicted that the ancestors will become a great nation (Gen. 12:2–3; 17:4–6, 16, 20; 18:18; 21:13,18; 25:23; 35:11; 46:3; 48:19). Futhermore, the Mari term for a nomadic settlement, *ḥaṣarum*, corresponds to the settlements, *ḥᵉṣērîm*, of the Ishmaelites (Gen. 25:16) as well as the Kedarite settlements of the Neo-Babylonian period (Isa. 42:11). But the manner of life of the Ishmaelites is contrasted with that of Israel's forefathers (Gen. 16:12; 21:20–21).

In contrast to the social and economic structures of nomadic society, which seem to emphasize groups bound together by kinship relations, the patriarchs represent single households augmented by various levels of subordinates, including bought and house-born slaves.[19] In Genesis 14 Abraham is able to arm 318 of his slaves for his night attack; yet there is no mention of any assistance from fellow tribesmen. Likewise the herdsmen who are mentioned in some of the stories are always viewed as part of the personal household of the patriarch, similar to the large household of Nabal, I Samuel 25, and not a reflection of a tribal unit.[20] The stories also speak of male and female slaves, and their role in these accounts is often of primary importance.[21] Such a slavery-based economy is not part of the nomadic way of life because it has no need for a cheap labor force, and there is nothing in the second millennium sources to suggest that nomads retained slaves as part of their social way of life. Slave ownership has its place in the settled urban economic system of antiquity with its stratification of society and its large private households, its royal and temple estates.[22] In this connection the term *bn byt* in Gen. 15:3 calls for some special comment. It appears to be equivalent to the Late Babylonian term *mār bīti* which has the

19. Gen. 12:5,16; 13:2; 14:14; 15:3; 17:12–13, 23, 27; 18:7; 20:14; 22:3f.; 24:2ff.; 26:13; 30:43; 31:1; 32:5ff.
20. Gen. 13:5–8; 26:15ff.
21. See especially chaps. 16; 21:8–21; 24.
22. On slavery see I. Mendelsohn, *Slavery in the Ancient Near East* (New York: Oxford University Press, 1949); idem, *IDB* 4: 383–91; R. deVaux, *Ancient Israel, Its Life and Institutions*, trans. J. McHugh (London: Darton, Longman and Todd, 1961), pp. 80–90. Cf. J. P. M. van der Ploeg, "Slavery in the Old Testament," *SVT* 22 (1972): 72–87. On pp. 81f. van der Ploeg comments on slavery among the patriarchs, but his comparisons with slaves among Arabs of recent times is hardly very helpful.

rather vague meaning of a "member of a household" in the sense of a functionary in the service of a household. These individuals were perhaps freemen above the rank of slave, but a large household may have had several *mār bītāti*.[23] Such a social structure, which includes slaves of various kinds as well as servants and hired hands of different rank and responsibility, has no relevance for a pastoral-nomadic society. It reflects the complex system of a settled economy.

Perhaps the most sedentary portrayal of all the patriarchs is that of Isaac in Gen. 26:12–13, in which he is presented as practicing agriculture. This is usually explained as a semi-nomadic transitional step which should not be used to deny the general nomadic character of the whole tradition.[24] However, the story itself does not really suggest this. First, one cannot speak here of any limited form of agriculture, but only of completely sedentary activity comparable to that of the local population (cf. also Gen. 20:15). Nor is Isaac temporarily settled on royal lands as was the case with the Benjaminites in the Mari texts which refer to nomadic agriculture. Isaac pays no tax for his produce and he does not leave of his own free will to care for his flocks; he is asked to leave. He also has a powerful independent household with flocks and herds of cattle, great wealth, and numerous slaves or retainers. In fact he is the envy of the Philistines. There is nothing in all of this to suggest a nomadic group, the only nomadic element being the rather incongruous reference to Isaac's tent in verse 25.

On the other hand, most scholars who speak of the nomadism of the patriarchs have in mind the population migration of the second millennium, with which Abraham in particular is associated. This was not just a matter of regular transhumance, but a massive movement into the settled lands. Such a migration may have resulted from overpopulation of the steppe region, periods of general famine leading to shortage in the usual grazing lands, or general weakness of the settled lands in resisting nomadic incursions. It was not the result of a wish by large numbers of nomads to suddenly become farmers, and the regions into which the nomads moved often re-

---

23. See *CAD* 2:295f.; G. Cardascia, *Les archives des Murasu* (Paris: Imprimerie Nationale, 1951), pp. 11–12. Cf. Mendelsohn, *Slavery* pp. 57–58; and *AHw* 2:616, where the meaning of "household slave" represents an older understanding of this term.
24. DeVaux, *Histoire* p. 222; G. von Rad, *Genesis*, trans. John H. Marks (Philadelphia: Westminster Press, 1961), p. 265.

mained predominantly pastoral.[25] Such major migrations have been identified with specific historical periods; so the question arises as to what extent the patriarchal stories reflect a very specific period of migration. In order to deal with this issue, it is necessary to enter into a more detailed review of the various nomadic migrations of the second millennium.[26] And since camels, tents, and Arab tribes are mentioned in the Genesis stories, the Arab migration of the first millennium will also have to be included. It is not my intention to give a survey of the political history of one and a half millennia, but only to clarify the historical nomadic background sufficient to evaluate the possible connection of the patriarchs with any of them.

The Amorites

The Amorites first make their appearance in historical records in the time of Sharkalisharri, King of Akkad, in the twenty-third century B.C. They are identified as the nomadic Semites associated with the region of Amurru, the "west-land."[27] This Akkadian term designated primarily the area of the Syrian desert north of the Palmyrene oasis, centering in Mount Bishri and enclosed by the Euphrates on the north and the Syrian mountains on the west.[28]

By the end of the third millennium B.C., during the Third Dynasty of Ur, the infiltration of Amorite nomads into the settled regions of Mesopotamia became a very serious problem.[29] While some of these West-Semitic immigrants were peacefully absorbed into the settled population of the valley, the tide of migration eventually became too great to hold back and gradually all the northern and western regions of the empire came under Amorite control. While the final blow to Ur itself was dealt by Elam, it was largely the Amorite migration which was responsible for the disintegration of power during the Ur III empire.

In Syria and Palestine during the late third millennium there is an almost complete absence of historical texts by which to evaluate their

---

25. Edzard, *The Near East*, pp. 183–85.
26. For a general treatment of Semitic migrations, see S. Moscati, *The Semites in Ancient History* (Cardiff: University of Wales Press, 1959).
27. On the Amorites, see Moscati, ibid., pp. 52–62; Kupper, *Nomades*, pp. 147–96; idem, *CAH*³ 2:1, 1–36; I. J. Gelb, "The Early History of the West-Semitic Peoples," *JCS* 15 (1961): 24–47; deVaux, *Histoire*, pp. 63–69.
28. Dossin, "Bédouins," pp. 38–39.
29. J. Bottero, *CAH*³ I:2, 559–66; C. J. Gadd, *CAH*³ I:2, 625–28; Edzard, *Zweit Zwischenzeit*, pp. 30–43; idem, *The Near East*, pp. 157–186.

situation. Yet it seems fairly clear from the archaeological remains that the whole region was overrun by nomadic groups that destroyed most urban centers of the country. The succeeding archaeological phase, the so-called Middle Bronze I period,[30] was largely nomadic, well attested by the many hundreds of tombs of this period that have been found throughout Palestine, but with very little evidence of any permanent settlements. The few references to Palestine in the contemporary Egyptian texts of the First Intermediate period and early Middle Kingdom seem also to confirm this picture.[31] Although many different explanations have been given for the appearance of MB I, the most persuasive is that which associates it with the Amorite nomadic movement, which was also felt in Mesopotamia at the same time.

In place of the unified empire of Ur III there arose a large number of individual "Amorite" kingdoms throughout Mesopotamia. In Syria it appears that urban life was also quickly restored, very likely by the settling down of these same nomadic groups. Hamath on the Orontes is perhaps the best example of this, having cultural contacts both with the nomadic MB I in Palestine and with the new urban centers of Upper Mesopotamia.[32] However, Palestine itself is somewhat different. The transition between MB I and the new urban phase of MB II A is quite sharp, and it would seem to indicate that after the new urban phase in Syria was already quite advanced, Palestine was colonized directly from the inland Syrian region. This situation in Palestine may also be reflected in the so-called "execration texts" of the late Middle Kingdom in Egypt.[33] These texts contain place names of Palestine and southern Syria along with the names of their chieftains or princes who were hostile to Egypt and so were ritually cursed. The personal names all belong to the northwest Semitic (Amorite) type and clearly link this development of urban civilization with the rest of the fertile crescent.

30. See most recently W. G. Dever, "The Peoples of Palestine in the MB I Period," *HTR* 64 (1971): 206–09.
31. *ANET*[2] pp. 414–418, 444–446. See also G. Posener, *CAH*[3] I: 2, 537–558; W. A. Ward, *Egypt and the East Mediterranean World, 2200–1900 B.C.* (Beirut: American University of Beirut, 1971), pp. 19–47.
32. See W. G. Dever, "The 'Middle Bronze I' Period in Syria and Palestine," in *Near Eastern Archaeology in the Twentieth Century*, ed. J. A. Sanders (Garden City, N. Y.: Doubleday, 1970), pp. 146–50.
33. *ANET*[2] pp. 528–29; see Posener, *CAH*[3] I: 2, 555–58 and literature cited there.

Nevertheless alongside of this developing sedentary civilization there were large numbers of West-Semitic peoples who still remained nomadic in varying degrees. This is particularly clear for the whole region between Syria and the Middle Euphrates, as revealed by the administrative archives of Mari.[34] Within the borders controlled by Mari there were some nomads such as the Haneans who were in the process of being settled, mainly in the Upper Euphrates region of the Balih and Habur rivers. Others, such as the Benjaminites, remained more nomadic and hostile, and their movement extended over the whole region from the Middle Euphrates to inland Syria. The situation for Syria and Palestine does not appear to be essentially different from this, though epigraphic evidence in the Mari texts for this region is rather sparse.

With the demise of the Twelfth Dynasty in Egypt this West-Semitic culture was able to gain a significant foothold in the eastern Delta region. At Tell ed Debʿa on the eastern branch of the Nile an urban settlement corresponding closely to those of Palestine was already established in the Thirteenth Dynasty.[35] These foreign occupants of the Delta eventually paved the way for the complete foreign control of Egypt by the Hyksos ($ḥq^{3}$ $ḥswt$, "foreign rulers"), who began the Fifteenth Dynasty.[36] These foreigners were not an obscure invading horde from the distant north but were clearly part of the West-Semitic civilization which dominated the whole of the fertile crescent at that time.

Now it should be pointed out that the term "Amorite" is often used as an academic convention indicating ethnic and linguistic affinity among all the West-Semitic nomads and sedentary population from the late third millennium to the mid-second millennium B.C. But this usage may lead to serious misunderstanding by students of the Old Testament. The term *Amurru* (Amorite) is of Mesopotamian origin and in South Mesopotamia it always seems to mean the nomadic peoples from the north-western steppe region.[37] It never

---

34. See the works in n. 2 above; also G. Dossin, "Les bédouins dans les textes de Mari," in *L'antica società bedouins*, pp. 35–51.
35. M. Bietak, "Vorläufiger Bericht über die dritte Kampagne der österreichischen Ausgrabungen auf Tell ad Dabʿa ... 1968," *MDIK* 26 (1970): 15–42; see also reports of J. Leclant, *Orientalia* 37 (1968): 98–100; ibid., 38 (1969), pp. 248–251.
36. On the Hyksos see J. Van Seters, *The Hyksos: A New Investigation* (New Haven & London: Yale University Press, 1966).
37. Dossin, "Bédouins," pp. 38–39.

applied to such peoples of Palestine, and the Egyptian terminology for these Asiatics is quite different. At Mari and Alalah, however, Amurru developed a special meaning, referring to a sedentary kingdom of central Syria.[38] In the later Amarna Age of the fourteenth century B.C. this Amurru emerges as a strong unified kingdom of central Syria. And this is the only use which Amurru has in the Egyptian sources of the Amarna and Ramessid periods or in the Hittite correspondence until the demise of this kingdom in the upheavals of the population migrations, about 1200 B.C. The term Amurru lived on in the cuneiform sources for many centuries, but it became a rather archaic and general designation for the region of Syria-Palestine with no precise ethnic or political delineation.[39]

Abraham and the Amorite Migration

The coming of Abraham to Palestine has frequently been explained as having been associated with this Amorite migration of the second millennium.[40] The Biblical traditions suggest two stages in the travels of Abraham's family. First there is a move from Ur in southern Mesopotamia to Harran, and then a migration from Harran to Palestine. Regarding the first phase the text speaks of "Ur of the Chaldeans," which is inappropriate for the second millennium, so many scholars strike out "Chaldeans" as an anachronistic gloss and consider the reference to Ur to be related in some way to the city under the Third Dynasty of Ur. The cause of the migration from Ur is usually attributed to the nomadic upheavals which destroyed the Ur III empire.

Objections to this reconstruction are many. Firstly, Abraham's family is represented as sedentary in Ur prior to their move. Secondly, the journey to Harran would have been directly against the tide of nomadic migration in this period and a move from one urban center to another. It is also not even certain that Harran existed in the Ur III period, and no texts as yet attest to any connection whatever between Ur and Harran in the second millennium. A movement from Ur to Harran in the early second millennium

---

38. Kupper, *Nomades*, pp. 179–81; idem, *CAH*[3] II:1,27; deVaux, *Histoire*, p. 27, n. 43.
39. J. Van Seters, "The Terms 'Amorite' and 'Hittite' in the Old Testament," *VT* 22 (1972): 64–81; deVaux, *Histoire*, pp. 68–69.
40. Bright, *History of Israel*, pp. 78–82; Albright, *From the Stone Age to Christianity*, pp. 236–40.

for migratory or other reasons is not at present historically explicable.[41]

The move from Harran to Palestine in the second millennium is also problematic. Harran is mentioned first in the so-called Cappadocian texts and in the Mari archives of the nineteenth and eighteenth centuries B.C.[42] While the town had some importance as a caravan station in trade to Anatolia, it was only a minor principality under the control of other major centers.[43] There were many nomads in the region, and some even had a treaty relationship with the king of Harran. But these nomads very likely came, whether permanently or seasonally, from the steppe region of the Syrian desert, a considerable distance south of Harran. In the same way nomads moved from the western edge of the Syrian desert into central Syria-Palestine, which has a climate and annual rainfall similar to that of Harran. This means that there is no sociological or historical reason to suggest that nomads migrated from Harran to Palestine.

On the other hand there must be some reason for the prominence given to the two cities of Ur and Harran and for their close association with one another. This can only reflect a time when both cities were at their height, and this exactly fits the Neo-Babylonian period and the reign of Nabonidus in particular. Harran, an Aramean city in the country of Bit-Adini, rose to a position of special importance in the Assyrian empire as a political and religious center from the mid-eighth century onward.[44] There is reason to believe that the god Sin of Harran was one of the major deities representing the Aramean population who, along with the gods of Assyria and Babylonia, confirmed the Assyrian kings in their kingship so that special status was given to the city and its temple. This continued into the Neo-Babylonian period and was especially evident in the reign of Nabonidus, who was apparently related to the royalty and priesthood of this city and gave to it exceptional honor. At the same time Ur, which also had an ancient temple to Sin (Nanna), received considerable attention from Nabonidus, who restored its temples and

---

41. See C. J. Gadd in *AOTS*, p. 94.
42. See references cited in deVaux, *Histoire*, pp. 189–90.
43. Kupper, *Nomades*, pp. 48–49.
44. See the extensive treatment on Harran by J. Lewy, "The Late Assyro-Babylonian Cult of the Moon and its Culmination at the Time of Nabonidus," *HUCA* 19 (1945–46): 405–489.

installed his daughter as the high priestess of Sin.[45] It is even speculated that Nabonidus was attempting to make Sin, a deity specially venerated by the Arameans, the principal deity of the empire with Ur and Harran the two main religious centers. Ur at this time was in the heart of that region dominated by the Chaldeans, the population group that had provided the previous rulers of the Neo-Babylonian empire. Nabonidus, however, was an Aramean who represented that element of the population in Southern Mesopotamia but at the same time was directly related to the Arameans of the Upper Euphrates. The Arameans had always maintained some antagonism toward the older population of Mesopotamia, particularly Babylon. Consequently, Babylon with its god Marduk represented a certain rivalry for honors with these cities and was never strong in its loyalty to the king.

Besides this close contact between Ur and Harran, there was another avenue of communication that was most important in this period. Quite early in his reign Nabonidus left Southern Mesopotamia and, proceeding by way of Harran, marched through Syria-Palestine to the oasis of Teima in North Arabia, where he established his residence for ten years.[46] His intention, though somewhat obscure, was probably to establish economic control over the important western incense trade which went from South Arabia by way of Western Arabia and the oases of the Ḥejaz to Palestine, Syria, Egypt, and beyond.[47] This move to Teima dramatically emphasizes the great importance of the "king's highway" from Harran to North Arabia. There are, of course, strong indications that during the Assyrian empire the importance of this trade route was already realized. Beginning in the mid-eighth century the Assyrian kings constantly campaigned against north Arabian tribes along this route and penetrated the desert as far as Adumatu (Al Jauf).[48] But it is entirely unjustified to read back into the second millennium this development of the "king's highway."

One can therefore conclude that the notion of the household of

---

45. J. A. Brinkman, "Ur: 721–605 B.C." *Orientalia* 34 (1965): 241–58; G. Roux, *Ancient Iraq* (London: Allen & Unwin, 1964), pp. 318–19.
46. *ANET*³, pp. 562–63.
47. See H. W. F. Saggs, *The Greatness That was Babylon* (New York: Hawthorn Books, 1962), pp. 145–49; Roux, *Ancient Iraq*, p. 322.
48. See the royal inscriptions from the time of Tiglathpileser III to Ashurbanipal, *ANET*², pp. 284–300.

Abraham moving from Ur of the Chaldeans to Harran and subsequently to Palestine fits most appropriately into the mid-sixth century B.C. Even if we admit that the connection with Ur may be a later extension of the tradition, the notion of a journey from Harran still fits best into a period toward the end of the Assyrian empire. This certainly seems preferable to those efforts that try to harmonize the movements of the patriarchs with the Amorite migrations of the early second millennium.

Israelites, Moabites, Edomites and Ammonites

The major migration of nomads that dominated the latter part of the second millennium B.C. resulted in the establishment, in Palestine and Transjordan, of the peoples of Israel, Moab, Edom and Ammon. We are not concerned in this study with the problem of evaluating the Biblical texts relating to the settlement of Israel and the Transjordanian nations as reflected in the exodus and conquest traditions of the Old Testament.[49] It is quite evident that they stand in sharp contrast to the patriarchal traditions, so that one must look outside of the Biblical settlement traditions if there is to be any possibility of associating the stories of Genesis with the late second millennium B.C. Such extra-Biblical sources are the so-called Amarna letters from Syrian and Palestinian princes to the Egyptian court and Egyptian royal inscriptions and other archival documents of the Eighteenth to the Twentieth Dynasties.[50]

The Amarna letters indicate that a nomadic people, the Ḫapiru,[51] were particularly active in Palestine in the late fifteenth and four-

---

49. For recent comprehensive treatments of the settlement see M. Weippert, *The Settlement of the Israelite Tribes in Palestine*; and deVaux, *Histoire*, pp. 443–620.

50. See especially W. Helck, "Die Bedrohung Palästinas durch einwandernde Gruppen am Ende der 18. und am Anfang der 19. Dynastie," *VT* 18 (1968): 472–80.

51. The literature on the Ḫapiru problem is now very extensive. However, the recent studies bearing most directly on the Amarna Age are: J. Bottéro, *Le problème des Ḫabiru à la 4e rencontre assyriologique internationale* (Paris, 1954); idem, "Ḫabiru," in *Reallexicon der Assyriologie und vorderasiatischen Archäologie*, eds. E. Ebeling and B. Meissner, 4 vols. (Berlin: W. de Gruyter, 1932–), vol. 4, pt. 1 (1972), pp. 14–27; M. Greenberg, *The Ḫab/piru* (New Haven: American Oriental Society, 1955); idem, "Ḫab/piru and Hebrews," in *World History of the Jewish People*, vol. 2, *The Patriarchs*, ed. B. Mazar (New Brunswick, N.J.: Rutgers University Press, 1970), pp. 188–200; Weippert, *Settlement*, pp. 63–102; idem, "Abraham der Hebraer?" *Biblica* 52:407–32; K. Koch, "Die Hebräer vom Auszug aus Agypten bis zum Grossreich Davids," *VT* 19 (1969): 37–81; R. deVaux, "Le problème des Ḫapiru après quinze années," *JNES* 27 (1968): 221–28; idem, *Histoire*, pp. 106–112, 202–208.

teenth centuries and, in cooperation with Labyu, ruler of Shechem, they probably controlled a large part of the hill country of Western Palestine. Under the military-minded Pharaohs Haremheb, Seti I and Ramesses II, vigorous campaigns were made against them. Ramesses carried his conquest as far as Moab in Transjordan.[52] Similar campaigns were conducted against the Shosu ($š3św$) in Edom and Seir and in southern Palestine, in the "hills of Ḫuru".[53] The Egyptian records from the Nineteenth and Twentieth Dynasties show both the Ḫapiru ($ʿprw$) and Shosu as state slaves and as Egyptian mercenaries, with considerable numbers settled in the Delta.

W. Helck has suggested that these nomadic peoples, the Ḫapiru and Shosu, were in fact the precursors of the Moabites, Edomites, and Israelites.[54] Moab and Edom are mentioned as places, and Israel as a tribe, for the first time in the texts of the Nineteenth Dynasty. In Ramesses II's campaign against Moab towns such as Dibon are mentioned, but nothing is said about any kings or princes of the region. Moab was probably only in the early stages of its settlement before any monarchy existed there. The land of Edom occurs in a document from the time of Merneptah which mentions Shosu from Edom being given access to the Eastern Delta in order to water their flocks. The nomadic Shosu are also associated with Seir, a synonym for Edom, in the documents from Ramesses II and III. In a stele of Merneptah Israel appears as the name of a tribe subdued by Egypt, but Helck has proposed that the stereotype listing of these names points to their earlier origin in the time of Ramesses II or Seti I.

The picture of the settlement of Israel and the Transjordanian peoples[55] which these texts suggest is that the process was a long and gradual one with its greatest intensity in the thirteenth century. It was not a very peaceful process for the settled communities of

---

52. K. A. Kitchen, "Some New Light on the Asiatic Wars of Ramesses II," *JEA* 50 (1964): 63–70.
53. R. Giveon, "The Shosu of Egyptian Sources and the Exodus," *Fourth World Congress of Jewish Studies: Papers I* (Jerusalem, 1967), pp. 193–96; idem, *Les bédouins Shosu des documents égyptiens* (Leiden: E. J. Brill, 1971); see also M. Weippert, "Die Nomadenquelle: Ein Beitrag zur Topographie der Biqaʿ im 2. Jahrtausend v. Chr.," in *Archäologie und Altes Testament: Festschrift für Kurt Galling*, ed. A. Kuschke and E. Kutsch (Tubingen: Mohr, 1970), pp. 259–272.
54. Helck, *VT* 18:472–80.
55. On the archaeological data for this region see N. Glueck, "Transjordan," in *AOTS*, pp. 429–453.

Western Palestine, though in Transjordan there was little settlement to offer resistance to the newcomers. However there must have been a fairly close association between the nomadic peoples of south Palestine and Transjordan in order to motivate such a deep penetration into Edom and Moab by Ramesses II.

The Biblical picture that suggests that Edom and Moab were already settled kingdoms before Israel arrived may have to be modified in the light of this evidence. These nomadic movements were all largely contemporary and closely related, and the development of separate nations was certainly a later stage. It is also likely that the Ammonites, perhaps related to a subsequent nomadic wave, came later when Moab and the eastern Israelite tribes were already settled.[56] This is not to suggest that the settlement of the Israelite tribes was not internally much more complex or that all of Israel settled at the same time. However there must have been some fairly definite relationship between these nomadic tribes of the fourteenth and thirteenth centuries and the later nations of Israel, Moab and Edom. These peoples were kept largely in check by the Egyptian authorities until the arrival of the "Sea-Peoples," after which Egyptian presence in Palestine ceased.

The stories of Genesis represent the patriarchs as related directly to the Edomites and somewhat more indirectly to the Ammonites and Moabites. The eponymous ancestors of these groups are presented as having migrated into Transjordan at the same time that the ancestors of Israel laid claim to Palestine through the divine promise. In their migrations as well as in their more pastoral or nomadic way of life they are contrasted sharply with the older autochthonous population. In these respects one might be inclined to recall the migrations of the fourteenth and thirteenth centuries described above. However it is doubtful if such a conclusion is warranted. Firstly, the tradition suggests that the Ishmaelite Arabs also belong to this same migration period, which is extremely unlikely. It further implies that the Arameans were already settled in their regions prior to the Israelite and Transjordanian settlement, which was certainly not the case.

Secondly, since Israel had traditions which specifically dealt with

---

56. Cf. G. M. Landes, "Ammon," *IDB* 1:108-114. This article presupposes that the patriarchal stories give primary historical data for the second millennium on which to reconstruct a history.

settlement of the land it is doubtful that the patriarchal traditions were ever viewed as a history of the settlement. On the contrary, the patriarchal age is kept quite distinct from the period of settlement as an era of promise. As such it functioned as a way of rationalizing and legitimating various territorial claims, relationships with neighboring groups of peoples and other political and social phenomena of later historical periods. Such a function for myths about eponymous ancestors and heroes was apparently quite common in Ancient Greece and can be assumed in these traditions as well.[57] In fact the presence of eponyms in the tradition actually takes for granted the later existence of these states and the relationships between them. But if one removes the eponyms of the Transjordanian states from the tradition then there is no longer any connection with the Late Bronze Age migrations mentioned above.

Thirdly, the atmosphere of the patriarchal stories is certainly far different from that portrayed in the Amarna letters and Nineteenth Dynasty inscriptions. There is no reflection whatever of the Egyptian presence in Palestine. Abraham's adversaries in Genesis 14 are from Mesopotamia and "Ḫatti" (?) but not from Egypt, which certainly doesn't fit this period. The sons of Jacob slaughter the inhabitants of Shechem, the one city that, in the Amarna letters, seems to cooperate so much with the Ḫapiru. The peaceful atmosphere which for the most part predominates in the patriarchal stories does not give any hint of the kind of nomadic movement which we have from the extra-Biblical sources of the late second millennium B.C. We must therefore conclude that any resemblance between the patriarchal stories and the migrations of the Late Bronze Age into Palestine and Transjordan is entirely superficial.

The Arameans

The origins and early history of the Arameans are beset with many difficulties.[58] When the Arameans came into the full light of history at the end of the twelfth century B.C. it is clear that they were still a nomadic people. The first reference to them is in the Assyrian

57. See especially the study of Martin P. Nilsson *Cults, Myths, Oracles, and Politics in Ancient Greece* (Lund: Gleerup, 1951).
58. R. A. Bowman, "Arameans, Aramaic, and the Bible," *JNES* 7 (1948): 65–90; idem, "Arameans," in *IDB* 1:190ff.; A. Dupont-Sommer, "Sur les débuts de l'histoire Araméene," *SVT* 1 (1953): 40–49; Moscati, *Semites*, pp. 64ff., 96f.; deVaux, *Histoire*, pp. 194–98.

royal inscriptions, where they are associated with the Aḫlamu. This name, along with another, Sutu, made its first appearance in the Mari Age, but the Aḫlamu only came into prominence in the thirteenth to twelfth centuries when the Assyrian kings attempted to control their movements in the Upper Euphrates region. Some scholars have tried to identify the Aḫlamu with the Arameans; indeed, the two terms appear linked together in the earliest reference to the Arameans, found in the inscriptions of Tiglath-pileser I. The term Aḫlamu is interpreted as a social designation meaning "nomadic confederates" or the like.[59] Moscati, however, has shown that the reasons suggested for this position cannot be maintained, and that it is only a case of two closely associated nomadic groups.[60] It is entirely likely that by the time of the appearance of the Arameans, or soon after, the terms Aḫlamu and Sutu had become rather general sociological terms for nomads and no longer carried any accurate ethnic connotations, as they did in the earlier references. The use of archaic traditional terminology alongside of more precise modern terms is quite characteristic of Assyrian royal inscriptions, as it is of Near Eastern documents generally.

The name "Aramean" itself is without adequate explanation. There has been some effort to see the name as associated with various places which occur in references as early as the Akkadian and Ur III periods. But these places are very distant from each other, located in the northern mountains of eastern Asia Minor and in the Diyala River region east of the Tigris—two locations which hardly commend themselves as the original homeland of these nomadic peoples. Supposed references to Arameans in certain personal names of the Mari age have also been firmly rejected as without foundation.[61]

On the other hand, a few possible references to individual Arameans occur in the Ugaritic texts along with a reference in a fourteenth century cuneiform text to *eqlêti aramima*, "the fields of the Arameans."[62] This expression probably points to the steppe region in northeastern Syria, but the location is not definite. It may correspond

---

59. Dupont-Sommer, *SVT* 1: 40ff.
60. S. Moscati, "The Aramean Ahlamu," *JSS* 4 (1959): 303–07; D. O. Edzard, "Mari und Aramaer?" *ZA* n.s. 22 (1964): 142–49.
61. Kupper, *Nomades*, pp. 112–113.
62. Dupont-Sommer, *SVT* 1: 46–47; deVaux, *Histoire*, p. 197.

to a reference in a text from the time of Amenophis III which mentions p₃ ꜣrmw, "the land of the Arameans."⁶³ The context of this inscription is also no help in locating the region.

Before 1200 B.C. the Arameans were scarcely considered a threat to the settled communities of the fertile crescent. However by the time of Tiglath-pileser I (1115–1077) there were large numbers moving into the Upper and Middle Euphrates regions and causing a serious threat to the political and economic stability of these areas. There is some reason to believe that famine was a principal factor in motivating the nomadic raids into the settled land. There is a complete lack of direct historical sources for Syria in this period, but the decline of both Hittite and Egyptian authority as well as the devastation caused by the Sea-Peoples left the Levant without an effective unified force to resist the hordes of hungry nomads. By the mid-tenth century the Arameans had firmly established their control of most of inland Syria and the Upper Euphrates, while Aramean nomads continued to raid Northwestern Babylonia.[64]

In the ninth century, during the time of Ashurnasirpal II, the first reference to the Chaldeans appears. In it a part of southern Babylonia is called *māt Kaldu*, and under Shalmaneser III, about 850, we learn the names of the principal tribes of the region as Bit-Dakkuri, Bit-Amukani and Bit-Jakin.[65] From this time on the Chaldeans were a major political and economic element in this region and a primary concern to the Assyrian Empire.

Whether the Chaldeans can be considered merely a part of the general Aramean migration is uncertain. Numerous smaller tribal groups which are specifically designated as Aramean began to appear in the Assyrian records only in the time of Tiglath-Pileser III (745–27). They lived in the eastern Babylonian region and in these documents are kept quite distinct from the Chaldeans even though they often made common cause with them against Assyria.

In Syria the Arameans founded a number of small kingdoms: Sobah, Bit-Rehob, Maʿakah, Geshur, Damascus, and Hamath in

---

63. E. Edel, *Die Ortsnamenliste aus dem Totentempel Amenophis III*, BBB 25 (Bonn: Hanstein, 1966), pp. 28–29; cf. Weippert, "Die Nomadenquelle," p. 260, where the reading is disputed.
64. About the impact of the Arameans on Assyria see G. Roux, *Ancient Iraq*, pp. 226ff.
65. See esp. J. A. Brinkman, *A Political History of Post-Kassite Babylonia*.

the south and central regions,⁶⁶ and in the north around Aleppo the Bit-Agushi, and in Upper Euphrates the Bit-Adini and the Bit-Bahiani. Alongside of these Aramean states were other older, urban populations which often created certain cultural and political antagonism. In Syria the Arameans shared land with the Canaanite-Phoenician cities that occupied the coastal plain and the Neo-Hittite kingdoms that dominated the inland region from Hamath to Carchemish, though the Arameans gradually took over control of most of these latter states. These Neo-Hittite kingdoms were founded, after the fall of the Hittite empire about 1200 B.C., by Anatolian peoples who moved into Syria.⁶⁷ In southern Babylonia the Chaldeans appear to have assimilated more readily with the Babylonian population even though they retained to a large extent their tribal structures. The Arameans, however, remained much more aloof and even hostile to the older population, though they cooperated fairly readily with the Chaldeans against their greater foe, Assyria.

By the ninth century the Aramean kingdoms of Upper Mesopotamia were incorporated into the Assyrian provincial system, and by the end of the eighth and early seventh centuries Assyrian military might was able to unify the whole of the fertile crescent under its control. This meant that all the Aramean political states along with the many other diverse ethnic elements were incorporated into the vast provincial system of the empire, with the exception of a few vassal kingdoms like Judah. Since the Arameans were such a large and important element in the population of Upper Mesopotamia and Assyria proper, Aramaic became the principal language of the empire.⁶⁸ The wealth and power of the Arameans was based on their success in controlling important trade routes from the Arabian Peninsula to the Euphrates, from Syria to the lands of the East, and from the Persian Gulf to Assyria.

Turning again to the stories of Genesis one is immediately struck by the strong sense of identity which the patriarchs seem to have with

---

66. B. Mazar, "The Aramean Empire and its Relations with Israel," *BA* 28 (1962): 97ff. (Reprinted in *BAR* 2:127-151).
67. See O. R. Gurney, *The Hittites* (Harmondsworth: Penguin Books, 1961), pp. 39-46; see also W. F. Albright, "The Amarna Letters from Palestine, Syria, the Philistines and Phoenicia," *CAH*², fasc. 51, pp. 43-46.
68. A. Jeffery, "Aramaic," in *IDB* 1:186-190.

the Arameans. The patriarchal origins are traced primarily to the region of Harran in northwestern Mesopotamia. This region is designated as either Aram-Naharaim, "Aram of the Upper Euphrates,"[69] or *Padan-Aram*, "country of Aram."[70] The relatives of the patriarchs in this area are called "Arameans." Even outside of Genesis, the cryptic liturgy of Deut. 26:5 states: "A wandering Aramean (*ᵃrammî ᵓōbēd*) was my father and he went down to Egypt." This last reference, however, could mean no more than "a perishing nomad" and refer to Jacob's forced descent to Egypt because of famine.[71]

The brief glimpses which the stories provide of the patriarch's Aramean kin (Gen. 11:32ff.; chaps. 24, 29–31) suggest that they have a close and peaceful association with the cities of Harran and Nahor. In Genesis 24 the Arameans are the sedentary dwellers of Nahor itself, while in the Jacob story Laban, the Aramean shepherd, is nevertheless a resident of Harran. This picture of the Arameans as settled in the Upper Euphrates (Naharaim) could reflect historical reality any time between the tenth and the fifth centuries, *but not any earlier.*

Some scholars are prepared to admit that the references to Arameans in the patriarchal stories are anachronistic.[72] However they are usually explained as resulting from a modernization of terminology of a more ancient tradition. Because the Arameans, like the Amorites, migrated from the same steppe region into the fertile crescent, they can be regarded as really reflecting the earlier Amorite migration in more modern terminology.[73] Against this suggestion it

---

69. On the meaning of this term see J. J. Finkelstein, "Mesopotamia," *JNES* 21 (1962): 73–92.
70. For this meaning see J. Simons, *The Geographical and Topographical Texts of the Old Testament* (Leiden: E. J. Brill, 1959), p. 7. Cf. Bowman, *IDB* 1:191, who translates the phrase as "road of Aram".
71. D. D. Luckenbill, "The 'Wandering Aramean,'" *AJSL* 36 (1920): 244–45, suggests that the Hebrew phrase corresponds to the expression "fugitive Aramean" in the Sennacherib Taylor Prism, col. 5:22f., with the general meaning of "nomad." See also Mazar, *BAR* 2:130, n. 8; and Albright, *From the Stone Age to Christianity*, p. 238.
72. See J. C. L. Gibson, "Observations on Some Important Ethnic Terms in the Pentateuch," *JNES* 20 (1961): 229–234; and deVaux, *Histoire*, p. 198.
73. This has led to the misleading term "Proto-Arameans" for Amorites of an earlier period. See Noth, *Die Ursprünge des alten Israel im Lichte neuer Quellen*, pp. 29–31; and deVaux, *Histoire*, pp. 198–201.

must be stated that the Old Testament knows nothing of such an identity between Amorites and Arameans. In fact it emphasizes most strongly its total distinction from the "Amorites." Furthermore, the explanation only has merit if it can be shown on other grounds that the patriarchs indeed belonged to the earlier nomadic movement of the second millennium. But I have given reasons against such a view, and I can find no evidence to suggest that an older tradition has been modernized in this way.

The question nevertheless persists as to how this feeling of kinship with the Arameans could have originated or developed in the time of the Israelite monarchies, since for the most part there was considerable warfare between Israel and the Aramean states of Syria during this period. Yet such a question overlooks the fact that the patriarchs are viewed as related not to the Syrian Arameans but to those around Harran. Only Laban by virtue of the reference to a territorial boundary with Jacob in the northeast Gilead region (Gen. 31:47ff.) suggests some association with Syria. But it is in this story also that Laban shows a certain hostility toward Jacob, although he is a resident of Harran.

One can only speculate as to what gave rise to the feeling of kinship with the Arameans of Northwestern Mesopotamia, but there are a few factors which might be considered. Firstly, the regions inhabited by Israel, the nations of Transjordan, and the Aramean states of Upper Euphrates all had the same basic economy, which was largely pastoral or semi-agricultural. And they had similar socio-political structures with an emphasis on tribal divisions. Secondly, the Assyrian Empire had united this whole Western region to a very large extent by the gradual abolition of national boundaries and the greatly increased communication between the regions. Thirdly, the Assyrians' deportation of a large number of Israelites to the Habur and Balih valley regions as well as the interchange of Arameans into Palestine would certainly have encouraged a sense of identity with the Arameans and the Harran region in the late monarchy. However it is likely that this sense of identity developed only after the demise of the Aramean states of Syria.

This rather late cultivation of a sense of identity with the Arameans seems reasonable in light of the late development of the important King's Highway from Harran to North Arabia and the extension of this route to Ur by the Aramean ruler of Babylonia, Nabonidus.

The Arabs

Another nomadic movement which forms part of the background for the patriarchal narratives is the coming of the Arabs on the scene of Near Eastern history.[74] The earliest reference to the Arabs in cuneiform sources occurs in an inscription of Shalmaneser III, which refers to a certain Gindibu, the Arab leading a contingent of 1000 camels as part of a coalition against the Assyrians at the battle of Qarqar in 854 B.C.[75] One may deduce from this that the Arab nomads, characterized by domesticated herds of camels, were becoming a significant political factor in the Near East by this time. Their military cooperation with the kings of Syria-Palestine also suggests economic relationships, probably centering on caravan incense trade between South Arabia and Syria-Palestine which had probably developed by this time.

References to Arabs, as well as to their camels, in cuneiform sources are rare until the mid-eighth century. From the time of Tiglath-Pileser III (745–727) of Assyria to that of Nabonidus (555–539) of Babylon the cuneiform texts make frequent mention of the Arabs of North Arabia. This permits a considerable knowledge about the various Arab tribes and subgroups of the region. It is clear that by the eighth and seventh centuries B.C. the Arab settlements in the oases of the Hejaz flourished, some having their own kings and queens. Arabs also occupied the region between North Arabia and the borders of Egypt, creating considerable pressure for the state of Edom and eventually for Judah. The source of their wealth was an active caravan trade in incense, gold, and precious stones, to judge from the booty in the Assyrian annals. These commodities, coming from the kingdoms of Southern Arabia by camel caravan, were destined for markets in Syria, Palestine, Egypt, and beyond. It was probably the control of these trade routes which motivated the Assyrian campaigns against the Arabs.

---

74. See Moscati, *Semites*; J. A. Montgomery, *Arabia and the Bible* (Philadelphia: University of Pennsylvania Press, 1934); A. Jeffery, "Arabians," *IDB* 1:182–83; and G. Ryckmans, "Het Oude Arabie en de Bijbel," *JEOL* 14 (1955/6): 73–84.
75. *ANET*^{2}, p. 279. For all the references to Arabs in cuneiform sources see T. W. Rosmarin, "Aribi und Arabien in den babylonischen-assyrischen Quellen," *JSOR* 16 (1932): 1–37; S. Parpola, *Neo-Assyrian Toponyms*, AOAT 6 (Kevelaer, Ger.: Butzon & Bercker, 1970); William J. Dumbrell, *The Midianites and their Transjordanian Successors* (Th.D. thesis, Harvard University, 1970), pp. 192–246.

In the Neo-Babylonian period the Arabs continued to be an important political and economic entity.[76] After Nebuchadrezzar's campaigns in Transjordan (582 B.C.) Ammon and Moab seriously declined as political entities and the Qidri (Kedarites), a major tribe among the Ishmaelites, infiltrated and occupied most of the region. Nabonidus made a campaign against the oasis of Adumu (Al Jauf), the heart of Kedar, and in his subsequent sojourn at Teima tried to come to terms with those Arab tribes through whose region the West Arabian caravan trade travelled.

There is some evidence to suggest that even before the fall of Babylon Cyrus the Great subdued North Arabia and took it out of Babylonian control.[77] In any case, soon after the decisive victory over Babylon in 539 B.C. the Cyrus Cylinder boasted of Persian hegemony over North Arabia by stating that, among others from the West, "the kings of Amurru dwelling in tents" paid him homage and tribute.[78] There can be little doubt that this phrase referred to the king of Kedar and related tribes and oases of North Arabia. Furthermore, under Cambyses the Kedarites assisted the Persians in their Egyptian campaign, providing support and water for travel through the region from Palestine to Egypt. The Kedarites at this time occupied the area as far north as Gaza, and perhaps as a result of their assistance to the Persians they gained control or access to a considerable part of the Eastern Delta. However the fact that they made an annual "gift" of 1000 talents of incense to the Persian authorities points to submission to Persia as well as to the source of their wealth and power through the incense trade.[79] The Kedarites continued to be a dominant presence in the region of North Sinai and South Judah throughout the Persian period and until the rise of the Nabateans, who replaced them.

In the tradition of Abraham, the patriarch is presented as the father of the Arabs. This comes out most clearly in the genealogies, but it is also expressed in the stories of Hagar and her son Ishmael.

---

76. For this and the subsequent period see A. F. Rainey, "The Satrapy 'Beyond the River,'" *Australian Journal of Biblical Archaeology* 1:2 (1969): 51–78; W. J. Dumbrell, "The Tell el-Maskhuta Bowls and the 'Kingdom' of Qedar in the Persian Period," *BASOR* 203 (Oct. 1971): 38–44.

77. R. P. Dougherty, *Nabonidus and Belshazzar*, YOS 15 (New Haven: Yale University Press, 1929), p. 109.

78. Ibid.

79. Rainey, "Satrapy," pp. 53–55.

The presentation of Ishmael in these stories is in keeping with the role and importance of the Ishmaelites from the late eighth century B.C. onwards. A. Jeffery states:[80]

> The description of Ishmael in Gen. 16:12 as a "wild ass of a man whose hand is against every man and every man's hand against him" suits remarkably well the Beduin of N. Arabia, whose raiding of settled folk has been a perennial factor in Near Eastern History. Gen. 21:20 speaks of him as dwelling in the desert area stretching from the land of Midian to the borders of Mesopotamia, which is precisely the area in which we find the Arab groups mentioned in the cuneiform inscriptions.

It is, likewise, noteworthy that in one of the Assyrian inscriptions a certain troublesome Arab queen, Samsi, is compared to a "wild ass-mare."[81]

Furthermore the extant patriarchal traditions suggest a long association between the Arabs on the one hand and the Arameans, Israelites, and Edomites on the other. Edom (Esau) is mentioned as intermarrying with the Ishmaelites. This represents the increasing Ishmaelite presence in the south Transjordanian region and the Negeb at the end of the monarchy and early exilic period. Likewise there is evidence that toward the end of the Assyrian Empire and in the Neo-Babylonian period there were strong cultural and economic connections between the Arameans of Harran and North Arabia.[82] It is little wonder, then, that the development of patriarchal associations with Aram-Naharaim should also include a sense of affinity with the Arabs of North Arabia. This was a view of the world in the mid-first millennium B.C. and can hardly be put into any earlier period.

Conclusion

In reviewing the conclusions reached thus far it should be emphasized that we are only concerned in this chapter with the question of nomadism in the patriarchal narratives. Most of the stories seem to

---

80. *IDB* 1:182.
81. *ANET*², p. 284.
82. See Lewy, *HUCA* 19:419ff., for these connections. For the earliest association of the Arabs with Babylonia see I. Eph'al, "'Arabs' in Babylonia in the 8th Century B.C.," *JAOS* 94 (1974): 108–115.

portray only a general pastoralism, whether of large or small livestock. The people's way of life is contrasted with that of the city-dwellers with a hint of antagonism towards this corrupt social form. Considering the basic characteristics of nomadism—transhumance, belligerence, and migrations—the stories, on the whole, reflect little of the nomadic way of life, and a distinction is made between the patriarchs and the full nomads of the desert or even the hunters. Abraham appears as the most nomadic of the patriarchal triad, but the frequent references to tents and camels point to first millennium phenomena. There is also little evidence of nomadic belligerence in their wanderings within the land of Palestine.

Furthermore, the patriarchal narratives do not present us with a nomadic migration in progress. There is nothing that points either to the Amorite migration of the early second millennium or to Israel's own settlement in the late second millennium B.C. The stories generally assume that the Arameans have settled in their respective regions, particularly the Upper Euphrates, and that the Arabs are already a fact of life in the desert and semi-desert regions to the south and east of Palestine and Transjordan.

Abraham's "migration" from Aramean Harran to Palestine and Jacob's journey to and from Harran suggest a period no earlier than the late Assyrian Empire. Abraham's move from Ur of the Chaldeans to Harran, on the other hand, is a specific historical allusion to the time of Nabonidus. These journeys can hardly be construed as nomadic migrations, and their function in the tradition must be sought in quite a different direction. There is nothing in this presentation of the "nomadic" patriarchs which is inappropriate to the portrayal of pastoral life in the period of the late Judean monarchy or exilic periods, but there is much that speaks against the choice of any earlier period.

CHAPTER 3

Personal Names, Peoples, and Places

One of the most frequent arguments used for placing the patriarchs in the early second millennium B.C. concerns their personal names.[1] It is suggested that these correspond very closely with West-Semitic ("Amorite") names of that period. But there are two fundamental problems with the argument based on personal names of the patriarchs. The first is that most of the names are eponyms of tribes, which means that while the tribal entities may all go back to the second millennium—that is, to the time of the Israelite settlement—the stories about the eponymous ancestors may all be much later. Consequently, a discussion about such names has significance for the question of the origin of the tribes and their settlement,[2] but no bearing upon the dating of the patriarchal narratives. For this reason we may immediately exclude from consideration the names of the twelve tribes of Israel as well as the names "Israel" and "Jacob." Even the name Isaac is an eponym, to judge by its occurrence in Amos 7:9,16 where it refers to the northern kingdom of Israel.[3] This leaves Abraham as the only important patriarchal name under consideration. It seems very unlikely that this name was ever an eponym for a tribal group; at least there is no indication of this in the Old Testament.

1. Bright, *A History of Israel*, pp. 70–71. Bright goes so far as to say that the names of the patriarchs "fit perfectly in the nomenclature of the Amorite population of the early second millennium rather than in that of any later day." See also Albright, *From the Stone Age to Christianity*, p. 237; deVaux, *Histoire*, pp. 190ff. Yet the argument by M. Noth that the West-Semitic population represented by these names is really "Proto-Aramean" is based primarily on the continuity of name types from the early period to the later Arameans, which would contradict Bright's statement. See Noth, "Mari und Israel, eine Personennamenstudie," *Geschichte und Altes Testament*, ed. G. Ebeling (Tübingen: Mohr, 1953), pp. 127–52, esp. 152; also J. C. L. Gibson, "Light from Mari on the Patriarchs," *JSS* 7 (1962): 51.
2. Noth, *The History of Israel*, pp. 53–68; cf. idem, "Mari und Israel," pp. 144–46.
3. See J. J. Stamm, "Der Name Isaac," *Festschrift A. Schädelin* (Bern: H. Lang, 1950), pp. 33–38.

The second problem with dating from names is that in the end it is so entirely inconclusive. The reason is that most of the features which characterize West-Semitic names of the early second millennium can be found in those of the late second millennium as well and in many Canaanite or Phoenician, Aramaic, Arabic, Nabatean and Palmyrene names throughout the first millennium B.C.[4] In fact, seventy years ago F. Hommel was so impressed with the similarity between the "Amorite" names of the Old Babylonian period and South Arabic names that he characterized the First Dynasty of Babylon as South Arabic.[5] Such a conclusion seems amusing in retrospect, but it is also very instructive. It is sufficient to recognize that the very conservative character of proper names, even when they are no longer understood, results in similar names and name formations for all the West-Semitic peoples over a very long period of time.

Nevertheless, it is necessary to give some consideration to the name "Abram," and its variant "Abraham."[6] One suggested explanation of the name "Abram" is that it should be associated with the Old Babylonian name, *abam-rama* (var. *aba-rama*).[7] With the loss of mimmation this would be represented in a consonantal text as אברם and incorrectly pronounced as Abram. This name, however, is not "Amorite" but native Akkadian. Nor is it limited to the Old Babylonian period but was apparently still in vogue in the Neo-Assyrian period as a male and female name.[8]

A more obvious and commonly accepted explanation of the name

4. The following are some of the primary collections and studies of personal names of the Ancient Near East. Amorite: Giorgio Buccellati, *The Amorites of the Ur III Period* (Naples: Instituto Orientale di Napoli, 1966); H. B. Huffmon, *Amorite Personal Names in the Mari Texts* (Baltimore: Johns Hopkins University Press, 1965). Ugaritic: F. Gröndahl, *Die Personennamen der Texte aus Ugarit* (Rome: Pontifical Biblical Institute, 1967). Akkadian: J. J. Stamm, *Die akkadische Namengebung* MVÄG 44 (Leipzig, 1939). Israelite: M. Noth, *Die israelitischen Personennamen im Rahmen der gemeinsemitischen Namengebung* BWANT 3, pt. 10 (1928). Phoenician and Aramaic: H. Donner and W. Röllig, *Kanaanäische und Aramäische Inschriften*, 3 vols. (Wiesbaden: O. Harrassowitz, 1962–64), vol. 3, "Index." Palmyrene: J. K. Stark, *Personal Names in Palmyrene Inscriptions* (Oxford: Clarendon Press, 1971). Pre-Islamic Arabian: G. Lankester Harding, *An Index and Concordance of Pre-Islamic Arabian Names and Inscriptions* (Toronto: University of Toronto Press, 1971).
5. F. Hommel, *The Ancient Hebrew Tradition* (New York, 1897), pp. 56ff.
6. For a general discussion with references to the literature see deVaux, *Histoire*, pp. 190–91; Noth, "Mari und Israel," pp. 143–44.
7. A. Ungnad, "Urkunden aus Dilbat," in *Beiträge für Assyriologie* 6, pt. 5 (1909): 82. It was popularized by W. F. Albright, "The Name Shaddai and Abram," *JBL* 54 (1935): 194. See also Bright, *History of Israel*, p. 70.
8. Stamm, *Akkadische Namengebung*, p. 292; deVaux, *Histoire*, pp. 190–91.

is to associate it with the West-Semitic form *abî-rām*, "(my) father is exalted."⁹ This style of nominal sentence name with these or corresponding elements was very common throughout the second and first millennia B.C. in West-Semitic names.¹⁰ In the name Abram the medial hireq, *î*, has quiesced, but this phenomenon is very common in Biblical as well as in Phoenician, Aramaic and Arabic names. Sometimes the same name is spelled with or without the hireq as in the cases of Abner and Absolom which rarely have the hireq, and Abishai which is rarely without it.¹¹

The name Ab(i)ram occurs in a few instances in the second millennium in texts from Ras Shamra,¹² but it is also possible that it occurs in a place name, *phqr ʾbrm*, "the fort of Ab(i)ram," found in the list of Shishak's campaign to be situated in southern Judah.¹³ There is no reason to suspect that the name has any connection with the patriarch. The two elements of the name, *abi* and *ram*, occur in both second and first millennium names. A number of Phoenician rulers have the name "Aḥiram" or "Ḥiram" in which the element *aḫi*, "brother," replaces *abi*, "father," a very common interchange in West Semitic names.¹⁴ Consequently, there is nothing about the name Abram that points especially to the second millennium more than the first.

The most obvious explanation of the variant "Abraham" is to consider it as a dialectic form of "Abram." In some Semitic dialects the weak verbal stems, particularly medial *waw*, may contain a secondary *hē*, for example Heb. *bôš* = Aram. *bht*.¹⁵ This dialectic

---

9. Noth, "Mari und Israel," p. 143; deVaux, *Histoire*, pp. 190–91.
10. See Noth, *Israelitischen Personennamen*, pp. 15ff., 145; and Huffmon, *Amorite Personal Names*, pp. 261–62. Note, however, that this name type is not so common in "Amorite" names but is very frequent in West-Semitic, Canaanite-Phoenician, and Arab names.
11. Albright (*JBL* 54:193) objects to the connection between Abram and Abiram because of the loss of medial *î*, which he regards as unusual. But this is a problem of the pronunciation tradition resulting from an alphabetic script. In early examples, such as Ugaritic *abrm*, *abmlk*, *aḫqm*, the hireq is not represented, but these probably correspond to Hebrew Abiram, Abimelek, Aḥiqam (see Gröndahl, *Personennamen aus Ugarit*, pp. 86–87. In Aramaic there occurs the name אחבר which corresponds in form to Hebrew אחאב, pronounced by MT Aḥab without the hireq. But Aramaic can also have forms written with the hireq, אביטב, which are similar to Hebrew אחיטב, Aḥitub (see Donner and Röllig, *Kan. und Aram. Inschriften* 3:53).
12. Gröndahl, *Personennamen aus Ugarit*, pp. 86–87.
13. B. Mazar, "The Campaign of Pharaoh Shishak to Palestine," *SVT* 4 (1957): 65.
14. See Donner and Rollig, *Kanaanäische und Aramäische Inschriften* 3: index.
15. So Albright, *JBL* 54:203; and deVaux, *Histoire*, p. 191.

phenomenon is found in a few instances in Ugaritic and Phoenician (though not with weak verbs) but is more characteristic of Aramaic and South Arabic. The name Abraham actually appears in the nineteenth century B.C. in the Egyptian execration texts as, *ᵓbwrhn*ᵓ (Aburahana), where it belongs to a ruler of a town *šmᶜn* (=Amarna Samḫuna) situated in Galilee.¹⁶ But the name also seems to occur in South Arabic as well.¹⁷ One can only conclude that the possible span for the use of "Abraham" is as great as for that of "Abram."

The other personal names which appear in the narratives are likewise inconclusive in dating the traditions. The name Laban is very likely a toponym, but the element *lbn* occurs in personal and geographic names over a long period of time.¹⁸ The name, Sarah (var. Sarai), "Princess," and its semantic equivalent, Milcah, belong to a class of feminine names that has a wide provenience in the Ancient Semitic world.¹⁹ Also common as a type are the feminine names related to animals, such as Leah, "cow", and Rachel, "ewe".²⁰ The meanings of some names, such as Lot and Rebekah, remain uncertain.

The patriarchal stories likewise abound in names of peoples, tribes, countries, and cities, and these names have also been used as arguments for the antiquity of the traditions.²¹ Consequently a review of these names, or at least those which may have any bearing on dating, will be undertaken below. Of course some names are more significant than others depending on how integral they are to a number of traditions. Other names are indecisive because their history may span the whole period under review. It is the overall

---

16. See W. F. Albright, "The Land of Damascus between 1850 and 1750 B.C.," *BASOR* 83 (1941): 34; deVaux, *Histoire*, p. 191. On the identification of *šmᶜn* see Y. Aharoni, *The Land of the Bible: A Historical Geography*, trans. A. F. Rainey (Philadelphia: Westminster Press, 1967), p. 106.
17. Albright, *BASOR* 83:34, cites both *ᵓbrhn* and *yhrhm* as occuring in South Arabic. These names appear as אברהן and יחרהם in vol. 2 of G. Ryckmans, *Les noms propres sud-sémitiques*, 3 vols. (Louvain: Bureaux du Muséon, 1934–35), but in Harding, *Index of Arabian Names*, they appear as *ᵓbrḥm* (p. 11) and *yhrm* (p. 689).
18. See J. Lewy, "The Old West Semitic Sun God Ḥammu," *HUCA* 18 (1944): 434, n. 39, pp. 455ff.
19. John Skinner, *Genesis*. International Critical Commentary, 2nd ed. (Edinburgh: T. & T. Clark, 1930) pp. 237–38; Noth, *Israelitischen Personennamen*, p. 10; J. J. Stamm, "Hebräische Frauennamen," in *Hebräische Wortforschung SVT* 16 (1967): 326.
20. Noth, *Personennamen*, p. 10; Stamm, "Frauennamen," p. 329.
21. See n. 1 above.

impression which the names suggest that is of decisive importance in the end.

The Israelites did not regard themselves as autochthonous in the land of Palestine, but as interlopers among another settled population. This population was designated by various names, such as Canaanites, Amorites, Hittites, and Philistines, known from historical sources of the second and first millennia B.C. There were other terms, however, such as Perizzites and Hivites, which are quite inexplicable or whose identity is very much debated. These terms, generally, do not seem to have been used in any very precise ethnic sense but are viewed as interchangeable for the same peoples. In some cases preference for a particular name seems to depend upon the literary source in which it is found, though caution should be used in making such terminology a strict criterion of source analysis.

As indicated in the previous chapter, an attempt has frequently been made to identify the patriarchs with the Amorites of the early second millennium B.C.[22] What is surprising about this attempted identification is how strongly the Old Testament contradicts it. The Amorites are mentioned in a stereotyped list of the autochthonous peoples along with the Canaanites and Hittites,[23] and in the Table of Nations (Gen. 10:15–19) they are regarded as only a subgroup of the Canaanites. In Gen. 15:16 the Amorites are regarded as the pre-Israelite population of Palestine in a way quite characteristic of Deuteronomy, especially with its strong pejorative overtones.[24] The distinction between these Amorites and Abraham and his descendents is clearly made. Gen. 14:7,13 suggests that the Amorites occupied the hill country of Judah around Hebron and as far south as the Judean towns of Hazazon and Tamar, but that beyond this point the nomadic Amalekites held sway.

Now it is true that the urban population of Syria and Palestine in the first half of the second millennium B.C. consisted of a prominent element of North-West Semitic peoples, commonly designated by modern scholars as "Amorite." This usage of Amorite, however, is

---

22. For the use of the term "Amorite" in the Old Testament see deVaux, *Histoire*, pp. 129–31; J. Van Seters, "The Terms 'Amorite' and 'Hittite' in the Old Testament," *VT* 22 (1972): 64–81; cf. Noth, "Nu 21 als Glied der 'Hexateuch'—Erzählung," *ZAW* 58 (1940/41): 181–89; and Gibson, *JNES* 20:220–24.

23. Gen. 15:20–21 (cf. Ex. 3:8,17; 23:23,28; 34:11; Deut. 7:1; 20:17; Josh. 24:11; Ezra 9:1).

24. See Van Seters, *VT* 22:72–78.

merely an academic convention and does not correspond to historical terminology in the second millennium B.C. Amorite (MAR.TU/ *Amurru*) is an Akkadian term, which in Old Babylonian was used for the direction west—that is, the western desert—or to designate the nomadic peoples of the Syrian steppes.[25] In the Mari archives of the Middle Euphrates and in the Alalah texts of North Syria, *Amurru* designates a specific political state in central Syria between Qatna and Hazor and is not a general term for nomad or west as in Babylonia. This special sense of *Amurru* as a political state also continues throughout the period of the Egyptian empire in Asia and is the only usage which is found. There is not a single instance from the second millennium B.C. in which the term Amorite includes Palestine or Transjordan or any parts of them.[26] After the demise of the kingdom of Amurru in the late thirteenth or early twelfth century B.C. there was no longer any distinctive ethnic group or political state known as Amorite.

The explanation for the Biblical use of the term Amorite as applied to Palestine comes from the royal inscriptions of the Neo-Assyrian Empire.[27] In these texts the term *Amurru* is used as a rather archaic designation for all the peoples of the West with whom the Assyrians came into contact. Consequently, with the Assyrian expansion of power in the eighth century all the states and peoples of Syria, Phoenicia, Palestine and Transjordan were regarded as belonging to the country of Amurru.[28] Its boundaries were given as extending from the Euphrates to the borders of Egypt, just as they are in the Old Testament, and in Gen. 15:18 in particular. The use of the term Amorite in the Old Testament generally, and in the Genesis

---

25. For the meaning of Amurru in the Old Babylonian period see G. Dossin, "Les bédouins dans les textes de Mari," *L'antica società bedouina*, pp. 38ff.; D. O. Edzard, *Die "zweite Zwischenzeit" Babyloniens* (Wiesbaden, 1957), pp. 30ff.; idem, *The Near East: the Early Civilizations* (London, 1967), pp. 180–186; J.-R. Kupper, *Les nomades en Mésopotamie au temps des rois de Mari*, pp. 147–196.
26. On the unhistorical nature of the traditions about the "Amorite" kingdoms of Transjordan see J. Van Seters, "The Conquest of Sihon's Kingdom: A Literary Examination," *JBL* 91 (1972): 182–197.
27. For all the Assyrian references see S. Parpola, *Neo-Assyrian Toponyms*, pp. 17–18.
28. See D. D. Luckenbill, *Ancient Records of Assyria and Babylonia*, 2 vols. (Chicago: University of Chicago Press, 1926–27) vol. 2, no. 239; *ANET*² p. 287. The recent work by A. Haldar, *Who Were the Amorites?* (Leiden: E. J. Brill, 1971), is quite unreliable. Among the many errors it contains is the attempt to read back into the second millennium the use of the term "Amurru" in these Neo-Assyrian inscriptions (p. 26)!

stories as well, is dependent upon this scribal development in Assyrian terminology.

The case is very similar for the use of the term "Hittite."[29] In Gen. 10:15f Hittite or its equivalent Heth occurs as a subgroup of the Canaanites second only to Sidon, and in Gen. 15:20 as one of the autochthonous inhabitants of Palestine alongside of the Amorites. Throughout Gen. 23 as well as in 25:9 and 49:29ff. the inhabitants of Hebron are called Hittites, although in Gen. 14:13 they are called Amorites, and in Judges 1:10 they are Canaanites. In Gen. 26:34; 27:46, and 36:2 mention is made of Esau marrying Hittite wives but these women are further identified as being Canaanite and women of the land (Gen. 28:1ff. and 36:2). There seems to be no clear distinction in Genesis among the terms Canaanite, Hittite, and Amorite, though a preference may be seen in the use of any one term by a particular literary source, and in this respect the term Hittite is usually assigned to the Priestly source.

In the Egyptian and cuneiform texts of the second millennium B.C. the land of the Hittites (*Ḫatti*) stood for the homeland of the successive Hittite kingdoms of Anatolia.[30] Following the destruction of the Hittite empire, about 1200 B.C., there was a migration of peoples from Asia Minor into North Syria. This led to the establishment of the so-called Neo-Hittite states of Carchemish, Aleppo, and Hamath,[31] with the result that this region became known as the "land of Ḫatti" in Assyrian inscriptions down to the ninth century B.C. However, with these "Hittite" states' complete loss of independence to the Assyrian empire and their incorporation into the provincial system of government and with the general tendency of the whole of inland Syria to become Aramaic, the term *Ḫatti* lost any specific ethnic or cultural connotation. It simply became an archaic designation for the political states of the West, frequently corresponding to Amurru.[32] Esarhaddon (680–669), for instance, includes among the "kings of Ḫatti" those of Tyre, Judah, Edom, Moab, Gaza, Ashkelon, Ekron, Byblos, Arvad, Samsimuruna, Beth Ammon and Ashdod—virtually the same list of nations that Sennacherib's

---

29. Van Seters, *VT* 22:66, 78–81; cf. Gibson, *JNES* 20:224–27.
30. On the Hittites see O. R. Gurney, *The Hittites* (Harmondsworth, England: Pelican Books, 1961); A. Goetze, *Kleinasien*, 2nd ed. (Munich: C. H. Beck, 1957).
31. Gurney, *Hittites*, pp. 39–46; W. F. Albright, *CAH*², fasc. 51, pp. 43–46.
32. See Parpola, *Toponyms*, pp. 157–58.

inscription calls "Kings of Amurru."³³ This understanding of the land of Ḫatti extends into the Neo-Babylonian period and even later.³⁴

The use of the word Hittite in Genesis corresponds only to this archaic and non-ethnic use from the late Assyrian empire onward. In fact while the term Ḫatti continued to be used for the whole region of the west and specifically for the sedentary population, Amurru took on a new specialized use by the late Neo-Babylonian or early Persian period and referred to the region of North Arabia.³⁵ This might account for the shift away from the Deuteronomic use of the term Amorite and the deliberate preference in the Priestly source for Hittite.

As mentioned above, the term Canaanite in Genesis is largely synonymous with Amorite and Hittite, and is a designation for the original inhabitants of the "land of Canaan" (Palestine) without implying a specific ethnic meaning.³⁶ The land of Canaan in the Old Testament, however, is not the equivalent of the "land of Amurru" or the "Ḫatti land" of the late Assyrian inscriptions but differs from them in two important respects. Firstly, the designation is completely absent from the Assyrian inscriptions of the first millennium B.C. Secondly, to judge from references outside of the patriarchal stories, the land of Canaan does not have the same geographical extent as the land of Amurru. The dimensions of the land of Canaan (Num. 34:2-12; Ezek. 47:15-20; Josh. 13:2-6, cf. Gen. 10:15-19) indicate that it extends only as far as Lebo—Hamath on the Upper Orontes and does not reach the Euphrates as does Amurru. Furthermore Canaan does not include any territory east of the Jordan even though it does include Damascus and the

---

33. Luckenbill, *Ancient Records*, vol. 2, no. 690; *ANET*² p. 291; cf. n. 28 above.
34. See D. J. Wiseman, *Chronicles of Chaldean Kings* (626-556 B.C.) (London: Trustees of the British Museum, 1956), pp. 69-70 for references in the text to Ḫatti, and pp. 25, 28, and 30-31 for commentary. For a Hellenistic reference see *ANET*², p. 317. DeVaux (*Histoire*, p. 133) overlooks these references when he states that the term Ḫatti disappeared from cuneiform texts after Esarhaddon. His general conclusions, however, are the same as mine. Note a similar development for the term Gutium in W. W. Hallo "Gutium," *Reallexicon der Assyriologie* 3, pt. 9 (1971): 717-19.
35. See Dougherty, *Nabonidus and Belshazzar*, p. 109.
36. The references to "Canaanites" are Gen. 12:6; 13:7; 34:30; cf. 34:2, where the same peoples are called "Hivites."

region east and north of it.[37] Since the dimensions of the land of Canaan do not correspond to Israel's boundaries at any time in its history it must also represent an idealization just as the land of the Amorites does. The question then arises as to how such a geographic designation arose and whether it has any bearing on the problem of dating the traditions which use it. This calls for a brief survey of the use of Canaan and Canaanites in extra-Biblical sources.[38]

Considerable confusion has been created by the current scholarly use of the term Canaanite to represent certain distinct cultural, archaeological or linguistic phenomena of the second millennium B.C. or earlier. It has also been suggested that the Canaanites were a Semitic migration of peoples which some place earlier and some later than the Amorites. In fact, such a modern usage of the term does not correspond to the ancient usage and can only lead to serious misunderstanding in any historical study of the second millennium B.C.[39]

The name of the country or people is entirely unknown until the early fifteenth century B.C., after which it occurs rather frequently throughout the period of the Egyptian Empire. Efforts to explain or delimit the term on the basis of etymology have not been very successful. The meanings "purple" and "merchants" are both probably secondary formations based on a certain contact with the people and products of Canaan, or at least a part of it. So while these meanings would point to the Phoenician coast, the term Canaan cannot be entirely defined geographically on that basis.[40]

37. See Y. Aharoni and M. Avi-Yonah, *The Macmillan Biblical Atlas* (New York: Macmillan Co., 1968), p. 41, map 50. The suggestion by M. C. Astour, in "The Origins of the Terms 'Canaan,' 'Phoenician,' and 'Purple,'" *JNES* 24 (1965): 348, that Canaan and Amurru are synonymous terms in Amarna and the Bible is incorrect and seriously weakens his study.
38. For a discussion of these sources see the following works: B. Maisler (Mazar), "Canaan and the Canaanites," *BASOR* 102 (1946): 7–12; Gibson, *JNES* 20: 217–20; Astour, ibid., 346–350; deVaux, "Le pays de Canaan," *JAOS* 88 (1968): 23–30; idem, *Historie*, pp. 124–26.
39. Such a usage is found, for instance, in W. F. Albright, "The Role of the Canaanites in the History of Civilization," *The Bible and the Ancient Near East*, ed. G. E. Wright (Garden City, N. Y.: Doubleday, 1961), pp. 328–62; K. M. Kenyon, *Amorites and Canaanites* (London: Oxford University Press, 1966); cf. Gibson, *JNES* 20:220; and deVaux, *Histoire*, pp. 135–40.
40. For a review of the various etymological approaches see deVaux, *JAOS* 88: 23–25; idem, *Histoire*, pp. 123–24.

The cuneiform and Egyptian sources are somewhat ambiguous about the location of Canaan. The earliest source, the statue of Idrimi from Alalaḫ seems to suggest a northern limit to Canaan in the region of the coastal town of Ammia, located a short distance north of Byblos.[41] The Amarna letters specify the towns in Phoenicia as far south as Acco and inland to Hazor as being part of Canaan and clearly indicate that the kingdom of Amurru to the north did not lie within its limits. Its more precise boundaries, however, are somewhat debatable. A suggestion that has recently been put forward is that Canaan was one of three provinces of the Egyptian Empire in Asia.[42] The farthest north was Amurru. The middle province was Upi, which included Damascus and northern Transjordan above the Sea of Galilee and the Beqa Valley with its center in Kumidi. The rest of the region to the south as far as Egypt, but not east of the Jordan, was included in Canaan, and its capital was at Gaza. Even after the kingdom of Amurru came under Hittite control the boundaries of the other two provinces remained stable until virtually the end of the empire. In general usage in the Nineteenth Dynasty, however, Canaan and Ḫuru (= the Hurrian land)[43] were largely synonymous terms which stood for the Egyptian holdings in Asia. Yet in spite of Ramesses II's campaigns in Transjordan there is no indication that Canaan or Ḫuru included this region.

The latest extant Egyptian reference to Canaan comes from a Twenty-second Dynasty (ca 9th to 8th century B.C.) inscription that mentions "a royal messenger of Canaan and Philistia."[44] This would suggest that with the establishment of the Philistine presence the designation Canaan may have become more restricted again to the Phoenician coastal region. There is some evidence to suggest that this more restricted Canaan was used by the Phoenicians themselves as the archaic name for their homeland.[45]

R. deVaux has recently pointed to the striking correlation be-

---

41. S. Smith, *The Statue of Idrimi* (London: British Institute of Archaeology in Ankara, 1949).
42. DeVaux, *JAOS* 88:27; idem, *Histoire*, p. 125.
43. See A. H. Gardiner, *Ancient Egyptian Onomastica*, 3 vols. (London: Oxford University Press, 1947) 1:180.
44. G. Steindorff, "The Statuette of an Egyptian Commissioner in Syria," *JEA* 25 (1939): 30–33.
45. For the late references see Maisler, *BASOR* 102:7–8; deVaux, *JAOS* 88:23.

tween the Egyptian administrative use of the term Canaan and the delineation of its boundaries in the Old Testament.[46] This is especially interesting in the case of Josh. 13:2ff. which states that the northern border of Canaan is the "boundaries of the Amorites." This is the only use of Amorites in the Old Testament which corresponds to Egyptian administrative terminology, and not to the idealized archaic usage of the Assyrian texts.[47]

DeVaux further suggests that this conception of the land of Canaan was adopted by the Israelite tribes when they first entered the land in the late Nineteenth Dynasty.[48] However this proposed dating has a number of serious weaknesses. First of all, the dimensions of Canaan were far beyond those gained by the early tribes, and it is hard to see how they could have appropriated such an ideal and felt themselves the inheritors of this land. It also specifically conflicted with their own historical reality of settling east of the Jordan River. Such a term could hardly have been functional to them, and one can scarcely imagine pedantic antiquarian interests on the part of the tribes to preserve it. The one population element with the greatest continuity from the period of the empire to the first millennium, the Phoenicians, apparently only retained at most a very restricted conception of Canaan applicable to themselves. Secondly, all the references to the precise dimensions of the "land of Canaan" are in rather late texts of the Old Testament, as deVaux also admits. The Ezek. 47:15–20 passage is particularly significant because it points to the fact that this "land of Canaan" was the land that formed the exilic ideal of the promised land and thus stands in contrast to the earlier "land of the Amorites," which dominates Deuteronomy. Thirdly, this careful delineation of all the borders of Canaan reflects a very scholarly sophistication and learning that is certainly not characteristic of tribal traditions but that was the result of scribal court education.[49]

In the light of these objections to an early date for the adoption of the term Canaan in its extended sense, I would propose a different solution. The suggestion of an Egyptian origin for the "land of Canaan" is very likely correct, and therefore its usage must have

---

46. deVaux, *JAOS* 88:29; idem, *Histoire*, pp. 126–27.
47. See Van Seters, *VT* 22:72–78.
48. deVaux, *Histoire*, p. 128; idem, *JAOS* 88:30.
49. See the "Letter of Hori" in ANET², pp. 476–77.

come into Judah at a time when Egyptian influence on the court was quite strong. This points to the Saite period in Egypt and the last days of the Judean monarchy.⁵⁰ The Pharaohs of this period revived Egyptian ambition for an Asian empire and were very much involved in Judean affairs. In support of this imperial dream were a consuming passion for the archaic and a revival of old terms and forms. It is true that there is no evidence from Egypt that the term Canaan was used at this time to designate Palestine. But there is some evidence that such archaic names as *Amor* and *Ḫuru* (the old synonym for Canaan) were revived and used through this period and down into later times.⁵¹

If this Egyptian use of Canaan was taken up during the Saite period (late 7th and 6th centuries B.C.), it would explain how a new ideal of the promised land arose after the western tribal territories had been lost. Its obvious archaic usage in Egyptian sources would have encouraged a similar use in Hebrew traditions about early times and would have given rise to the notion that the autochthonous population was "Canaanite." Certainly no corresponding Egyptian use of the term "Canaanite" existed in the time of the empire. There are also some indications of attempts at scholarly harmonization of the two different scribal traditions: the Assyrian and the Egyptian. One way was to assign the Amorites and Hittites (and other primitive peoples) to the hill country, while the Canaanites were said to "dwell by the Sea and along the Jordan" (Num. 13:29). This division probably recognized a Western Asian definition in

50. On the general characteristics of the Saite period see A. H. Gardiner, *Egypt of the Pharaohs* (Oxford: Clarendon Press, 1961), pp. 352–363.
51. In the "decree of Canopus" from the Hellenistic period the two names are given side by side as p^3 $t^š$ p^3 ^ʾImr p^3 $t^š$ n^3 $Ḫ^3$ rw, "the region of Amor, the region of the Ḫuru," and this is said to correspond in the Greek to ^ʾék $tē$ $Syrías$ $kaì$ $Phoiníkēs$, "from Syria and Phoenicia." (See Gardiner, *Onomastica* 1:180*–181*.) In a late demotic text, R. A. Parker, *A Vienna Demotic Papyrus on Eclipse—and Lunar—Omina* (Providence: Brown University Press, 1958), pp. 6–7, one finds the following list of foreign countries: p^3 *Grty*, "the Creatans," ^ʿybr (var. *ybr*), "the Hebrew (land)," p^3 ^ʿyrm, "the Amorite land," p^3 $t^š$ p^3 ^ʾIšur, "the land of the Syrians" (or Mesopotamia?). The text is Roman but its *Vorlage* may be Hellenistic or Persian. D. B. Redford in "The 'Land of the Hebrews' in Gen. XL 15," *VT* 15 (1965): 531–32, wants to date the original as early as the Saite period. Weippert's argument (*Settlement*, p. 93, n. 162) for an even earlier date suggests a serious misunderstanding of the text. The form and influence may have been Babylonian but there was certainly not a "Babylonian original" of this text. For additional late references to Ḫuru see H. Gauthier, *Dictionnaire des noms géographiques*, 7 vols. (Cairo: Société royale de géographie d'Egypte, 1925–31) 4:151–52.

which Canaan meant the Phoenician coast. Another method of harmonization is found in the Table of Nations (Gen. 10:15-19). There the list of primeval nations was construed in such a way as to make Canaan the father of all the primeval peoples but with Sidon as the first-born and Heth (Ḫatti) the next in line. The list gives special emphasis to the Phoenician cities, but the mention of "Hamathites," while not quite accurate according to the stricter boundary limitations, may be an allusion to the northern border of Lebo—Hamath. In the patriarchal stories themselves the authors are content for the most part merely to let the various terms stand as synonyms for one another (see also Ezek. 16:3). On the basis of this reconstruction one would have to assign the use of the term Canaanites, when it has reference to the greater land of Canaan, to the period of the late Judean monarchy at the earliest.

Another name which is used for the primitive population of Palestine is the Hivites. Besides appearing in the list of indigenous nations, it occurs in Gen. 34:2 as the designation of the population of Shechem. There has not as yet been any identification made between the Hivites and any historical people of the Near East. In the story of Genesis 34 the father of the eponym Shechem is called Hamor, which is the Hebrew word for "ass." Some attempt has been made, on the basis of the Septuagint, to regard the term Hivite as originally Horite, but the change is not supported by the other versions and seems arbitrary.[52] Consequently the term Hivite must remain inexplicable and of no concern to the present subject.

On the other hand, the name Horite does seem to correspond to a Near Eastern people, the Hurrians.[53] They were a movement of non-Semitic peoples largely contemporaneous with that of the Amorites but with their center of radiation in Armenia. Consequently their primary impact was on Upper Mesopotamia, where they established their first kingdoms in the early second millennium. They did not become a major power until after the founding of the

---

52. On the Hivite question see deVaux, *Histoire*, p. 134.

53. For a recent survey of the Hurrians see deVaux, "Les Ḫurrite de l'histoire et les Horites de la Bible," *RB* 74 (1967): 481–503; idem, *Histoire*, pp. 69–71, 86–91; also Van Seters, *The Hyksos*, pp. 181–190. For evidence of at least a few Hurrians in Palestine in the earlier OB period see A. Malamat, "Syro-Palestinian Designations in a Mari Tin Inventory," *IEJ* 21 (1971): 35–36; also the text discussed by A. Shaffer in W. G. Dever et al., *Gezer I: Preliminary Report of the 1964–66 Seasons* (Jerusalem: Keter Press, 1970), pp. 111–113. The archaeological findspot of this text, however, makes the dating uncertain.

kingdom of Mitanni in the Upper Euphrates region in the late sixteenth century B.C. About this time they also became strong enough to penetrate into Syria-Palestine in considerable numbers. They were not a nomadic movement but a military elite that had a reputation as charioteers, or *maryannu*. There is no evidence that their presence was the result of conquest, although some became rulers of various cities. While they were probably always a minority and largely Semiticized, the Egyptians recognized the importance of this elite urban element by calling the whole region of Syria-Palestine under their control the Ḫuru land.[54] This name came into common use in the Amarna Age and through the Nineteenth Dynasty. Yet long after the empire ended the Egyptians commonly referred to Syria-Palestine and its inhabitants by this archaic geographic term, even when there was virtually no ethnic trace of the Hurrians left.

A difficulty which thus arises with the Biblical Horites is how they came to be regarded as the original inhabitants of Edom (Gen. 14:6; 36:20–30; Deut. 2:12).[55] It seems inappropriate to associate charioteers of this group with such a region, and at any rate archaeological evidence suggests no great urban settlement in the area in the Late Bronze Age. Perhaps the explanation is that the authors of these references knew from Egyptian sources the name Ḫuru as an archaic designation for the people of Palestine. However in trying to localize the primitive nations in relation to later peoples they associated the Hurrians, most inappropriately, with Edom. There is, of course, no exact period with which to connect this development, although it more likely belongs to a time of Egyptian influence in Israel's court than to any other. As with the term Canaan, this would suggest the Saite period.

The Philistines are brought into the patriarchal stories by one author who identifies Abimelech, the king of Gerar and his people as Philistines (Gen. 26:1ff.) and the region around Gerar as the "land of the Philistines" (Gen. 21:32). The Philistines are not regarded as one of the autochthonous nations, for Israel knew the tradition which remembered that they had come from Crete (Amos 9:7). But there are also some indications to suggest that the Philistines were regarded as already present in the land when Israel entered (Judg. 3:3), and this would be consistent with the source

---

54. Gardiner, *Onomastica*, 1:180*–186*
55. See deVaux, *Histoire*, pp. 133–34.

in Genesis. Nevertheless many scholars who argue for the antiquity of the patriarchal traditions are prepared to admit that this reference to Philistines is an anachronism. However this still does not settle the question of the dating of such an anachronism so the history of the Philistines in Palestine will be briefly considered.[56]

At the end of the thirteenth century B.C., the Levantine coast received a devastating attack from a group of migrating peoples, called in Egyptian records the "Sea-Peoples." They came by both sea and land, and among the group which took part in the decisive battle against Ramesses III were the *prst*, "the Philistines." The Egyptians were successful in stopping the invasion of Egypt, and the Philistines were apparently settled in the destroyed cities of the southern coastal plain of Palestine. There they formed a pentapolis of Gaza, Ashkelon, Ashdod, Gath and Ekron. The Philistines apparently inherited the territorial administration of Palestine from the Egyptians. Biblical accounts about the early period of Israelite history refer to the rulers of the five Philistine cities as $s^eran\hat{\imath}m$, a foreign word which has been associated with the Greek *tyrannos*, or "tyrant." The Philistines remained the dominant power in Palestine until the rise of the Davidic monarchy, after which time they were largely confined to the coastal region from Gaza to Ekron. In spite of periodic disputes over territory between Judah and the Philistines the region of Philistia, known by this name in Egyptian and Assyrian sources, remained fairly stable. The names of the five principal cities and their kings also occur frequently in accounts of the wars of the Neo-Assyrian and Neo-Babylonian kings. Finally Nebuchadrezzar put an end to Philistine independence and exiled many of its inhabitants. Only the history of individual cities of the region continues, though remembrance of the archaic name of this region lived on into Roman times, when the name given to the whole land was "Palestine."

The references in Genesis are rather inconsistent with the historical outline. This book does not use the term *seren*,* the oldest term for the ruler of a Philistine city, even though this title was in use as late

---

56. See the recent surveys in J. C. Greenfield, *IDB* 3: 791–95; M. L. and H. Erlenmeyer, and M. Delcor, "Philistines," *DBS* 7, cols. 1233–88; T. C. Mitchell, "Philistia," in *AOTS*, pp. 405–429; deVaux, *Histoire*, pp. 468–74; W. F. Albright, *CAH*[2], fasc. 51, pp. 24–33; R. D. Barnett, "The Sea Peoples," *CAH*[2], fasc. 68; J. C. Greenfield, "Philistines," *Encyclopaedia Judaica*, 13: 399–403.

as the united monarchy. Genesis also speaks about a Philistine king of Gerar, but this is not one of the five royal cities, and there is no other historical record of a Philistine monarchy at Gerar or at any other city apart from the pentapolis. Furthermore, when Abraham and Isaac enter into treaties with the Philistines no other ruler except Abimelech (with a Semitic name!) is mentioned. Yet in the book of Judges and in the stories from the time of Saul and David, the five rulers of the Philistines always act in concert.

The solution to this problem is partly literary, but also partly historical. As I hope to show below, the earliest version of the story spoke only of a king of Gerar without any ethnic qualification. It was a later writer who identified Gerar as a place "in the land of the Philistines" and therefore, he had to regard the king as a Philistine. Yet this connection would only have been possible after the pentapolis had been broken and only a vague notion of a region called Philistia remained. This, in my judgment, seems to point again to the exilic period.

In a few instances in Genesis the patriarchs are called Hebrews,[57] although these references are rather isolated from the main body of patriarchal traditions. In Gen. 14:13 Abraham is called a Hebrew (ᶜibri) in a context in which Mamre (an eponym for Hebron) is called an Amorite—both terms clearly intended as ethnic. However Genesis 14 is regarded by many scholars as separate from the rest of the Abraham stories and often considered as "late midrash."[58] All the other occurrences of "Hebrew" in the patriarchal stories are in the Joseph story, which is also regarded as not integral to the Jacob traditions, but a separately created novella.[59] Here Joseph is called a Hebrew by the Egyptians (Gen. 39:14,17; 41:12). He describes his own origin as from the "land of the Hebrews" (Gen. 40:15), which is synonymous with "land of Canaan" in the rest of the story. The brothers are called Hebrews, as distinct from Egyptians (Gen. 43:32). All these references are clearly ethnic, and the choice of Hebrew over Israelite or Jew is probably intended to avoid an obvious anachronism.

57. For discussion of the biblical references see deVaux, *Histoire*, pp. 202–08; Gibson, *JNES* 20: 234–36.
58. DeVaux, *Histoire*, p. 211.
59. See most recently the full discussion by D. B. Redford, *A Study of the Biblical Story of Joseph, Genesis 37–50, SVT* 20 (1970).

It is difficult to date the use of the term Hebrew as an equivalent for Israelite within any very narrow limits. The term Hebrew occurs in the book of Jonah (1:9), which is admittedly a late work, and it also appears in both Jewish and non-Jewish literature of the Hellenistic and Roman periods.[60] Hebrew with the meaning of Israelite also occurs in Deut. 15:12–17 and Jer. 34:9,14—texts of the late monarchy—but these are usually regarded as interpretations of an earlier law on the Hebrew slave in Exod. 21:2–6 that cannot be so easily dated. In the story of the Exodus the term Hebrew is regularly alternated with Israelite. It is also found in the accounts of warfare between Israel and the Philistines (I Sam. 4:6ff.; 13:3ff.; 14:11,21; 29:13). On the basis of these occurrences it has sometimes been suggested that the term Hebrew belongs to the pre-monarchy period. But this argument is misleading. The dating of these stories is debatable and may very well be late. Hebrew (ʿibri) is always used in a context in which Israelites are in contact with foreigners, and such stories are abundant in the period of time before the monarchy and after the exile but rare during the monarchies of Judah and Israel.[61]

The question about dating the term Hebrew has been confused by a further issue: whether or not the term is ever used in a non-ethnic, sociological sense. It has been argued that the earlier use of the term was in fact non-ethnic, and that only later did it take on an ethnic meaning equivalent to Israelite or Jew.[62] But a non-ethnic meaning of the term is not obvious in any of the passages in which it is used and certainly not in Genesis. In fact the issue only arose because the term Hebrew was identified with the non-Biblical designation Ḫapiru used in the second millennium B.C. Because of the very extensive discussion of this question in the scholarly literature some consideration must be given to it here.[63]

The name of this people occurs in various forms throughout the second millennium B.C. In cuneiform texts it is written either with the ideogram SA.GAZ or in syllabic writing as ḫapiru. In the alphabetic script of Ugarit it is written as ʿpr and in Egyptian hieroglyphs as ʿprw. The earliest references to the Ḫapiru occur in the

60. See deVaux, *Historie*, p. 202.
61. See also Redford, *Joseph Story*, p. 201–03.
62. See Koch, *VT* 19:37–81.
63. See the works cited in Chap. 2, n. 55.

Old Assyrian texts followed by frequent occurrences in the Mari and Alalaḫ archives. These all suggest a rather bellicose and nomadic people located primarily in the region of North Syria and the Upper Euphrates. Very early the ideogram SA.GAZ "bandit," was applied to them and became a regular ideogram for Ḫapiru with its strongly negative connotation. The Ḫapiru appear most often in the texts as bands of soldiers, either as belligerents or as mercenaries.

Essentially the same picture emerges in the latter part of the second millennium B.C., whether in the Idrimi inscription from Alalaḫ, the Hittite treaties with Ugarit and Amurru, the Amarna letters, or the Egyptian texts. These texts give considerable information about the activity of the Ḫapiru in Syria and Palestine. On the other hand, the portrayal of Ḫapiru as militant nomads in these texts is complicated by the fact that in texts from the fifteenth century B.C. at Nuzi, east of the Tigris River, they appear as entering into a contractual servitude in return for their livelihood. However this situation may be due largely to their geographic isolation from the main body of Ḫapiru in the West and cannot be construed as normal for an understanding of the term Ḫapiru elsewhere. Similarly the presence of Ḫapiru as slaves in Egypt from the Eighteenth to Twentieth Dynasties indicates that they were probably prisoners of war, much as other ethnic groups were in this period.[64]

The diversity of references to the Ḫapiru in time, place, and manner of life has given rise to the notion that the Ḫapiru do not represent a specific people but are, instead, a social class. In further support of this judgment is the fact that their personal names do not belong to one particular ethnic group.[65] On the other hand attempts to derive a sociological meaning for Ḫapiru from etymological study have not been very successful.[66] Against such a sociological usage is the fact that it is difficult to see why a foreign term would be used in Akkadian and Egyptian documents for different social phenomena instead of using native terms.

R. de Vaux has recently suggested that Ḫapiru should be viewed as an ethnic term in spite of their geographic dispersion and varying social status. Their role in the Near East is paralleled to a large

---

64. This was apparently the case with the Shosu in Egypt. See R. Giveon, *Les bédouins Shosu des documents égyptiens* (Leiden: E. J. Brill, 1971), pp. 219–31.
65. See Greenberg, *Ḫab/piru*, p. 87.
66. See deVaux, *Histoire*, pp. 109–110; Weippert, *Settlement*, pp. 81ff.

extent by other bellicose, nomadic groups, such as Sutu, Lulahhu and Shosu.[67] The fact that some persons such as Idrimi of Alalaḫ lived for a time among them does not argue against this, for Idrimi is never actually called a Ḫapiru.[68] It still seems to me most reasonable to regard the term as an originally ethnic one that acquired some sociological and derogatory connotations such that it could apply to similar or only loosely related nomadic groups. It was not unlike the development of the term Aramean of a later day.[69]

We now come to the question of whether there is any connection between the term Ḫapiru and Hebrew, and there are two aspects to this question that should not be confused. Firstly, there is the historical question of whether or not the Israelite settlement in Palestine is a part of the larger Ḫapiru nomadic movement, and secondly there is the question of whether or not the two terms are linguistically equivalent. In our earlier discussion we accepted the historical arguments which suggested that there was some relationship between the two groups. However this cannot be taken to immediately solve the linguistic question of whether or not the term Ḫapiru can be equated with the term Hebrew (ʿibri). It is not so easy to account for the difference—that is, the shift from p to b—since both terms are West Semitic, and there would be little reason for a corruption in any primitive and virtually contemporary tradition.[70] It is possible that the term ʿibri is a late degenerated archaism of the earlier Ḫapiru (ʿapiru), which was revived along with other archaic terms that also suffered some corruption.[71] On the other hand it might have had an entirely different origin that is now much more difficult to discover. Yet at some stage in Israel's history the term Hebrew was used to imply an ethnic unity of both Judeans

---

67. *Histoire*, pp. 111–12.
68. Weippert's criticism of deVaux, in "Abraham der Hebräer?" *Biblica* 52 (1971): 412ff., rests on the reference in the Idrimi inscription: "I lived for seven years among the SA.GAZ (Ḫapiru) people." Weippert interprets this to mean that he became a Ḫapiru. But it can also be taken as similar to the situation of the exile Sinuhe who lived for several years among the ʿamu, although he always remained an Egyptian.
69. Another parallel would be the Shosu (*šʒsw*) nomads of Southern Palestine in Egyptian sources of the Late Bronze Age. It is likely that the name is still preserved in Hebrew *šōse/šōsîm* (1 Sam. 14:48; Judg. 2:14,16; 2 Kings 17:20; Isa. 17:4; Jer. 30:16, 50:11) in which it has the meaning of "robbers," "plunderers." In late Egyptian and Coptic *shos* means "shepherd" but also "Arab." See R. Giveon, *Les bédouins Shosu*, pp. 261–64.
70. Cf. the linguistic arguments by Weippert, *Settlement*, pp. 74–82.
71. See above, no. 70, for a similar development of Shosu.

and Israelites vis à vis foreign nations, and this is why it always occurs in such contexts in the historical traditions. It was, likewise, a most suitable term for designating the ancestors of the people in relation to foreigners; thus, it was used in the patriarchal stories. There is certainly no compelling reason to believe that it is early and every reason to suspect that it is late. However in spite of all the discussion about the term Hebrew, it remains very inconclusive in dating the patriarchal narratives.

In the previous chapter the relationship of the patriarchs to the Arameans, particularly those of Upper Mesopotamia, was discussed. Now the various toponyms and tribal names associated with the Arameans in the patriarchal narratives must be considered. The general region in which the ancestral home of Harran is situated is called Aram-Naharaim in the Old Testament.[72] The last element in this name occurs first in the Eighteenth Dynasty in the Egyptian sources as *Nhrn*, and in the Amarna letters as *Naḥrima*.[73] It was apparently a word for the region within the bend of the Euphrates as far east as the Habur, possibly with some extension west of the Euphrates as well. It does not seem to have been either an Akkadian term or one used in the region itself but a creation of the scribes of Syria-Palestine. At some time after the Arameans settled in that general region the refix "Aram" was applied to the term, which is how it appears in the Old Testament.

A synonym for Aram-Naharaim that appears in the P redaction of Genesis is Paddan-Aram (Gen. 25:20; 28:2,6,7; 48:7). This is the Aramaic equivalent of the Hebrew $śědē$-*Aram* "field of Aram" or "country of Aram" (Hos. 12:12[13]).[74] Both Aram-Naharaim and Paddan-Aram are devoid of any political connotations and reflect neither the time of the independent Aramean states nor that of the later Assyrian provinces in the region. As they stand the terms simply suggest an area in which Arameans lived; they give little indication of any historical period.

Abraham's origin in Aram Naharaim is further stressed in the tradition by the association of a number of place names in the region of Harran with Abraham's immediate family (Gen.

72. Gen. 24:10; Deut. 23:5; Judg. 3:8; 1 Chron. 19:6; Ps. 60:2.
73. See the discussion of this term by J. J. Finkelstein, "Mesopotamia," *JNES* 21 (1962): 73-92.
74. Simons, *Geog. and Topog. Texts*, #19, p. 7; cf. R. A. Bowman, in "Arameans," *IDB* 1:191, who interprets the expression as "road of Aram."

11:22–32).⁷⁵ Abraham's father is called Terah, which corresponds to the town name Til Turaḫi (var. Til ša Turaḫi), while the name of his brother (or grandfather?) Nahor may be seen in the place name Naḫuru (OB) or Til Naḫiri (Assyr.).⁷⁶ The name of Abraham's other brother, Haran (with h instead of ḫ), cannot be so easily identified with Harran (Heb. Ḥaran), especially since the city is thought to have existed before the family arrived from Ur. The father of Nahor is Serug, whose name corresponds to Sarūgi, another town in the area. All these places are listed in the Neo-Assyrian texts as being in the Balih valley region near Harran. The fact that Harran and Nahor (Naḫuru) appear in second millennium sources from the Old Assyrian texts and Mari archives has led some to stress the importance of these names as indicative of the antiquity of the tradition.⁷⁷ But two of the names do not occur, and one of them, Sarūgi (Serug) seems to have been a different name, Batna, in the Old Babylonian period.⁷⁸ The father of Serug is Reʾu (Gen. 11:21–22), and this name is connected with Ruʾua, an Aramean tribe of southeastern Mesopotamia and is known from the mid-eighth century onward.⁷⁹ The significance of this name in the genealogy must be to emphasize the original connection between the Arameans of southern Mesopotamia and those of the Upper Euphrates.

Another list of Arameans is found in Gen. 22:20–24, in two parts. In the first part eight sons of Nahor by his wife Milcah are listed, and of these four names can be clearly identified as place or tribal names.⁸⁰ Chesed represents the Chaldeans of Southern

75. See the treatment of this genealogy by A. Malamat, "King Lists of the Old Babylonian Period and Biblical Genealogies," *JAOS* 88 (1968): 163–73 (esp. p. 166); also deVaux, *Histoire*, pp. 189–90. For the Assyrian sources see Parpola, *Toponyms*, pp. 306, 354–56.
76. On the use of *Til* in these names see Malamat, *JAOS* 88:166, n. 13. There are some names in Assyrian texts that alternate in the use of Til, for example Barsip and Til Barsip, so the prefix Til cannot be used as an argument against the Assyrian form of the name.
77. W. F. Albright, *From the Stone Age to Christianity*, pp. 236–37; J. Bright, *A History of Israel*, p. 70; deVaux, *Histoire*, p. 190.
78. Finkelstein, *JNES* 21:77–78.
79. B. Moritz, "Die Nationalitat der Arumu—Stämme in Südost—Babylonien," *Oriental Studies Dedicated to Paul Haupt*, ed. C. Adler and A. Ember (Baltimore: Johns Hopkins University Press, 1926), p. 193.
80. See Simons, *Geog. and Topog. Texts*, #19, 40, 48, 68; cf. Albright, "Dedan," *Geschichte und Altes Testament, Festschrift A. Alt*, ed. G. Ebeling (Tübingen: Mohr, 1953), pp. 8–9, n. 2.

Mesopotamia. Buz and Hazo are known from Assyrian sources (primarily seventh century) as two oases, Bazu and Hazu, situated in Northeastern Arabia. Uz is known from the Book of Job to have been in the North Arabian region, but its exact location remains uncertain.[81] The other four names in the list may be personal names exclusively, since they cannot at present be identified as eponyms.[82] The second part of the list names four sons of the concubine Reumah, and of these Tebah and Maacah share their names with Aramean regions of Syria known from first millennium sources.[83] This genealogical scheme suggests that in the view of its author the primary group of Arameans in the Upper Euphrates had most important connections with the peoples of southern Mesopotamia, both with the Chaldeans and with certain north Arabian regions close by, which may have been Aramaic-speaking. What is surprising is that the relationship with the Syrian Arameans is given such a lowly status after the complete decline of the Syrian Arameans in the late Assyrian and Neo-Babylonian empire. This reconstruction of Aramean relations very likely reflects the world of the seventh or sixth centuries B.C.

In the previous chapter it was noted that in the Hagar-Ishmael stories Abraham was considered to be related to the Arabs of North Arabia. In further support of this connection Genesis 25 gives two lists of Arab peoples descended from Abraham through secondary wives.[84] The first group (vv. 1–5) are the offspring of Keturah, a name clearly related to Heb. $q^e\underline{t}\hat{o}ret$ "incense," and it is therefore very likely that the author has organized the list to include those involved in the incense trade.[85] The names of the first three sons, while Arabic in character, cannot be identified with certainty as place names. On the other hand, the tribe of Midian is very familiar,

---

81. Albright, "Dedan," p. 8; but cf. Simons, *Geog. and Topog. Texts*, #19, p. 8.
82. Kemuel is a personal name in Num. 34:24 and 1 Chron. 27:17. Bethuel is a personal name in the story of Laban (Genesis 24). Pildash and Yidlaph are not easily explained as Semitic names.
83. Simons, *Geog. and Topog. Texts*, pars. 19, 766 (see index).
84. For a recent full discussion of these names see F. V. Winnett, "The Arabian Genealogies in the Book of Genesis," *Translating and Understanding the Old Testament*, ed. H. T. Frank and W. L. Reed (Nashville: Abingdon Press, 1970), pp. 171–96 (esp. 188–96). See also Montgomery, *Arabia and the Bible*, pp. 42–46; A. Jeffery, "Arabians," *IDB* 1:182–83; Albright, "Dedan," pp. 9–12; Skinner, *Genesis*, pp. 349–54.
85. This was a suggestion made in a seminar of the Department of Near Eastern Studies, University of Toronto, by Professor Israel Ephal in the winter of 1972. See also Skinner, *Genesis*, p. 350.

referring to the Arabs living in northwestern Arabia along the east coast of the Gulf of Aqaba. The Old Testament knows them as merchants of spices in Isa. 60:6, along with Ephah, a "son" of Midian. The sons of Midian, Ephah and Epher, are mentioned in eighth-century Assyrian inscriptions as Haiappa and Apparu and have been identified with the towns Ghwāfah and ʿOfr. Another son Hanoch may be the eponym of the town Hanakiya in the same region. Abida has been linked with the tribe Ibadidi, regularly associated with the Thamud. It may also have given its name to the modern Badʿ, an important oasis in ancient Midian. Eldaʿah is not listed as a place name, but it does occur as an Arab royal name in Assyrian and Sabean inscriptions and may point to southern connections.[86]

Following Midian among the names of Keturah's sons are two closely related regions, Ishbak and Shuah. These appear in the Assyrian sources as Yasbuq and Suhu and are located in the steppe region of northern Syria.[87] Their place in this genealogy indicates that they must have been the northernmost Arab tribes involved in the incense trade. Similarly, the presence of Sheba and Dedan, the sons of Jokshan (variant for Joktan), in this list must have a different function from that in Gen. 10:7,26. They were both important centers in the incense trade. Sheba (Saba) was, of course, the southern terminus, while Dedan was a major emporium located in the oasis of elʿUla in the northern Hejaz. It is mentioned in both Biblical and Arabic sources from the sixth century B.C. onward, but not earlier.[88] Dedan's absence even from Assyrian sources, given

---

86. For the occurrence of two royal names in the table of nations see M. C. Astour, "Sabtah and Sabteca, Ethiopian Pharaoh Names in Genesis 10," *JBL* 84 (1965): 422–25.

87. Albright, "Dedan," p. 9, nn. 4 and 5. However, there is no need to consider that these tribes "migrated from much further south" because close geographical affinity is not the organizing principle. Cf. Winnett, "Genealogies," p. 193. Jeffery (*IDB* 1: 182–83) regards the connection of a southern Sheba with northern Dedan as strange and looks for a northern Sheba, relating it to the Sabai of the Assyrian texts. However, these Sabai cannot be easily located.

88. See Albright's treatment of Dedan. However, his use of the Table of Nations to find a reference as early as the tenth century B.C. has no independent historical value; cf. Winnett, "Genealogies," p. 172, who regards the Genesis references as exilic. Furthermore, Albright's identification of Tidnu/Didnu of the Ur III period with Dedan may be firmly rejected; cf. J. Bottéro, *CAH*², fasc. 29: 30, where he identifies Tidan/Didan with the region of Mt. Basar in North Syria. See also A. van den Branden, "La chronologie de Dedan et de Lihyan," *Bi. Or* 14 (1957): 13; and F. V. Winnett and W. L. Reed, *Ancient Records From North Arabia* (Toronto: University of Toronto Press, 1970) pp. 31, 99–101.

their intense interest in the region, is significant. The sons of Dedan, Asshurim, Letūshim and Leummim, are rather enigmatic. One suggestion is to identify Asshurim as "Syrians," since Ashur ('šr) is mentioned with this meaning in late texts.[89] It may be that the names suggest foreigners or a mixture of peoples resident at Dedan in merchant colonies there. In any case this text on the sons of Keturah, under the guise of a genealogy, gives a picture of the wide-ranging incense trade carried on by the various Arab tribes and localities in the sixth century B.C.

The second list of Arab tribes (Gen. 25:13-16) gives the genealogy of Hagar-Ishmael. These two names were very likely quite distinct tribal groups which the author has linked together as mother and son in order to relate them both to Abraham. Both Hagrites and Ishmaelites are mentioned in Ps. 83:7 (ET:6) as Arab tribes hostile to Israel, similar to the statement in Gen. 16:12. The Hagrites are situated in Moab while the Ishmaelites are in Edom. The mention of Edom could refer to the Negeb as well as the country east of the Arabah if the psalm is postexilic. While it has been dated quite early by some, this seems hardly likely.[90] The reference to Gebal, v. 8(ET:7), is to an Arab tribe that was in this Transjordanian region in the latter part of the sixth century, according to a recent archaeological discovery.[91] There is considerable evidence that the whole of Transjordan was dominated at this time by Arab tribes who largely replaced the older states and who constituted a threat for Judah as well.[92] This development is also reflected by the Chronicler (I Chron. 5:10,15ff.) when he anachronistically places the Hagrites in Transjordan in the time of Saul and also mentions them as the chief inhabitants of Transjordan at the time of the settlement. But these are merely the reflections of the Chronicler's own day, when the Hagrites and the closely related Itureans (Jetur) were the principal population element in Transjordan.

It is doubtful that the Hagrites can be identified with the Ḥaga-

89. Winnett, "Genealogies," p. 190.
90. B. Mazar, "The Historical Background of the Book of Genesis," *JNES* 28 (1969): 79-80.
91. See S. H. Horn, "Chronique," *RB* 79 (1972): 425, which mentions the discovery of an ostracon dated about 525 B.C. and containing a reference to the Benē Gubla. This tribe is also mentioned by Josephus, *Ant.* 9:188 as the Gabalitai.
92. See W. J. Dumbrell, "The Tell el-Maskhuta Bowls and the 'Kingdom' of Qedar in the Persian Period," *BASOR* 203 (Oct., 1971): 40-41.

ranu of the eighth-century Assyrian texts.[93] Against it is the difference between Heb. h and Akkadian ḫ, as well as the fact that the Ḫagaranu appear to be an Aramean tribe of southern Mesopotamia.[94] Yet the Assyrian references do suggest a close association between the Ḫagaranu and the Nabatu similar to the connection between Hagar and the Nabaioth in the genealogy of Hagar-Ishmael (v. 13). The Hagrites, however, are known from the classical geographers and pre-Islamic sources as Arab tribes living in North Arabia.[95] The Ishmaelites, on the other hand, are very probably identified with the *Sumuʾil* of the Assyrian annals dating from the time of Sennacherib onward.[96] The king of Sumuʾil is also called the "king of Arabia" or the "king of the Qidri" (Kedar). One of the gates of Nineveh, the "Desert Gate," was so called because "the men of Sumuʾil, the men of Tema" entered the city through it with their royal tribute. This connection of the Ishmaelites with Teima (Tema) is further strengthened by the discovery near ancient Teima of two inscriptions in ancient Teimanite script that refer to a tribe or kingdom of *SMᶜL*.[97] Elsewhere in ancient North and South Arabic the name is rendered by ysmᶜl, though there is evidence of orthographic inconsistency.[98]

Among the sons of Ishmael in Gen. 25:13–16 those attested in Neo-Assyrian and Neo-Babylonian sources are the Arab tribes of the Nabaioth (*Nabaitu*), Kedar (*Qidri*), Massa (*Masai*) and Adbeel (*Idibaʾili*). The prominence given to Nabaioth has always tempted an identification with the Nabataeans but against this is the difference (t/ṭ) in the two names. Furthermore the name written as *nbyt* with unemphatic t has actually been found in inscriptions in the

---

93. See Parpola, *Toponyms*, p. 141.
94. However, see Naḥrima for Naharaim cited above (p. 58).
95. Simons, *Geog. and Topog. Texts*, #102, p. 39. See also Giveon, *Les bédouins*, pp. 166–67, for Egyptian *hkrw* from the Persian period.
96. For this identification see J. Lewy, "The Late Assyro-Babylonian Cult of the Moon and its Culmination at the Time of Nabonidus," *HUCA* 19 (1945–46): 432, n. 143. See also the discussion in Winnett and Reed, *Records from North Arabia*, pp. 93–96. A parallel for the Assyrian rendering of Sumuʾil for Ishmael is the Assyrian Siriʾil for Israel.
97. Winnett and Reed, *Records*, pp. 93–96.
98. Harding, *Index of Arabic Names*, lists smᶜ (p. 328) and bnw smᶜym (p. 329), but also smᶜl (p. 328) ysmᶜl and ysmᶜl (p. 671) and ʾsmᶜl (p. 46), as personal or tribal. There also seems to be a tribal group ḥjrm as in the phrase šᶜbn smᶜy ḏ ḥjrm (p. 177), as well as a tribal group hjrm (p. 609). Are these merely orthographic variants? See G. Ryckmans, *Les noms*, p. 307.

neighborhood of Teima.[99] In the Neo-Assyrian and Neo-Babylonian periods the Qidri seem to be the leading tribe of the Ishmaelites and play an important political role in the west.[100] Included also among the sons of Ishmael are the eponyms of two important oases: Tema and Dumah (*Adumu/Adumatu*), both of great importance in the late Assyrian Empire and throughout the Neo-Babylonian Empire. The last three names on the list belong together because they probably represent tribal elements of Transjordan. Two of them, Jether (Itureans) and Naphish, are Hagrites (I Chron. 5:19), and Kedemah also belongs in the eastern Moab region (Deut. 2:26). Mibsam and Mishma were probably Ishmaelite or Kedarite tribes in south Judah. By the time of the Chronicler they were so fixed in the region that they appear as part of the tribe of Simeon (I Chron. 4:25). Nothing can be said about the name Hadad, which is otherwise unknown. The list seems to represent a confederacy of tribes that lived on the southern and eastern borders of Judah (Gen. 25:18; cf. 16:12; 21:20–21) with an extension of their influence or control as far as the major oases of northern Arabia. The same reality is reflected in a number of Old Testament texts from the late monarchy to the postexilic period in which these Arab tribes play a major political and economic role.[101]

The lists of Arameans and Arabs may be interpreted as representing a view of these peoples in the sixth century B.C. but not much earlier than this. These lists should not be regarded as simply late material added to old traditions. On the contrary, they are quite consistent with the way in which the stories speak about the Arameans and Arabs. Their authors' intent, at least in part, was to relate the ancestors of Israel (and therefore Israel itself) to the two major peoples which dominated the world of the Neo-Babylonian period. It was most appropriate to endeavor to express this relationship in the language of eponymous ancestors and mythical origins.

---

99. Winnett and Reed, *Records from North Arabia*, pp. 38–39, 113–20. Cf. now E. C. Broome, "Nabaiati, Nabaioth and Nabataeans," *JSS* 18 (1973) : 1–16.

100. Dumbrell, *BASOR* 203: 40–44; A. F. Rainey, "The Satrapy 'Beyond the River,'" *Australian Journal of Biblical Archaeology* 1 (1969): 51–78.

101. Job 1:13ff.; 2:11; 6:19; 32:2,6; Isa. 21:1–17; 60:6–7; Jer. 2:10; 6:20; 25:23; 49:7–8, 28–30; Ezek. 25:13; 27:20–22; 38:13. For recent discussion of Isaiah 21 see Dumbrell, *BASOR* 203:41.

CHAPTER 4

The Social Customs of the Patriarchs

This chapter will take up the question of the Near Eastern background for family customs, laws, and other social forms reflected in the patriarchal narratives.[1] While it may be argued by some that an account of an ancient tradition can always be updated by changes in terminology for peoples and places, it is much harder to do so in the case of social customs. They are often so integral to the course of the story, as for instance the practice of giving a maid to one's husband, that it is difficult to see how the custom could be updated without changing the whole tradition. Indeed, many scholars have seen in these patriarchal customs the strongest criterion for considering the Genesis stories to be of great antiquity.

Most students of Old Testament literature have by now become quite familiar with the references to legal materials from the second millennium B.C. which have been used for comparative purposes. The various law codes of the second millennium are quite accessible through the translations in J. B. Pritchard's *Ancient Near Eastern Texts*[2] as well as the translations and legal commentary by G. R. Driver and J. C. Miles.[3] Alongside of these codes and at least as important in this discussion are the various collections of legal documents that pertain to family laws and business contracts.[4]

---

1. See deVaux, *Histoire*, pp. 230–243. This is easily the best general treatment of the subject at the present time and has a comprehensive bibliography which does not need to be repeated here. Cf. Bright, *History of Israel*, pp. 78–79, who takes an apologetic approach in defense of an early date and does not fairly represent the critical views and contrary evidence presented by Greenberg, Tucker, and Van Seters.
2. *ANET*[2], pp. 159–197; *ANET*[3], pp. 523–528.
3. G. R. Driver and J. C. Miles, *The Assyrian Laws* (Oxford: Clarendon Press, 1935), cited as DMAL; idem, *The Babylonian Laws*, 2 vols. (Oxford: Clarendon Press, 1952–55), cited as DMBL. A new German translation of the law codes is available in R. Haase, *Die keilschriftlichen Rechtssammlungen in deutscher Übersetzung* (Wiesbaden: O. Harrassowitz, 1963). A comprehensive bibliography can be found in the article "Gesetze," *Reallexicon der Assyriologie*, vol. 3, pt. 4 (1966): 243–97.
4. A sampling of these may be seen in *ANET*[2], pp. 217–20; *ANET*[3], pp. 542–47.

Blocks of such materials have come from many of the major archives of the second millennium. Among these collections, the Nuzi texts have played a very prominent role because of the unusually large number of family archival documents which have come from this site and from the related site of Arrapḫa.[5] These have given rise to the most extensive discussion of parallels with the family customs of the patriarchs, especially by C. H. Gordon and E. A. Speiser.[6] The numerous studies on comparative family law have concentrated almost exclusively, up until now, on second-millennium sources.

Far fewer social and legal materials from the early to mid-first millennium exist. There are only a few fragments of a Neo-Babylonian code,[7] although texts of older codes were preserved into the later period.[8] In addition there are some collections of family and business documents, primarily from Assyria and Babylonia but also the important Aramaic papyri from Elephantine.[9] Only this last

5. For the publication of the texts see: E. Chiera and E. R. Lacheman, *The Joint Expedition with the Iraq Museum at Nuzi*, Publications of the Baghdad School, 6 vols. (Philadelphia: University of Pennsylvania Press, American Schools of Oriental Research, 1927–39) cited as JEN; E. Chiera et al., *Excavations at Nuzi*, 8 vols. (Cambridge: Harvard University Press, 1929–62), also known as the Harvard Semitic Series, vols. v, ix, x, xiii–xvi, xix, and cited as HSS v, etc.; C. J. Gadd, "Tablets from Kirkuk," *RA* 23 (1926): 49–161, cited as Gadd. See also the transliterations and translations in E. A. Speiser, "New Kirkuk Documents Relating to Family Laws," *AASOR* 10 (1930): 1–73; R. H. Pfeiffer and E. A. Speiser, "One Hundred New Selected Nuzi Texts," *AASOR* 16 (1936); E. M. Cassin, *L'adoption à Nuzi* (Paris: Adrien-Maisonneuve, 1938). For general treatments with bibliography see R.-J. Tournay, "Nouzi," *DBS* 6 (1960): 646–74; C. J. Mullo Weir, "Nuzi," *AOTS*, pp. 73–86; M. Dietrich, O. Loreta, W. Mayer, *Nuzi-Bibliographie*, *AOAT* 11 (Kevelaer, Ger.: Butzon & Bercker, 1972).

6. C. H. Gordon, "Biblical Customs and the Nuzi Tablets," *BA* 3 (1940): 1–12 (reprinted in *BAR* 2:21–33); various essays by E. A. Speiser in *Oriental and Biblical Studies*, ed. J. J. Finkelstein and M. Greenberg (Philadelphia: University of Pennsylvania Press, 1967); also throughout Speiser's commentary on Genesis.

7. *ANET*², pp. 197–98; DMBL 2:324–347.

8. The lexical series *ana ittišu* is only found in Neo-Assyrian copies, while fragments of the Hammurapi code have been found in both Neo-Assyrian and Neo-Babylonian texts.

9. Note the following collections: J. Kohler and A. Ungnad, *Hundert ausgewählte Rechtsurkunden aus der Spätzeit des babylonischen Schrifttums* (Leipzig: E. Pfeiffer, 1911); idem, *Assyrische Rechtsurkunden* (Leipzig: E. Pfeiffer, 1913); J. Augapfel, *Babylonische Rechtsurkunden aus der Regierungszeit Artaxerxes I und Darius II*, Denkschriften der Akademie der Wissenschaften Wien, Phil.-hist. Klasse 59/3 (1917); M. San Nicolò and A. Ungnad, *Neubabylonische Rechts- und Verwaltungsurkunden*, vol. 1 (Leipzig: J. C. Hinrichs, 1935); E. W. Moore, *Neo-Babylonian Business and Administrative Documents* (Ann Arbor: University of Michigan Press, 1935); G. Cardascia, *Les archives des Murašû* (Paris: Imprimerie Nationale, 1951); M. San Nicolò, *Babylonische Rechtsurkunden des ausgehenden 8. und des 7. Jahrhunderts v. Chr.*, Abhandlungen des Bayerischen Akademie der Wissenschaften, Phil.-

group has had any extensive discussion. Yet most of the first millennium materials have been available for a long period of time, much of it before the major part of the second millennium materials even came to light.

This raises an important issue in the whole approach to comparative analysis of Biblical and non-Biblical materials. Far greater attention has been paid to the legal corpus of the second millennium than to that of the first millennium. No doubt this has been due partly to the greater volume of texts from the earlier period. But the primary reason is certainly the prejudicial treatment that the second millennium has had in the area of law and social customs, which was a direct influence from Old Testament studies. The demand for knowledge about the second millennium was high because of the interest in the question of Israelite origins, but interest in the later period for the same materials was very meagre. There was simply an assumption beforehand that the patriarchal folk culture must be second-millennium and that anything later was irrelevant.[10] Such an assumption is completely rejected in this present study. In fact no fair assessment can ever be made of parallels with the older material unless some consideration is given to the question of cultural continuity or change in the later periods. The fact that the Code of Hammurapi was still highly esteemed in the later period certainly suggests considerable continuity. On this basis alone it would be very unwise to conclude that earlier practices were completely forgotten in later times.

Another problem with current comparative analysis is the way in which parallels have been forced on the Old Testament narratives with a rather strong hand. Admittedly narrative style does not

---

hist. Klasse, N.F. 34 (1951); M. San Nicolò and H. Petschow, *Babylonische Rechtsurkunden aus dem 6. Jahrhundert v. Chr.*, ibid. N.F. 51 (1960). For the Elephantine texts see: A. Cowley, *Aramaic Papyri of the 5th Century* B.C. (Oxford: Clarendon Press, 1923); E. G. Kraeling, *The Brooklyn Museum Aramaic Papyri* (New Haven: Yale University Press, 1953); R. Yaron, *Introduction to the Law of the Aramaic Papyri* (Oxford: Clarendon Press, 1961); B. Porten, *Archives from Elephantine* (Berkeley and Los Angeles: University of California Press, 1968), pt. III. See also the study of J. J. Rabinowitz, "Neo-Babylonian Legal Documents and Jewish Law," *Journal of Juristic Papyrology* 13 (1961): 131–175. A small sampling of these texts may be found in *ANET*², pp. 221–23; *ANET*³, pp. 547–49. I have extended this list of later texts because they are largely ignored in any general discussion of patriarchal customs, including deVaux's survey (see n. 1 above), which is otherwise quite complete.

10. The attack by Morton Smith on this attitude (*JBL* 88: 31) is entirely justified.

correspond to legal style; yet this should not be an excuse for license but a reason for caution. It is not legitimate, in making such comparisons with extra-biblical material, to give a wholesale reconstruction of the tradition "as it must have been" in order to make the parallel fit, or to emend the narrative to include certain details vital to the comparison. Such a method would allow one to prove almost any relationship, early or late. Similar to this is the propensity among some scholars to create "distinctive" customs which are, in fact, artificially constructed by either a narrow consideration of the material or a combining of heterogeneous materials which have nothing to do with each other. It is too easy to lead non-specialists of cuneiform astray by the supposed reconstruction of certain customs which cannot stand up to very careful scrutiny.

This study would be greatly burdened by consideration of every parallel of a legal or social custom which has been drawn to the patriarchal stories. I have tried, therefore, to make a judicial selection of those which seem most central to the discussion of dating and which appear most influential in the creation of current opinion about the age of the patriarchs. I have likewise tried to cover a broad range of types as well as most of the Abraham, Isaac, and Jacob cycles in spite of the limits of my basic concern with the Abraham tradition itself. However, I have largely excluded consideration of parallels in the Joseph story because this tradition piece is separate from the rest, and the parallels in it have been thoroughly dealt with in a recent study by D. B. Redford.[11] His conclusions are largely in harmony with those of the present study, and I would have little to add to them.

These general remarks must now be tested by the treatment of specific examples.

The Childless Wife

One of the examples of marriage customs in the patriarchal stories which has frequently been cited as reflecting the second millennium background is the account in Genesis 16 of the childless Sarah giving her handmaid Hagar to Abraham, her husband, so that he may have children by her.[12] The childless Rachel does the same

---

11. *A Study of the Biblical Story of Joseph, Genesis 37–50*, SVT 20 (1970).
12. See Gordon, *BA* 3: 2–3 (same as in *BAR* 2: 22–23); Speiser, *Genesis*, pp. 119ff. Cf. my fuller treatment of this story in "The Problem of Childlessness in Near Eastern Law and the Patriarchs of Israel," *JBL* 87 (1968): 401–08.

thing (Gen. 30:3) by giving her maid Bilhah to Jacob, and even Leah, who already has sons but has stopped bearing, gives her maid Zilpah to Jacob in order to increase her offspring (Gen. 30:9).

The parallel that has frequently been drawn to this custom is the law in CH #146 which states:

> If a man has married a priestess and she has given a slave girl to her husband and she bears sons, (if) thereafter that slave girl goes about making herself equal to her mistress, because she has borne sons, her mistress shall not sell her, she may put the mark (of a slave) on her and may count her with the slave girls.[13]

The purpose of the priestess' (*nadītu*) giving the slave girl to have children was to circumvent the law which prevented her from having natural offspring of her own. Marriage contracts of Babylonia in this period that have to do with such priestesses confirm the fact that the regulation was for the wife's benefit but also show that this practice was restricted to priestesses who were childless by law.[14]

On the other hand there is an Old Assyrian marriage contract from the nineteenth century B.C. that provides that if the wife is still childless within two years she must purchase a slave woman who will bear a child for the husband.[15] Afterwards the wife may sell the slave woman (contrary to the provisions in CH #146). A very similar situation is provided for in an adoption and marriage contract of Nuzi from the fifteenth century B.C.[16] However, it is not clear in this document what power the wife retains over the slave or her offspring.[17] These texts differ from the Old Babylonian laws and

---

13. The translation is taken from DMBL 2:57; see also the commentary in DMBL 1:245–65, 305–06. Cf. the translation by T. J. Meek in *ANET*[2], p. 172.
14. See M. Schorr, *Urkunden des altbabylonischen Zivil—und Processrechts* (Leipzig: J. S. Hinrichs, 1913) nos. 3 & 4. See also those examples reproduced in DMBL, 1:253ff. The situation cited in Schorr, no. 205, in which the sons of the slave girl are regarded as the sons of the first wife, is regarded by Driver and Miles (ibid., p. 304) as an exception. But this is not the case. The document only states that on the day when inheritances are distributed the wife will inherit any future children of the slave girl as well. It is clear from the witnesses that the first wife has eight sons, and it is against their possible claim that the tablet is made. Thus, the text is not relevant to the Genesis stories.
15. See J. Lewy, "Old Assyrian Institutions," *HUCA* 27 (1956): 8–10; *ANET*[3], p. 543. In this contract the husband is allowed to marry a *qadištum* priestess in Asshur, but presumably she cannot bear him any children; see DMBL 1:369–70.
16. HSS v:67. Cf. Speiser, *AASOR* 10, no. 2, pp. 31–32; *ANET*[2], p. 220; Gordon, *BA* 3:2–3.
17. Cf. Speiser's different rendering of the text in *Genesis*, p. 120.

contracts in that the childless women are not priestesses. In this respect they are closer to the Old Testament examples. But they differ from the Genesis stories in that the provision in the contracts is for the benefit of the husband, so that he may have offspring. This is especially clear since both contracts forbid the husband's taking any other non-priestly wife. In contrast, the provision in the patriarchal stories is for the sake of the wife, in order that she may have children of her own. This is stated in Gen. 16:2 even though it is known from the context that Abraham is also childless. It is clear in the Jacob story, however, that Jacob already has children, and thus it is only at the wishes of his wives that the maids bear more children.[18]

In an Egyptian document of the late twelfth century B.C. there is an account of how a childless couple together bought a female slave who then bore three children, a son and two daughters.[19] At some point after this the husband died, but the wife raised the three children as her own. These three children along with the husband of the eldest daughter all inherited the property from the wife and mother as freemen with equal shares in the estate. There is every indication in this text that the action of having children by a slave girl was for the benefit of the wife as well as the husband.

There is another text from Nimrud, dated about 648 B.C., that is a marriage contract.[20] The relevant portion states that if the wife does not bear offspring the husband may take a maid and the wife will deposit her dowry for the future children. The maid's children then become her children, and the wife is also warned against treating the maid improperly. The text is certainly the closest one of all to the patriarchal narratives because the whole provision for having children is presented from the wife's viewpoint. The children become hers and inherit her dowry. And the warning against improper treatment of the maid certainly highlights Sarah's behavior towards Hagar. While there is obviously a long continuity of legal custom, there also seems to be evidence of some social development in terms of the specific rights of the wife. The patriarchal customs would seem to reflect more closely the latter part of this continuum, the

18. See Van Seters, *JBL* 87:403.
19. A. H. Gardiner, "Adoption Extraordinary," *JEA* 26 (1940): 23–29.
20. B. Parker, "The Nimrud Tablets 1952—Business Documents," *Iraq* 16 (1954): 37–39, ND 2307; Van Seters, *JBL* 87: 406–07.

mid-first millennium, than the early or mid-second millennium as formerly proposed.[21]

"Wife-Sister" Marriages

The stories about the patriarch who pretends, for his own safety in a foreign land, that his wife is his sister (Gen. 12:10–20; 20; 26:1–11) call for special attention. It has been proposed by E. A. Speiser that behind these stories lies a distinctively Hurrian marriage custom, found elsewhere only in the Nuzi texts, in which the wife was also adopted by her husband as a sister and thereby gained a status superior to that of ordinary marriage.[22] Such a custom, it is said, is reflected in a "sister-adoption document," *ṭuppi aḫatūti*.

There is some doubt as to whether Speiser has represented the Nuzi material correctly. The clearest example of a sister-adoption document is JEN 78 which states:

> Document of sister-adoption of Zikipa son of Ehel-Tešup; his sister Hinzuri for sister-adoption to Hutarraphi with 4 *ammusni* he gave. Hutarraphi will give Hinzuri in marriage to whomever he pleases and his money he will receive, and Hutarraphi 1 ox, ... sheep, 1 homer of grain, 2 minas copper, 9 minas wool, equal to 20 shekels of silver to Zikipa has given and thus Zikipa: "20 shekels of silver, the dowry [*riḫtu*] to Hinzuri my sister in the hem of Hinzuri I have bound; to Hutarraphi I have handed her over." If Hinzuri has a claimant, then Zikipa will clear her and restore her to Hutarraphi. The declaration of Hinzuri in the presence of these witnesses. Thus she spoke: "with my consent for sister-adoption to Hutarraphi he gave [me]." Whoever among them breaks the contract shall pay as fine one mina of silver and one mina of gold. This tablet was written according to the proclamation in the entrance of the palace in Nuzi.[23]

---

21. See also the recent opinion by deVaux, *Histoire*, pp. 233–34; cf. Bright, *History of Israel*, p. 79.
22. "The Wife-Sister Motif in the Patriarchal Narratives," *Biblical and Other Studies*, ed. A. Altmann (Cambridge: Harvard University Press, 1963), pp. 15–28, reprinted in *Oriental and Biblical Studies*, pp. 62–82.
23. Based on the transliteration and translation by P. Koschaker, *Neue keilschriftliche Rechtsurkunden aus der El-Amarna Zeit*, Abhandlungen der Sächsischen Akademie der Wissenschaften, Phi.-hist. Klasse 39/5 (Leipzig, 1928), pp. 173–74. Cf. a similar text, HSS xix:68.

It is clear from this text that Zikipa, the natural brother is *not* giving his sister in marriage to her future husband. He is giving her to an adoptive brother who in turn will have the responsibility of giving the girl in marriage to a future husband who is unknown at the time the document is drawn up. In any case, Hutarraphi will not be Hinzuri's husband, and any future husband Hinzuri may have will not be regarded as a brother. As Koschaker pointed out long ago, the form for "sister-adoption" is essentially the same as that of the adoption formula for "daughter-adoption."[24] The only difference in the two situations is that instead of the girl's father transferring to another his responsibility to give his daughter in marriage, in the *ahatūtu* situation it is the brother of the woman who transfers his obligations towards his sister to another person. This latter situation only arises when the father is dead, and a brother, usually the eldest, must assume some legal responsibility on behalf of his sister. However, the brother's authority is inferior to that of a girl's father; he does not receive the *patria potestas*, so he must have the consent of his sister in any such transaction.[25] Marriage, of course, is the ultimate intention in both daughter-adoption and sister-adoption, but this should not have led Speiser to regard the wife in the latter instance as having a special wife-sister status. The eventual marriage in both cases to someone other than the adopter is simply the usual marriage form.

This same understanding of sister-adoption, *ahatūtu*, is emphasized by two court declarations, HSS v:26 and SMN 1009. In the first text an unknown woman declares before witnesses:

> "[To] Akawatil son of Elli upon the street my wealth I offered, and as sister [*ana ahatūti*] I have been adopted. And Akawatil shall manage my possessions; what is in my stores is in his stores; since he has adopted me as sister he shall be of assistance

---

24. Ibid., pp. 90ff. See also the discussions in DMAL, pp. 161–68; M. Burrows, *The Basis of Israelite Marriage* (New Haven: American Oriental Society, 1938), p. 23; A. van Praag, *Droit matrimonial Assyro-Babylonien* (Amsterdam: N. V. Noord-Hollandsche Uitgevers Maatschappij, 1945), pp. 79ff. All of these studies follow Koschaker's lead, which disagrees basically with Speiser's position. Yet Speiser has completely ignored all of them.
25. A. Skaist, "The Authority of the Brother at Arrapha and Nuzi," *JAOS* 89 (1969): 10–17. In this article Skaist criticizes Koschaker's theory, in "Fratriarchat, Hausgemeinshaft und Mutterrecht in Keilschriftrechten," *ZA* 41 (1933): 1–84, that Nuzi society contained vestiges of a fratriarchal society. Skaist's criticisms are also applicable to Speiser's wife-sister marriages and also to the ideas about fratriarchy in the patriarchal stories by C. H. Gordon, "Fratriarchy in the Old Testament," *JBL* 54 (1933): 223–231.

to me. And Akawatil shall receive from my [future] husband 20 shekels of the money [paid] for me, and shall have the usufruct of it [*ikkal*]; and 20 shekels of silver my brother Elhinnamar shall use [*ikkal*].[26]

In this document a woman entrusts herself to some public agent(?) who will act as a brother to her and give her in marriage even though she has a natural brother. The brother may be a minor but his rights are still safeguarded. Once again the adopter does not marry the adopted sister but only offers to arrange a marriage with a future husband. In the second document, SMN 1009, a woman has formerly been given in marriage by her brother, but now both this brother and her husband are dead. Consequently, in a public act her younger brother is obligated to act as her legal guardian with the primary duty of finding another husband for her. The resumption of this responsibility by the brother is called "sistership," *aḫatūtu*, the same terminology used for the obligations of the adoptive brother as well.[27] In HSS v:79 a brother gives his sister as a "daughter-in-law" (*ana kallūti*) to a man who will give her to one of his sons.[28] The woman declares in the document that she is in "sister relationship" *aḫatūti* to her real brother, and he continues to have some legal obligations toward her.

There are three texts, however, (HSS v:80,69,25)[29] which require special consideration because they have given rise to Speiser's misunderstanding about "sistership." The document HSS v:80 is a marriage contract (*ṭuppi riksi*) in which a brother gives his sister in marriage to a third person. The bride-price is the equivalent of 40 shekels of silver of which 20 go to the brother and 20 are returned to his sister as a dowry. This text is similar to others[30] and would call for no special consideration except for its connection with the other two. HSS v:25, which must be taken with HSS v:80, is a court declaration in which all the principals—brother, sister, and bridegroom—declare their agreement and consent to the terms of the contract.

26. *AASOR* 10, no. 29, pp. 62–63. Similar documents are HSS xix:70 and Gadd, no. 31.
27. *AASOR* 16, no. 54.
28. *AASOR* 10, no. 25, pp. 57–58.
29. *AASOR* 10, nos. 26–28, pp. 59–61. Cf. the treatment of these texts in Koschaker, "Fratriarchat" *ZA* 41:14ff.
30. Cf. *AASOR* 16, no. 55.

The third document, HSS v:69, constitutes the problem.³¹ In this document, called a *ṭuppi aḫati*, the brother gives his sister to a third party "as sister," *ana aḫati*, for 40 shekels of silver. Since all the principals are the same as those in the marriage contract, HSS v:80, Speiser has interpreted this transaction as complimentary to the other so that the sister is both wife and adopted sister to the third party. However, there is a more likely alternative. If *ana aḫati* is the equivalent of *ana aḫatūti*, "for sister adoption," as seems most likely, then HSS v:69 is an act of sister-adoption like the others. But this action in HSS v:69 was probably carried out *before* the marriage agreement of HSS v:80 with the full intention that the third party would act only as the adoptive guardian. The subsequent desire of the adoptive brother to marry the girl himself required another document of marriage from the real brother with the sister's consent and replaced the former act.

It certainly cannot be proven on the basis of these three documents and to the exclusion of all others considered that women were adopted as sisters and then married by their adoptive brothers as a special kind of marriage. Nor can it be shown that a woman involved in an *aḫatūtu* act gained anything more than legal protection from the natural or adoptive brother, who was a guardian who could then offer her to a prospective husband.³² This was no more than any woman would have expected from her natural father or brother.

Furthermore, the only right or obligation of the brother that is involved in the Nuzi texts is the brother's duty to give his sister in marriage in the absence of the woman's father. But this custom is otherwise known from the Old and Neo-Babylonian periods and from the Elephantine papyri, so it constitutes nothing particularly Nuzian or Hurrian.³³ The peculiarity of Nuzi society is its fondness for using the adoption formula for commercial transactions even to the point of making marriage and the right to give in marriage a salable commodity. But this did not necessarily create a variety of different marriage types or place women on varying levels of social status, as Speiser suggests.³⁴ Consequently, the whole comparison

---

31. This text is Speiser's point of departure in the study cited in n. 11 above.
32. See especially the conclusions reached by Skaist, *JAOS* 89:17.
33. Schorr, *Urkunden*, no. 3; San Nicolò and Petschow, *Babylonische Rechtsurkunden*, nos. 1 & 3; Yaron, *Laws of the Aramaic Papyri*, .p. 45.
34. See also Burrows, *Israelite Marriage*, p. 23, where he denies that there is any evidence to suggest that the social status of women "adopted" for the purpose of being given in marriage was thereby affected in any way.

between the supposed "wife-sister status" and the wife-sister motif of the patriarchal stories completely disintegrates. There is no way of usefully associating the *aḫatūtu* transactions of Nuzi with these episodes.[35]

Turning again to the stories of Gen. 12:10–20; 20; 26:1–11, it remains now to consider those aspects of the story which deal with marriage customs. In all three stories the patriarch pretends to be the brother of his wife. This would imply a change in status from a husband to a woman's guardian. In this latter pretended capacity Abraham, in the first two accounts, apparently is regarded as having given Sarah in marriage to the respective kings of Egypt and Gerar, and in the first story, at least, he received ample compensation for doing so. While the marriage is not described, it is clear that Sarah is considered the wife of both Pharaoh and the king of Gerar, while in the last story marriage to another was only a possibility. It has already been noted that the practice of a brother giving his sister in marriage is well known from both the second and first millennia, so the narrative makes good sense without any alternate explanation.

Nevertheless it is possible that the narrator of the original story (Gen. 12:10–20) is deliberately implying a *double entendre* in the words of the patriarch, "She is my sister." The intention of the stratagem is to have the foreigners take the meaning in the quite strict sense of a blood relative and legal guardian. But another sense possible for more astute readers would be to understand the terms "brother" and "sister" as affectionate synonyms for husband and wife.[36] It is particularly interesting to note that in Egyptian marriage contracts from the sixth century B.C. the wife is referred to as "sister," although it is quite clear from the context that the man's wife is not related to him by blood.[37] In Gen. 20:12 a more explicit

---

35. Two studies on this problem that were not available to me when my own study was made are: C. J. Mullo Weir, "The Alleged Hurrian Wife-Sister Motif in Genesis," *Glasgow Oriental Transactions* 22 (1967–70): 14–25; D. Freedman, "A New Approach to the Nuzi Sistership Contract," *The Journal of the Ancient Near Eastern Society of Columbia University* 2 (1969): 77–85. S. Greengus, in a paper, "Sisterhood Adoption/Marriage in Nuzi and the Bible" (American Oriental Society, Santa Barbara, Calif., 1974), also reached conclusions similar to those above.
36. This usage is frequent in the Song of Songs and Tobit.
37. E. Luddeckens, *Ägyptische Eheverträge*, Ägyptologische Abhandlungen 1 (Wiesbaden: O. Harrassowitz, 1960), nos. 3 & 4, pp. 13–15. It may also have occurred in no. 2 from the seventh century (the text is defective at this point), but it is not present in the ninth century contract (no. 1), nor does it appear in any of those from the fifth century onward.

reason for exonerating the patriarch of lying is made by giving more concrete truth to his words.

The second feature of the story reflecting social attitudes is the possibility of great moral wrongdoing as a result of taking the patriarch's wife in marriage. In Gen. 12:17 the seriousness of the sin involved is implied in God's judgment of a plague on Pharaoh's house. In Gen. 20:9 the predicament is recognized as a "great sin," and similar terminology is used in Gen. 26:10. All the ancient Near Eastern law codes recognize adultery as a crime worthy of capital punishment. On the whole, however, they stress that the offense is against the husband and that he has the power to a certain degree to mitigate the punishment. It is interesting to note, however, that in a document from Ugarit of the late thirteenth century B.C. and in Egyptian marriage contracts from the ninth to the sixth centuries B.C., adultery is actually referred to as the "great sin."[38] In the Egyptian documents the following formula is used:

> If I divorce the wife PN, my sister, who belongs to me ... except for the great sin which one might find in a woman, I will give her ...

Here both the suggestion that a wife may be called a man's sister and a reference to the "great sin" as adultery occur together, just as they do in the Genesis narratives. It is the customs and attitudes reflected in these Egyptian texts, which may have been common also in the neighboring Phoenician region, that provide the *Vorlage* for these patriarchal stories and not the Nuzi texts as proposed by Speiser. There is no reason whatever, on the basis of the present stories, to look for a period distant from the first millennium narrators to understand the customs reflected in them.

The Marriage of Rebekah

The proposed marriage of Rebekah to Isaac in Genesis 24 has been described by Speiser as "a reasonable facsimile of a standard Hurrian *aḫatūtu* document."[39] Now as shown above the document for sister-adoption has to do with the transfer of guardianship of an

---

38. W. L. Moran, "The Scandal of the 'Great Sin' at Ugarit," *JNES* 18 (1959): 280–81; J. J. Rabinowitz, "The 'Great Sin' in Ancient Egyptian Marriage Contracts," *JNES* 18 (1959): 73. For the texts see Lüddeckens, *Ägyptische Eheverträge*, pp. 10–17.
39. Speiser, "Wife-Sister Motif," p. 26; see also idem, *Genesis*, pp. 181–82.

unmarried woman from the real brother to an adoptive brother who subsequently gives her in marriage to a prospective husband. But Genesis 24 is about the marriage agreement of Rebekah itself and there is no indication of any transfer of the duty of a brother to the servant. It is Abraham, the father of the bridegroom, who is arranging through the servant the marriage for his son as is the usual practice in ancient Near Eastern law.

On the other hand, Bethuel, the father of the bride, is probably dead, and his name in v. 50 is only a gloss as Speiser suggests.[40] So Laban acts along with his mother in his father's place. But the mother is not "incidental and without legal standing" as Speiser declares her to be. She is prominent throughout the whole transaction from v. 52 onward and should probably be substituted for the name of Bethuel in v. 50 as involved in the initial marriage declaration. Furthermore, the gifts are given by the servant to both mother and brother together. In comparative Near Eastern law there are documents from both the Old and the Neo-Babylonian periods in which the mother and brother of the bride act together in giving a daughter and sister in marriage.[41]

After the marriage has been agreed upon in vv. 50–51, mention is made of gifts which are given to Rebekah, her mother, and her brother. These cannot be regarded as the bride-payment (Bab. *terḫatu*, Heb. *mōhar*) which was usually a fixed sum paid only to the guardians and as part of the agreement. The gifts here (v. 53), made subsequent to the agreement, are in the nature of ornaments, and correspond much more to the betrothal gifts of Assyrian Laws.[42]

The element of the story which Speiser regards as "most significant of all"[43] for his early dating is Rebekah's consent. It has already been noted that in the Nuzi texts a man, in giving his sister in marriage (HSS v:25) or in giving her into sister adoption (JEN 78), was required to have her consent. This was probably necessary because the brother's authority was not as great as the father's. But in the Biblical story it is a question of exactly to what Rebekah consents. In v. 51 the marriage has already been agreed upon: "Behold,

---

40. Speiser, "Wife-Sister Motif," p. 26; idem, *Genesis*, pp. 181–82.
41. For the OB period see van Praag, *Droit matrimonial*, p. 79. For NB texts see San Nicolò and Petschow, *Babylonische Rechtsurkunden*, nos. 1 & 3.
42. See DMBL 1:265ff.; DMAL, pp. 193ff.
43. Speiser, "Wife-Sister Motif," p. 27; idem, *Genesis*, p. 185.

Rebekah is before you, take her and go, and let her be the wife of your master's son, as the Lord has spoken." The discussion in vv. 55ff. seem to be concerned with whether Rebekah will remain for a few days before departure. Her answer to the question, "Will you go with this man?" is "I will go," which may mean no more than that she has agreed to set out for a distant land without the privilege of a prolonged leave-taking.

Even if it is granted that Rebekah's answer is ultimately a consent to marriage, this should not be regarded as so exceptional. Once a woman became free of the *patria potestas* through the death of her father or through marriage she could have property of her own, either an inheritance portion or a dowry, and she often had sufficient means to arrange a second marriage after her first one ended, or even a first one after her father's death. The Code of Hammurapi and the Assyrian Laws recognize this liberty.[44] If, however, a marriage was arranged through a brother as guardian, which was usual in the case of virgins, consent from a woman of age would certainly be expected. Neither the Nuzi texts nor the Biblical story need be regarded as in any way unusual.

In conclusion, it is safe to state that in neither the stories about the patriarchs acting as the brothers of their wives nor the account of the marriage of Rebekah and Isaac is there any basis for comparing these accounts with the *aḫatūtu* transactions of the Nuzi texts. The stories are quite intelligible on the basis of Near Eastern customs in the first millennium B.C., the time of the narrator, and any features that they share with the Nuzi documents are common to other areas and times as well.

Jacob's Marriages

In the discussion of patriarchal marriage customs a large place has been given to Jacob's marriages to the daughters of Laban as illustrating a special type of marriage called an *errebu* marriage, which some believe is mentioned in cuneiform texts of the second millennium B.C.[45] It was argued that such a form of marriage existed in

---

44. CH #177.
45. M. Burrows, "The Complaint of Laban's Daughter," *JAOS* 57 (1937): 259–76; idem, "The Ancient Oriental Background of Hebrew Levirite Marriage," *BASOR* 77 (1940): 3ff.; E. Neufeld, *Ancient Hebrew Marriage Laws* (London: Longmans, Green, 1944), pp. 56ff.

cases where a man adopted a son for the purpose of marrying him to his daughter. In a recent review of this subject, however, I have attempted to show that the whole notion of an *errebu* marriage as a special type practiced in the Near East is a modern fiction.[46] Under Near Eastern law it was quite possible for an adopted son to marry the daughter of the adopter because they were not related by blood. This logically involved some special considerations, such as the fact that no bride-payment was necessary since the father of the bride and of the groom were now one and the same. However, the marriage itself was certainly no different from any other normal marriage. Nevertheless, since C. H. Gordon has emphasized that certain adoption texts of Nuzi which also contain provisions for marriage between the adopted son and the adopter's daughter are close parallels of the Jacob story, the comparison requires some consideration.[47] The fundamental issue in the alleged similarity is Jacob's adoption by Laban. If this cannot be demonstrated then the whole basis upon which the Nuzi parallels to Jacob's marriages have been built is completely destroyed.

Gordon seeks a basis for Jacob's adoption in the original encounter between Jacob and Laban (Gen. 29:13f.). But neither the general expression of kinship, "my bone and my flesh" which could express kinship as broad as a whole tribe (2 Sam. 19:12f.), nor the remark that Jacob "stayed" with Laban can be regarded as pointing to declarations of adoption.[48] Adoption formulas are nowhere suggested in the story. Nor can it be argued from silence in the early part of the story that Laban had only daughters when Jacob arrived, which would have led to Jacob's adoption. Sons are mentioned as in charge of the flocks of Laban (Gen. 30:35) only fourteen years after Jacob's arrival and only seven years after his marriages, and in Gen. 31:1 the sons are Jacob's rivals.

Another argument used to suggest that Jacob was adopted is Laban's outburst in Gen. 31:43: "The daughters are my daughters, the children are my children, the flocks are my flocks and everything you see belongs to me." If there is any literal truth to Laban's

---

46. J. Van Seters, "Jacob's Marriages and Ancient Near Eastern Customs: A Reexamination," *HTR* 62 (1969): 377–395.
47. C. H. Gordon, "The Story of Jacob and Laban in the Light of the Nuzi Tablets," *BASOR* 66 (1937): 25–27; idem, "Biblical Customs" *BA* 3:5–6. Cf. J. H. Tigay, "Adoption," *Encyc. Jud.*, col. 299.
48. Cf. S. Feigin, "Some Cases of Adoption in Israel," *JBL* 50 (1931): 186–200.

claim then this would certainly point toward Jacob's adoption. But the context makes it clear that it is only a cry of frustration that Jacob has derived all his family and goods from him and left him much poorer for it. It is an empty denial of Jacob's claims in Gen. 31:38–42 that he earned fairly everything he has as a result of twenty years of service. Laban has, in fact, previously admitted Jacob's right to his wives and property as well as his right to leave (Gen. 30:25–34; 31:27–32). Consequently the arguments for Jacob's adoption are entirely lacking.

Arguments against Jacob's adoption by Laban are quite decisive. Laban refers to Jacob as his kin, which he was, but never as his son. Similarly, Jacob never regards Laban as his father but only the father of his wives (Gen. 31:4ff.), while Isaac remains Jacob's father and his paternal home is in Canaan (Gen. 30:25; 31:13,18). This entirely contradicts the Near Eastern adoption documents in which the adopter and adoptee are considered father and son, and any statement by either to the contrary is a recision of the adoptive tie. In adoption no connection is retained with the adoptee's original family or ancestral home.

Jacob has his own household (Gen. 30:30) and his own possessions entirely separate from Laban's property, earned by wages and not by inheritance (Gen. 30:31ff.; 31:6ff.; cf. 30:43; 31:1,18). In Near Eastern adoption formulas, however, the adoptee does not own property independent of the adoptive father, and he acquires right to his property only by inheritance. To leave the adoptee's household would be to break the adoptive tie and forfeit the right to the property. Furthermore, the fact that Jacob paid bride-money for his wives while they were still in their father's house (Gen. 29:15–30; 30:26; 31:41), cannot be reconciled with adoption because it is never required when the adoptive father of the groom and the father of the bride are the same person. Only if the adoptive tie is broken must the bride-money be paid retroactively as a penalty.[49]

In conclusion, it is safe to say that Jacob cannot possibly be considered an adopted son of Laban. The details that speak against this are both numerous and essential to the story, while the arguments used to support the notion of adoption are fanciful reconstructions from silence. The Nuzi texts, HSS v:67 and Gadd 51 used by

---

49. See esp. Van Seters, "Jacob's Marriages," *HTR* 62:383–86 for the parallel material.

Gordon in a comparison with the Jacob story disagree on the most essential point—that of adoption.

Another passage in the Jacob-Laban story (Gen. 31:14–16) calls for some discussion, since it has also been compared with these Nuzi texts. It states:

> Then Rachel and Leah answered him (Jacob), "Is there any portion or inheritance left to us in our father's house? Are we not regarded by him as foreigners? For he has sold us, and he has had continuous use of what was paid for us.[50] All the property which God has taken away from our father belongs to us and to our children; now then, whatever God has said to you, do."

First of all, the daughters of Laban suggested that they had a right to expect an inheritance portion of the paternal estate, but that there was no longer any hope of attaining this. Some scholars have suggested that since there were sons in the family, the sons would stand to inherit all the property.[51] This would interpret the remark of the two daughters as a complaint against their father for having begotten natural sons, which is nonsense. Sons were certainly expected, and they had already been in the family by the time of the daughters' marriages. Besides, the presence of sons in the family did not necessarily eliminate the rights of the daughters to inherit property in Near Eastern law.[52]

The normal way for daughters to receive a share of the paternal estate was through the dowry at marriage.[53] It was marriage and subsequent alienation from the father's household, along with the

---

50. There is a technical phrase used in v. 15b which is often missed in translation, *wayyōʾkal gam ʾākôl et kaspēnû* does not mean "he has used up the money given for us" (RSV), but means only to have the usufruct or profit from it. The capital, that is what Jacob now has, belongs to them. This use of the verb *ʾkl* "to eat" derives this legal meaning from the literal meaning in which in an inheritance document a share of land can be designated to a son before the death of the father, but the father may continue to eat (*akālu*) the produce of this field in his lifetime. This usage was extended to the use of money as well, and its usage was current in both the OB and NB periods. See CH #171, 178, 180, 181, and DMBL 1:377–78; CAD 1/1, pp. 251–53.

51. Burrows, *JAOS* 57:263; see also Gordon, *BASOR* 66:26.

52. DMBL 1:335ff.; see also Gardiner, *JEA* 26:23–29.

53. DMBL 1:271ff. In the NB period an inheritance share (*zittu*) was often given as a bridal gift or dowry (*nudunnū*); see San Nicolò and Ungnad, *Neubabylonische Rechtsurkunden* 1, nos. 3 & 4.

receiving of a dowry that included their respective maids that eliminated any further right to their inheritance—not the fact that they had brothers.

The most obvious explanation from the story itself is in the remarks of the daughters and their brothers. The sons of Laban lament in Gen. 31:1: "Jacob has taken all that was our father's; and from what was our father's he has gained all this wealth." They are concerned that there will not be any property left for them. So also the daughters consider that with what Jacob has already gained from their father they can hardly expect anything in addition, especially since his attitude toward Jacob has changed to disfavor (Gen. 31:2). This is one reason why the wives may regard Jacob's property as their own as well (Gen. 31:16).[54]

The second complaint (v. 15) also permits two explanations. According to the first explanation Laban has treated his daughters as "foreigners" by the way in which he has used the bride-payment.[55] A father had the right in Near Eastern law to keep the bride-payment and to use it for himself. It was common practice, however, as early as the Old Babylonian period and in the Nuzi texts to return a part of the bride-payment to the bride as her dowry.[56] Yet this same practice was not limited to the second millennium, for in the Elephantine papyri and in Arabic society of a more modern period the whole of the bride-payment (*mhr*) was usually returned to the bride.[57] It is possible, therefore, to interpret the daughters' complaint as an objection to Laban's not returning the bride-payment to them. If they had been given Jacob's service as their dowry, then all Laban's wealth gained after the first fourteen years would have been theirs. In the subsequent six years this same wealth had returned to Jacob, so that they could feel justified that God had restored to them what was their rightful dowry and inheritance.[58]

On the other hand, a somewhat different interpretation of the passage is also possible. From the time of the Middle Assyrian Laws

---

54. See Burrows, *JAOS* 57: 263–64.
55. On the bride-payment in Near Eastern law see DMBL 1:249ff.; DMAL 142ff.; Burrows, *Israelite Marriage*, pp. 16ff.; van Praag, *Droit matrimonial*, pp. 130ff.
56. DMBL 1:253ff.; Speiser, *AASOR* 10:22–24; Burrows, *JAOS* 57:27ff.
57. Yaron, *The Law of the Aramaic Papyri*, pp. 47ff.; deVaux, *Ancient Israel: Its Life and Institutions*, p. 27; Van Praag, *Droit matrimonial*, pp. 152ff.; Burrows, *Israelite Marriage*, p. 44.
58. Burrows, *JAOS* 57:271ff.

onward the practice of giving a bride-payment, *terḫatu*, seems to be in decline.[59] In fact, the term *terḫatu* does not seem to occur in cuneiform sources of the first millennium. In its place there is frequent mention of the bride-gift, *nudunnū*, which was either a gift given by the parents of the bride as a dowry or a settlement of property given by the bridegroom directly to his wife.[60] This was the regular procedure in the Neo-Assyrian and Neo-Babylonian marriage contracts. But there is a Neo-Assyrian text from the late seventh century B.C. that treats marriage as a purchase transaction.[61] The relevant portion of the text states:

> Niḫtešaru has come to an agreement with Nabu-riḫtu-uṣer concerning Ninlil-ḫaṣina his daughter and for 16 shekels of silver she has taken possession of her as a wife for Ṣiḫa her son. The wife of Ṣiḫa she is. The money is completely paid.

The interesting feature of this text is that it does not use the terminology familiar in marriage contracts, for nothing is said about a *nudunnū* or a *terḫatu*. Instead the language is borrowed directly from documents of purchase agreements having to do with slaves and land.[62] Here evidently a father has "sold" his daughter into marriage and in the latter part of the text he waives all right on the part of the family to redemption or claim before the law. It is possible that a crass form of "purchase-marriage" was still continued in the late Assyrian period in which on rare occasion the marriage agreement could resemble very closely a slave sale transaction.

The similarity of this Neo-Assyrian marriage document to the complaint of Laban's daughters becomes quite clear. Originally they could have expected from their father a sizeable marriage gift. But instead their father has treated them as foreigners, i.e., slaves, and has *sold* them into marriage. It is the dowry they could have rightfully expected at their marriage that Jacob has won back and that belongs to them.

59. DMAL, pp. 191ff.
60. DMBL 1:265ff.
61. J. Kohler and A. Ungnad, *Assyrische Rechtsurkunden*, no. 37, pp. 33ff.; cf. p. 451.
62. On the significance of the phraseology: *tupiš* PN *ina libbi* × *šiklu kaspi ... talqi*, which is used in this text, see *CAD* 4:231. See Kohler and Ungnad, *Assyrische Rechtsurkunden*, nos. 38–40, pp. 34ff., where the same terminology is used for the sale of slaves, and no. 36, pp. 32ff., for the sale of property.

It may be difficult to decide which marriage custom provides the best explanation of the Biblical passage: the one in which the bride-payment became a part of the dowry, or the one in which the "purchase-marriage" of the Neo-Assyrian period actually resembled a slave purchase in contrast to a marriage with a dowry, *nudunnû*. To my mind, the second explanation comes closer to the actual words of the daughters with their mention of being "sold" *mkr* and explains more clearly the bitterness expressed in it. However, even if one retains the first explanation, it certainly cannot be used to establish a second millennium date since the *mōhar* was still quite common among the Jews at Elephantine. Even Burrows, who adopts the first explanation, considers the viewpoint reflected in the story as a development later than that reflected in Nuzi.[63] A date in the late monarchy of Israel is, in fact, entirely possible as a setting for these remarks.

There are two other minor points of comparison that are made between Jacob's marriage and the Nuzi texts. Firstly, Laban gives both his daughters a maid as a marriage gift (Gen. 29:24,29), and this custom is also found in Nuzi, HSS v:67. Speiser attaches a great deal of importance to this detail.[64] However, this practice was common in Ancient Mesopotamia and is particularly well-attested during the Neo-Babylonian and Persian periods.[65]

Secondly, Laban demanded of Jacob an oath that he would not take another wife besides the two daughters and that he would not mistreat his wives (Gen. 31:51–54). Either or both of these conditions are found in a number of texts from Nuzi and the Old Assyrian contracts.[66] But again, such regulations are common in marriage contracts of the mid-first millennium as well.[67]

We may summarize the analysis of the marriage customs in the Jacob-Laban story thus: firstly, some parallels have been proposed between the Biblical story and the Nuzi texts; these were based on a

---

63. Burrows, *JAOS* 57:270ff.
64. Speiser, *Genesis*, pp. 226–27.
65. See San Nicolò and Petschow, *Babylonische Rechtsurkunden*, nos. 2 & 3, pp. 3ff., and San Nicolò and Ungnad, *Neubabylonische Rechtsurkunden*, nos. 5 & 11.
66. For Nuzi see Gadd 12, 51; also HSS v:67,80; ix:24. For Old Assyrian see Lewy, *HUCA* 27:6–10; *ANET*³, p. 543a.
67. For late references see Yaron, *The Law of the Aramaic Papyri*, p. 60. To these add: San Nicolò and Petschow, *Babylonische Rechtsurkunden*, no. 1; and San Nicolò and Ungnad, *Neubabylonische Rechtsurkunden*, no. 2.

serious misunderstanding of the cuneiform sources. This is the case with the so-called *errebu* marriage. Secondly, some parallel customs are common to both the second and the first millennia B.C. and so are completely indecisive for the dating of the traditions. Thirdly, there may be some elements of the story, such as the remarks of Laban's daughters, that actually seem to reflect more closely the situation expressed in the texts of the mid-first millennium B.C. At least there is nothing here that would contradict the composition of the Jacob-Laban story at this late date.

The "Adoption" of Abraham's Servant

The text of Gen. 15:2–3 is another example of rather undisciplined speculation about parallels with second millennium adoption practices mostly drawn from the Nuzi archives. Part of the problem is the obscurity of the Hebrew text, which has allowed for various interpretations. For the sake of the present discussion we will give the translation of the RSV, which states:

> But Abram said, "O Lord God, what wilt thou give me, for I continue childless, and the heir of my house is Eliezer of Damascus?" And Abram said, "Behold, thou hast given me no offspring; and a slave born in my house will be my heir."

W. F. Albright found in this text a primary support for his theory that Abraham was a great donkey caravaneer in the early second millennium.[68] He explained these verses in the following way:

> Soon after the discovery of the Nuzi tablets from the fifteenth century B.C. it was recognized that Abraham had adopted Eliezer in much the same way that the capitalists of Nuzi had themselves adopted by persons who borrowed from them. Since—at least in theory—a man could not alienate his property, which belonged to his family, he simply adopted the money-lender in order to provide collateral for a loan in time of need. ... It stands to reason that an organizer and head of caravans [Abraham] would need ample credit in order to purchase donkeys and buy supplies of all kinds before starting out on a trading expedition.[69]

---

68. W. F. Albright, "Abram the Hebrew," *BASOR* 163: 36–54.
69. Ibid, p. 47.

This is an amazing statement because, even though it is repeated over the course of thirty-five years,[70] it is never documented with any reference to cuneiform sources and is, in fact, a complete misunderstanding of the Nuzi adoption texts. It should be obvious that if property could not be legally alienated then it could not function as collateral for a loan. And what land did Abraham own so that he could enter into such an arrangement with a financier of Damascus?

It has long been recognized that there are two types of adoption documents mentioned in the Nuzi texts.[71] The first type is the *true* adoption in which a childless couple adopt a son in order to have him care for them in their old age. In return for his faithful service he would receive the inheritance. This type of adoption was not restricted to Nuzi but was common to other periods and places. Besides this type, however, there was the rather distinctive *sale* adoption document. Since immovable property, land and buildings, could not be alienated from a family because they involved feudal service, the Nuzians carried on a legal fiction by which a person was "adopted." His "inheritance" was a specific piece of property carefully delineated and handed over immediately in return for a "grant" (*qištum*); that is, the price of the land. It was a sale, and there was no further obligation to either party. These transactions had nothing to do with whether a man had children or not. Agreements of loans by merchants for commercial ventures were of an entirely different character.

Furthermore the Hebrew text in v. 2b is very obscure: *ûben mešeq bêtî hû dammešeq ʾelîʿezer*, and the RSV is admittedly only a guess based on the parallel in v. 3. But *ben mešeq bêtî* certainly does not mean "heir" and the search for parallels from Ugaritic and elsewhere are too ambiguous to be of any help. The final phrase *hûʾ dammešeq ʾelîʿezer* is syntactically impossible and has led to the conjectures that it contains a gloss of either one or the other names. It is perhaps safest to regard the entire half verse as corrupt and to build no arguments upon it.

The parallel in v. 3 uses the term *ben bayt*. H. L. Ginsberg has recently suggested the meaning of "steward" for this phrase, based on this meaning in Roman Hebrew.[72] But this meaning may be a

---

70. W. F. Albright, *The Archaeology of Palestine and the Bible* (1932), pp. 137–38; idem, *Yahweh and the Gods of Canaan* (1968), pp. 65–66, n. 3.
71. See Speiser, *AASOR* 10: 7–18.
72. H. L. Ginsberg, "Abram's 'Damascene' Steward," *BASOR* 200 (Dec. 1970): 31–32.

development from the older Akkadian term *mar biti*, meaning a "member of the household" although not directly a member of the family. Such a person would be a servant of non-slave status among the higher rank of servants. This usage is only known from the Persian period. There is, of course, no warrant for seeing in such a term a wealthy financier. The problem is whether or not such a person could inherit his master's property. The answer to this question has usually been given in terms of *real* adoption.[73] Many adoption texts from OB to NB indicate that the adopted son will inherit the property of his adoptive father unless there is a natural son, in which case the principal heir will be the natural son and the adopted son will have to take second place. However, he is not excluded from inheritance. Yet if Abraham had adopted a household servant there is no indication of any such shared inheritance in the rest of the story. On the contrary it is clearly excluded.

Since the Hebrew text actually says nothing about adoption it is perhaps best to take it at face value as meaning that servants of this status could actually inherit property.[74] While support for such a suggestion is rare there is a reference in Prov. 17:2 that indicates that a servant could "share in the inheritance as one of the brothers." It may also be suggested by the story of Ziba, Saul's servant, who received part of the paternal estate (2 Sam. 16:1–4; 19:29). There is little in Gen. 15:2–3 that points to customs of an archaic period, much less to an elaborate theory about the patriarch's economic way of life.

The Right of the First-Born

The patriarchal stories reflect a social custom which may be designated "right of the first-born."[75] This right implies that a special privilege was attached to being the eldest son; this was usually demonstrated in the size of the inheritance he could expect in comparison with that of his brothers. While the patriarchal stories make reference to this right by the use of the term $b^e k\hat{o}r\bar{a}h$,

---

73. Gordon, *BA* 3:2; cf. Albright, *Archaeology of Palestine* (1932), p. 138 where he originally expressed a preference for this explanation.
74. Z. W. Falk, *Hebrew Law in Biblical Times* (Jerusalem: Wahrmann Books, 1964), p. 166.
75. See the discussions by deVaux, *Histoire*, pp. 225, 238–39; J. Henninger, "Zum Erstgeborenenrecht bei den Semiten," *Festschrift W. Caskel*, ed. E. Gräf (Leiden: Brill, 1968), pp. 162–83; idem, "Premiers nés," *DBS* 8, cols. 467–82; H. Cazelles, "Premiers-nés," *DBS* 8, cols. 482–91.

they do not give any clear indication of exactly what advantage it had. In fact there is some ambiguity in the matter. In the Abraham story two sons are involved, but one is the son of a slave woman, so in spite of the fact that he is regarded as Abraham's full son his position is ambiguous. And since he is not fully accepted by Sarah as her son he can be deprived of any inheritance alongside of the natural child of the wife (Gen. 21:10). Much like Hagar, Keturah is also regarded as a concubine. Her sons received gifts before Abraham's death, but no inheritance is left them (Gen. 25:6).

In the Isaac-Jacob story the right of the first-born comes to the fore because both Jacob and Esau are sons of the same mother, and although they are twins, Esau is regarded as the elder. However, in the story of Esau's sale of his birthright to Jacob (Gen. 25:29-34), there is no indication as to what advantage this had for Jacob. Presumably it is to be taken with the earlier prediction about the fate of the two nations, Edom and Israel, in which it is hinted that Esau's rash action led ultimately to Israel's superiority. Yet the matter is complicated by the story of chapter 27, in which Jacob steals the death-bed blessing which apparently still belonged to Esau in spite of his loss of birthright. The blessing also predicts superiority over the other brother. But the story does not clarify anywhere how birthright is related to the two sons' inheritance.

Genesis 48 contains the account of Jacob's adoption of Joseph's two children as his own with the explicit intention of giving them each a share equivalent to that received by Reuben and Simeon (v. 5f.). This implies that all the brothers were thought to inherit equally, and that preference could only be given to the favorite son by the adoption of his two children.[76] However, in vv. 14 and 17-20 occurs the blessing of the two sons in which the younger instead of the first-born receives the patriarch's blessing. But it is difficult to see how this blessing can have anything to do with a change in the first-born status as some have suggested, since only as Joseph's children would one have an advantage over the other, but not as Jacob's children. Finally Joseph himself is given a special gift of Shechem (v. 22), but this may again be interpreted only as a gift to the favorite before death and not as the primary inheritance portion.

---

76. It is hard to see how this verse can mean that Ephraim and Manasseh were substituted for Reuben and Simeon, the first and second born, or given their preferential shares, although 1 Chron. 5:1-2 seems to interpret it this way.

On the other hand, it was perhaps possible to lose the rights of the first-born through some crime or serious misdemeanor. This is indicated in Gen. 49:3–4, in which Reuben loses the first position, and vv. 5–7 suggest that Simeon and Levi lose their places in the succession and even their inheritance for similar reasons. Consequently Judah, as the next in line, falls heir to the right of the first-born (v. 8). Yet in all these passages it is not clearly specified what advantages the birthright is thought to have apart from a certain destiny which it bestows on the eponymous ancestors. But this is presumably mediated more effectively through the power of the "blessing" which does not directly coincide with the birthright. It can scarcely be said that the stories of the patriarchs take the matter of primogeniture very seriously.

The right of the first-born in cuneiform sources of the second millennium, as reflected in laws and legal dispositions of inheritance, is far from uniform. It would seem that generalizations about its practice even within a fairly limited period of time and region are quite unwarranted. For instance, the Code of Lipit-Ishtar and the Code of Hammurapi state that the sons in a family should inherit equally, but the documents from Southern Mesopotamia from this same period of time often indicate a preference for the first-born.[77] This tendency to favor the eldest son above the rest is most explicit in the texts of Nuzi and Arrapḫa and in the Assyrian Laws of the late second millennium B.C. These suggest that the first-born's inheritance portion was double that given to any of the other sons.[78] Nevertheless, there is considerable diversity of practice represented in the Nuzi texts, for while the "double portion" *šinnišu ina zitti* may have been customary it was not obligatory, and it was within the power of the testator to stipulate that the shares should be equal, even between sons and daughters.[79] In some cases an offending son could be denied his share, or a son who had acquired property by other means could be passed over.[80]

The favored inheritance share could also be affected at Nuzi by considerations of a polygamous marriage or by terms of adoption. In

---

77. DMBL 1:331.
78. M-AL B 1:8–12; for the Nuzi texts see Gadd 5 & 6; HSS v: 21,72 (same as in *AASOR* 10:8,21): E. M. Cassin, *L'adoption à Nuzi*, pp. 286, 292.
79. HSS v:65,74 (same as in *AASOR* 10, no. 7, 23); HSS xix:17, discussed by E. A. Speiser, "A Significant New Will from Nuzi," *JCS* 17 (1963): 65–71.
80. See HSS v: 7,72 (same as in *AASOR* 10, nos. 4, 21).

the case of the former, the son of the favorite wife might inherit a larger portion than the son of a second wife.[81] In adoption agreements, on the other hand, the adopted son might have to give place to any future natural-born son, but his document of adoption usually guaranteed him against sharing inheritance with any subsequent adoptee, so he generally stood a good chance of gaining all of the property.[82]

The situation at Mari may have been a little different, although it is dangerous to generalize on the basis of a single text. In one adoption document the adopted son is guaranteed two-thirds (*šittīn*) of the inheritance.[83] It is unlikely that natural sons are contemplated since both man and wife together adopt the son and if they acquire any future sons their total share will only be one-third. Such adoption was usually for the purpose of caring for the adoptive parents in their old age and for conducting the funerary rites. Thus adoption by childless couples usually meant that the one adopted would stand to gain the entire inheritance. So the rather high two-thirds guaranteed inheritance may be a special condition of adoption in place of a restrictive clause against any future adoption, and may not reflect the right of the first-born, as Noth has recently suggested.[84] The terminology designating the eldest son is not used in this text, and there is no other information on this from Mari as yet.

Furthermore, a number of scholars have emphasized the father's right, as shown in certain documents from Nuzi and Alalaḫ, to designate which of their sons would be the "first-born" regardless of age.[85] This situation, however, only arose in the case of marriage contracts which envisaged a polygamous marriage. In such a situation a marriage contract might indicate that the first male offspring of a particular wife would always have priority over the children of the second wife. Likewise in adoption, of course, the adopted son might have to give way to the natural-born sons. But it was unlikely,

---

81. See HSS v: 71 (same as in *AASOR* 10, no. 19).
82. See HSS v: 48 (same as in *AASOR* 10, nos. 1, 2, 33), 60, 67.
83. G. Boyer, *Archives Royales de Mari* 8, *Textes Juridiques* (Paris: Imprimerie Nationale, 1958), 1:24. Boyer translates *šittīn* as "double part." See also his commentary, pp. 178–182. J. J. Finkelstein in *ANET*³, p. 545, also renders it as "double share." But Noth, *Ursprünge des alten Israel*, pp. 19ff., argues on the basis of regular Akk. usage (see Ch #64) that *šittīn* means "two-thirds." However, I see no justification for Noth's remark that the adoptee was "*vielleicht eines Slaven.*" It is most unlikely.
84. Noth, *Ursprünge*, pp. 19–20.
85. See Speiser, *Genesis*, p. 212.

except for cases of serious wrongs, for a father to make an arbitrary choice from among the sons of one wife as to which would be the "first-born," and to my knowledge no such instance has ever been cited.

This second-millennium B.C. material is the background against which the Old Testament customs regarding first-born rights have been compared. At the same time the legal material related to the order of succession in inheritance and preferential treatment of heirs from the first millennium has been ignored or categorically dismissed.[86] Nevertheless some interesting observations may be made on these late texts.

There is a marriage contract from the Neo-Babylonian period that tells of a man taking a second wife because his first is childless. One of the conditions of the marriage, however, is that "on the day that PN, his first wife, shall bear a son, two-thirds (2-ta $q\bar{a}t\bar{e}$) of the property shall belong to him." The child of the second wife will get only one-third ($šalšu$). But if the first wife dies childless all the property will go to the second wife and her children.[87] The mention of two-thirds in this document is not just a special condition of this situation as might be argued in the case of the Mari text discussed above. This proportion is repeatedly mentioned as an inheritance share in several texts of the period and must be regarded as a customary preferential share.[88] There is, in fact, a sixth-century will in which the property is distributed by a mother to her two daughters. The elder one gets two-thirds, while the younger one gets one-third.[89] A similar will from this period divides property between two sons, distinguishing between the eldest and the second son, although the proportions of the inheritance cannot be determined.[90] An adoption document of the mid-seventh century states that even if the adoptive parents should subsequently bring seven heirs into the world, the adopted son would remain the oldest heir.[91] Yet in spite of this

---

86. The study by Henninger, "Erstgeborenenrecht" (cited in n. 66 above), makes no mention whatever of any later Babylonian and Assyrian material, and is therefore quite incomplete.

87. San Nicolò and Ungnad, *Neubabylonische Rechtsurkunden* no. 1, pp. 1–4. See also N-BL #15 in *ANET*[2], p. 198; DMBL 1: 341–42.

88. San Nicolò and Ungnad, *Neubabylonische Rechtsurkunden*, nos. 12, 15, 19.

89. Ibid., no. 19.

90. San Nicolò and Petschow, *Babylonische Rechtsurkunden*, no. 7; cf. also no. 4 (= *ANET*[3], p. 547).

91. Kohler and Ungnad, *Assyrische Rechtsurkunden*, no. 41; cf. also no. 46 where one son gets the largest share, and eight other brothers divide the rest.

frequently expressed preference for the eldest son there are also documents that divide the property equally among the children.[92]

The only text in the Old Testament that deals with the inheritance share of the first-born is Deut. 21:15–17. The law in this passage forbids a man from showing any preference for a favorite wife by designating her son as first-born. Instead, "if the first-born is hers that is disliked, then on the day when he assigns his possessions as an inheritance to his sons ... he shall acknowledge the first-born, the son of the disliked, by giving him two-thirds (*pī šᵉnayim*) of all that he has. ..." Many have taken *pī šᵉnayim* to mean "double share," but Noth is probably correct in arguing on the basis of Zech. 13:8 that it means "two-thirds."[93] The best extrabiblical parallel to this text is not the Mari document of adoption, as Noth suggests, but the Neo-Babylonian text and the N-BL #15 mentioned above,[94] which refers to the two-thirds/one-third disposition of the inheritance between the two wives. Deuteronomy is, in fact, forbidding the preference shown by demanding a strict chronological priority. There is no reason to see an archaic remnant of an ancient practice from Mari here.

As to the patriarchal stories, there is no indication of what the preferential inheritance share of the first-born was thought to be, apart from the suggestion in Jacob's adoption of Ephraim and Manasseh in which all the brothers seem to share equally (Gen. 48:5–6). On the other hand, Jacob does seem bound originally to recognize Reuben as his first-born, and only because of wrongs done to his father does Reuben lose this status (cf. 1 Chron. 5:1). There is no instance where the patriarchs ever knowingly gave a son other than the first-born that status. Furthermore, Deut. 21:15–17 and its close association with Neo-Babylonian texts are sufficient evidence that the custom of special privilege for the first-born was still prominent in Israel at a late date. Consequently, there is little basis for arguing that the patriarchal stories especially reflect the customs of the second millennium regarding the rights of the first-born.

Nevertheless, some episodes in the patriarchal stories have been

---

92. San Nicolò and Ungnad, *Neubabylonische Rechtsurkunden*, nos. 2, 10; San Nicolò and Petschow, *Babylonische Rechtsurkunden*, no. 6.
93. Noth, *Ursprünge*, pp. 19–20.
94. See above, n. 90.

interpreted as reflecting special situations related to the rights of the first-born in the Nuzi texts. One such story is the sale by Esau of his birthright to Jacob. This has been compared with a Nuzi text (JEN:204), in which a man transferred a piece of property to his brother for three sheep.[95] However, this action was done through the process of sale-adoption, a very common means of sale transaction in Nuzi, and there is no way of telling whether it was a good or bad deal. Furthermore, the ability to transfer one's inheritance rights before they were even received is not at all uncommon in the Neo-Babylonian and Achaemenid documents.[96] Sometimes they were given as gifts and sometimes sold. One broken text even seems to suggest that a man gave his brother his two-thirds portion—his birthright.[97]

Another episode pertains to Rachel's theft of her father's *teraphim*, a term which should probably be rendered as "household gods." These domestic deities are mentioned in the Nuzi texts under the term *ilāni* and are sometimes listed among the properties disposed of in a will. Since such deities were usually left to the eldest son, some scholars interpreted them as a way of designating priority in the inheritance. Thus possession of the family gods established the right of the first-born and priority in the family as a whole. Consequently, Rachel's theft of *teraphim* was carried out in order to insure Jacob's priority in her father's household.[98]

M. Greenberg, however, has recently shown that this parallel is quite spurious. In the first place, there is no evidence that the domestic deities, as such, had any legal status as to the designation of who was the principal heir. This was established, in the event of any doubt (as in adoptions or polygamous marriages), by a written document that did not even need to mention the gods. And the deities stolen by Rachel could have no legal claim without a document or witnesses giving her the right of possession. As objects of a theft they could

---

95. See Gordon, BA 3:5; cf. deVaux, *Histoire*, p. 238.
96. San Nicolò and Ungnad, *Neubabylonische Rechtsurkunden*, no. 3; Moore, *Neo-Babylonian Business Documents*, no. 160; Kohler and Ungnad, *Assyrische Rechtsurkunden*, no. 48.
97. San Nicolò and Ungnad, *Neubabylonische Rechtsurkunden*, no. 15.
98. See Gadd 51 (same as in *ANET*[2], pp. 219–20, erroneously called a "sale-adoption" instead of a "real adoption"). See the discussion by Gordon, *BA* 3:5–6; A. E. Draffkorn, "Ilâni/Elohim," *JBL* 76 (1957): 216–24; Speiser, *Genesis*, pp. 249–51. Note in HSS xvii:7 the *ilâni* did not go directly to the eldest son; see E. Cassin, "Nouvelles données sur les relations familiales à Nuzi," *RA* 57 (1963): 115.

only be a grave liability. Also, since Jacob was leaving Laban's homeland when Rachel stole them they could certainly have no significance for any subsequent inheritance, quite apart from the fact that Jacob was not an adopted son. Greenberg suggests that they were taken for purely religious reasons. His parallel with the first century A.D. custom of a Parthian woman taking the domestic deities with her when taken from her homeland is much more convincing.[99]

A final instance of a Nuzi parallel to birthright concerning the deathbed blessing of Isaac has been drawn by Speiser. In reference to this episode he states in his Genesis commentary:

> Birthright in Hurrian society was often a matter of a father's discretion rather than chronological priority. Moreover, of all the paternal dispositions, the one that took the form of a death bed declaration carried the greatest weight.[100]

Speiser then goes on to refer to a Nuzi text,[101] which deals with a legal dispute over the deathbed disposition of a slave girl by a father to his youngest son because he did not yet have a wife. The older brothers, who were married, contested the right of the youngest to his possession but the latter brought witnesses to the event and eventually won the case.

It should be noted that this was not a matter of passing over the right of the older brothers to their appropriate share of the estate. On the contrary, CH #166 made special allowances for expenses out of the estate for the marriage of a younger unmarried son, so this was the legitimate right of the youngest brother.[102] The deathbed act was also a legal process with witnesses, whether or not it was recorded on a tablet, and as such it was binding in a court of law. There is nothing extraordinary about the whole event.

On the other hand, nothing in the biblical story of Isaac's blessing suggests a legal process. There were no witnesses in the formal sense and no actual property being disposed of. The story clearly distinguishes between the birthright and the blessing (Genesis

---

99. M. Greenberg, "Another Look at Rachel's Theft of the Teraphim," *JBL* 81 (1962): 239–48.
100. Speiser, *Genesis*, p. 212; see also idem, "I Know Not the Day of My Death," *JBL* 74 (1955): 252–56.
101. Speiser, *AASOR* 16, no. 56.
102. See DMBL 1: 326.

27:36). The blessing is not property and has no parallel in the Nuzi documents. Furthermore, Isaac's intention was to bless his *eldest* son, Esau, and if it had been a matter of legality Jacob would certainly have lost his claim in a court of law. The only parallel between the Nuzi text and the Genesis story is the expression of the last wishes of an old or dying father, which is such a universal phenomenon as to be of no significance in understanding the cultural background of the story.[103] Consequently, there is no justification for seeing in the patriarchal references to birthright, *teraphim*, or blessings allusions to special customs of the second millennium B.C.

Jacob the Shepherd

Jacob's life as a shepherd and particularly his terms of employment by Laban (Gen. 30:27-34; 31:38-40) have been the subject of comparison with parallels from the second millennium B.C.[104] CH #261-267 gives a number of laws which have to do with the conditions of employment of shepherds and their assistants provided by owners of large flocks and herds. There is also a number of contracts from this period, both state and private, which records the hiring of shepherds and the terms of their employment and wages.[105] One such contract is the subject of a study by J. J. Finkelstein, who compares the terms of the contract with those of Jacob and Laban.[106]

The Old Babylonian document in question consists of a list of the sheep and goats that are put under the care of a shepherd who assumes liability for them. It further stipulates that if the shepherd's assistant suffers any loss through neglect (*ḫiṭum*) he will be held responsible for it, but the shepherd himself will also have to forfeit some of his wages, which apparently consisted of a certain fixed amount of grain per year.

The actual points of comparison between this document and the

---

103. See Psalm 72, interpreted in the tradition as the last words of David to Solomon with some similarity in the blessing.
104. Speiser, *Genesis*, p. 247.
105. See F. R. Kraus, *Staatliche Viehhaltung im altbabylonische Lande Larsa*, Mededeelingen Kon. Ned. Academie van Wetenschappen, Afd. Letterkunde 29/5 (Amsterdam, 1966); DMBL 1:453-61.
106. J. J. Finkelstein, "An Old Babylonian Herding Contract and Genesis 31:38f.," *JAOS* 88 (1968): 30-36.

Jacob story are surprisingly few for the claims that are made for it, especially when one realizes that such work contracts with shepherds are not found exclusively in any particular period. In the Jacob story there are only two parties involved, not three, and Jacob's wages are in sheep and not in grain. The only link that remains, which is most significant to Finkelstein, is the liability for loss due to neglect of duty (*ḥiṭum*), a usage for this word peculiar to the Old Babylonian period.[107] This statement of liability is compared with Jacob's protest to Laban about his faithfulness as a shepherd, in Gen. 31:39, which Finkelstein translates as follows, "The ones fallen prey to wild beasts I did not charge to you [lit.: bring to you] —I myself *made good the loss*, whether it was snatched by day or by night."[108] The italicized words are Finkelstein's rendering of *ʾaḥaṭṭennah* which is construed as a piel of *ḥṭʾ* with the basic meaning of "to err, miss, sin" and in the piel "to purify, cleanse." Thus the meaning proposed here would be unique in the Old Testament, and Finkelstein therefore feels that it reflects the OB *ḥiṭum*, or "loss." This leads him to affirm that the Jacob-Laban story reflects "the precise terminology current in Old Babylonian herding contracts."[109]

But some serious questions may be raised about this proposed connection. Firstly, a substantive, *ḥiṭum*, is being compared with a verb, *ḥṭʾ*. But the Akkadian verb *ḥaṭû*, comparable to the Hebrew *ḥṭʾ*, is found with both cultic and profane usage from Old Babylonian to Neo-Babylonian, and in the D stem (=*piʿel*) it is almost always found in the later period.[110] Secondly, the translation proposed by Finkelstein is still difficult because at best the verb would have to mean "to damage, lose" and not its opposite. To argue on the analogy of the cultic meaning for such a shift is rather risky when only one example exists. Thirdly, loss as a result of wild

---

107. Ibid., p. 32; see also deVaux, *Histoire*, p. 242.
108. Finkelstein, *JAOS* 88:30. Note that Finkelstein seems to have omitted the phrase *miyyādî tebaqšennāh*, "from my hand you demanded it." Cf. R. Fraukena, "Some Remarks on the Semitic Background of the Chapters xxiv–xxxi of the Book of Genesis," *OTS* 17 (1972): 58, who suggests (on the basis of T. Onkelos) that the phrase *ānōkî ʾaḥaṭṭennāh* should be rendered, "what was lacking," but it is difficult to see how this clause can be made the object of the following verb.
109. Finkelstein, *JAOS* 88:32.
110. *CAD* 6:156–58. For possible exceptions see W. G. Lambert, "A Vizier of Ḫattuša? A Further Comment," *JCS* 13 (1959): 132.

animals can hardly be construed as "loss through negligence," as Finkelstein himself makes quite clear. So the problem in translation remains.

It is possible that the verb ᵃḥaṭṭennāh is not related to the verb ḥṭʾ at all, especially since the orthography is defective and lacks the aleph. There is another verb used in Babylonian contracts in both the old and late periods, the Akkadian ḫâṭu, which has the meaning "to weigh out (money), to pay compensation."[111] The general meaning, "to pay," in a sense equivalent to nadānu is particularly common in Neo-Babylonian and Achaemenid period documents. It would be quite simple to construe the Hebrew as a qal (=G stem) ᵃḥiṭennāh and thus a verb which would correspond to Akkadian ḫâṭu. The passage would then mean: "the victim of wild animals I did not bring to you, but I myself paid for it...." Whether or not this solution is acceptable, the connection with the Old Babylonian herding contracts has little to commend it, and if there is Babylonian influence in terminology it may well be late.

There are, however, some herding contracts from the Neo-Babylonian and Achaemenid periods that may throw more light on the Jacob story than the Old Babylonian ones can. These belong generally to a type of contract known as the "dialogue document," in which is recorded the conversation that preceded the agreement.[112] The prospective shepherd approaches the owner of the sheep or his representative and states his willingness to graze a certain number of sheep and goats, guaranteeing a certain return to the owner in new lambs and by-products, and arranging an agreement on unpreventable deaths. Above all this he has his own profit. The owner of the sheep agrees, and a contract is drawn up repeating these terms and setting the date on which the contract starts. Allowing for the narrative style of the biblical story, this is the form which is found in Gen. 30:27-34. Laban urges Jacob to name his own wages, and Jacob proceeds to specify very clearly those sheep and goats which will be his wage as distinct from Laban's guaranteed

111. *CAD* 6:161–62. For its use in contracts of NB see H. Petschow, "Die neubabylonische Zwiegesprächsurkunde und Genesis 23," *JCS* 19 (1965): 122.

112. For a general treatment of form see the work of Petschow (in n. 111 above), pp. 103–120. For examples of such herding contracts see J. Augapfel, *Babylonische Rechtsurkunden aus der Regierungszeit Artaxerxes I und Darius II*, pp. 83–86; G. Cardascia, *Les archives des Murašu*, pp. 155–57; J. Kohler and A. Ungnad, *Hundert ausgewählte Rechtsurkunden*, nos. 48–50, 62.

increase.¹¹³ The folkloric element has entered the story to make the terms unusual, but the form of the agreement is not essentially different. Furthermore, the terms that Jacob mentions—taking only the spotted and striped animals—is of particular interest in the light of these late contracts, since they refer to the sheep and goats as "the white ones and black ones," *piṣāti u salmāti*.¹¹⁴ If one is looking for contractual forms and agreements behind the Jacob-Laban story, a better case can be made for associating the story with the herding contracts known from the Neo-Babylonian and Achaemenid periods than with those suggested from Old Babylonian times.

Abraham's Purchase

The Genesis 23 story about Abraham's purchase of Machpelah as a grave site for Sarah, his wife, has produced considerable discussion about second millennium parallels. The mention of Hittites at Hebron has encouraged M. R. Lehmann to interpret the purchase procedures in the light of Hittite law.¹¹⁵ This chapter presents Abraham, a landless resident alien (*gēr wᵉtôsāb*), endeavoring to buy a burial place from the native population. There are lengthy negotiations in which Abraham finally buys not only a cave but also the field in front of it for a high price. Lehmann interprets Ephron's offer to *give* the field to Abraham as his eagerness to sell the whole of his holdings in conformity with laws #46 and 47 of the Hittite Code which specify that the feudal service (*ilku*) attached to a property is only transferred to a new owner when the entire holdings of the previous owner are sold.¹¹⁶ It is suggested that Abraham wanted to avoid this obligation and so only asked for the cave. However, he was forced to buy the field as well and thus assumed Ephron's *ilku* service.

While this interpretation of the story won considerable support,¹¹⁷

---

113. A very brief reference to this parallel occurs in DMBL 1:457, n. 5.
114. Cf. Finkelstein, *JAOS* 88:33.
115. "Abraham's Purchase of Machpelah and Hittite Law," *BASOR* 129 (Feb. 1953): 15–18.
116. For the Hittite Laws see *ANET*³, p. 191. For further discussion on these see H. van den Brink, "Genesis 23: Abrahams Koop," *Tijdschrift voor Rechtsgeschiedenis—Revue d'histoire du droit* 37 (1969): 469–88.
117. Albright in *BASOR* 129:18, n. 14; Bright, *History of Israel*, p. 72; C. H. Gordon, "Abraham and the Merchants of Ura," *JNES* 17 (1958): 29.

it contains many difficulties.[118] The most obvious way of interpreting the proceedings is to view them as exaggerated politeness and protracted negotiations characteristic of oriental business dealings. The offer of the field in addition to the cave has been compared with Arauna's offer to David of both his threshing floor and in addition the oxen, harness and threshing sledges (2 Sam. 24:22–23a; 1 Chron. 21:23).[119] There is certainly no question of any feudal duties involved here. Both cases show polite ways of trying to get the most out of the deal. There is no hint in the Genesis story of any feudal service or of the sale of Ephron's entire property. This would certainly have given him an inferior status in the city. The basic difficulty with Lehmann's comparison is that it must supply the story with the missing point of comparison and then reconstruct the rest to agree with it. Lehmann also ignores the question of how the Hittites obtained sovereignty over Hebron in the late second millennium B.C.[120]

More recently another legal background has been proposed for this chapter, namely, sale contracts from the Neo-Babylonian and Achaemenid periods known as "dialogue documents" (*Zwiegesprächsurkunde*).[121] In this form one party approaches another party with an offer either to buy or to sell, which is recorded in direct speech in the document. The second party agrees (lit.: hears, *išmē*) and the purchaser then pays out the amount (*iḥiṭma iddaššu*) named in silver. The transfer and description of the property is recorded along with the usual quitclaim, penalty clauses, witnesses, and date.

The story in Genesis 23 follows this model completely. Abraham makes a proposal to purchase the cave in Ephron's field. Ephron makes a counterproposal that includes the field as well. Abraham then agrees to pay for both cave and field, and the price is set at four hundred shekels. Abraham agrees to (lit.: "hears," *šmʿ*) the price

---

118. See the criticisms by G. M. Tucker, "The Legal Background of Genesis 23," *JBL* 85 (1966): 77–84.
119. Tucker, *JBL* 85:78.
120. Van den Brink, "Abrahams Koop," pp. 479–82, tries to meet this problem by suggesting that the original tradition related to the region of Aram-Naharaim from which Abraham came. Such a solution must ignore much in the current story and remain completely speculative.
121. So Tucker, *JBL* 85:80–84; also Petschow, "Zwiegesprächsurkunde und Genesis 23," *JCS* 19:103–120, for a full treatment of this form. See also the earlier suggestion by J. J. Rabinowitz, "Neo-Babylonian Legal Documents and Jewish Law," *JJP* 13:131–35.

and weighs out the named amount of silver. The story then records the transfer of the property along with its precise description and with the suggestion that it was all duly witnessed.

Now it is possible to take certain individual features of the story such as the mention of the "full price" (v. 9) or the weighing out of the silver (v. 16) and find Old Babylonian parallels for these as well.[122] This only points to the continuity of legal procedures and terminology over a very long period. Nevertheless, the "dialogue document" schema is a legal form restricted to the late Assyrian, Neo-Babylonian, and Persian periods, and the Genesis 23 story fits this particular pattern in structure and vocabulary to a very remarkable degree.[123] One can also add to this the fact that the reference to Hittites does not correspond to the second millennium but to its use in this same period. Consequently, if there are any older elements to this tradition they must be of a very limited nature, and the general statement that the tradition has been reworked is scarcely adequate to account for so many late features in this chapter.

The Covenant of Abraham

The account of the covenant with Abraham in Gen. 15:7–22 has played a major role in discussions about the history of the Abrahamic traditions. In this passage many have looked for the nucleus of an ancient tradition of land promise. It is therefore necessary to deal with any arguments that have to do with the dating of this pericope or a part of it. Such arguments are primarily concerned with the nature of covenant-making preparations that reflect the practice of ancient Near-Eastern oath-taking.

Already in the work of Frazer extensive parallels to the covenant with Abraham were drawn from Near Eastern, Classical, modern Arab and primitive tribal sources.[124] Frazer outlined the two basic types of explanation for the act of cutting the animals in half and passing between the pieces. The first is the *retributive* theory. "According to it, the killing and cutting up of the victim is symbolic of the retribution that will overtake the man who breaks the covenant or violates the oath; he, like the animal, will perish by a violent

---

122. See Tucker, *JBL* 85:80.
123. See the conclusions of Tucker, *JBL* 85:84; Petschow, *JCS* 19:119–120. See also the Neo-Babylonian period example in Jer. 32:8–12.
124. James G. Frazer, *Folk-Lore in the Old Testament* (London: Macmillan, 1918), pp. 391–428.

death."[125] But Frazer did not think that this fully accounted for the act of passing between the pieces, so for this part of it at least he adopted W. Robertson Smith's sacramental or purificatory explanation in which the parties by their action partook of the lifegiving power released by the victim's death. His final conclusion was that the rite in the covenant of Abraham was a combination of both the retributive and sacramental elements.[126]

The problem with Frazer's solution is that it attempts one general explanation for all rites of cutting animals, but this is hardly necessary. It is directly denied by the Near Eastern example, which he quotes,[127] of the treaty between Ashurnirari V and Maticilu which specifies that the animal used for the oath is not for sacrifice.[128] The biblical example of Jer. 34:18–20 can also hardly be interpreted in a sacramental or purificatory way. The individuals who passed between the pieces in this way took the oath upon themselves, and it need have no other meaning.

There have been subsequent efforts to find an element of sacrifice in Genesis 15, but these attempts are scarcely convincing.[129] Most recently the question has been formulated somewhat differently by Loewenstamm.[130] He remarks that while the rite of self-curse is originally and functionally quite distinct from sacrifice there is a certain treatment of the story in Genesis 15 that is reminiscent of sacrificial procedures. This is seen in the careful prescription of the types of animals and the non-division of the birds. He points out that the animal terminology is not that used by the priestly writers and tries to find another cultic locus for it, which he proposes as Shiloh in the premonarchy period. This last suggestion is very speculative and need not be considered further. However, it should be pointed out that Loewenstamm seems to confirm the basic identity of this rite as a self-curse with the biblical and Near Eastern sources of the first millennium B.C.

---

125. Ibid., p. 399.
126. Ibid., p. 425.
127. Ibid., p. 401.
128. See D. J. McCarthy, *Treaty and Covenant*, Analecta Biblica 21 (Rome: Pontifical Biblical Institute, 1963), pp. 195–97; *ANET*³, pp. 532–33.
129. J. Henninger, "Was bedeutet die rituelle Teilung eines Tieres in zwei Hälfen?" *Biblica* 34 (1953): 344–53.
130. S. E. Loewenstamm, "Zur Traditionsgeschichte des Bundes zwischen den Stücken," *VT* 18 (1968): 500–06.

In a recent discussion of this Abrahamic covenant, M. Weinfeld has pointed to what he regards as a similar oath made by Abba-El of Yamhad which dates to the seventeenth century B.C.[131] Abba-El takes an oath by cutting the neck of a lamb and saying to Yarimlim, "(May the gods do so to me) if I take back what I gave you." This is a reference to the gift of the city of Alalaḫ to the vassal ruler in exchange for the destroyed Irridi. To this text Weinfeld links another, which he interprets as a reference to Yarimlim supplying the animal for the same event *as a sacrifice*.[132] He points out that in Genesis 15 the inferior party also supplies the sacrificial animals while the superior party takes the oath. He then argues that in the first millennium oaths of this kind, the sacrificial element is no longer present so that Genesis 15 must reflect the more primitive usage.

This presentation, however, has a number of basic weaknesses. The argument about Yarimlim's sacrifice rests on a broken passage in which there is no mention of animals whatever. The subject of the verb *ušēli* "he caused to go up, brought up" is also not clear so that D. J. Wiseman may have been right when he suggested in his publication of the text that it is Abba-El who brought Yarimlim to the temple of Ishtar [*ana bît*] *^dIštar* for the purpose of installation into office.[133] It is also possible to read the text as [*šum*] *^dIštar ušēli* in the sense of "he raised the name of Ištar [in an oath]," which would fit the context.[134] With such a broken text, however, nothing can be very definite, and it is best to base no arguments upon it.

The second weakness with Weinfeld's position is his misuse of Loewenstamm's arguments for the sacrificial character of the rite.[135] For Loewenstamm this is only part of the revision (*Bearbeitung*) of the tradition and cannot be functionally original to the rite itself. There is no altar mentioned, though it occurs elsewhere in

---

131. M. Weinfeld, "The Covenant of Grant in the Old Testament and in the Ancient Near East," *JAOS* 90 (1970): 196; also D. J. Wiseman, "Abban and Alalaḫ," *JCS* 12 (1958): 126; A. Draffkorn, "Was King Abba-AN of Yamḫad a Vizier for the King of Ḫattuša?" *JCS* 13 (1959): 94–97. See the translations in McCarthy, *Treaty and Covenant*, pp. 185–86.
132. *JAOS* 90:196.
133. *JCS* 12:126.
134. Weinfeld follows the restoration of *CAD* 4:130 but cf. p. 135 where the use of *ušēli* in the sense of "taking an oath" is cited. Both the meanings of "offer" and "take an oath" are uncommon for OB but attested for NB.
135. *JAOS* 90:197 n. 118; cf. S. E. Loewenstamm, "The Divine Grants of Land to the Patriarchs," *JAOS* 91 (1971): 509–10.

the Abraham stories. There are no terms for sacrifice used, no burning of the animals or other sacrificial procedures. The sacrificial elements of the story are, at best, superficial. It is likewise questionable whether any of the covenant cutting rites of the second millennium had a sacrificial character to them.

On the other hand Weinfeld has not taken seriously enough the actual form of the Genesis 15 rite, which is the halving of the animals and the passing between the parts. None of the descriptions from the second millennium fits this very well. They describe the rite as cutting the throat or just as killing. The later texts are much more instructive. The inscription of Sefire I speaks of cutting the calf in two (*gzr*); this verb corresponds to the term for "pieces" *gzrm* in the Hebrew text of Gen. 15:11.[136] But the closest parallel is still that of Jer. 34:18–20, and there is no need to look beyond this. Whether the oath is made by the inferior or superior party and who provides the animals do not matter. The same oath form is often used for a variety of different judicial and political or diplomatic procedures. The text of Gen. 15:9ff. is really saying that God is making a solemn oath that in other passages is stated as swearing by himself (Gen. 22:16; 26:3; cf. Deut. 32:40, Jer. 22:5).

In conclusion, there is nothing in the form of covenant-making in this chapter that to my mind points to an early date. The best parallel is still the biblical one that comes from the end of the monarchy. There may be reasons *on the literary level* why the rite has taken on some characteristics of sacrificial preparation. This is undoubtedly due to the fact that the subject of the oath-taking is deity and not man so that the animals used must be very carefully specified as to number and treatment. Yet for this very reason the description of the rite would never have to correspond to any actual instance or practice of such a ceremony. As I hope to show below, Genesis 15 is a mixture of many forms in a literary conglomerate that is strongly suggestive of a late date.

---

136. J. A. Fitzmyer, *The Aramaic Inscriptions of Sefire*, Biblica et Orientalia 19 (Rome: Pontifical Biblical Institute, 1967) Cf. I A: 7 where *gzr* is used in the sense of "conclude" a covenant, but in I A: 40 it has the literal meaning of "cut in two;" see also the commentary, pp. 32–33, 56–57. Fitzmyer observes (p. 57) that the "calf," ʿglʾ is the same animal as used in Jer. 34:18 and Gen. 15:9. See also McCarthy, *Treaty and Covenant*, pp. 189–92.

CHAPTER 5

Archaeology and the Patriarchs

Frequently the phrase "archaeological evidence" is used in connection with the patriarchs to include the whole range of materials that have been discussed thus far. But our concern in this chapter is with evidence related directly to excavations in Palestine and the correlation of the patriarchal narratives with archaeological phases and data.

The Middle Bronze Age

There are two archaeological periods for Palestine in the early second millennium B.C. with which the patriarchs have been associated: the periods known as Middle Bronze I (= Intermediate Bronze Age) and Middle Bronze II A–C (= Middle Bronze I–II).[1] In much of the discussion about the archaelogy of the early second millennium B.C. the distinction between these two phases is often obscured. This is partly because of the choice of nomenclature (MB I, MB II A–C) which suggests some continuity between them. It is generally recognized, however, that the two periods are quite distinct, and thus efforts have been made to introduce new, more appropriate terminology. What this means for this discussion is that if the cultural milieu in which the patriarchs lived is viewed as fairly homogeneous throughout the "patriarchal age," then a choice has to be made as to which of these two periods provides the more suitable historical context.[2]

---

1. There is still confusion at the present time over archaeological nomenclature. Two systems are in current use:

    Middle Bronze I (Albright) = Intermediate Early Bronze-Middle Bronze (Kenyon)
                                           or Intermediate Bronze Age (Lapp)
    Middle Bronze II A (Albright) = Middle Bronze I (Kenyon)
    Middle Bronze II B–C (Albright) = Middle Bronze II (Kenyon)

2. This issue is sometimes obscured, as in G. E. Wright, *Biblical Archaeology*, pp. 45–52; J. Bright, *History of Israel*, pp. 76–78; ibid., 2nd ed., pp. 83–85, where the dates for the patriarchs are given as between the twentieth and seventeenth centuries B.C.

W. F. Albright and Nelson Glueck have maintained rather firmly in recent years that Abraham can only be associated with Middle Bronze I.[3] Glueck states:

> Either the Age of Abraham coincides with the Middle Bronze I period between the twenty-first and nineteenth centuries B.C. or the entire saga dealing with the Patriarch must be dismissed, so far as its historical value is concerned, from scientific consideration. The flesh and blood personage of Abraham ... could not have existed later than the nineteenth century B.C., at the end of Middle Bronze I, for otherwise there would have been no historical framework into which his life could have been set.[4]

This view is based upon the judgment that the region of Transjordan and the Negeb must have been settled in order to account for the stories of Sodom and Gomorrah, the invasion of the foreign kings in Genesis 14, and Abraham's unhindered wanderings in the Negeb—particularly his trips between Palestine and Egypt. Glueck and others have firmly established by their archaeological surveys of Transjordan and the Negeb that this whole region was quite densely covered with numerous MB I sites.[5] However, a long occupational gap exists for the subsequent periods lasting until the end of Late Bronze in Transjordan and into the Iron Age in the Negeb. Consequently, if the Abraham stories suggest a settlement in these regions then the only appropriate period prior to Israel's own settlement would be MB I.

This position, however, is basically weak at a number of points. First of all, the Genesis stories do not suggest that there were any settlements in the region.[6] If Abraham's way of life had been purely nomadic this would constitute no problem. Nomads did enter Egypt from Palestine and Transjordan in the second millennium. However, if one takes the nature of Abraham's retinue at face value, as Glueck does, then it would have been difficult without support stations to travel from Palestine to Egypt. But this is really a denial of the patriarch's nomadic way of life.

3. See Chap. 1, n. 5 above.
4. Glueck, *Rivers in the Desert*, p. 68.
5. N. Glueck, *Explorations in Eastern Palestine I–III, AASOR* 14, 15, 18–19 (1934–39); idem, *Rivers in the Desert*, Chap. 3; B. Rothenberg, et. al., *God's Wilderness: Discoveries in the Sinai* (London: Thames and Hudson, 1961).
6. See the criticisms of Y. Aharoni in *AOTS*, p. 387; M. Noth, "Der Beitrag der Archäologie," *SVT* 7 (1959): 265ff.

The real problem with the view taken by Glueck and Albright is in their evaluation of the MB I culture. K. M. Kenyon has quite appropriately characterized this period as one in which there was widespread semi-nomadic occupation between two periods of more advanced town life, EB III and MB II A–C.[7] Kenyon insists that there is no significant cultural continuity with either the preceding or following periods. She lists these considerations: 1) there is a clear stratigraphic break both before and after this phase at every excavated site where it occurs, 2) there are no walled towns in this period, no monumental architecture such as temples, palaces, fine houses, that would characterize the preceding and following town life, 3) the burial customs, with large shaft tombs and predominantly individual burials, are quite distinct from the preceding or following phases and are a distinctive feature of this period, and 4) the artifacts such as pottery and metal objects have little continuity with the other archaeological phases.

Within the broad homogeneity of the MB I culture there seem to be indications of tribal distinctions characterized by "families" of pottery styles and differences in burial customs although still within the shaft-grave type.[8] Nevertheless, the uniformity of the culture generally is quite remarkable within the whole region of Palestine, Transjordan and the Negeb with some extension northward into inland Syria. On the other hand, the relationship of the MB I culture to coastal Syria, especially Byblos and Ugarit, is quite limited.[9] One question still under debate is the direction from which this nomadic culture came. P. Lapp has argued for an Analotian origin, but this suggestion has not been very convincing.[10] Most recently, W. Dever has associated it with the "Amorite" migration of nomads from the Syrian steppe, although admittedly the evidence

7. K. M. Kenyon, *Archaeology in the Holy Land* (New York: Praeger, 1960) pp. 135–161; idem, *CAH*[3], 2/1, pp. 77–88; see also W. G. Dever, "The 'Middle Bronze I' Period in Syria and Palestine," *Near Eastern Archaeology in the Twentieth Century: Essays in honor of Nelson Glueck*, ed. J. A. Sanders, (Garden City, N.Y.: Doubleday, 1970), pp. 132–163; idem, "The Peoples of Palestine in the Middle Bronze I Period," *HTR* 64 (1971): 197–226, esp. pp. 206–9; idem, "Middle Bronze Age I Cemetries at Mirzbaneh and Ain-Samiya," *IEJ* 22 (1972): 95–112, esp. p. 109.
8. See Kenyon's emphasis on grave types and Dever's on pottery "families" in works cited in n. 7 above.
9. See Dever in *Near Eastern Archaeology*, pp. 146–50 and his criticism of Kenyon on this point.
10. P. W. Lapp, *The Dhahr Mirzbaneh Tombs: Three Intermediate Bronze Age Cemetries in Jordan* (New Haven: American Schools of Oriental Research, 1966). Cf. Dever, *HTR* 64:197–226. This later article was written as a direct response to Lapp's theories.

is not very plentiful.[11] So Albright's suggestion that MB I represents a cultural lag of several centuries from the civilization of Mesopotamia may be firmly rejected.[12] Apart from some slight resemblances in pottery forms, the MB I culture of Palestine and the late-third-millennium-civilization of Mesopotamia are different in every way. One unsolved problem is where these people went, if anywhere, at the end of the period, since there is so little in common with the subsequent MB IIA.

When MB I is compared with the stories of Abraham, it becomes clear that the Old Testament descriptions of cities, a sedentary way of life, and political forms are quite inappropriate to this period. The Old Testament stresses the difference between the pastoral population represented by Abraham and the urban population of Shechem, Gerar, Hebron, and the cities of the Jordan Valley. But none of the settlements of MB I, whether in Palestine, Transjordan or the Negeb, can be interpreted as urban centers of this kind. The whole economy of MB I appears to be only pastoral. It should also be noted that both Shechem and Beersheba have no MB I settlements. And in spite of the many settlements of Transjordan, there is still no adequate context here for the Sodom and Gomorrah story or the invasion of foreign kings as in Genesis 14. The Old Testament also suggests a continuity in the indigenous urban population, the "Canaanites," with the people living in the land at the time of the settlement. But MB I represents a discontinuity with the periods that follow. In the matter of chronology, Albright has tried to accommodate the MB I period to the Old Testament by dating it as late as the eighteenth century.[13] This makes it possible for him to get the patriarchs into Egypt at the time of the Hyksos. But such a low chronology for MB I is clearly unacceptable, and there is a fairly broad agreement now toward a higher date.

A much more attractive archaeological correlation is the association of the patriarchs with MB II as advocated by G. Ernest Wright.[14]

11. Dever, *HTR* 64:217ff.; see also deVaux, *Histoire*, pp. 61–69.
12. *BASOR* 163:39; cf. his later discussion in "Remarks on Chronology," *BASOR* 184 (Dec. 1966): 30–35.
13. Cf. my criticism of Albright's chronology in *The Hyksos*, pp. 9ff. Kenyon's dating for the whole period, in *Amorites and Canaanites* (London: Oxford University Press, 1966), p. 35, is 2300–1900 B.C. See most recently Dever, "The 'MB I' Period," pp. 135–144.
14. Wright, *Biblical Archaeology*, p. 47; idem, *Shechem: The Biography of a Biblical City* (New York: McGraw-Hill, 1965), pp. 128–38. This follows Albright's view in *Stone Age to Christianity*, pp. 179–84.

MB II replaced the semi-nomadic occupation of MB I with a slowly developing urban civilization which eventually rose to quite remarkable heights.[15] The excavations of various sites reveal that many places achieved an advanced form of town life with large temples and palaces and strong fortifications. These features point to the proliferation of city-states and petty kingdoms throughout Palestine. And this civilization had strong cultural and ethnic connections with similar kingdoms stretching from Palestine throughout the fertile crescent as far as Lower Mesopotamia. The development of these petty states is reflected in the Execration Texts from Egypt and a little later in the Mari archives, which also make mention of cities in North Palestine.[16] There is a strong cultural continuity that extends from the beginning of MB II down to the end of Late Bronze—the time of the Israelite settlement.

The advantages of this period over MB I as a choice for the patriarchal age are obvious. A distinction between the urban and the pastoral population is now possible. This time also allows for the association of the Sojourn in Egypt with the Hyksos rule in the Delta, a connection favored by many scholars. However, it still does not solve the problem of a lack of settlement in Transjordan, a settlement necessary for the story of the invasion of foreign kings, Genesis 14.[17]

Even though MB II may fit the patriarchal stories better than MB I, this is by no means decisive since a similar case could be made for Late Bronze. Furthermore, since Palestinian kings are mentioned only for Jerusalem and Gerar in "the land of the Philistines," but no kings are associated with Hebron and Shechem (which were regarded as having urban life), it is possible to argue that the period most fully parallelled by this description is the time of the Judean monarchy. Nor can one make a connection with the Hyksos on the

---

15. For a general treatment of this period see *The Hyksos*, pp. 19–84; Kenyon, *Archaeology in the Holy Land*, pp. 162–94; G. E. Wright, *The Bible and the Ancient Near East*, pp. 88ff.; deVaux, *Histoire*, pp. 71–75.

16. See most recently A. Malamat, "Northern Canaan and the Mari Texts," in *Near Eastern Archaeology in the Twentieth Century*, pp. 164–77; idem, "Syro-Palestinian Designations in a Mari Tin Inventory," *IEJ* 21 (1971): 31–38.

17. The cavalier dismissal of this problem is well illustrated by S. Yeivin in "The Patriarchs in the Land of Canaan," *World History of the Jewish People*, ed. E. A. Speiser and B. Mazar (London: W. H. Allen, 1964–70), vol. 2 (1970), *The Patriarchs*, p. 217. Yeivin seems to suggest that the periods can be easily run together. Cf. Wright, *Biblical Archaeology*, p. 50.

basis of the reference in Num. 13:22, which states: "Hebron was built seven years before Zoan (=Tanis) in Egypt." Tanis was not founded until the Twenty-First Dynasty, about 1100 B.C., as is now commonly acknowledged.[18]

Wright, however, attempts to find archaeological confirmation from MB II for quite specific traditions associated with Shechem in the stories of the patriarchs.[19] In fact he links Abraham and Jacob with certain architectural features which belong to the MB II A phase of the city.[20] His argument is as follows. In the western sector of MB II city there was an important sacred area (*temenos*) that, according to Wright, had a long history and passed through several stages of development. In the earliest stage, MB II A, there seems to have been "a kind of platform, ca. 1 m. high, the outer sides of which are faced with stone, while the interior is made of packed earth and stones topped by a layer of fine yellow (marly) earth."[21] Wright speculates that it may have had a use similar to a large earthen altar at Megiddo dating from the same period, but lack of any other evidence for the Shechem structure makes its use unknown. Wright also suggests that the structure was outside the city because this platform was built "before the earliest known city fortification at Shechem, wall D, was built."[22]

The next four developmental stages of this area of the mound, MB II B, are represented by a large building that Wright describes as a "courtyard temple." This building had four phases of alterations over a period of about 100 years. From the beginning of this period onward the area was situated within the city fortifications and was apparently also separated from the rest of the city by a temenos enclosure wall. Following the "courtyard temple" phase a new structure was built in MB II C, the so-called "fortress-temple," which survived through various subsequent stages down to the time of the Judges.

Wright endeavors to relate this archaelogical data to the Biblical narratives by identifying the altars that Abraham and Jacob are

---

18. For a discussion of this problem see *The Hyksos*, Chap. 9; cf. also the review of *The Hyksos* by J. von Beckerath in *JAOS* 90 (1970): 312 in which he suggests that "nearly all Egyptologists" reject the identification of San el Hagar (Tanis) with Avaris.
19. Wright, *Shechem*, pp. 128–38.
20. Ibid., pp. 110–122.
21. Ibid., p. 111.
22. Ibid., p. 112.

said to have built outside of Shechem (Gen. 12:6–7; 33:18–20) with the earliest structure of the temenos area: the raised platform of MB II A. Wright further suggests that the continuity of the area's sanctity would account for the preservation of the tradition about its origin.[23]

There are many problems with this reconstruction, such as the fact that it is difficult to discover the purpose of the raised area, and on Wright's own admission this must remain a serious weakness.[24] He also suggests that it was outside the city but then admits that no city walls were found for this phase. So we cannot assume that it was outside. There were other structures in the area—a few wall fragments, a tannur (oven) and a drain—that suggest some permanent occupation and not a completely isolated "altar." The history of the area is badly obscured by the apparent clearing of existing structures for later installations, but it is reasonable to assume that whatever the platform was, it was *within* the city and not outside of it.

Whether the area had a specifically sacred character in the following MB II B period is also open to question. The building that Wright describes as a "courtyard temple" does not seem to me to be a temple at all, and his comparison with Hittite temples is not persuasive.[25] The contents, in particular, speak against the suggestion. In two phases of the building there were infant burials. While such burials were not uncommon in private dwellings I do not know of any in temples. Apart from this there were, as possible religious objects, two free-standing pillars in two different courts of the fourth phase. These Wright interprets as sacred pillars (*maṣṣeboth*). But this evidence seems to me insufficient to identify the building as a temple, especially when it would make this type very unique for the whole of Syria-Palestine. In fact the building resembles much more a multi-roomed palace similar to others of the period in

23. It is important to note that Wright is following the lead of Gunkel, Alt and Noth, who suggested that traditions were tied to sacred places and transmitted by the sanctuaries (Wright, *Shechem*, p. 129). Here he apparently does not follow the criticism of the notion of *Ortsgebundenheit* by J. Bright in *Early Israel in Recent History Writing* (London: SCM, 1956), although in other respects the positions of Wright and Bright are very similar.
24. In a subsequent exploration and report on the platform, J. F. Ross, in "The Fifth Campaign at Balâtah (Shechem)," *BASOR* 180 (1965): 27, states: "The purpose of the platform remains obscure. It is now difficult to designate it as an altar. Perhaps it was merely a terrace."
25. Cf. the discussion of such courtyard temples in O. R. Gurney, *The Hittites*, pp. 145ff.

Alalaḫ and Mari.[26] Consequently, there seems to be no convincing reason for ascribing a sacred character to this area before the building of the so-called "fortress-temple"—a type very well attested from other sites. If this is so then the argument based on archaeological continuity of a sacred place going back to MB II A is without foundation.

Quite apart from the archaeological arguments, serious problems still remain. It seems to me most unlikely that the non-Israelite population of Shechem would associate the origin of their worship of El or Baal[27] with a passing nomad such as Abraham or with Jacob and his sons, whom the same tradition makes responsible for a bloody slaughter of the population. One cannot imagine more unlikely bearers of the patriarchal traditions than the "Hivites" at Shechem or more unlikely worshippers of the patriarchal deity. It is much easier to suppose that the association of El (or Baal) of Shechem with the God of Israel is the result of a much later syncretistic development in the history of Israel and is now only minimally reflected in biblical tradition. But this is a different approach to the history of the traditions and cannot be dealt with here.

There is one site that raises a large query over this whole archaeological approach, and that is Beersheba. It has often been stated that the partiarchal traditions were preserved at local sanctuaries and that the emphasis on altars in the stories points to their use as means of legitimating the sanctity of these places. This, as we saw, is the line of argument used by Wright in connection with Shechem and he even draws a direct parallel with Beersheba.[28] In this respect Beersheba certainly does play an important role in many stories. All three patriarchs built altars there, and Isaac and Jacob both had theophanies there as well. However, recent archaeological excavation at Beersheba reveals that there was no settlement there before the Iron Age.[29] In the period of the Judges it was only a village and first became an important fortified town under Solomon. It is likely, though not as yet confirmed, that there was a temple at Beersheba during the time of the Judean monarchy. It remained an

26. Cf. my discussion in *The Hyksos*, pp. 38–39.
27. Note the discovery of a bronze "Baal" figurine at Shechem dating to LB, cited in *BASOR* 180 (1965): 24f.
28. Wright, *Shechem*, p. 129; idem, *AOTS*, p. 359.
29. See most recently Y. Aharoni, "Excavations at Tel Beersheba," *BA* 35 (1972): 111–127.

important city to the end of the monarchy, when it suffered serious destruction.

What is one to make, then, of these altars, theophanies, and sacred trees at Beersheba? Perhaps all these patriarchal allusions reflect only the sacredness of the place in Israelite times with no great antiquity to the stories. There is nothing unusual about such a theory. The only problem is one of dating the traditions, but if they are late as we have repeatedly suggested then this problem vanishes. Moreover, if such a hypothesis is possible for Beersheba it is also possible for Shechem, Hebron and Bethel. The implications of this archaeological site for the problem of tradition-history will be taken up below.

In conclusion, I can find no archaeological evidence based upon excavations conducted in Palestine that points to the early second millennium B.C. Either the archaeological period is entirely different from that reflected in the patriarchal stories, as in MB I, or it is not sufficiently distinct from other periods to make a decision possible, as in MB II. In my opinion, our extensive archaeological knowledge of Palestine in the early second millennium B.C. has not clarified a single feature of the patriarchal stories. In contrast to this, Beersheba artifacts from the Judean monarchy period have forced a very serious reconsideration of the character and function of the Genesis narratives about sacred places.

Abraham's Victory over the Eastern Kings

Genesis 14 is regarded by most exponents of the early-second-millennium argument as one of the strongest supports for their position.[30] Yet there are others who view this chapter as a late legend with no historical value whatever.[31] Both of these opinions arise from conflicting evaluations of the royal names, kingdoms and

---

30. For a recent survey on the historical views of this chapter see M. C. Astour, "Political and Cosmic Symbolism in Genesis 14 and in its Babylonian Sources," *Biblical Motifs: Origins and Transformations*, ed. A. Altmann (Cambridge: Harvard University Press, 1966), pp. 65–112; also Bright, *History of Israel*, 2nd ed. pp. 82–83; Speiser, *Genesis*, pp. 105ff.; Albright, *Yahweh and the Gods of Canaan*, pp. 68–69; Yeivin in *World History of the Jewish People* 2:215–17; W. Schatz, *Genesis 14: Eine Untersuchung* (Bern & Frankfort: H. Lang & P. Lang, 1972). (This last work came to my notice too late for extensive use here.)

31. Gunkel, *Genesis*, pp. 288–90; Skinner, *Genesis*, pp. 271–76; deVaux, *Histoire*, pp. 108–12.

international political events that are mentioned. If there is any hope of finding an actual historical context for the patriarch Abraham then it should be in this episode.

The chapter consists of two basic components. The first, vv. 1–12, describes an invasion by foreign kings seeking to subjugate the region of Transjordan and to put down a rebellion of five cities in the valley region of the Dead Sea. Included among the captives is Lot, a resident of Sodom (v. 12). This provides a link with the second part, vv. 13–24, which presents the rescue by Abraham. He defeats the foreign kings, restoring Lot along with the booty and the rest of the captives. I am not concerned, at this point, with discussion of the literary character of this chapter or with arguments having to do with its composite nature. Primary attention here must focus on the first component, vv. 1–12, the part of the story most significant to arguments relating to the matter of dating.

With respect to the identity of the four foreign kingdoms in the coalition, the following observations may be made. Elam, which is considered the primary power, is clearly the state on the north-east of the Persian Gulf. Its king, Chedorlaomer, apparently bears an Elamite name although only the initial element, Chedor = Kudur, is intelligible as Elamite.[32] This particular name cannot be found among the rather complete list of Elamite kings in the early second millennium B.C.[33] Shinar almost certainly stands for the region of Babylonia, as it does elsewhere in the Old Testament.[34] But the old identification of Amraphel with Hammurapi is now generally discarded, and there is scarcely any other likely candidate from the early second millennium. Tidal, on the other hand, can be identified as the Hittite royal name Tudḫaliaš, which belongs to a number of Hittite kings between the seventeenth and thirteenth centuries B.C. The name of Tidal's kingdom, "Nations" (*gōyîm*) has puzzled scholars. Some have suggested a derivation from *Umman Manda*.[35]

32. Albright, *BASOR* 163:49; Astour, "Genesis 14," pp. 91–94.
33. W. Hinz, *CAH*² fascs. 19 & 21; idem, *Das Reich Elam* (Stuttgart: W. Kohlhammer, 1964), pp. 57–83, 149–50.
34. Shinar is often identified with Sumer (see Speiser, *Genesis*, p. 106). But the correct identification apparently is with Sumer and Akkad, derived from *Singi-Uri*. See S. N. Kramer, *The Sumerians* (Chicago: University of Chicago Press, 1963), p. 297; Astour, "Genesis 14," p. 76. This archaism, "Sumer and Akkad," was frequently used by the Neo-Babylonian kings to refer to Babylonia.
35. Speiser, *Genesis*, p. 107.

But the Manda peoples were enemies of the Hittites so they are hardly appropriate. The term is also used as the traditional designation for "hordes," which does not correspond with the term *gōyîm*, meaning "political states." This must be a case in which a writer is substituting one term, "Nations," for another, "Ḫatti." But the only period in which "Nations" could represent "Ḫatti" is the mid-first millennium, when Ḫatti meant the whole collection of western petty kingdoms and states. If the source from which the name was derived mentioned Tudḫaliaš as the great king of Ḫatti then a later writer could interpret this to mean a king who ruled over several petty kingdoms (*gōyîm*) of Syria-Palestine.

Arioch, king of Ellasar, represents a problem in the names of both the king and the place. Attempts have been made to associate him with a minor vassal prince, Arriwuk, mentioned in the Mari archives. But this is very improbable since he could hardly be in league with three other major powers.[36] The same problem arises in the name of the kingdom, Ellasar. It must surely stand for a kingdom commensurate with the other powers, Elam, Babylon, and Ḫatti, and the only one that would fit is Assyria. The name has been plausibly explained as a phonetic reading of the ideograms $A.LA_5.SAR$ (=Aššur).[37] Elsewhere in the Old Testament the name Assyria is clearly written as Asshur. But just as cuneiform scribes enjoyed writing the names of Asshur and Babylon in archaic forms it is quite possible that this writer also liked to demonstrate his erudition by transcribing what he thought was an archaic form. If this identification is correct it would mean that the four kings represent the rulers of the four quadrants: East-Elam, West-Ḫatti, North-Asshur, and South-Babylon.

The tendency of the approach to find an early date for the story in Genesis 14 has been to seek parallels from the early second millennium B.C. at any price, whether it yields any ultimate sense to the account or not.[38] No serious attempt has been made to use these

---

36. For criticism of this identification see M. Noth, "Arioch-Arriwuk," *VT* 1 (1951): 136–40.
37. Astour, "Genesis 14," pp. 78 and 86.
38. One proposal (Yeivin in *World History of the Jewish People* 2:217) makes the raid of Chedorlaomer an attempt to keep a monopoly of the Transjordanian highway from his rival Hammurapi of Babylon. Another suggestion (Albright, *BASOR* 163:50 n. 68) makes the real object of the campaign the overthrow of the Twelfth Dynasty of Egypt. Such reconstructions are without merit. They do violence both to our present knowledge of the period's history and to the Biblical account of the story.

clues to reconstruct the actual historical event. The reason for this is quite plain. The notion of a coalition between the Hittites, Babylonians, Assyrians and Elamites is fantastic, and no historian of the early second millennium B.C. can seriously entertain such a suggestion. The Hittites never acted in consort with any of these powers. They sacked the city of Babylon and so brought an end to the First Dynasty of Babylon. The other three powers were almost always at perpetual enmity throughout their history. At no time did they ever engage in any joint military activity in the west, and at no time did even one of these powers campaign as far south as Palestine. There was certainly no Elamite empire in the west as the twelve years of servitude imply. Nor is it possible to dismiss these statements by suggesting that our ignornace of such a campaign may be due to lacunae in our records. Our knowledge of the period is, in fact, sufficiently complete for us to know that there is no period or setting which could any longer accommodate such an event.

Equally problematic is the objective of the military expedition. There were no national states in Transjordan during the second millennium prior to the Ammonites, Moabites and Edomites. Nor was there any pentapolis of the Jordan Valley. The effort of Glueck to interpret the MB I ruins in this way is hardly convincing. They were not much more than nomadic shelters. A great military campaign to subjugate such impoverished settlements seems ludicrous. And after MB I there is virtually nothing. Some scholars, such as Speiser and Albright, have attempted to read into the story quite different objectives of the campaign. But such efforts are quite gratuitous since no supporting evidence is ever cited to support these suggestions.

Furthermore, this joint military venture would have involved several thousand troops since the resources of one power were deemed insufficient. Yet we are expected to believe that one chieftain with a band of three hundred and eighteen men could, by a surprise attack at night, completely rout such a mighty force. There was no follow-up of this victory, no retaliation by the defeated, and no evidence of political effects on the states involved. And this same victorious Abraham, a short time later, was presented, in the petty state of the city of Gerar, as fearful to the point of misrepresenting his wife as his sister. The whole account is so problematic that it cannot possibly have historical significance and must be viewed in an entirely different manner.

Some effort at salvaging the antiquity of vv. 1–12 has been made by suggesting that behind it lies a cuneiform source of the second millennium from which some of the elements may have been derived.[39] It is considered by some that this source may have been legendary and not historical at all.[40] But even this suggestion is questionable. What could such a document contain? It is extremely unlikely that there would have been a Babylonian legend about a coalition with Babylon's traditional enemies, and one that would have given preeminence to Elam! It certainly could have said nothing about Transjordan, an area totally outside of their concern. It is unlikely that it would have glorified the victory of a small group of nomads over their king. There is nothing whatever in Gen. 14:1–12 that suggests a Mesopotamian viewpoint or interest. There is only one detail, that of the name of Tidal, that must go back to the second millennium. But many first-millennium sources contain this much information about the second millennium, so I see little need for positing a second-millennium document as a source for any of it.

The nonhistorical character of this chapter is further indicated by the nature of the names given to the five kings who ruled the cities of the Dead Sea basin. They are not personal names at all but are abbreviated pejorative epithets.[41] This is clear in the case of Bera, "in evil" and Birsha, "in injustice," the kings of Sodom and Gomorrah respectively. The name of the city, Bela, means "destroyed" but it is likely that originally this was the name of the king of Zoar. Astour has recently suggested that Shemeber is to be read Shemabad, on the evidence of the Samaritan version and the Genesis Apocryphon with the meaning "the name is lost." These last two names would then represent the fate of these two kings. The name Shinab is the most difficult. But if it is read as $Śn^ɔb$ and regarded as consisting of $śn^ɔ$, "to hate" $+ {}^ɔab$, "father," it would mean "the one who hates the father [of the gods]." Astour has argued that such epithets as these occur in Assyrian and Babylonian inscriptions as characteristic of rebel kings so they are most appropriate here. They also occur in royal psalms as descriptive of the

---

39. For a review of the various theories about a cuneiform original see J. A. Emerton, "Some False Clues in the Study of Gen. XIV," *VT* 21 (1971): 29–46.

40. This seems to be Emerton's preference in "The Riddle of Gen. XIV," *VT* 21 (1971): 436.

41. See Astour, "Genesis 14," pp. 74–75; see also Speiser, *Genesis*, p. 101; Skinner, *Genesis*, p. 259.

king's enemies; that is, those who hate God, who devise evil and plot mischief, who will be "consumed" by divine wrath, and whose offspring (=name) will be destroyed.[42] The author clearly knows the tradition of these cities as supreme examples of wickedness, but he has no tradition of any royal names. So he merely creates names that are most appropriate to the reputation of these cities.

Concerning their names Astour points out that there seem to have been two independent traditions about the destruction of these cities.[43] A northern tradition reflected in Hosea 11:8 knows only of the annihilation of Admah (var. Adamah or Adam) and Zeboiim, and both of these are located a fair distance north of the Dead Sea in the region of the Jabbok River in the Jordan valley. On the other hand a southern tradition, reflected in Amos, Isaiah, Jeremiah, and Ezekiel, mentions only Sodom and Gomorrah as examples of complete destruction. And their location is given as south or southeast of Judah. The location of the fifth city, Zoar, which escaped destruction, is ambiguous.

These two streams of tradition are combined in Deut. 29:23, an addition made by an exilic editor. Of course the combining of names from such widely separated regions created a certain confusion that is still reflected in Genesis. In the story of Lot's separation from Abraham the valley of the Jordan, in which the cities are located, is the region directly east of Bethel and Ai and therefore north of the Dead Sea. But the story of the destruction of the cities in Gen. 18:16 through 19:29 suggests a southern location more appropriate to being viewed from the vicinity of Hebron. Consequently the cities of Genesis 14 represent a late combination of traditions about two different groups of cities, and any attempt at archaeological confirmation of an ancient pentapolis in the southeastern region of the Dead Sea is futile.[44]

Another similarity with the exilic revision of Deuteronomy is the antiquarian interest in the ancient inhabitants of Transjordan and the Negeb. The list in Deut. 2:10–12, 20–23 and 3:9–13 is very similar to Gen. 14:5–7, with the Rephaim in Bashan, Emim in

---

42. See for example Psalm 21.
43. Astour, "Genesis 14," pp. 72–73.
44. About the location of these cities see Simons, *Geog. & Topog. Texts* #404–414, in which he argues for a northern location. J. P. Harland, "Sodom and Gomorrah: The Location of the Cities of the Plain," *BA* 5 (1942): 17–32, supports a southern location. If one adopts the two-traditions theory then the conflicting evidence can be easily explained.

Moab, Horites in Edom and Zamzumim (=Zuzim) in the region of the Ammonites. It is possible to dismiss the similarity by stating that the list of names simply derives from an older tradition.[45] But in fact the texts give every indication to the contrary. In the various discussions about the primeval peoples two types of sources appear to be used. One is mythological, and in it the primeval inhabitants are the Anakim or Rephaim, which were generally thought to be Nephilim, or "giants."[46] The other type of source is the use of archaic names such as Amorites and Hittites. These, as I have shown above, cannot date before the eighth century B.C. Deuteronomy shows a tendency to identify the Amorites, a name of one category, with the mythological Anakim or Rephaim.[47] But the process is carried one step further in Deuteronomy 2. Here the author displays his erudition by indicating that the mythical Rephaim, who originally inhabited the whole of Transjordan as well, are the same people as those called Emim by the Moabites and Zamzumim by the Ammonites. These designations, however, were foreign and not part of Israel's own traditions as the text makes very clear. The author of Genesis 14, however, has taken the tradition a step further by restricting these terms to very specific regions as if they were distinct peoples corresponding to the distinct political states of a later day. The dependence, therefore, must be of Genesis upon Deuteronomy, but it could scarcely have gone in the reverse direction.

Astour also points to the similarity of the route taken by the invading kings and the route, in reverse, that Israel took from Kadesh to Transjordan. Considered by itself this similarity might indicate no more than that both sources were familiar with important commercial "highways" that became important during the monarchies of the Transjordanian and Israelite states. But a curious feature of the Genesis story is the very indirect route taken to arrive at the destination of the cities in the valley. Taken with the other indications of dependence upon the names of the primeval peoples, the possibility of the author of Genesis 14 using the route in Deuteronomy 1–3 is greatly increased.

Such a dependence by Genesis 14 upon Deuteronomy 1–3

---

45. So Emerton *VT* 21:405 against Astour.
46. Note the frequent rendering of all three terms in the Septuagint by *gigantes*.
47. See Van Seters, *VT* 22:74–75.

implies a rather late date for the Genesis story. J. A. Emerton has recently challenged this late dating by suggesting a date in the time of the Davidic monarchy. Emerton makes the statement: "The possibility that such records [i.e., historical records that told of the relations of vassal states to a foreign overlord] existed as early as the reign of David cannot be denied."[48] This statement, however, can certainly be challenged. The only possible records that he could have in mind are some which came down from the Amarna period in which Jerusalem, but not the cities of the Jordan Valley, were subject to Egypt. Apart from the improbability that such records were ever preserved, there is nothing in Genesis 14 that even remotely suggests such a background.

The basic question to be answered is this: When could a story about such an invasion from the direction of Mesopotamia be written? The answer to this question is that such a story is scarcely possible before the domination of Palestine and Transjordan by an Eastern power from the mid-eighth century onward. An author of the Davidic period simply could not have thought in these terms. Such a threat was non-existent in his day, and such conditions of servitude to a Mesopotamian or Elamite power had never existed prior to that time. Astour has characterized very well the account of Genesis 14 in terms of the political situation in the late monarchy. He states:

> What it [Gen. 14] describes is a typical situation of the period between the eighth and sixth centuries, many times experienced by Israel and Judah and occurring with distressing monotony in the Assyrian royal inscriptions: a king is forced to recognize Assyrian overlordship, and promises to pay the heavy tribute imposed upon him. A few years later he stops paying tribute, and seeks help from other rebel vassals or outside powers. Then, usually the very next year, an Assyrian punitive expedition, often led by the king, invades the country, devastates it, subdues it again, and carries off to Assyria all movable goods and a large number of people... Phrases like "turning" of the conquering army in the course of its campaign (Genesis 14:7) and "the rest fled to the mountains" after defeat (Genesis 14:10) are quite common in Assyrian war descriptions.[49]

48. Emerton, *VT* 21:437.
49. Astour, "Genesis 14," pp. 70–71. He also cites Luckenbill's *Ancient Records* nos. 237 and 244 as good examples.

Astour is probably also correct in associating the manner of presentation here with the annalistic style of the Deuteronomist who in turn clearly imitates the form of the Assyrian and Babylonian records. However, one can go a step further. While the Assyrian royal inscriptions are predominantly in the first person singular as the personal account of the king, another style developed independent of it using the third person as an objective account. This new chronicle style does not come into vogue until the end of the Assyrian period but is very characteristic of the Neo-Babylonian period.[50] And it is this particular objective style that is the model for the Deuteronomist and for writers of other late accounts such as Genesis 14.

It seems reasonable to conclude from these observations that Genesis 14 is not based on any historical sources from the second millennium. It has all the marks of being composed by a Judean author, perhaps in Babylon, no earlier than the exilic period. His terminology and pseudo-historiographic style also point strongly to this time. He used Israelite traditions in the form contained in the latest recension of Deuteronomy. His use of Mesopotamian documents was probably as no more than a source for the names of the rulers of the four foreign kingdoms. Yet it remains a puzzle as to how he could have done so badly in the transcription of these names into Hebrew, in which only one name and half of another are intelligible. In arguing for a late date I have not made use of any interpretation of the author's intention or message because only after one has fixed the general historical background can that issue be discussed at all.[51] In any case there is little support for any antiquity of the patriarchal age in this chapter of Genesis.

Summary to Part I

The conclusion that may be drawn from our investigation thus far is largely a negative one. That is, attempts to portray a "Patriarchal Age" as a historical context for the stories of Genesis in the

---

50. See my discussion of this in "The Conquest of Sihon's Kingdom," *JBL* 91 (1972): 187–89. However, one correction of my earlier remarks is necessary. A. K. Grayson, in a private communication, suggested to me that the chronicle style was not directly dependent upon the royal inscriptions but was an independent development.

51. This is the method employed by Emerton in *VT* 21:403–39, but to my mind it becomes completely circular.

second millennium B.C. must be viewed as failures. The "Abraham of history" can no longer be recovered from the traditions as we now have them, even to the limited extent of reconstructing his "life and times." Instead, the following features in the stories tend to support the fact that they were written from the historical and cultural perspective of a later day.

1) There is no real portrayal of a nomadic pre-settlement phase of Israelite society, nor any hint of the migratory movements or political realities of the second millennium B.C. Instead, the stories recognize the spread of Aramean settlement in upper Mesopotamia, Syria and even lower Mesopotamia. The tradition recognizes the threat of hostile Arab nomads (Ishmaelites), with all their various sub-groups, on the borders of the settled regions of the Levant.

2) The few nomadic details that occur in the stories, such as the references to camels and tents, the patriarchs' presence and movement primarily in the Negeb, and their contact and political agreement with the established "Philistines" in the border region, all point strongly to the social and political circumstances of the mid-first millennium B.C.

3) The archaic designations for the indigenous population are not used according to the historical realities of the second millennium, but represent the idealized and ideological use of a much later period.

4) The reference to Ur of the Chaldeans and its association with Harran and a route to the West reflect the political circumstances of the Neo-Babylonian period. The place names of Palestine are those which have a special place in the history of the monarchy.

5) While the social customs and institutions reflected in the patriarchal stories are, generally, a very poor means of dating the traditions, the few indications of date they do contain all point to the mid-first millennium rather than to the earlier period.

6) The attempts by archaeologists to find patriarchal connections with MB I or MB II have been quite unconvincing. On the other hand, the strong association of the patriarchs with Beersheba, which did not become a significant site until the Judean monarchy, points again to a late date.

7) The efforts to find an archaeological and historical background for the Genesis 14 story about the invasion of the eastern kings has not met with any successs. There is no time in the second

millennium B.C. when such an eastern coalition could or would have invaded the West. The placing of such invasions before the mid-first millennium B.C. is an anachronism.

Thus far the conclusion reached is that the tradition as it stands reflects only a rather late date of composition and gives no hint by its content of any great antiquity, in terms of biblical history. This conclusion has important implications for the study of the literary history of the tradition, which will follow in Part II. Our investigation calls into question the presumption of antiquity that has for a long time been the basis of so many studies on the literary form and history of tradition of the partiarchal stories. If the tradition only reflects its latest stage one must review with great caution any attempt at reconstructing an older form of the tradition by any purely literary methodology. Let us now proceed to a review of literary and traditio-historical method.

PART II

Abraham in Tradition

CHAPTER 6

Method I: A Critique

Source Criticism

It is true to say that the problem of the literary sources of the Pentateuch, and that of Genesis in particular, has never been satisfactorily solved, and that a consensus seems even further away today than it was fifty years ago.[1] The point of departure for most literary criticism is still the Graf-Wellhausen documentary theory, which proposes four principal literary sources for the Pentateuch under the symbols J, E, D, and P, or for the study of Genesis, J, E, and P. This does not exclude the possibility of Deuteronomistic glosses in the Tetrateuch (Gen.–Num.), but little attention has been paid to a comprehensive literary study of these.

With respect to literary analysis of the Pentateuch perhaps the greatest agreement has been reached in the case of P, the "Priestly" writer's contribution to the final corpus, although debate continues about its dating, its relation to the other sources, and its extent outside of the Tetrateuch.[2] The question of dating and of P's presence in the book of Joshua need not greatly concern us in this study. But the question of the relationship of P to the pre-priestly sources is an

---

1. For recent reviews of the history of pentateuchal studies see Otto Eissfeldt, *The Old Testament, An Introduction*, trans. Peter R. Ackroyd (New York: Harper and Row, 1965); G. Fohrer, *Introduction to the Old Testament*, trans. David E. Green (New York and Nashville: Abingdon, 1968); H. Cazelles, "Pentateuque," *DBS* 7:687–858.
2. Y. Kaufmann, *The Religion of Israel from the Beginnings to the Babylonian Exile*, trans. M. Greenberg (Chicago: University of Chicago Press, 1960), pp. 175–200. Kaufmann considers P to have been the earliest source, and he is followed, at least in part, by a number of Israeli scholars. I. Engnell, *A Rigid Scrutiny: Critical Essays on the Old Testament*, trans. John T. Willis (Nashville: Vanderbilt University Press, 1969), pp. 50ff., regards P as the compiler of the Tetrateuch. For him there was no prior literary work in these four books corresponding to the classical "documents." This view stems from Engnell's theory of tradition-history. Most scholars who follow the generally accepted literary analysis restrict P to the Tetrateuch. However, on the presence of P in the later books see S. Mowinckel, *Tetrateuch-Pentateuch-Hexateuch BZAW* 90 (1964); also J. G. Vink, *The Origin and Date of the Priestly Code* (Leiden: E. J. Brill, 1969).

important issue in the Abraham tradition and one which I do not regard as clearly settled. P. Volz raised the question forty years ago as to whether P was to be considered as an independent *narrative* source, or simply a priestly editor who supplemented the earlier corpus with legal discussions, cultic institutions and theological discourses.[3] On the other hand he denied that such a narrative as Genesis 23 belonged to P. In contrast to Volz, most literary critics still regard P as a separate source utilized by the last redactor Rp as the basis for the final form into which the earlier material was placed.[4] Yet I do not consider the question settled, and it must again receive some attention, especially as regards Genesis 17 and 23, as well as the nature of P's framework in the Abraham tradition.

Much more difficult, however, are the problems that surround the so-called J and E sources. The initial point of departure for distinguishing sources generally has been the presence of doublets—parallel accounts of essentially the same episode. It was primarily on the basis of conclusions drawn from studies of these parallels that the other criteria were developed and the general theory of pentateuchal criticism was established. The conclusions drawn from a study of doublets were that they pointed to two independent sources, and that one source had a preference for the divine name Yahweh (J) while the other source used the generic term Elohim (E) to designate the Deity. In single accounts where both divine names are used the two sources were separated from one another on the theory that in these instances an editor had combined elements from two similar accounts to produce one extant version. Other criteria used to distinguish such a redactional process have been the evidence of repetition, contradiction, variation in vocabulary, and breaks in narrative continuity. But all these criteria are quite secondary to the notion of two independent parallel traditions and the alternation in the use of the divine name.

Yet these criteria have created as many problems as they have solved and have rarely been applied absolutely. The divine names, for instance, seem to distinguish certain clear blocks of material for

---

3. Paul Volz and Wilhelm Rudolph, *Der Elohist als Erzähler: ein Irrweg der Pentateuchkritik? BZAW* 63 (1933): 13, 135–142.

4. Martin Noth, *Überlieferungsgeschichte des Pentateuchs* (Stuttgart: Kohlhammer, 1948). English translation, *A History of Pentateuchal Traditions*, trans. B. W. Anderson (Englewood Cliffs, N.J.: Prentice-Hall, 1972), pp. 8–19.

the two sources. But in other cases the alternation in the use of the divine name has resulted in the complete fragmentation of otherwise unified stories and episodes. The issue was raised long ago how it was that the sources could be so dissimilar in the doublets on the one hand but so completely similar in the unified accounts such as Genesis 24.[5] While most literary critics still hold to the notion of two independent sources, J and E, a strong dissenting view has continued to exist from the time of Volz's criticisms to the present.[6]

Now it is precisely in the Abraham tradition that the doublets between J and E predominate. This has led M. Noth to state:

> The situation in the Abraham tradition seems so obvious to me that here, above all, the problem of literary analysis of the old Pentateuch tradition must become clear, leaving only the question as to whether the results gained here are valid also for the whole of the Pentateuch.[7]

This means that the doublets must constitute an important starting place for any new attempt at a literary analysis of the Abraham tradition.

Furthermore, many scholars have felt that the J source was also not a unity of sources but two independent ones, both of them prior to E.[8] There has been little agreement, however, on the division of the Yahwistic corpus, largely because of a lack of convincing criteria. Thus one reads of a Lay source (L), a Southern source (S), a Kenite source (K), or a Nomadic source (N), all suggesting by their names that the division is made on the basis of specific content instead of the usual literary criteria. This is largely true also of earlier attempts at a division of J into J_1 and J_2 or the like. However, generally speaking the distinguishing feature used to make the source separation arises out of a rather limited amount of material, and then this is forced through the rest to construct a "document." But the question is scarcely raised as to whether the element or theme used

5. W. Staerk, "Zur alttestamentlichen Literaturkritik: Grundsatzliches und Methodisches," *ZAW* 42 (1924): 61; also P. Volz, *Der Elohist als Erzähler*, pp. 13–25.
6. See F. V. Winnett, *The Mosaic Tradition* (Toronto: University of Toronto Press, 1949), pp. 20–24; idem, "Reexamining the Foundations," *JBL* 84 (1965): 1–19; S. Mowinckel, *Erwägungen zur Pentateuch Quellenfrage*, Norsk Theologisk Tidsskrift, 1 (1964): 59–118.
7. Noth, *Pentateuchal Traditions*, p. 22.
8. For a survey of such attempts see Fohrer, *Introduction*, pp. 106ff.; N. E. Wagner, "Pentateuchal Criticism: No Clear Future," *CJT* 13 (1967): 225–32.

as a source criterion is really part of the traditional material (oral or written) that the narrator inherits or a genuine expression of his own perspective. Literary sources should be separated, first of all, on the basis of literary criteria. Other features, such as ideological perspective, geographic setting, or "nomadic" characteristics, can only be evaluated when more controlled literary principles are first applied to the material.[9] Now it happens that there is a literary doublet within the so-called J corpus, Gen. 12:10–20 and 26:1–12, so this will afford a good opportunity to examine the whole question on a more controlled basis.

Besides the need for dividing the sources there is the problem of explaining the similarity of the variants when the same or similar stories are attributed to each source. Since it has become a basic presupposition of literary critics of the Pentateuch that the sources were originally independent of each other, at least for J and E, Noth proposes, as a solution, a *Grundlage* (G), which was the basic source from which J and E drew their versions.[10] Whether this *Grundlage* was already in a written form or was a body of oral tradition he regards as uncertain but also unimportant; his concern is only that it existed in a rather fixed form. As far as its content is concerned he states: "Everything in which J and E concur can be attributed with some certainty to G. . . . It is quite clear that the major themes of the Pentateuch tradition, arranged in the sequence with which we are familiar, were contained already in G."[11] But this general statement really begs the question of G's content because it does not face the problem of the doublets. Which version was the one in G, and why did either J or E depart from it? And if such a departure from the *Grundlage* was possible, for whatever reason, then it was also possible between an earlier and a later source, between J and E, and Noth's criticism of Volz against the creation of a 'parallel recension' is without any weight. Of course, the problem is only compounded when there are three independent sources, since this would necessitate at least two "groundworks," G_1 and G_2, as Fohrer has recently suggested.[12] Yet this whole notion of a basic

---

9. The uncertainty of the geographical criterion has been pointed out by Wagner, *CJT* 13:229–30.
10. Noth, *Pentateuchal Traditions*, pp. 38–41.
11. Ibid., p. 39.
12. Fohrer, *Introduction*, pp. 127ff.

stratum of fixed tradition (G) is conceived almost entirely in terms of its theoretical necessity for the old literary theory. If one does not divide the sources in a manner similar to Noth or believe that the sources are independent, then this need for a basic stratum vanishes.

Just as there is a need for groundworks to explain an original unity, there is also a corresponding need for a series of redactors to bring the various sources together again. Staerk suggested many years ago that the use of the device "R" in literary criticism was perhaps the most serious problem of the Pentateuch, especially the redactor R_{JE}.[13] And the problem is only compounded if one adds another "document" such as Fohrer's N. There is also considerable confusion about the character and extent of the redactor's own work. Noth suggested, on the basis of the preponderance of Yahweh over Elohim, that the redactor used the Yahwist as the basis of the Pentateuchal tradition and supplemented it with material from E, but this does not work so easily if there are two sources behind J. In theory the redactor's work is described in such a way as to make him almost indistinguishable from an actual writer such as J or E, since these writers are also regarded as collectors and editors of the tradition in G. In the actual practice of literary criticism the redactor functions mainly as a *deus ex machina* to solve literary difficulties.[14] In fact the whole elaborate system of redactors and groundworks is unnecessary if it can be shown that the various *writers* who succeeded one another (and who were admittedly also compilers and editors) were directly dependent upon the works of their predecessors and incorporated these works into their own. This would of course also have to be true of P in its relationship to the JE corpus.

One way of stating this alternative is the suggestion by Volz that the major narrative work is the Yahwistic corpus, and that this was augmented by two successive redactions, a so-called Elohistic and a Deuteronomistic redaction, before the time of the priestly writer.[15] These redactions, however, made rather minor additions to the basic Yahwistic work. Volz's study actually concerned itself only

---

13. Staerk, $\mathcal{Z}AW$ 42:66.
14. See, for example, the descriptions of the redactor's activity in K. Koch, *The Growth of the Biblical Traditions: The Form-Critical Method*, trans. S. M. Cupitt (New York: Charles Scribner's Sons, 1969), pp. 57–59; cf. Fohrer, *Introduction*, pp. 190–192.
15. Volz, *Elohist*, p. 13.

with a discussion of the relationship and limits of the E "additions" to J in Genesis and did not carry through an investigation of the so-called Deuteronomistic redactor. He simply accepted the suggested references to the latter in the critical literature. He also maintained the basic ordering of the material given by the critics as J E D and P.

There is still another possibility. This lies in a new appraisal of the Deuteronomistic redactor in the Pentateuch, particularly in Genesis.[16] His contributions to the larger corpus cannot easily be isolated on literary grounds, so that he is simply invoked whenever the language and perspective of a text seem to reflect Deuteronomy. But it is particularly significant that at many points the Deuteronomistic material is integral to the Yahwistic corpus. This suggests that there may have been only a very limited amount of the patriarchal, or specifically Abrahamic, tradition prior to E, and that the major Yahwistic narrative work of which Volz speaks is actually subsequent to E. Such a scheme would yield the pattern J_1 (for the oldest material) supplemented by E (the second stage of development) edited with considerable additions and arranged basically in its present order by J_2 and finally reedited by P.[17] The problem of the divine name would also be solved if it could be shown that J_2 made use of both forms of the designation for deity, as also happens in some other books of the Old Testament where no division on this basis is suggested.

Nevertheless, this scheme too is purely hypothetical, in spite of

---

16. This problem has been discussed primarily on the basis of Exodus and Numbers. The most usual approach is that of M. Noth, *Pentateuchal Traditions*, p. 30, n. 106, and his commentaries on Exodus and Numbers. A different approach is given by Winnett, *Mosaic Tradition*, pp. 155–71. Some scholars have begun to speak of a pre-Deuteronomic source or redactor in the Tetrateuch: N. Lohfink, *Das Hauptgebot; eine Untersuchung literarischer Einleitungsfragen zu Dtn 5–11* (Rome: Pontifical Biblical Institute, 1963), pp. 172ff.; J. Scharbert, "Formgeschichte und Exegese von Ex. 34, 6," *Biblica* 38 (1957): 130–50; C. Brekelmans, "Die sogenannten deuteronomischen Elemente in Gen. — Num., Ein Beitrag zur Vorgeschichte des Deuteronomiums," *SVT* 15 (1965): 90–96; A. Besters, "'Israel' et 'Fils d'Israel' dans les livres historiques (Genése–II Rois)," *RB* 74 (1967): 5–23; idem, "L'expression 'Fils d'Israel' en Ex i–xiv. Un nouveau critère pour la distinction des sources," *RB* 74 (1967): 321–55; M. Caloz, "Exode xiii, 3–14 et son rapport en Deuteronome," *RB* 76 (1969): 321–50, 481–507; cf. R. C. Dentan, "The Literary Affinities of Exodus 34:6f.," *VT* 13 (1963): 34–51; W. Fuss, *Die deuteronomistische Pentateuchredaktion in Exodus 3–17*, BZAW 126 (1972).

17. See Winnett, *JBL* 84:1–19; N. E. Wagner, "A Literary Analysis of Genesis 12–36," (Ph.D. diss., University of Toronto, 1965).

all its apparent literary advantages, until it is actually demonstrated by specific examination of the textual evidence. It may be noted, however, that the Abraham corpus does contain important examples of what have been characterized as Deuteronomistic redaction, so all the ingredients for testing this and the other literary reconstructions lie within this tradition complex. In my literary examination I am not beginning with any assumptions about dependence or independence of sources or about the accepted order of those sources. All of the possibilities must remain open.

Form-criticism: What is "Saga?"

Such problems of literary criticism as we have been considering above have been largely pushed into the background in the past few decades by the new concerns of form-criticism and tradition-history arising out of the pioneering work of Hermann Gunkel. In his work on Genesis,[18] Gunkel attempted to go behind the literary authors of the texts to a stage in which the stories, as he believed, were primarily in the medium of oral tradition. The basic form for this medium was *Sage*, or legend.[19] He did not give any precise definition of the term *Sage* but used it, as he says, according to the current usage. He speaks of it as "folkloristic tradition in poetic narrative dealing with persons and events of the past."[20] As a kind

---

18. Gunkel, *Genesis, übersetzt und erklärt*, 8th ed. (a reprint of 3rd ed. 1910) (Göttingen: Vandenhoeck & Ruprecht, 1969). The introduction from the first edition was translated as *The Legends of Genesis* (1901) and reprinted by Schocken Books, New York, 1964, (with a new foreword by W. F. Albright). However, there are some important changes between the first and third editions.

19. The prevailing practice of translating *Sage* as "saga" in recent works on Old Testament subjects is a serious mistake. Strictly speaking, saga is derived from the Norwegian term *saga*, which refers to a genre of Icelandic and Norse literature of the Middle Ages. *Sage*, on the other hand, is a broad category of folklore which includes many genres of oral tradition. The Norwegian term for German *Sage* is *sagn*, which is kept quite distinct from *saga*: see C. W. von Sydow, "Kategorien der Prosa—Volksdichtung," (1934) in *Selected Papers on Folklore* (Copenhagen: Rosenkilde and Bagger, 1948), pp. 61ff. English-speaking folklorists regularly use the term "legend" for the German *Sage*: see W. D. Hand, "Status of European and American Legend Study," *Current Anthropology* 6 (1965): 439–46. Confusion on the term saga is already evident in the work by H. M. and N. K. Chadwick, *The Growth of Literature*, 3 vols. (Cambridge: Cambridge University Press, 1932–38), p. 2, where saga is defined as "prose narrative preserved by oral tradition." In their work no distinction is made between Norse and Icelandic sagas and the folklore category of *Sage*. Cf. also W. F. Albright in Gunkel, *Legends*, pp. xi–xii, who is quite wrong on this point. I will continue to use the term legend for German *Sage* throughout this study.

20. Gunkel, *Genesis*, p. viii. This definition is missing from *Legends*.

of scholarly and liberal apologetic he was primarily concerned with emphasizing that Genesis was not history in the modern sense of the term. Instead, its view of reality corresponded much more to the traditions of ordinary people, to a popular presentation of the past, unconcerned with matters of state and politics. So for Gunkel *Sage* meant, first of all, a certain way of thinking about the past by the unlettered *Volk*.[21]

Gunkel's form-critical observations on *Sage*, on the other hand, have to do largely with two areas: a classification of *Sage* types, and a treatment of the artistic form of *Sage*. Gunkel recognized in Genesis what is a prominent feature of European *Sagen*, namely etiology, and most of his *Sage* types in Genesis have to do with the various kinds of etiology. Yet Gunkel did not give any structural analysis of these stories in a form-critical sense, or any classification of the episodic units as a whole, but only a rough categorization of the various etiological statements.[22]

In the area of artistic form Gunkel followed the rather debatable notion that poetic forms of folklore are more original than prose forms, and he tried to argue that while Genesis was prose, it still retained much of the earlier poetic character of the original legends.[23] Such a position could scarcely be defended in current folklore studies. More important, however, was the fact that Gunkel enumerated many folkloristic features common to the Genesis stories and supplemented the later editions of his commentary by frequent references to A. Olrik's "Epic Laws of Folk-literature."[24]

Gunkel's approach to Genesis had a tremendous impact on the study of Genesis and the Pentateuch as a whole, especially in Germany. In the works of Alt, Noth and von Rad, for instance, it was largely considered established that the narrative basis of Genesis was an oral tradition of ancient *Sagen*, and their scholarly interest shifted from a literary criticism of the written sources to a history of the pre-literary stage of the legend-traditions.

21. Gunkel, *Legends*, pp. 1–12.
22. Ibid., pp. 13–36.
23. Ibid., pp. 37–38; cf. the longer discussion in *Genesis*, pp. xxvii–xxix, where Gunkel takes issue with Sievers that a poetic version lies behind Genesis. Consequently Albright's remarks in *Legends*, p. viii, about the poetic nature of the original "sagas" is a serious misrepresentation of Gunkel's position, and his discussion of "saga" is of no value in the current investigation.
24. A. Olrik, "Epische Gesetze der Volksdichtung," *Zeitschrift für deutsches Altertum* 51 1909): 1–12.

Such a wholesale acceptance was certainly premature, however, since some very serious questions may be raised about Gunkel's treatment of legends in Genesis. As to the matter of form, recent studies on etiology in narratives, particularly the form-critical studies of Brevard Childs and Burke Long have rather convincingly shown that the etiological statements in the various stories are almost alway secondary and not the reason for relating the narrative as a whole.[25] These etiological elements are viewed instead as having "been added as a redactional commentary on existing traditions."[26] This greatly undermines Gunkel's classification system and his principal form-critical argument for calling the Genesis narratives *Sagen*.

Likewise his appeal to folkloristic characteristics in Genesis, such as those set forth by Olrik, suffers from the same weakness as the etiological argument. A few scattered examples of formulae common to folklore is not enough to establish a sweeping generalization about oral tradition or *Sage* in particular.[27] Some of these artistic features may be present in literary works as well, while most narratives in Genesis fit Olrik's epic laws rather poorly. Gunkel himself seems sufficiently sensitive to this last point to suggest that a number of stories give evidence of a more discursive style characteristic of written composition, but he does not elaborate on the relationship between the oral tradition and the literary sources.[28] It is also curious how later scholars, such as Noth, can speak of this discursive style as a "discursive saga style" and simply make it a later phase of oral tradition![29]

25. B. S. Childs, "A Study of the Formula 'Until this Day,'" *JBL* 82 (1963): 179–92; Burke O. Long, *The Problem of Etiological Narrative in the Old Testament*, *BZAW* 108 (1967). See also J. Fichtner, "Die etymologische ätiologie in den Namengebungen der geschichtlichen Bücher des AT," *VT* 4 (1956): 372–96; I. L. Seeligmann, "Aetiological Elements in Biblical Historiography," *Zion* 26 (1961): 141–69 (Hebrew); idem, "Hebräische Erzählung und biblische Geschichtsschreibung," *TZ* 18 (1962): 305–25. A different line of criticism against etiology was taken by J. Bright, *Early Israel in Recent History Writing: A Study in Method* SBT 19 (London: SCM, 1956), pp. 91ff. But cf. Mowinckel, *Tetrateuch*, pp. 78ff.
26. Childs, *JBL* 82:290; quoted with approval by Long, *Etiological Narrative*, p. 85. This judgment, however, is still predicated on the assumption that the traditions are oral and prior to the final literary work. I am skeptical about Long's opinion that the etiological statements belong to a body of older variant traditions, and I do not see any justification for regarding them as redactional additions to the literary works. I hope to show below that they are part of the style of these literary works themselves.
27. Koch's attempt, in *Biblical Tradition*, pp. 148–51, to apply Olrik's laws is much too vague and imprecise.
28. *Legends*, pp. 82–85.
29. Noth, *Pentateuchal Traditions*, pp. 57, 65, 75, *et passim*.

Gunkel also raised the question of how faithfully oral tradition was preserved and transmitted. He answered this question by an appeal to certain tenets of literary criticism as he understood it. Since there are variants of the same story which are almost identical in two different sources (his example is the wooing of Rebekah in Genesis 24), and since the sources are independent, then the oral tradition behind the variants must have been transmitted with the greatest fidelity. However, if one cannot accept such a literary theory, then the fidelity of oral tradition rests on shaky ground.[30] It should be obvious that the nature of oral tradition ought not to be explained on the basis of what is necessary for a hypothesis of literary criticism but on an objective description of the phenomenon in its own right.

Gunkel's initial contribution moved into two basic directions of development: that of form-criticism having to do with the nature of *Sage*, and that of tradition-criticism, the development of the pre-literary stage of the tradition. Both lines of development must be briefly traced.

Very important historically for the discussion of *Sage* in Genesis is the book by Andre Jolles, *Einfache Formen*[31]—a work that has been used by several German scholars including M. Noth, G. von Rad, C. Westermann, K. Koch, and others. Jolles suggested that *Sage* is not what is usually meant by this term in German (and therefore, by implication, what Gunkel meant by it), but has its true form in the Icelandic saga (which is also the real equivalent of the English term "saga"). Depending heavily upon Andreas Heusler's treatment of Icelandic saga (1914), Jolles held that the Icelandic sagas go back in all essentials to oral tradition beginning with the time of the island's settlement in the tenth to eleventh centuries and developing into "fixed oral narratives" from which the extant written texts are derived. Of the three main categories of sagas (family sagas, king sagas, and sagas about olden times), the family sagas are the most original and most indigenous and considerably influenced the shaping of the others. The family sagas themselves are the artistic end product, even on the oral level, of the development of more basic units of *Sagen*. The latter have, as their mental preoccupation, family tradition and domestic matters rather than

---

30. Even if his literary theory was correct, the similarity of the supposed sources could be explained on the basis of mutual dependence upon a common *literary* source, as was admitted by Noth, ibid., p. 41.

31. A. Jolles, *Einfache Formen*, 2nd ed. (Tübingen: Niemeyer, 1958), pp. 62–90.

affairs of state and the activities of political leaders. And hero sagas (*Heldensagen*) are only properly so-called when the hero is the progenitor of a tribe or the symbolic embodiment of his family. Such a popular frame of mind is only possible at an early stage in a people's history—at the time of their settlement when the basic unit of society is still the family, before the rise of the political state. For the state is concerned with political history and national affairs which are antithetical to the development of the saga (legend).

Jolles went on to suggest that the patriarchal stories of Genesis also belong to the category of *Sage* as he had defined it, and this suggestion was taken up by German Old Testament scholars. It is Westermann, above all, who has recently applied Jolles' principles to the narratives of Genesis, largely in an effort to overcome Gunkel's weakness of calling the legends etiological.[32] So, by analogy, the patriarchal stories would be more original than the primeval history, equivalent to sagas of olden times, and earlier than the stories of the "judges" and kings, which would correspond to the king sagas. Westermann also follows Jolles in the theory that the family saga is the more original form from which the other two types are derived and uses this to explain the similarity and priority of the patriarchal stories to the primeval history and the stories in Judges. Like the family sagas also, the patriarchal stories are derived from oral tradition in the early settlement period before the rise of the state under the monarchy.[33] Both family sagas and the patriarchal stories are governed by the context of family life, involving bloodties, marriages, genealogies, and inheritance and are unaware of a broader political, social, or religious context. Westermann, likewise, remarks that hero legends never devloped in ancient Israel, and that the patriarchal stories certainly do not belong to this genre.

What is rather disconcerting about this appeal to Jolles is the degree to which Westermann and others have accepted this highly unconventional understanding of *Sage* and have been completely oblivious to the severe criticism that folklorists working in this field have leveled at it.[34] It was rejected from the start, and the study of

---

32. Claus Westermann, "Arten der Erzählung in der Genesis," *Forschung am Alten Testament*, TB 24 (Munich: Chr. Kaiser, 1964), pp. 36–47.
33. Previously Noth, *Pentateuchal Traditions*, p. 44.
34. Cf. von Sydow, *Folklore*, pp. 61ff.; L. Petzoldt, ed., *Vergleichene Sagenforschung* (Darmstadt: Wissenschaftliche Buchgesellschaft, 1969), p. vii.

Sage has not included Icelandic sagas. The latter belong to a special literary genre quite different from almost every subcategory of *Sage*. There is one category of family legend of the type "What my grandfather told me," but this rarely becomes the property of the *Volk* as a whole, so its place within folklore and *Sage* is therefore disputed.[35]

But quite apart from this criticism by folklorists of Jolles' view of *Sage*, there is also his complete distortion of the character and development of Icelandic sagas. Heusler's views of 1914, which Jolles follows, have all been questioned and largely dismissed since that time.[36] Many authorities on Icelandic sagas regard them as primarily literary works with only a limited amount of oral tradition behind them. The present debate in Icelandic saga studies between "free prose" and "book prose" has to do largely with the degree to which gifted writers used traditional materials as well as other native and foreign literary works for their own compositions. The family sagas are not necessarily older than the other types; in fact the king sagas and family sagas come largely from the same period, and a few may have a common author.[37] Most of them date generally to the thirteenth century, the period which saw the fall of the republic and the rise of Norway's state control of Iceland.[38] There is certainly no basis in this Icelandic literature for the discussion of primary forms of oral tradition that could then be applied to Israel's traditions.

Furthermore, even the name "family saga" is freely acknowledged as a complete misnomer because, although they deal with family units, they are hardly domestic in content. Virtually all have the same basic structure, which has to do with the development of a conflict between two individuals or families leading to a violent confrontation and tragic death. This leads in turn to revenge by the injured person's family. In the end there is usually a reconciliation

---

35. See the type *Memorat* in von Sydow, *Folklore*, pp. 73–74; cf. Hand, "Status," *CA* 6:443.
36. For a history of saga criticism see T. A. Andersson, *The Problem of Icelandic Saga Origins* (New Haven and London: Yale University Press, 1964).
37. See E. O. Sveinsson, *Njals Saga: A Literary Masterpiece*, ed. and trans. Paul Schach (Lincoln: Nebraska University Press, 1971), pp. 28ff.
38. For the historical background of this period see E. O. Sveinsson, *The Age of the Sturlungs* (Ithaca, N.Y.: Cornell University Press, 1953). What Sveinsson emphasizes is that Norway's control of Iceland was not simply a change in constitution, but the imposition of foreign rule with which the Icelanders did not wish to identify. So it hardly represents an appropriate analogy for the early history of Israel.

of the families involved, often by means of action by the larger political unit, the assembly. It has also been recently argued that this basic framework is an adaptation of heroic epic models for the presentation of the "traditional" Icelandic saga material.[39] Nor are the family sagas any less national in their political, social, or religious character than the king sagas. The families are all part of the broader political life with membership in the local assemblies, representation in the national assemblies, and awareness of political and religious authorities beyond. These sagas are not small episodic units, but very complex literary works that often run several hundred pages in translation! Consequently, there is scarcely a single point in Westermann's comparison that is not completely different from what he has stated.

The recent discussion of "saga" in Koch's handbook on form-criticism also suffers from a number of weaknesses.[40] While Koch draws on a wider range of scholarly discussion, including recent anthropological studies on *Sage*, he often uses statements and opinions of various scholars in combination that are mutually exclusive. For instance, he follows Gunkel in applying Olrik's epic laws to the patriarchal narratives, but then adopts Jolles' concept of *Sage* as family tradition. But Jolles and Olrik have two quite different bodies of material in mind.[41] Furthermore, many of the criticisms of both Gunkel and Westermann apply *mutatis mutandis* to Koch as well.

In the end Koch admits that *Sage* is not a very precise "literary" genre, but is more of a "thought process" (*Geistesbeschäftigung*). There is some discussion in current studies on this aspect of *Sage*, but it does not function as a form-critical criterion.[42] Such discussion deals with material that is already known on other grounds to belong

---

39. See T. A. Andersson, *The Icelandic Family Saga: An Analytic Reading* (Cambridge: Harvard University Press, 1967).
40. Koch, *Biblical Tradition*, pp. 148–58.
41. Koch's references to the works of L. Röhrich, "Die deutsche Volkssage: Ein methodische Abriss," *Studium Generale* 11 (1958): 664–91, and W. E. Peuchert, *Sagen, Geburt und Antwort der mythischen Welt* (Berlin: E. Schmid, 1965), are also problematic since they are in clear contradiction to Jolles' approach.
42. See Rohrich, "Volkssage," *SG* 11:667, Hand, "Status," *CA* 6:441. But, against Koch, *Legende* is a subcategory of *Sage* that is not structurally different and does not have a different "mental process." The two forms may also be quite contemporary with each other. The more important difference in *Geistesbeschäftigung* is between *Sage* and *Märchen*, but Koch does not take up this matter.

to one of the subcategories of *Sage*. But Koch superimposes a *Geistesbeschäftigung*, taken from Jolles, upon the material that he presupposes to be oral tradition and *Sagen*. This is no different from the old "idea-criticism" that form-criticism was intended to replace as a more controlled and objective exegetical method.

This means that there is no adequate basis at the present time for speaking about *Sage*, "saga," or legend as a form-critical category for the stories in Genesis. Present day folklorists seem to agree that *Sage* or legend is not an adequate form-critical category, and therefore it should not be used as such in Old Testament studies.[43] Not even the subcategories are of much help, since they are merely means of classifying what is already known to be oral tradition from carefully collected materials and are not useful for making judgments about the oral basis of written literary works.[44] It may be possible to assess the amount of folklore in Genesis by a careful application of criteria such as Olrik's laws *to particular units*, but simply discovering a few signs of folklore cannot make the whole of Genesis *Sage*. Quite independent of the literary and form-critical questions there may be considerable value in comparing the traditionist perspective of the Old Testament with that of legend in general to see what characteristics they share in terms of a pre-modern historical way of thinking. There may, in fact, be various levels of historical consciousness, rationalization, or other such elements evident in the Old Testament. But to suppose at the same time that the ability to write or compose written literature automatically changes one's way of thinking from legendary to historical is a serious fallacy.[45] What is an even worse error is to suppose that the small literate circle of the court in the time of the Israelite monarchy was in any way representative for the people as a whole. Their local oral traditions might have continued, in fact, long after the state came into being. At any rate the whole discussion of *Sage* since the time of Gunkel has done little to clarify the form of the tradition in the Abraham stories.

43. Rohrich, "Volkssage," *SG* 11:667.
44. For recent attempts at general classification within the area of folklore studies see Hand, "Status," *CA* 6:420ff. See also the articles on this subject collected in Petzoldt, *Vergleichende Sagenforschung*.
45. Note the large amount of folklore in Herodotus, especially for the early historical period. See W. Aly, *Volksmärchen, Sage und Novelle bei Herodot und seinen Zeitgenossen*, 2nd ed. (Göttingen: Vandenhoeck & Ruprecht, 1969).

The History of Traditions

Let us now turn to the other line of development from Gunkel, that of the history of the traditions. Gunkel's suggestion about the great antiquity of the oral tradition behind the patriarchal stories and the fidelity of their transmission has led to an extensive search for the earlier pre-literary levels of the tradition and their use in reconstructing the earliest period of Israel's history and religion. A. Alt, in his essay, "The God of the Fathers,"[46] accepted Gunkel's form-critical judgment of the Genesis stories as legends, but he was particularly concerned with those parts of the tradition that had a cultic or religious reference. His object was to deal with the question of whether it was possible to say anything about the pre-Yahwistic patriarchal religion.

As indications of this possibility in the first instance, Alt pointed to the fact that Yahweh was a deity only known in the tradition as related in covenant to all of the tribes together, and whose identity therefore presupposes the settlement of Israel. On the other hand, the tradition itself gives some evidence of tension between Yahweh and the various Elim—viewed as local numina of old sanctuaries throughout Palestine. But these Alt did not regard as appropriate to a nomadic group entering the land because of their close association with the sedentary centers within the land. Yet the tradition also suggested to Alt a certain distinction between Yahweh and the God of the Fathers. He saw this especially in the so-called E version of the call of Moses in Exod. 3, where in v. 14 the God of the Fathers is identified with Yahweh. For Alt this was a clear recognition that the form of the partiarchal religion was different from that of the Mosaic-Sinai tradition.

On the other hand, the stories of Genesis presented a problem in trying to deal with this religious history of the patriarchal deities because virtually every reference to them was in a context that showed extensive literary activity by the later writers. Only in a few instances, such as in the story of the treaty between Laban and Jacob in Genesis 31:53 and in Gen. 46:1-3, was it possible to see more original archaic references to this type of deity. From these,

---

46. A. Alt, *Der Gott der Väter* [The God of the Fathers] 1929, in *Essays on Old Testament History and Religion*, R. A. Wilson, trans. (Oxford: Blackwell, 1966), pp. 1-77. Note that in this work *Sage* is translated by "saga" instead of "legend."

however, one could hardly develop a very clear notion of this kind of religion. By contrast, the references to the Elim and the legends associated with them seemed to be much closer to their primitive form.

To solve this problem Alt attempted to reconstruct a possible form of nomadic religion of a personal deity based on Nabataean inscriptions of the first and second centuries A.D. This model was admittedly not from a nomadic context, but from the settled regions a few centuries after these nomads had given up the desert life. Nevertheless Alt found in these sources references to cults whose deities were identified by their association to a specific historical person, presumably the founder, and supported by a group of followers. In most instances the deity was simply known as "the God of PN." Since the patriarchal tradition contained a considerable variety of legends and deities associated with them Alt felt justified in applying this historical analogy—the idea of a personal "God of the Fathers"—to the stories and in reconstructing its history on the basis of it.

According to Alt, the history of the patriarchal cultic traditions consisted of two distinct phases. In the first phase (the period in the wilderness before the entry into the land), the patriarchal cults of the personal deities came into being and were associated with certain tribal groups, although they preserved the names of the cult founders. After the settlement in the second phase they took over the sanctuaries throughout the land, but they had to relate their traditions to these new places of worship and to the new conditions of settlement. So virtually all their old etiological legends connected with the cults of the fathers, with the possible exception of Genesis 15, died out and were replaced by the cult legends of the local sanctuaries of the land of Palestine. But in most cases the patriarchal deity replaced that of the local El as the principal numen of that place. In this way the house of Joseph supplanted a number of local El numina at Shechem, Bethel, and Penuel by the "God of Jacob". The "God of Isaac" became the chief deity of Beersheba and the "God of Abraham" was established at Mamre-Hebron. In time, through the interaction of the tribes and particularly by means of pilgrimages from all three groups to Beersheba, a gradual unity was created out of the three deities and a genealogical association between the cultic founders was established. The final stage in the development was for the national deity, associated with non-patriarchal sanctuaries, to eventually win out over all the other local cults as well and to be identified with the God of the three patriarchs.

In this brief review of Alt's famous essay I am not concerned with the question of whether it is possible to reconstruct a pre-Yahwistic religion.[47] The primary focus here is on the question of Alt's method of tradition-history, since it plays such a major role in subsequent historical and literary studies.

My first point of criticism is that since Alt accepted Gunkel's conclusions about etiological legends in the patriarchal stories all the weaknesses of Gunkel apply equally to Alt. Form-critically it becomes very doubtful if any of the references to the El numina constitute etiological legends that legitimate sanctuaries. In most instances they are more like appendages attached to stories of a quite different character. Only the theophany at Bethel (Genesis 28) looks like a reference to the founding of a sanctuary, but this is viewed by Alt as thoroughly reworked by the writers so that to him it does not reflect a very primitive level of the tradition.[48] On the other hand, he places great importance on Genesis 15 as an etiological legend: "A distinct and independent saga almost undoubtedly lies behind this passage."[49] But this is not a form-critical judgment because there are no etiological elements in the chapter, and Alt even admits that he doesn't know what the form would look like, since there are no such legends associated with his model in the Nabataean sources. Form-critical evaluations of Genesis 15, in fact, yield quite different results. In the end Alt cannot point to a single cult legend in Genesis with which he can associate the two phases of his historical reconstruction.

It is also important for Alt's thesis that Beersheba should have been an important pre-Israelite site with a prominent sanctuary, and that it should have continued to be such in Iron I—the period of the settlement and the Judges. But in fact, as noted above, Beersheba did not exist before the Israelite period, and in Iron I it was

---

47. Cf. Frank M. Cross, Jr., "Yahweh and the God of the Patriarchs," *HTR* 55 (1962): 225–59; H. Weidmann, *Die Patriarchen und ihre Religion im Light der Forschung seit Julius Wellhausen*, FRLANT 94 (Göttingen: Vandenhoeck & Ruprecht, 1968).
48. Alt, *Essays*, pp. 17–19.
49. Ibid., p. 65.

no more than a village. It was only made a prominent town under the united monarchy, and it probably first developed an important cult place under the Judean monarchy. I fail to see how it could have been the nucleus of early pilgrimages in the pre-monarchy period or the repository of patriarchal legends.

The most serious weakness of all is that Alt has really abandoned an examination of the traditions themselves because he is uneasy about their form, which he admits is in most cases freely composed literature and therefore scarcely close to the form of oral legends at all. In its place he substitutes as his overriding criterion a kind of "idea-criticism" that can take him behind the received traditions to traditions that no longer exist. From the point of view of method it does not matter whether his concept of a "God of the Fathers" religion accurately corresponds with a form of Nabataean religion or not. He has lost any objective control over his method so he can always make it fit. One can begin with virtually any idea as a historical analogy, reconstruct the original "lost" traditions and then account for how they were reworked by later writers. One may be impressed with the way the pieces (admittedly selective) fit together, but given the freedom that Alt allows himself that is a demonstration of ingenuity and nothing more.

The work of G. von Rad represents quite a new departure in the tradition-history of the Pentateuch.[50] Von Rad attempted to show that not only the individual units of tradition in Gunkel's sense, but also the confessional or thematic framework into which these units were put belong to the oldest traditional material. He suggested that the Hexateuch's thematic structure derived from an early confessional formula or creed such as is found in Deut. 26:5–9; 6:20–24; or Joshua 24:2b–13. Its original setting (*Sitz im Leben*) was in the earliest cultic life of pre-monarchic Israel, and its use was the common confession of this "cult legend" by the tribes of the settlement period. This credo, consisting of a series of saving events, ultimately provided a structure into which all the various traditions were fitted.

A number of criticisms of interest to our methodological concerns have been raised against von Rad's thesis. First of all he is hard put

---

50. G. von Rad, *Das formgeschichtliche Problem des Hexateuch*, BWANT 4/26 (1938). English translation, *The Problem of the Hexateuch and Other Essays*, E. W. T. Dicken, trans. (New York: McGraw-Hill, 1966), pp. 1–78.

to establish the antiquity of the credo in any of its forms since they are all now so thoroughly Deuteronomic in phraseology.[51] His efforts to find a special festival in which the credo was used (the Feast of Weeks) and a special sanctuary (Gilgal) may also be seriously disputed. These Deuteronomic summaries also omit a great deal that is important to the Hexateuch, such as the promises to the patriarchs and the Sinai tradition. These traditions must then be accounted for in some other way, perhaps as cult traditions of other sanctuaries and cultic celebrations. The separation of such themes from one another has not been accepted by a number of scholars who are inclined to substitute another model, for example the covenant/treaty model, and who make their own reconstructions of the earliest traditions on that basis.[52]

The most decisive criticism of von Rad's thesis, however, comes from a form-critical study by Childs.[53] He points out that in the treatment of the exodus by the credos of Deuteronomy 26 and 6 the Reed Sea episode is omitted, and in this they are consistent with Deuteronomic usage. But in the Tetrateuch the Reed Sea episode is quite central to the treatment of the exodus, so that the credo formulations could hardly have formed a basis for the Tetrateuchal treatment of them. The alternative origin for the credos that would thus commend itself would be "Deuteronomic abbreviations of fuller traditions which, in the later Dtr. redaction, continued to develop the form of summaries of salvation history through secondary expansion."[54] However, this raises the very serious question of whether any of the thematic structures in the Pentateuch can be traced back to an oral tradition basis, or whether they are not all the result of literary composition by a redactor/collector. The full impact of this question can only be appreciated by considering M. Noth's work on the Pentateuch.

As a presupposition to his study of the history of pentateuchal

51. See Fohrer, *Introduction*, p. 118 for a review of the criticisms with bibliography.
52. See W. Beyerlin, *Origins and History of the Oldest Sinaitic Tradition*, S. Rudman, trans. (Oxford: Blackwell, 1965).
53. Brevard S. Childs, "Deuteronomic Formulae of the Exodus Traditions," *Hebräische Wortforschung, Festschrift Walter Baumgartner*, SVT 16 (1967): 30–39.
54. Ibid., p. 39. Could it also point to the fact that the Tetrateuchal tradition is Post-Deuteronomic? Why do the latest forms of the historical summaries contain the Reed Sea episode, Ps. 136; Neh. 9:6ff.; but also Josh. 24:2b–13? See also George W. Coats, "The Traditio-historical Character of the Reed Sea Motif," *VT* 17 (1967): 253–65; B. S. Childs, "A Traditio-historical study of the Reed Sea Tradition," *VT* 20 (1970): 406–18.

traditions, Noth adopts the view that the Pentateuch represents a long history of development from the pre-literary stage of oral tradition through a complex literary stage to its final form. However, he makes the primary focus for his study the pre-literary history of the tradition and states: "The decisive steps on the way to the formation of the Pentateuch were taken during the preliterary stage, and the literary fixations only gave final form to material which in its essentials was already given."[55]

Noth regards the process by which the Pentateuch developed as quite different from that of the literary histories of Samuel-Kings and Chronicles. Whereas the histories were deliberate literary compositions by "authors" who carefully assembled their sources (oral and written) and gave the work its perspective and structure, the structure and basic themes of the Pentateuch were supplied by the process of oral tradition itself as well as the filling out of these themes in all their essentials at the pre-literary level. Noth regards this difference as demonstrated in the work of von Rad and uses the latter's study in an attempt to go beyond Gunkel's concern for individual units of tradition. Thus Noth includes in this stage also the development of the larger structure and basic themes of what he calls the "Pentateuchal tradition." Yet Childs' criticism of von Rad, mentioned above, would deny that the Pentateuch was different from the literary histories in its development, so that the same method of redactional criticism ought to be employed for both literatures. In fact, unless other very strong reasons are suggested for doing otherwise I can see no alternative but to trace the tradition-history of the Pentateuch on the basis of redaction criticism.

Noth's views on tradition-history are also very closely related to his reconstruction of Israel's history.[56] Here Noth advocates two basic considerations. First, the focus of the pentateuchal tradition is "all Israel," so that its formation can only derive from a period after the occupation of the land by the various tribes and after they had developed a clear sense of common identity. The second factor in determining the date of the tradition is, according to Noth, its character as legend. Noth does not define "saga-tradition" in strict form-critical terms, but on the basis of Gunkel's description about how this tradition has grown from an oral base. Noth further states that the only appropriate soil in which such a "saga-tradi-

---

55. Noth, *Pentateuchal Traditions*, p. 1.
56. Ibid., pp. 42–45.

tion" can grow is in a community of tribes where there is a degree of democratic rule, and *not* during a period of strong centralized authority under a state goverment. The evidence cited for this is the Icelandic sagas, which are said to "constitute the most important example open to historical investigation of a saga-formation in this sense."[57] Consequently, the period for the formation of the pentateuchal tradition must be the pre-monarchic period of the tribal league, which was also the period of the Judges.

There are some serious questions that can be raised about Noth's historical context for the pentateuchal tradition. Noth acknowledges that the "hero stories" of the Book of Judges belonged primarily to the individual tribes and were only secondarily given an "all-Israel" orientation. Yet Noth goes to this same source to glean evidence for his theory of an all-Israel amphictyony, which in turn becomes the context for the pentateuchal tradition. He does not explain how such different "historical" traditions can arise in the same period from essentially the same group of tradents but with such different tribal/national perspectives. His characterization of the tribal orientation in the Book of Judges seems to me correct and therefore the strongest argument against any amphictyonic unity or all-Israel orientation in the pre-monarchic period.[58]

Concerning Noth's appeal to the Icelandic sagas as evidence for a pre-state saga age, I have already indicated that there is little support for such a suggestion in current Icelandic studies. There are no grounds for any comparison between either the two literatures or the two historical situations. On the other hand, in a recent work on oral tradition, J. Vansina indicates that traditions that have a general all-tribe orientation are only found in centralized societies—in states—and "never among tribes with a political structure which depends entirely upon kinship links."[59] It is difficult to see how any all-Israel orientation could develop in the tradition before the time of the monarchy.

The most important test of Noth's tradition-history is the way in

---

57. Ibid., p. 44, n. 152.
58. For recent criticisms of the notion of a tribal amphictyony see G. Fohrer, "'Amphictyony' und 'Bund,'" *TLZ* 91 (1961), cols. 801–16, 893–903. See also de Vaux, *Histoire*, pp. 487–510, in which he gives strong arguments for a disunity between the southern tribes in Judah and the northern tribes of Israel before the time of David. This is a serious difficulty for Noth's tradition-history.
59. J. Vansina, *Oral Tradition: A Study in Historical Methodology*, H. M. Wright, trans. (London: Routledge and Kegan Paul, 1965), p. 155.

which he views the incorporation and development of the Pentateuch's basic themes into the main body of tradition already at the pre-literary level. We do not need to deal here with his discussion of all the themes, but only the one that primarily concerns this study, the "promise to the patriarchs."[60] Noth builds directly on Alt's presentation of the God of the Fathers, but Noth's special concern is how these patriarchal traditions became a part of the pentateuchal tradition as a whole. Originally the patriarchal traditions arose and developed separate from the rest of the pentateuchal tradition. The two main localities and groups of patriarchal traditions were the Jacob traditions of the central highland region (along with the eastern Jacob traditions) and the Abraham-Isaac traditions of the southern Judah and Negeb regions. These patriarchal traditions each developed, independent of the other, the theme of promise of land and progeny, made to the nomadic fathers along with the fulfillment of that promise in their settlement of the land. Since the land promise theme competed with the similar theme of Yahweh's guidance into the arable land in the pentateuchal tradition, the two traditions became related by identifying the "God of the Fathers," who was the author of the promises, with the God of Israel of the exodus and conquest traditions. The promise to the fathers was then placed prior to the Egyptian sojourn and the specific fulfillment of land possession was replaced by the conquest theme. This process of amalgamation of tradition, Noth suggests, took place first with the Jacob traditions within the central highland tribes, and only later were the southern Abraham-Isaac traditions, which had the same basic theme, added. This was done by the construction of a genealogical framework in which Abraham and Isaac were added to Jacob by a backward extension.

The first problem with this reconstruction is that Noth makes no attempt to demonstrate that the promise theme is primary to the traditions and not just a framework for them. Even Alt and von Rad argued that it was originally present only in Genesis 15, in the Abraham tradition. They saw its use elsewhere as part of the kerygmatic framework constructed by the literary activity of the Yahwist, who also combined it with the other pentateuchal themes. Unless one can, in fact, show that the promise theme is primary in the

---

60. Noth, *Pentateuchal Traditions*, pp. 54–58.

Jacob stories, it is difficult to see how his thesis about the combining of these themes on the pre-literary level can be maintained.[61]

Furthermore, Noth does not deal with the question of who the bearers of these separate pentateuchal and patriarchal traditions in the central highlands were. He suggests that one group of tribes developed a strong sense of unity through their identity with a common ancestor, Jacob, and the promises of his god to him. He does not make clear, of course, how an individual historical figure in the religious cult form "the God of PN" could become a tribal eponym. Nor does he explain which group was left in this region to develop an alternative sense of identity through the exodus and conquest themes, to regard itself as "Israel," and to have its own way of legitimizing its settlement. At what point in time and under what circumstances did the need arise for forming a common identity? Noth would have to rule out the beginning of the settlement period, with its encounter between new tribal groups, because of his theory about the gradual and ununified nature of the settlement. However, to suggest that the amalgamation of the tradition themes was a gradual process begs the question. Two groups with different identities through their different traditions, laying claim to the same territory, could only result in bitter rivalry unless unusual circumstances, such as one conquering the other, created a common unity out of both. But nothing in the tradition itself suggests this.

One other aspect of Noth's study calls for comment. That is the association of the patriarchal traditions with particular places, their *Ortsgebundenheit*. This was already a concern of Alt in his discussion of the Elim numina and their sanctuaries and of the absorption by some patriarchal traditions of some original El cult legends. But Noth, in his treatment of all the traditions, went much further and seems to associate most of them (outside of the Joseph story) with particular localities and sanctuaries. Some places, such as Gerar, don't work very well, and in other cases more than one patriarch is associated with the same place. This usually suggests to Noth that traditions original to one patriarch were transferred already on the pre-literary level to the other patriarch. Yet the whole notion of *Ortsgebundenheit* is predicated on the notion that the stories are

61. H. Seebass, *Der Erzvater Israel*, *BZAW* 98 (1966), has attempted this. But his point of departure is Deut. 26:5ff., which he regards as having a very old liturgical tradition behind it. However, Childs' study, noted above, certainly makes this problematic.

etiological legends. But they are not. And it is well known from Greece that heroes and eponyms may be freely associated with a large number of sanctuaries and other places with which they have no ancient connection.[62] Such connections with accompanying stories were being produced for various motives in the full light of the Greek historical period. So place names by themselves constitute a very uncertain criterion for deciding on a tradition's origin.

On cannot dismiss these criticisms of Gunkel, Alt,.von Rad, Noth, Westermann, and others as of little consequence. So serious are the basic weaknesses of their treatments that it seems to me they have not made a case for regarding the traditions of Genesis as either ancient or deriving from an oral base. They have not established the form of the stories, their function, the identity of the bearers of these traditions, or the process by which they might have arrived at their extant shape. Furthermore, I do not see any great merit in a further critique of later traditio-historical studies that follow the basic principles and methods of the above mentioned scholars.[63]

Dating the Literary Tradition

After the above review of the basic literary, form-critical and traditio-historical questions it is now possible to give some attention to the dating of the earliest extensive literary treatment of the Abraham tradition, the Yahwist. Fortunately, this subject has recently received an extensive treatment by Norman E. Wagner, which will serve as a helpful point of departure for the discussion here.[64]

The first important aspect of the problem, as Wagner points out, is the scope of the J work. There is still considerable debate over whether it should be limited to the Tetrateuch or extend as far as Joshua. This is the basic difference between Noth and von Rad.[65] Yet their arguments are not basically literary at this point; differing views on the history of the tradition and the difficulties with both views of tradition-history have been noted above. There are some

---

62. See especially M. P. Nilsson, *Cults, Myths, Oracles, and Politics in Ancient Greece* (Lund, Sweden: C. W. K. Gleerup, 1951), esp. pp. 65–80.

63. Such studies as R. Kilian, *Die vorpriesterlichen Abrahamsüberlieferungen*, BBB 24 (Bonn: P. Hanstein, 1966) add nothing new to the history of method. Yet the discussion of this and other similar traditio-historical studies will be treated in detail below.

64. Norman E. Wagner, "Abraham and David?" *Studies on the Ancient Palestinian World, Festschrift F. V. Winnett*, ed. J. W. Wevers and D. B. Redford (Toronto: University of Toronto Press, 1972), pp. 117-40.

65. Other scholars who see J in Joshua as well are Mowinckel, *Tetrateuch-Pentateuch-Hexateuch*; and Fohrer, *Introduction*, pp. 196–205.

scholars who extend the work of J to the historical books as well, but then the Abraham traditions become only an extensive source within the whole.⁶⁶ The question of the broad extent of the J work beyond Genesis cannot be a primary concern within the limits of this study.

On the other hand, the establishing of the scope of J within the Abraham tradition itself is still something of an open question, as indicated above. This, in itself, can serve as a most important criterion for the assessing of J's limits elsewhere as well. Very much a part of this task is the evaluation of the relationship of J to the other so-called sources of the Pentateuch. As long as it is assumed that J is the earliest source in the Pentateuch this question does not have much value. But as soon as any other possibility is considered the question becomes inevitable.⁶⁷

With respect to the various proposals for the dating of J, Wagner points out that there has been a considerable shift from the time of Wellhausen to the present.⁶⁸ Wellhausen dated both J and E rather close together and placed them both in the early period of classical prophecy, the eighth century B.C.⁶⁹ Since then J has been redated to the tenth century, while E has remained about where it was. The arguments for E's dating have not changed to any extent since the time of Wellhausen, but for J they have gone in quite a new direction. It was largely as a result of the new traditio-historical approach of von Rad and Noth to the pentateuchal traditions that J was now regarded as the culmination of this whole process in the early monarchy. It is perhaps true to say that the present views on the tradition-history of the Pentateuch, especially those which follow the lead of von Rad and Noth, provide the strongest motivation for maintaining an early date for J.⁷⁰

Besides the general argument from tradition-history, a number of specific clues have often been put forward for the dating of J.⁷¹ One such suggestion is that there is no evidence in J for a division of

---

66. See Wagner, "Abraham and David?", p. 125.
67. This point is not sufficiently stressed by Wagner, even though he favors a late date for J.
68. Wagner, "Abraham and David?", p. 118.
69. Julius Wellhausen, *Prolegomena to the History of Ancient Israel*, pp. 360–61.
70. See Hans W. Wolff, "The Kerygma of the Yahwist," *Interpretation* 20 (1966): 131–58; R. E. Clements, *Abraham and David* SBT 2/5 (London: SCM, 1967).
71. See Wolff, *Interpretation* 20:134–35; Peter F. Ellis, *The Bible's First Theologian* (Notre Dame, Ind.: Fides Publishers, 1968), pp. 40–42.

Israel into two separate states or for any tension between Judah and the northern tribes. This, it is said, would point to the Solomonic period, before the schism of the two regions. The most obvious objection to this argument is that there is no such division reflected in any of the sources. On the other hand, one could interpret Genesis 34 as a rather late southern polemic against a paganized "Samaritan" north and against any intermarriage or other dealings with the people of that region. Furthermore, the Davidic-Solomonic period cannot be regarded as a period of ideal unity between north and south, since there was considerable tension between the two regions, and each region was quite separately related to the king.[72] It is still a moot question as to whether "Israel" ever included Judah in the United Monarchy. It may even be argued that only after the demise of the northern kingdom could an idealized "greater Israel," an ideal which becomes most important in the late monarchy and exilic periods, develop. At any rate, the "all Israel" motif is not a sure clue for an early date.

A second argument that has been suggested is that the various peoples mentioned by J: Philistines, Canaanites, Arameans, Amalekites, Ammonites, Moabites, and Edomites, were all a part of David's empire (2 Sam. 8). Of course, these same peoples were the neighbors of the two kingdoms throughout their history so their mere mention does not suggest anything very specific. Nor can their relationship to the patriarchs be regarded as a prototype for the relationship of David and Solomon with these states since they were altogether different. Furthermore, as we have seen, the use of some of these terms in a particular manner in J cannot be made to fit the United Monarchy, for example, the reference to a Philistine king of Gerar.

Some have tried to see a specific historical reference in the "blessing" to Esau (Edom) in Gen. 27:40: "By your sword you shall live, and you shall serve your brother; but when you break loose you shall break his yoke from your neck." This has been associated with

---

72. In "The Monarchy in the Kingdoms of Israel and Judah," *Essays on Old Testament History and Religion*, pp. 241–43, Alt argued that the Davidic monarchy abolished the "original" tribal federation and created two entities, a northern and a southern one, and that this concept of a duality continued to the end of the northern kingdom. He states rather emphatically that he cannot find a single trace of any appeal against this duality to an original unity of the confederation. If one has grave doubts about any such unity *before* the monarchy the only conclusion left is that the unity was an idealistic creation after the fall of the northern kingdom.

the reference to a certain Hadad, an Edomite who gave Solomon some trouble (1 Kings 11:14ff.). But this really fits the "blessing" rather poorly. The closest parallel is, in fact, the revolt by Edom under Joram (2 Kings 8:20–22) around 850 B.C., but it is not clear that this was the last revolt for there seems to have been some domination of the Edomites by Amaziah as well (2 Kings 14:7) until the time of Ahaz (2 Kings 16:6). The historical allusion in Genesis 27:40, therefore, can hardly be regarded as very precise.

Another line of argument suggests that J belongs to the period of "Solomonic Enlightenment," a new literary age which is also reflected in such works as the Court History of David (2 Sam. 9–20; 1 Kings 1–2).[73] Attempts have been made to see similarities in literary style and thematic treatment between J and the Court History but there is scarcely anything in these comparisons that is very convincing.[74] Nor can we regard the dating of the Court History to the Solomonic period as established. To regard this scandalization of the monarchy as originating in the Solomonic court is to my mind entirely incredible.[75] At any rate, arguments based on the notion that J reflects the spirit of this period, as if we could really gauge what this was, are too vague to be useful.

Recently there has been an increasing effort to associate Abraham with David and to see in this part of the Yahwist the most specific reflection of the Davidic period.[76] It is suggested that the close connection between Abraham and Hebron (Mamre) gave to David a means of legitimizing his monarchy on the basis of this tradition, since his own power base was originally from Hebron in Judah. This legitimation, it is argued, can be seen in the special stress on the covenant of Abraham (Genesis 15), which provided the model for the Davidic covenant (2 Sam. 7), and the promises of great progeny and the gift of the land of Canaan, which were all fulfilled in David.

This argument develops a curious circularity, especially in the

73. See von Rad, *Old Testament Theology* vol. 1. *The Theology of Israel's Historical Traditions*, trans. D. M. G. Stalker, (New York: Harper & Row, 1962), pp. 36–56.
74. J. Blenkinsopp, "Theme and Motif in the Succession History (2 Sam. xi 2ff.) and the Yahwist Corpus," *SVT* 15 (1966): 44–57; W. Bruggemann, "David and his Theologian," *CBQ* 30 (1968): 156–81.
75. R. N. Whybray, *The Succession Narrative: A Study of II Sam. 9–20 and I Kings 1 and 2* SBT 2/9 (London: SCM, 1968).
76. See R. E. Clements, *Abraham and David*; G. E. Mendenhall, "Covenant Forms in Israelite Tradition," *BA* 17 (1954): 71–72; idem, *IDB* 1:717–718.

recent presentation of it by Clements.⁷⁷ He admits that the form of the covenant and promises in the Yahwist have already been influenced by royal dynastic ideology. But he believes that these themes were also pre-Davidic from the original Abrahamic tradition and were used to shape the royal ideology itself. It is then on the basis of this conviction that Clements attempts to reconstruct the tradition-history, with a considerable dependence on the theories of Alt and Noth as well. But in such a proposed tradition-history there are no historical or literary controls. If the tradition-history of Alt and Noth cannot be accepted, neither can that of Clements. If, on the other hand, the promises in J were influenced by dynastic ideas this could have happened anytime during the monarchy or later. But that an Abrahamic covenant ever influenced the Davidic covenant can never be proven. On the other hand, there are several arguments against any early connection between Abraham and David. Firstly, in all the passages that make reference to the royal ideology throughout the history of the monarchy, not once is Abraham mentioned. How can these traditions be important for royal legitimation if they were never used as such? The histories often use the device of promise and fulfillment and make these connections very specific. Why did they not do so in the case of Abraham and David? The argument that it is there in a subtle form is not very convincing. An instance of quite direct prediction, Gen. 15:13–16, is usually excised from the Yahwist, though for no good literary reasons.

Secondly, the most important means of royal legitimation in the ancient Near East (and in most dynastic monarchies) is genealogical connection.⁷⁸ But this is not used in the case of David.⁷⁹ Isaiah can go back no further than Jesse when he speaks about a new dynastic beginning for the Judean monarchy (Isa. 11:1). The form of genealogy used for legitimation of office is the linear genealogy. But the

77. *Abraham and David*, pp. 58–59. Cf. the criticisms by Wagner, "Abraham and David?" pp. 133–34.
78. The best treatment of the function of genealogies in the ancient Near East and in the Old Testament is the thesis by R. R. Wilson, "Genealogy and History in the Old Testament: A Study of the Form and Function of the Old Testament Genealogies in their Near Eastern Context," (Ph.D. diss., Yale University, 1972). See also A. Malamat, "King Lists in the Old Babylonian Period and Biblical Genealogies," *JAOS* 88 (1968): 163–73. Malamat's reconstruction of the Davidic genealogy (pp. 170–73) is entirely artificial and never existed as such in the history of the monarchy.
79. The late genealogical additions in Ruth 4:17b–22 can hardly be regarded as serving this purpose.

form of those in Genesis involving the patriarchs are all segmented genealogies whose function is quite different. Such genealogies indicate status and relationship of various subgroups, tribes, clans, families, etc., within a larger whole. Nothing in Genesis suggests a concern for royal legitimation of any kind.

Thirdly, it can hardly be doubted that the function of the Yahwistic presentation of the patriarchal tradition is to articulate Israel's identity and destiny. But how could such a presentation of the national tradition be made from the Jerusalem court of the Davidites without any clear suggestion that the monarchy was at the heart of this identity? It cannot be argued that it is subtly implied. On the contrary, it is clear that the monarchy is quite superfluous to this national identity. This may be stated in spite of the inclusion within the Yahwist work of two poetic allusions to the monarchy in Gen. 49:10 and Num. 24:17. These are very likely not original to the Yahwist, as most critics admit, and they are very vague in what they suggest. They are hardly central to the Yahwist's own thematic structure. I frankly find it difficult to conceive how this ideological presentation could stand side by side with the royal ideology of the Davidic covenant, and I see no evidence that in fact it ever did.[80]

In general I concur with Wagner that the heart of the problem of dating, as well as the understanding of the Yahwist's "message," lies in one's evaluation of the promises to the fathers. The question of dating can only be taken up after the literary, form-critical and traditio-historical treatment of these promises, and especially Genesis 15, has been finished. I have attempted to indicate here why the question must remain open for the present.

---

80. This is an important methodological issue on the formation and function of tradition, whether oral or written. See esp. Vansina, *Oral Tradition*, chap. 4.

CHAPTER 7

Method II—Some Guidelines

In the preceding discussion I outlined the present doubtful state of literary criticism in pentateuchal studies. It is scarcely possible to adopt the current approach of the discipline for the following literary study of the Abraham traditions. It is not just a question of a slight modification of the old methods, as seems to be the vogue in the present methodological studies.[1] Instead I want to outline step by step a fresh approach to the various types of literary problems that we face in this part of the tradition—an approach that will be as open and unbiased as possible. At the same time, in the execution of a new method in the following chapters a dialogue must be carried on (within reasonable limits) with other views so that a fair appraisal may be made of the new analysis offered in this study.

Source-Analysis

To begin a fresh literary approach one must come to the Abraham traditions with the first basic question: is it a unified work, the product of a single author? The answer to this question is that it is not, since there are certain obvious indications of a plurality of sources among the various stories. For instance there are the doublets of the same story plot, which could scarcely be thought of as coming from the same author. These are the story of a patriarch in a foreign land calling his wife his sister, Gen. 12:10–20; 20; 26:1–11, or the story of the flight or dismissal of Hagar in Gen. 16 and 21:8–21. There is also the double presentation of a kerygmatic theme, as in the two separate covenants with Abraham in Genesis 15 and 17. Besides

---

1. See the recent book by K. Koch, *The Growth of the Biblical Tradition*; also W. Richter, *Exegese als Literaturwissenschaft* (Göttingen: Vandenhoeck & Ruprecht, 1970). Although both works suggest that the principles they enunciate are applicable to the Pentateuch only a very limited reference is actually made to it, so they fail to come to terms with the real problems.

these doublets there are some awkward points of tension or contradiction between stories, such as the story of the birth of Isaac. In Genesis 18 Abraham and Sarah, an aged couple, are promised a son and in chap. 21 he is born. Yet in chap. 20 Abraham is able to pass his wife off as his sister, and does so presumably because she is very beautiful, so that she is taken into Abimelech's harem. The context, however, clearly suggests that she is both old and pregnant. Similarly, in chap. 25, Isaac and Rebekah already have two full-grown sons, and both parents are now old. Yet in chap. 26 Isaac pretends that Rebekah is his sister because she is so beautiful, and he fears that his life is threatened. Likewise the chronological framework in which the stories are now set often provides a problem. In the story of Hagar's expulsion from Abraham's household, 21:8–21, Ishmael is still clearly a child, but the larger context suggests that he must have been about sixteen years of age (cf. Gen. 17:25). These rather obvious examples are enough to suggest that the Abraham tradition is a combination of sources. It would also indicate the first steps toward literary analysis: a recognition that the framework may be an artificial means of holding together originally independent stories, and a comparison of the various doublets that may be used to separate the sources from one another. Since most of the stories are not duplicated one would have to rely upon their similarity and internal connection with the stories of the doublets in order to carry through the source division of the whole Abraham tradition.

The task of source division, however, is not settled by this process alone, for the unity of the individual stories themselves has also been questioned. This is not the same kind of problem and becomes much more difficult to deal with. A particular narrative unit may give evidence of disunity for two different reasons. First, the unit may consist of a complete story or episode from a certain source to which secondary additions have been made. It would then be a legitimate task to decide which was primary and which secondary. On the other hand, a unit may consist of a story which is a conflation of two or more earlier versions that are only partially utilized in the final version. This second case must be clearly recognized as an act of composing a narrative and not as an editorial procedure. The end product, therefore, must be considered as a literary work, a source in its own right, and unless one actually has the prior versions that were utilized, a further separation into sources becomes very doubtful indeed. It is not the task of source analysis to do so.² This means that for the individual unit source-analysis will be concerned only with the decision of what is a primary and what is a secondary addition.

The next question that arises is: what are the criteria by which one may distinguish between the primary source and the secondary additions? Some criteria that have been suggested in the past have not been very helpful and have even been misleading. One of these is the principle of repetition of words and phrases. This is often grouped together with the principle of the story doublet, but it is not the same at all.³ Repetition within a story or other prose narrative passage can have a large variety of reasons depending upon an author's style, intention, or source material. Only in the case of awkward repetition that breaks the continuity of thought and action would source division be indicated.

Another criterion that has often been used for source division is that of distinctive terminology, especially as it has to do with divine names and the like.⁴ However, this criterion may be helpful in the task of source *identification* but rarely in source division; that is, not for the purpose of separating the sources from one another but of grouping the various units belonging to a particular source, only after the separation. I am very skeptical about making a division between two verses or parts of verses within the same unit only on the basis of vocabulary, such as the alternation of the divine names Yahweh and Elohim.

A criterion that is quite helpful and necessary, on the other hand, is that of logical, dramatic or grammatical discontinuity and contradiction.⁵ Yet this principle is not entirely certain. It often depends upon the analyst's preconception of the unit's genre whether or not

---

2. Cf. Richter, ibid., pp. 53f.; idem, *Die sogenannten vorprophetischen Berufungsberichte* (Göttingen: Vandenhoeck & Ruprecht, 1970), pp. 58-72. Richter attempts to separate Exodus 3 into two fragmentary sources that were combined by a redactor. Since the results of such a separation will always be fragments this kind of source analysis remains very hypothetical and unconvincing. A different approach to the problem of an account that is the result of a conflation of two or more sources may be seen in my treatment of Num. 21:21-35, in "The Conquest of Sihon's Kingdom," *JBL* 91 (1972): 182-197.

3. Richter, *Exegese*, pp. 53-54. But he immediately cites examples in which repetition is a feature of style. Cf. idem, *Berufungsberichte*, pp. 59-62, in which he speaks of Exodus 3 as a conflation of doublets. His analysis here, and therefore his sole application in the Pentateuch, is very much in doubt.

4. Richter, *Exegese*, p. 56.

5. Richter, ibid., p. 59; Koch, *Biblical Tradition*, p. 70.

there is a logical or dramatic discontinuity within the passage. This means that prior to the source analysis of a particular unit there must be some decision about its *form* and *structure*. At this point I part company with many present-day literary critics who suggest that form criticism only comes *after* source criticism.[6] All too often the division of a unit has been carried through on the basis of defective source division criteria with the result that the form and structure of the passage is broken instead of elucidated. On the other hand, the analysis of the form and structure of a passage can be an effective control on source division. This is often the case even when narrative prose does not always yield a clearly defined genre or when there is a complex combination of genres or formulae. So each unit of tradition must be scrutinized from the viewpoint of internal consistency and continuity and with the use of form-critical and structural analysis[7] to arrive at an evaluation of its unity or division into primary and secondary sources.

We now turn to the most serious problem of literary criticism: how to account for the relationship of the sources to each other. The answer that has been given to this question for the last century or more is that the sources are independent of each other and united only by a subsequent editorial process. This position has virtually become dogma in that the opposite possibility of *dependence* of one source on another is never given any consideration. Thus the way in which one accounts for all similarity between sources is by appealing to the notion of a "common tradition" behind the sources. This solution to the problem of similarity is most insidious, in that it immediately stops all serious comparison between sources. Yet unless one can say something about this common tradition, its form and content, and the way in which the two versions depart from it one has said nothing at all.

6. Richter, *Exegese*, pp. 72ff. where he insists that literary criticism must precede form-criticism. In *Berufungsberichte*, pp. 72–127, he attempts a form-critical analysis of the two fragments, but it is certainly not evident how the source division has clarified the form. Koch, ibid., pp. 77–78, also suggests that literary criticism should precede form-criticism, largely for the reason that it did historically in the development of the discipline. Yet Koch also makes literary criticism just a branch of form-criticism.

7. Structural analysis as the search for an obvious literary pattern in a piece of literature may be highly useful. But there is a type of structural analysis by some anthropologists that attempts to impose a rather dubious interpretive scheme on Biblical narratives, as in the work of E. R. Leach and C. Levi-Strauss. For a review of this method see R. C. Culley, "Some Comments on Structural Analysis and Biblical Studies," *SVT* 22 (1972): 129–142.

Oral Tradition

It is generally assumed, at the present time, that this common tradition for the Abraham stories was oral in its origin and basic development. It is this supposed oral character of the tradition that is regarded as answering the most questions about the diversity of the tradition and the variant sources into which it finally developed. There is a large number of misconceptions about oral tradition used to support this view of a common oral Abraham tradition, and since we will encounter them in the subsequent literary discussion we might briefly consider them here.[8] One of these fallacies is that of a fixed oral prose tradition. Folklorists are generally agreed that the prose narrative forms are the least likely to be preserved in any fixed manner. On the contrary, they allow the greatest freedom, and the most widespread use of this freedom, for artistic creativity. This includes those genres generally classed as folk tales, but also those which would be considered myths, legends, and historical narratives.

Another misconception has to do with the tradents, or so-called "circles of traditionists." To the degree that various types of tradition had to be "fixed" and preserved in an illiterate society for the proper functioning of the state, for example the genealogy of the royal dynasty, this task of preservation was committed to special persons who maintained the memory of these traditions for public recital at the appropriate times. Yet each type of tradition that had to be preserved was the responsibility of a different group of tradents, and the degree of fixity as well as the mechanisms for such preservation varied somewhat from group to group.[9]

Furthermore, one can expect that a literate society in antiquity placed the same value on the same kind of traditions and for the same social purposes as the illiterate society. But the fundamental difference is that the mechanism of preservation is now changed. In such literate societies scribal traditions develop that commit to written documents, as a more reliable means of preservation,

---

8. See especially Vansina, *Oral Tradition*; Ruth Finnegan, *Oral Literature in Africa* (Oxford: Clarendon Press, 1970); R. C. Culley, "An Approach to the Problem of Oral Tradition," *VT* 13 (1963): 113–25.

9. See especially Vansina, ibid., for a study of this whole process. There is no analogy in any of these anthropological studies for a "circle of traditionists" who preserved all kinds of tradition and lore of the past: poetry and prose, songs and stories, lists and laws, and all in a highly complex combination such as now exists in the Pentateuch. This is the view of Engnell (*A Rigid Scrutiny*, pp. 58ff.) and of E. Nielsen, *Oral Tradition* SBT 11 (Chicago: Allenson, 1954), but it is largely the product of Engnell's imagination.

materials to be handed on to posterity.[10] This does not mean that in such societies all oral tradition or folklore came to an end. But it does mean that where a particular "tradition" had to be preserved for the benefit of the state it was soon committed to writing. Yet it would be wrong to suppose that all local traditions immediately became national in character with the rise of the monarchy or with the creation of a hypothetical amphictyonic league prior to that time. The "all-Israel" orientation given to early tribal or local traditions cannot be dated in any easy way. They could have become "fixed" in writing at various times during the history of the monarchy, and there is certainly more than one explanation of an impulse to do so.[11]

At this point we are faced with the debatable subject of the classification of prose narrative genre such as might lie behind the stories of Genesis. Yet it is sufficient to note that at the present time folklorists are inclined to see the genres of myth, legend, and historical narratives as not *functionally* distinct in that they all seem to serve as "community-making" tradition and are therefore sacred.[12] The only difference among them seems to be the degree of remoteness from the time of the narrator, which a tradition seems to assume. Furthermore, in *form* they may be no different from popular folktales except that the former categories are taken more seriously. There is no warrant for the notion that the origin of folktale and legend is necessarily distinct; that is, that the former is based on imaginative fantasy while the latter rests on a chain of tradition that always goes back to a historical kernel. Myths and legends may very well be the products of creative narrators such that the amount of received tradition is of little significance in the work as a whole. Even though oral tradition might deal with historical subjects and might be taken quite seriously by the society in which it exists, this is no warrant for believing that such traditions contain very much actual historical material. The degree of reliability of oral prose traditions diminishes in a rather brief period of time.[13]

The Abraham tradition is generally classified as legend (*Sage*),

---

10. See A. Leo Oppenheim, *Ancient Mesopotamia* (Chicago and London: University of Chicago Press, 1964), pp. 7–30, for a discussion of the scribal traditions of Mesopotamia.
11. Cf. Noth, *Pentateuchal Traditions*, pp. 42–45.
12. See most recently Finnegan, *Oral Literature*, pp. 361–372.
13. Finnegan, ibid., p. 372. See also R. C. Culley, "Oral Tradition and Historicity," in *Studies on the Ancient Palestinian World*, ed. J. W. Wevers and D. B. Redford (Toronto: University of Toronto Press, 1972), pp. 102–116, for a survey of the problem and literature.

but this descriptive term says nothing about its period of origin or the degree to which the present literary form derives from oral tradition. Gunkel, in his Genesis commentary, listed some criteria which would point to an oral source of the literature and made reference to Olrik's "epic laws" as a support for his views.[14] Recently these epic laws have come into use again, and since we will also use them in our own literary analysis it may be helpful to enumerate them briefly:

1) The stability of the introduction and conclusion. By the use of typical formulae the setting is clearly given. In prose there is also a tendency to avoid an abrupt conclusion by an extension through an etiological connection to a place name or the like.
2) Repetition. This is used to fill out the action in a story and to move it forward towards the climax.
3) The number three. This is the highest number of persons with which storytellers usually work. There is also a love for threefold repetition of events.
4) Scenic duality. Only two people ever share a scene in any active role. Others in the story, if they are present, remain completely neutral. In such scenes there is often a love of contrast or polarity between the principles.
5) Law of the twin. Two persons of the same rank and status are often treated as one.
6) Singleness of direction that does not drop back to make up for missing, prerequisite data. Oral prose uses a very clear structural schematization.
7) Concrete details of the main scene. Few details are given that are not essential and clear to the form of the whole story.
8) Logic. The story may be presented according to natural or supernatural perspective, but the logic of either form is consistently maintained.
9) Consistency of treatment. Olrik stresses that where there is a quite new treatment of a theme, this is the surest sign of literary reworking.

---

14. A. Olrik, "Epische Gezetze der Volksdichtung," *Zeitschrift für deutsches Altertum* 51 (1909): 1–12. See also a later discussion of these laws by K. Krohn in *Folklore Methodology*, trans. R. L. Welsch (Austin and London: University of Texas Press, 1971), chap. 13.

10) Focal concentration on the principal person. Olrik calls this the highest law of oral tradition.

The significance of these laws or principles will become clearer when we discuss their application in specific instances in the Abraham tradition.

It needs to be pointed out that even if an application of Olrik's epic laws does reveal some indications of oral folklore behind some parts of the tradition this does not mean that the tradition as a whole, or even these parts of it, derive from a pre-literate period. The narrators of the written tradition, whenever they lived, had access to large amounts of folklore, which they could have used in various ways without any of it being of a very primitive character. The application of Olrik's laws may be useful in understanding the sources of a narrator and his mode of composition without saying very much about the history of the tradition.

Types of Variants

We may now turn from this digression on the subject of oral tradition back to the problem of how to evaluate the relationship of the sources to each other, and particularly the problem of variants. How are we to account for more than one version of the same story in the present body of the tradition? The first step in a solution to this problem, it seems to me, is to make a careful distinction between the different types of possible variants. The term "variant" is most at home in the field of textual criticism and has to do with the establishment of the best text out of a number of parallel manuscripts that contain various scribal errors, deviations, pluses, etc. We may speak of these variants as *transmission variants*. The scribe responsible for the parallel text intended to pass on a faithful copy of a *fixed* text, but not to present it as his own. The variants that result from such a transmission process follow certain patterns that have been frequently discussed by text critics.[15] The degree of variation will depend upon the "canonicity" of the text and the care and competence of the copyists.

Transmission variants may also be present in oral tradition if the latter consist of fixed traditions that must be carefully handed down

---

15. E. Würthwein, *The Text of the Old Testament* (New York: Macmillan, 1957), pp. 71–75.

by means of memorization and a carefully controlled chain of testimonies. The differences between oral and written transmission variants are not necessarily of degree but of kind, directly related to the type or genre of tradition and the medium of transmission. There is also an important difference in the mechanism of preservation. For the illiterate society the cumbersome manner of transmitting the tradition means that it will only maintain a tradition as long as it remains functional to the society, whereas the "scribal tradition" can preserve a greater quantity that may be much less actively used.

Besides transmission variants, whether written or oral, there is another category of variants, which we may call *composition variants*. These have to do with similar material occurring in different works by different authors. A writer, for instance, may borrow from one or more sources in order to create his own work. The degree of similarity will vary but, generally speaking, the difference between composition variants will be greater than between transmission variants. Composition variants may appear in a wide range of literary types and over a considerable period of time. Some examples in prose narrative may be found in Assyrian and Babylonian royal inscriptions,[16] the Synoptic Gospels of the New Testament, early Arabic literature,[17] and Icelandic sagas. In all these cases the presence of composition variants means the dependence of one literary work on another. Clarification of this dependence is most important for any literary and historical appreciation of these works.

Time does not permit any detailed treatment of these literatures, but a few guidelines on the relationship of variants to literary dependence might be useful to our discussion. 1) The account with the simplest form and structure will most likely be the earliest one. The tendency in written composition is toward form-critical complexity resulting from the incorporation of heterogeneous material into an earlier account.[18] 2) The second version often shortens or summarizes the material that it borrows from the first one, although by

---

16. W. de Filippi, "The Royal Inscriptions of Assurnasir-apli II," (Phil.M. thesis, University of Toronto, 1972); L. D. Levine, "The Second Campaign of Sennacherib," *JNES* 32 (1973): 312–17.

17. G. Widengren, "Oral Tradition and Written Literature among the Hebrews in the Light of Arabic Evidence, with Special Regard to Prose Narratives," *Acta Orientalia* 23 (1959): 201–262.

18. See Widengren, "Oral Tradition," pp. 234ff.; Sveinsson, *Njals Saga: A Literary Masterpiece*, pp. 12ff. So also the Synoptic Gospels.

METHOD II: SOME GUIDELINES

adding new material of its own it may result in a longer story.[19]
3) Occasionally, in a later version there occurs a "blind motif;" that is, some unexplained action or detail that assumes consciously or unconsciously that the earlier account is known. Where such cases exist this is a clear indication of literary dependence and the direction of borrowing.[20] 4) The strongest evidence for literary dependence is verbal similarity. This, of course, does not include popular sayings or common expressions used generally in narrative. But verbal similarity related to the distinctive content of the story, especially in prose composition variants, is evidence of direct literary borrowing.[21]

There are also composition variants in free oral tradition, but they differ from those in written literature because the modes of composition are quite different.[22] Variation in oral composition means that basically the same theme or plot is used in more than one tale or song by either the same, or a different, singer or storyteller. Unlike written composition the question of sources and dependence is not very significant for free oral composition. The following points of comparison may be noted between oral and written composition variants:

> 1) Oral variants will usually be in the same genre but differ in the non-typical detail. A theme may go from one genre to another; that is, from a song to a tale, but a combination of genres is a literary phenomenon.
>
> 2) Oral variants do not summarize, and any new material is added in the same genre since the tradent usually masters only one form.
>
> 3) Oral tradition does not assume knowledge of various aspects of the story, so the "blind motif" does not exist. If an important aspect has been lost from lapse of memory the storyteller will have to supply it with something new.

---

19. See Sveinsson, *Njals Saga*, p. 23; idem, *Dating the Icelandic Sagas* (London: University College, Viking Society, 1958), pp. 80–83. This also holds for Matthew and Luke's relationship to Mark.
20. See esp. Sveinsson, *Njals Saga*, p. 20; idem, *Dating the Sagas*, pp. 78–79.
21. See Sveinsson, *Dating the Sagas*, pp. 79–80. This, of course, is basic to Synoptic criticism.
22. See A. B. Lord, *The Singer of Tales* (Cambridge: Harvard University Press, 1964), esp. pp. 124–138.

Consequently, there are four basic types of variants: written and oral transmission variants, and written and oral composition variants. These reflect four quite distinct situations so it should be possible, theoretically, to identify any variant as one of these four types. Scholars have often begun their study of the Abraham tradition with the assumption that there is a long history of oral transmission behind these narratives, thereby immediately limiting their choice to one possibility, that of oral transmission variants. But one must first evaluate the variants to see to which type they belong and only then face the problem of the history of the tradition.

In a literate society such as Israel the scribal tradition would not be dependent any longer upon an oral mechanism for the preservation and transmission of a fixed tradition. It may, of course, augment an earlier tradition by drawing upon either an open oral tradition or its own creative literary activity. But it is difficult for me to accept the idea, suggested by the current view of literary criticism, that through the whole course of Israel's history from the United Monarchy to the Post-exilic period the various literary sources of the Pentateuch were all dependent upon a body of fixed oral tradition but quite independent of each other. On the contrary, it is much more reasonable to assume that each successive stage of the literary development had access to the previous scribal tradition. The variation between the sources is not the result of the process of oral *transmission*. Nor could the doublets in the Abraham story be viewed as the result of errors in scribal transmission.[23] This means that in actual fact the choice is only between oral and written *composition* variants. If the doublets in the Abraham tradition are written composition variants then the sources are dependent upon one another, but if they are the result of using free oral composition variants then the written sources are independent of each other.

The Method of Procedure

The procedure suggested by the above discussion will be as follows. We shall begin with an examination of the doublets in order to make a fresh evaluation of the tradition's sources and their relationship to each other. The first set of doublets to be dealt with are the stories about the threat to the forefather's beautiful wife (Gen. 12:10–20;

---

[23]. Thus, the whole notion of a fixed *Grundlage*, whether oral or written, out of which the variants are said to have arisen must be completely rejected.

20; 26:1–11). In close connection with these are the episodes having to do with the covenant between Abraham/Isaac and Abimelech of Gerar (Gen. 21:22–34; 26:12–33). The second set of doublets to be considered are the stories of Hagar's flight (Genesis 16) and the expulsion of Hagar and her son (Gen. 21:8–21). This last story cannot be properly analyzed without also including the story of the promise and birth of Isaac (Gen. 18:1–15; 21:1–7). These doublets provide the basic clue to the nature of the tradition's development, whether it was by direct dependence of a later source upon an earlier one in which the tradition grew by direct supplementation, or whether it was by the common use of a much freer form and body of oral tradition by various independent sources.

In the case of each particular narrative unit and as part of the method of comparison of doublets, some form-critical and structural analysis will be attempted to determine the unity and limits of a piece and to evaluate to what extent oral tradition may lie behind any part of the tradition and what role it played in the formation of the whole. Here the use of Olrik's epic laws will serve as a valuable aid in such an evaluation. Likewise form-criticism and structural analysis will serve as a control over the division of the tradition into sources and will give some indication of the use of genres from the distinctly literary sphere of the writers themselves. Some stories may have features akin to oral tradition genres while others betray the features of literary composition variants. From a comparison of the doublets, then, it will be possible to formulate the basic characteristics of the tradition's development and its various sources, and to assign the remaining parts of the tradition to the appropriate source stratum.

There are two groups of stories which do not have doublets, but which have many similarities in form and vital points of contact with the other stories, and it is therefore best to consider these next. The first group is the Lot-Sodom story (Gen. 13:1–13; 18:16 to 19:38) which is tied to the initial itinerary and, at the end, to the story of Isaac's promised birth. The second group follows on Isaac's birth and childhood and includes the near-sacrifice of Isaac (Genesis 22) and the finding of a wife for him (Genesis 24), in all of which Isaac plays a very passive role. These two episodes are connected to each other by a genealogical bridge (Genesis 22:20–24). Our interest in these stories will focus on the question of evidence for oral tradition and on their relationship to the literary sources. Some observations will also be made on the themes that these passages suggest.

Quite different in form and character from all the preceding stories of Abraham mentioned thus far is the chapter on the promises to Abraham of progeny and land (Genesis 15). This chapter represents the center and focus of the whole thematic framework that encloses and permeates the literary corpus of stories discussed to this point. The problems of form, unity, and source identification of Genesis 15 will first be dealt with. But at this point in the study the very nature of this unit demands that primary attention be given to the question of the historical context of the development and use of the Abraham tradition by this literary source. Included in this must be a consideration of the whole thematic framework of the patriarchal promises and of how they relate to the use of the Abraham tradition in the rest of the Old Testament.

The covenant of circumcision in Genesis 17 should be considered next because it actually represents a doublet or variant to chap. 15, as well as to some other references in the other stories. It has long been recognized as an important theological statement by the priestly writer, and it affords an excellent opportunity to examine the literary and ideological relationship of P to the other literary corpus. Quite a different form is that of the story of Sarah's burial, Genesis 23, but it is still generally regarded as the work of the priestly writer, and so it will also be considered here. The story of Abraham's war against the eastern kings, Genesis 14, is certainly the most problematic and very likely the last addition to the Abraham tradition.

These, then, are the principles and the plan to be carried out in the following chapters for clarifying the development of the tradition in its present literary form in Genesis.

CHAPTER 8

The Problem of the Beautiful Wife

I want to begin the discussion of variants in the Abraham tradition by quoting a remark about doublets from Gunkel:

> Let the investigator make his first observations on these twice-told tales; when he has thus acquired the keen eye and found certain lines of development, then let him compare also the legends which are told but once.[1]

What is both surprising and disheartening to me is the almost total neglect of this principle by scholars who claim to follow in the footsteps of Gunkel. It invariably happens now that presuppositions from literary criticism and tradition-history are imposed on these stories so that the eye is seriously dimmed from the outset. In order to acquire the keen eye again all the literary possibilities must be kept open at the beginning.

The Form:

The first question that confronts us in the three stories of Gen. 12:10–20; 20; 26:1–11, is the problem of form.[2] These stories are generally recognized as three variants of a folktale, but there is no clear agreement about which of the three represents the oldest form of the story. Gunkel argued, against some of the older critics, that the account in 12:10–20 was the oldest.[3] This judgment was based on the enumeration of general folkloristic characteristics that seemed to him most prominent in this account but much weaker in the others. He even suggested that it was not original with the patriarch at all but a type of popular story that was secondarily applied to him.

---

1. Gunkel, *Legends of Genesis*, p. 100.
2. See the studies of C. A. Keller, "Die Gefährdung der Ahnfrau," *ZAW* 66 (1954): 181–91; Kilian, *Abrahamsüberlieferungen*, pp. 210–19; Koch, *Growth of the Biblical Tradition*, pp. 111–132; cf. now G. Schmitt, "Zu Gen 26:1–14," *ZAW* 85 (1973): 143–56.
3. Gunkel, *Genesis*, pp. 225–26; see also Skinner, *Genesis*, p. 365.

Noth, on the other hand, came at the problem from an entirely different perspective and concluded that the account in 26:1-11 was primary.[4] This judgment was not based on form-critical considerations and contains no critique of Gunkel's arguments. It rests entirely on his broader theory of tradition-history in which he regarded all the traditions connected with Beersheba and the south as originally belonging to Isaac and only secondarily transferred to Abraham. The only "form-critical" statement about 26:1-11 is that it appears in a "profane" form. This statement is made in spite of the theophany to Isaac, part of which at least is regarded as original. The fact that the divine intervention does not occur within the story itself does not make it closer to folklore since quite the opposite is generally true. There is in Noth's treatment no form-critical analysis at all, and yet this is now the position most often repeated on this matter.[5]

On the matter of form Gunkel admitted that the story in Gen. 12:10-20 was not of the etiological type, but instead it had a certain "novellistischen" origin.[6] Its function was to celebrate the cleverness of the patriarch, the beauty and submission of his wife, and the faithful help of Yahweh. These general remarks are enough to give us a clue to a large body of folk literature which has as one of its themes the cleverness or foolishness of a man who has a beautiful wife who is either faithful and submissive or unfaithful. A story is then told of a situation that is meant to illustrate these characteristics. The primary motivation for such stories was clearly entertainment.[7]

Their structure is relatively simple and straightforward and would consist of the following elements:

a) a situation of need, problem, or crisis
b) a plan to deal with the problem (wise or foolish)
c) the execution of the plan with some complication
d) an unexpected outside intervention
e) fortunate or unfortunate consequences

4. Noth, *Pentateuchal Traditions*, pp. 102-09.
5. See von Rad, *Genesis*, p. 266; Koch, *Biblical Traditions*, pp. 125-26; Kilian, *Abrahamsüberlieferungen*, pp. 213-15.
6. Gunkel, *Genesis*, p. 173.
7. Examples of such stories may be found in Hans Schmidt and Paul Kahle, *Volkserzählungen aus Palestina*, 2 vols. (Göttingen: Vandenhoeck, 1918 and 1930). See esp. "Die verkleidete Frau," 1:45-53, no. 24.

Such a story is a self-contained unit and fulfills the basic structural requirements of Olrik's laws. It runs a single course of action with a balance between the various parts. This structure, of course, is much broader than the motif of the "beautiful wife" and forms the basis of a great variety of story themes although it is not necessarily the only pattern for folktales. Yet it is a genre of folk literature that can be tested against examples both within the body of folk literature generally and in the Genesis stories in particular.

In Genesis 12:10–20 this same structure appears. There is a crisis (a) in that the famine in Canaan (v. 10) has forced Abraham and Sarah to travel temporarily to a foreign and potentially hostile region, Egypt. Because Sarah is very beautiful such a situation could endanger the life of her husband, Abraham. So the patriarch devises a plan (b) that they act as brother and sister. This means that Abraham, as her guardian, will be well-treated for her sake. It may also suggest that Abraham could forestall any suitors for the duration of the famine. The plan is put into effect (c) and is successful as far as Abraham's life is concerned, but with a complication. Sarah is taken into the royal harem. There is, however, an unexpected intervention by God (d) who plagues Pharaoh, and thereby the inadvertent act of adultery is disclosed. Yet since Pharaoh is as threatened by the circumstances as is Abraham, the danger to the patriarch is neutralized and Pharaoh merely expels the man and his wife from the land (e). In the end Abraham is greatly enriched by the whole turn of events.

This structure of the story is likewise interesting from the standpoint of its balance of the various elements. The setting, which reveals the problem, is given in v. 10. The plan is set forth in vv. 11–13 and its execution and complication in vv. 14–16. The divine intervention and consequences are given in vv. 17–20. This fine balance of the various parts is certainly not an ad hoc invention but part of the whole art of storytelling, in which each element receives its due for the enjoyment of the whole. This is the first principle of Olrik's epic laws.

Likewise, all the other laws that were enumerated in the previous chapter fit this presentation very well. Repetition is seen in the correspondence between the plan and its execution. There is singleness of direction without the need to return to any previous point in the story. There is a clear situation as a point of departure and an appropriate summing up at the end. The actions and reactions of all the story participants are lucid and logical. The principle of scenic duality first with Abraham and Sarah and then with Abraham and Pharaoh is consistently maintained. Yet the story also has three main persons, with Sarah remaining in a completely passive role, though vital to the whole. The concentration of the story remains on Abraham throughout, focusing on his actions and his fate. A finer example could scarcely be found to illustrate Olrik's epic laws.

Furthermore, the story is a self-contained unit. There is nothing in it that ties it to anything previous, and there is nothing that follows as a sequel. It is in every way complete.[8] In fact, it has often been noted that Lot, who appears previously (v. 4–5) and in the episode that follows (13:1ff.), has no place in this story at all. It is also generally agreed that 12:9 and 13:1–2 are secondary bridge-passages to bind the story into its present context.[9] But this literary tension between the story and its context can mean different things to different people. Gunkel, for instance, took it to be an indication of a different literary source and thus characterized it as J^b.[10] Its inclusion into the present context is the work of a redactor, R^j. This literary tension, however, does not indicate a separate "source" for Noth but simply a story from "the circle of the older Abraham narratives set in the Negeb," which J as a redactor fitted into his present collection.[11] Yet Noth never faced the question on the literary level of how both 12:10–20 and 26:1–11, two variants as he admits, could exist in the same source, especially on the basis of his own avowed principle of doublets indicating separate sources. If J as redactor could combine these two variants there is scarcely any need for a separate source for E in chap. 20. One need only speak of another "tradition." The matter can only be clarified by a comparison of the variants.

We may summarize our observations on 12:10–20 (story A) by stating that it corresponds rather closely to a folktale model. It contains an obvious narrative structure and other compositional characteristics well suited to popular storytelling. There is very little adaptation of the story to the Abraham tradition as a whole,

---

8. See Koch, *Biblical Traditions*, pp. 115–17.
9. Skinner, *Genesis*, p. 251; von Rad, *Genesis*, pp. 162–63.
10. *Genesis*, pp. 168ff.; see also Skinner, *Genesis*, p. 251.
11. *Pentateuchal Traditions*, p. 233; similarly Kilian, *Abrahamsüberlieferungen*, pp. 215–19.

either in terms of its internal content or in terms of its connections with its present literary context.[12]

Let us now compare the folktale model outlined above with Genesis 20 (story B). When we do so certain incongruities become apparent immediately. First of all there is no famine in the land, so there is no problem situation that can serve as an effective point of departure for the story. Why does Abraham need to go near Gerar? One could, of course, conjecture that the final redactor omitted the reason, as various commentators are inclined to do, but this approach is highly prejudicial to objective literary analysis.[13] As the text stands there is nothing in the situation to suggest any threat whatever to the patriarch. The next two elements in our model, the plan (b) and its execution (c), which made up at least half of story A are here diminished to half a verse, v. 2a. Furthermore, the remark by Abraham "She is my sister," is completely inexplicable in its present context and is not explained until much later, vv. 11ff. Such a resumptive or proleptic style is a feature of literary style, as Gunkel recognized,[14] but according to Olrik's laws it is not a feature of oral storytelling. It is also not clear why the king should suddenly have taken Sarah as his wife. There is scarcely any preparation for such an abrupt action. Considering the length of this account, which is almost double that of the previous one, the economy of detail expressed in v. 2 is far too great if this is an independent account of the same story.[15] The only way in which the cryptic character of v. 2 can be explained is that the other story is known and can be assumed, and therefore Abraham's plan and its execution need not be recounted again in full. The two essential features of the earlier story —that Sarah is called Abraham's sister, and that she becomes the wife of the king—are enough to recall the general situation described more fully earlier.

The remarks of Abraham later in the story also make it quite clear

---

12. Cf. Kilian, *Abrahamsüberlieferungen*, pp. 6–8. The attempt to find redactional additions in vv. 13 and 16 is without any clear warrant.
13. Ibid., p. 190. Koch, *Biblical Traditions*, p. 117.
14. Gunkel, *Genesis*, p. 221, compares the use of this literary style to the Book of Jonah, in which Jonah's actions at the beginning of the story are not explained until the latter part of it.
15. Kilian's statement (*Abrahamsüberlieferungen*, p. 190) "doch fehlt nichts Wesentliches oder gar Notwendiges" indicates literary insensitivity at this point.

that the narrator has the earlier episode in mind. He states, v. 13:

> When God caused me to wander from my father's house, I said to her, "This is the favor which you must do for me: at every place to which we come, say of me, 'He is my brother.'"[16]

The statement "at every place to which we come" is meant to suggest that this is not an isolated incident but rather a general practice, which then could include the earlier situation of their trip to Egypt. It is clearly a modification of Abraham's plan in story A, which was meant for that specific crisis. The narrator of this episode, however, had to account for the fact that it happened again at Gerar.[17] Furthermore, the statement "When God caused me to wander from my father's house" also takes us back to Chap. 12, in this case to the literary context in which the first episode is set. It suggests that the narrator knew the previous story, not just as an isolated tale but in a particular framework that included at least 12:1.

The introduction to story B, likewise, points to the fact that this is not simply an isolated variant of story A. The story is very much tied into an itinerary of Abraham suggested in v. 13 as well. It cannot here be regarded as a redactional addition, for v. 1 provides the only setting and introduction for the story. It is true that in the present state of the text it is not entirely clear to what the phrase "from there" (*miššām*) refers. But this is additional reason for not regarding it as simply redactional. The continuation of the story at the conclusion of the episode has also been obscured by the passage 21:1–21, which is out of place in the present text. Consequently the events in 21:22–34 followed directly on 20:17(18), and these have to do with subsequent relationships between Abraham and Abimelech. As I hope to show below, a whole new episode has been appended to the original story.[18]

When these features are judged by the law of fixed beginning and ending it becomes clear that we do not have an oral story variant. Similarly, all the other "laws" that work so well for story A break

---

16. The text in MT has an initial plural verb that would suggest a plural subject, "gods." But the Samaritan text and the versions give support for a singular verb, and the translations generally have followed this meaning.
17. How could the original form of chap. 20 have included a reference to famine in the light of this verse? Cf. Koch, *Biblical Traditions*, p. 124.
18. See Mowinckel, *Pentateuch Quellenfrage*, p. 101. Cf. Koch, *Biblical Traditions*, pp. 117–
18. He does not see any connections with the subsequent episode.

down in almost every case in story B. What is involved in this instance is a deliberate literary recasting of the story for quite different purposes. The pleasure of telling a good tale is nowhere evident in this account.

These clues strongly suggest that story B, generally ascribed to E, is not an independent version of the previous account in story A. On the contrary, it is another version of the same theme, which has the older account very much in mind and which seeks to answer certain important theological and moral issues that the narrator felt were inadequately treated in the earlier account.[19] These issues that were raised by the latter part of the earlier story occupy virtually the whole account here. They have to do with God's relationship to the innocent king, vv. 3–7, Abraham's reply to the king's accusation, vv. 8–13, and the subsequent relationship of the king to Abraham, vv. 14–17(18).[20] In contrast to the use of monologue in the earlier account, here there is the effective use of dialogue to clarify the issues with which the narrator wishes to deal. This is a much more sophisticated literary technique and quite a departure from the original concern of the folktale.[21]

The first set of questions raised by 12:17 (story A) is why God should have punished Pharaoh, who did not know that Sarah was Abraham's wife, and how it was that the king knew that Sarah was the cause of divine displeasure.[22] Ch. 20:3–7 answers these questions by suggesting that God appeared to the king in a dream and accused him of his fault, and when the king protested his innocence God provided a way by which the consequences of his action could be averted. It is important to note that in this dialogue there is a form taken from the cult—the complaint of the falsely accused.[23] The

---

19. P. Volz, *Der Elohist als Erzähler*, pp. 34–36; cf. Noth, *Pentateuchal Traditions*, p. 22; Mowinckel, *Pentateuch Quellenfrage*, p. 100.
20. Whether v. 18 belongs to the rest of the story in its original form is questionable. Besides the change in the divine name to Yahweh there is the lack of consistency with v. 17, which has in mind a disease affecting Abimelech as well.
21. Gunkel, *Legends*, p. 84.
22. Koch's remark (*Biblical Traditions*, p. 123) that this element of the story has been lost from story A is unacceptable. Such an inclusion would have destroyed the focal concentration on Abraham and was quite unnecessary for the comic perspective of the story. The frequent suggestion by Koch and others that parts of the original versions have been lost is a questionable methodological approach to tradition-history.
23. See S. Mowinckel, *The Psalms in Israel's Worship*, trans. D. R. Ap-Thomas, 2 vols. (Oxford: Blackwell, 1962), 2:1–25; cf. Koch, *Biblical Traditions*, p. 123.

king is accused of adultery with the possible penalty of death. He makes a confession that he is innocent (*ṣaddîq*) and invokes the liturgically important phrase: "With a clear conscience and clean hands (*betām lebābî ûbeniqyōn kappay*) I have done this." He is told that Abraham is a prophet and as such is able to pray on his behalf so that he will live. This whole episode is no longer dealt with by popular storytelling motifs but on the basis of Israel's cultic experiences. It is a serious theological lesson with which the author is concerned.[24]

The author is also troubled by two other features in the earlier story, that of the plague that God brought upon Pharaoh's household, which would suggest unjustified punishment, and that of Sarah's moral position. The author of the second story specifically states that God prevented the king from touching (ng^c) her (v. 6), and the means by which he did so was the disease. This is vaguely suggested in v. 7 in the reference to Abraham praying for Abimelech, but it is not specifically stated until v. 17, which states that as a result of Abraham's prayer God healed Abimelech and his household. This is another clear instance in which the author has to assume the knowledge of story A.

One also notes that in story B the focal concentration on Abraham has changed to that of Abimelech, so he is certainly the main figure in the story even though he is not appropriately introduced as such. In fact, the focus has become confused because the author's intention is not on the storytelling level. This is certainly a long way from any oral base.

The second set of issues has to do with Abraham's apparent lie and his reply to the king's accusations. In story A Abraham makes no reply to Pharaoh's charges, which would certainly be interpreted as an admission of guilt. But here he justifies himself by stating that she was in fact his half sister, whom he married. Many have pointed out that this custom is strictly forbidden in a number of laws, but D. Daube's study of these suggests that injunctions against marrying a half sister are rather late additions to the codes and, in fact, Ezek. 22:11 may be the earliest statement against this practice.[25]

---

24. On this see Keller, *ZAW* 66:188–89; cf. Koch, *Biblical Traditions*, p. 122. I cannot agree with Koch's criticism of Keller on this point.
25. D. Daube, *Studies in Biblical Law* (Cambridge: Cambridge University Press, 1947), pp. 78–82.

Abraham also defends himself by suggesting a religious motif that is lacking in story A: "I did it because I thought, there is no fear of God here. ..." The story up to this point has, of course, given no reason for such a view. To the contrary, the king and his servants do fear God greatly, as seen in v. 8. On the other hand, if 21:25ff. goes with this passage there was some justification for Abraham's apprehension. But from the storytelling viewpoint this is certainly out of place.

Finally, there are some questions that deal with Abraham's relationship to the king subsequent to the disclosure. In story A Abraham received all his wealth *before* the disclosure and as a direct result of Sarah's being a member of Pharaoh's harem. Such acquisitions, the result of his lying about his wife, may be viewed as morally questionable. But in chap. 20:14 Abraham receives all these goods as gifts *after* the disclosure of Sarah as his wife. Abraham is not expelled, as in story A, but is allowed to live wherever he pleases—an acknowledgment of his just position. In fact, it is the king who seeks vindication from Abraham at a very high price (a thousand shekels of silver), as if the king were the guilty one and not Abraham. And only after such restitution does Abraham pray for the king and his family, who are then healed as a sign of divine forgiveness. Consequently, the whole relationship between Abraham and the king is reversed from that of story A in order to give great moral stature to the patriarch.

It seems to me that one can only conclude from these observations that story B is not simply a variant tradition that has slowly evolved somewhat differently from that of story A. It bears no marks of such an oral tradition, either in its basic structure or in its manner of telling. At every point where there is a difference between story A and story B, the latter has given up the folktale point of interest for moral and theological concerns. Finally, story B exhibits a number of "blind motifs," foreshortening, and backward allusions that can only be accounted for by viewing it as directly dependent upon story A.

When the parallel episode in 26:1–11 (story C) is brought into the discussion, it raises the rather complex problem of its relationship to both of the other accounts. This problem suggests a considerable variety of theoretical possibilities, but all of these need not be debated since this would make the present investigation rather tedious. Therefore, I shall endeavor to defend the thesis that the account in chap. 26:1–11 is the latest version and is directly dependent upon the other two.

As I indicated above, there is an initial problem as to whether story A and story C were from the same source, J. On purely literary grounds Gunkel is certainly correct in holding that story A stands so clearly apart from its Yahwistic context and is so entirely different in style and presentation from the variant in story C that it is hard to see them as belonging to the same source.[26] For those like Noth and Koch,[27] however, who hold to the unity of the Yahwistic source, J simply becomes a redactor of variant oral traditions, in this case an already existent collection of old stories about Isaac, which had to be incorporated into his work as a block. The question is not whether or not there are two separate sources but at what level they were separate. Did they belong to two separate literary sources as Gunkel suggested, or were they only of separate origin at the level of oral tradition, as Noth suggests? Noth's position against Gunkel would only be tenable if one could show that story C was at least as close to oral tradition as that of story A.

If we apply the form-critical criteria of the folktale model and the "epic laws" to story C it becomes clear that we are not dealing with an independent folktale in the latter instance. If v. 1, or a part of it, states the situation, there is a long interruption, vv. 2–5, which presents a theophany completely negating any sense of crisis created by v. 1. And only in v. 7 do we have a rather weakened allusion to the "plan" and its execution. But the subsequent events hardly make the plan necessary, and Isaac is made to look completely foolish. The story does not have a fixed conclusion, since v. 11 does not resolve the question of what happened to Isaac and Rebekah but continues on in vv. 12ff. Nor are the epic laws very well observed, for there is considerable lack of clarity and focal concentration, and one's feeling about the hero is certainly ambivalent. In comparison with story A, story C does not appear to be close to an oral source at all; consequently Noth's position must be abandoned.[28] Gunkel seems entirely justified in seeing a separate Yahwistic source in story C.

26. Gunkel, p. 299.
27. Noth, *Pentateuchal Traditions*, pp. 114ff.; Koch, *Biblical Traditions*, p. 131.
28. Cf. Koch, *Biblical Traditions*, pp. 122–27. Koch's general discussion seems to me to contradict his final conclusion.

Even though I agree with those who would make story C part of a different source from story A, they have not shown that it is independent in its origin. This has simply been taken for granted on the basis of the old documentary hypothesis. But just as story B was a literary revision of story A, story C is a further revision of both stories A and B. Let us test this theory by a more detailed examination of the text.

Story C begins:

> There was a famine in the land (in addition to the previous famine which occurred in the time of Abraham) so Isaac went to Abimelech, king of the Philistines at Gerar.

This verse alone clearly indicates that the writer knows both accounts in stories A and B and has tried to combine elements from both of them, but he does so in a rather awkward fashion.[29] For instance, he refers to a famine in the land and specifically mentions the previous episode in story A. Most commentators overcome this problem by invoking a redactor for the phrase "in addition to the previous famine which occurred in the time of Abraham." But this solves nothing, for Abraham's response to a famine was to go to Egypt, which would be unaffected by lack of rainfall in Palestine. But Isaac goes instead to Gerar which is "in the land" and would be no help at all.[30] The detail of the sojourn in Gerar, however, is taken from story B, in which there was no mention of famine or of any need for such a motive. Isaac is prevented from going down to Egypt by divine command, v. 2, but no reason is given for this.

Isaac is also described as going "to Abimelech, king of the Philistines." Are we to imagine that this is a state visit by a group of nomads at a time when the food supply is scarce? Such a notion hardly fits the rest of the story. The only reason Abimelech is immediately introduced in this awkward way is to remind the reader of story B, which is already known. The reference to Abimelech is a literary device and no more, so the incongruity of referring to the same king for the two patriarchs is not considered. This one verse is enough to establish the perspective of the writer for the whole story. He has no interest whatever in the folktale but only in

---

29. Cf. Kilian, *Abrahamsüberlieferungen*, pp. 202–09.
30. Cf. Koch, *Biblical Traditions*, p. 116. He is aware of the appropriateness of going to Egypt in the first story but fails to see that a visit to Gerar would be no help in story C.

the use of previous narrative elements to construct a history of Isaac.

There is one further detail that must be noted in this story's prologue, and that is the identification of Abimelech as "king of the Philistines." This should not be interpreted as a casual historical comment, but as an important ideological statement.[31] An altogether different view of this foreign realm is introduced into the story. The difference is not, as frequently suggested, that the Yahwist regards Abimelech as Philistine while the Elohist thinks of him as Canaanite or Amorite, since rhetorically speaking all these designations mean the same thing in the Old Testament, and they are clearly all negative.[32] They all mean an irreligious person or people, and this is not stated in story B where the king and his people are clearly God-fearing. The addition of the designation Philistine in story C means that an altogether different view of the patriarch's relationship to the king and his people is thereby suggested.[33]

Since vv. 2–5 are usually considered as largely redactional additions we shall return to this section at the end. Verse 6 simply takes up where v. 1 left off and adds nothing new. The action of the story resumes in v. 7, which states:

> When the men of the place asked him about his wife, he said, "She is my sister;" for he was afraid to say, "[She is] my wife," [thinking to himself], "lest the men of the place should kill me because of Rebekah;" because she was beautiful.

Here again is a case of conflation of the two previous stories. The first statement, v. 7a, is modeled on the statement in 20:2 "Abraham said about Sarah, his wife, "She is my sister." The verbal affinities are very close and quite obvious. The next statement, v. 7b, has its closest parallel in 20:10–11: "What were you afraid of ($y\bar{a}r\bar{e}t\bar{a}$)[34] that you did this ...." "Because I thought ... 'they will kill me because of my wife.'" An addition in both clauses, however, is the

---

31. Kilian, *Abrahamsüberlieferungen*, p. 203, misses the point of this reference by making it a redactional addition.
32. See my discussion of the ideological use of such designations in "The Terms 'Amorite' and 'Hittite' in the Old Testament," *VT* 22 (1972): 64–81.
33. Whether "king of the Philistines" is redactional or not must be answered by whether the view of Abimelech is consistently negative in chap. 26 as compared with chap. 20, and not by whether it would be anachronistic.
34. Instead of MT $r\bar{a}^{\jmath}\bar{\imath}t\bar{a}$.

curious expression "the men of the place" (*anšēy hammāqôm*), instead of the expected "men of Gerar" or the like. Yet in 20:11 and 13, the same word, *māqôm*, is used twice, "in this place" and "in every place," so the carry-over of this designation with the rest is understandable. This close verbal correspondence cannot simply be dismissed as possible on the basis of oral tradition alone, especially since both stories B and C show characteristics of written composition and are not close at all to story A. This must be a case of literary dependence.

Yet there is one remark, the very last one about Rebekah's beauty, that is derived from story A (12:11).[35] But even here the difference with story A is significant for the order in it is clear and logical, beginning with the remark about Sarah's beauty, then the threat that this poses, and finally the plan to get around this. In story C this order, in abbreviated form, is completely reversed, creating a very confusing statement. This literary reworking has completely destroyed the clear oral pattern of the earlier story and abolished the repetition of plan and execution by an awkward telescoping.

In v. 8, story C presents a complete departure from the earlier two stories. The text states:

> When he (Isaac) had been there for a long time, Abimelech, king of the Philistines, looked out of the window and discovered Isaac fondling Rebekah his wife.

This shift in the story comes precisely at that point in which story A created serious problems that story B sought to answer; namely, how did the king discover that the woman was really the wife of the patriarch? And was the chastity of the woman ever in jeopardy? Since in story C Rebekah does not become the wife of the king this alleviates the problem of illicit sexual contact for the patriarch's wife. And it also makes it easier to suggest a rather "natural" means of discovery, especially important since we are now dealing with a godless Philistine.

This solution by the author of story C, however, ultimately raises more problems than it solves. The story has not made it clear why the king should be involved at all. The narrator may have assumed that the king was informed about Rebekah, as in the case of

---

35. Kilian, *Abrahamsüberlieferungen*, p. 207, attributes this connection to a redactor.

Sarah in 12:15, but for what purpose if he did not marry her? This is another example of blind motive in a literary variant. Furthermore, the original model of the folktale has been completely dissolved at this point. How is it possible that the men of the place should ask about her and then, discovering that she is both beautiful and "unattached," not seek her hand? Such a lack of interest in the folktale theme can only be explained by suggesting that the author's interest is elsewhere. I therefore find it quite remarkable that some scholars see in this verse an important clue to the oldest level of the legend.[36] There is no basis whatever for such a judgment.

The confrontation scene between the monarch and the patriarch, vv. 9–10, is given in two parts, which are divided by the speech of Isaac. In comparing this scene with the other two accounts it is clear that the first speech has been drawn from story A while the second part comes from story B, though with some rearrangement of details. This may be illustrated by setting the passages down in parallel columns.

Story A—Chap. 12	Story B—Chap. 20	Story C—Chap. 26
18. Pharaoh called Abram and said, …	9. Abimelech called Abraham and said, …	9. Abimelech called Isaac and said, …
19. "Why did you say, 'She is my sister?' … Now there is your wife … .		"Surely she is your wife. How could you say, 'She is my sister?'"
	11. Abraham answered, "Because I thought … I might be killed on her account."	Isaac answered him, "Because I thought I might be killed on her account."
18a. "What is this you have done to me?"	9a. "What have you done to us? … For you have brought a great sin (ḥaṭāʾa, gᵉdōlā upon me and my kingdom."	10. And Abimelech said, "What is this you have done to us?… You might have brought guilt (ʾāšām) upon us."

36. See Noth, *Pentateuchal Traditions*; p. 105; von Rad, *Genesis*, p. 266; Kilian, *Abrahamsüberlieferungen*, p. 214; cf. Koch, *Biblical Traditions*, p. 125.

As can be observed from the chart, the first statement by Abimelech in story C has its parallel only in story A, but is completely absent in story B. This is because it was already dealt with in 20:5 and is implied again in Abraham's defense in 20:12. However, the rest of the scene in C is taken from B. Isaac's defense is a shortened version of Abraham's remarks in 20:11. Obviously, Isaac could not claim that Rebekah was his half sister since the tradition was quite clear about her parentage. Abimelech's second accusation, in C, corresponds with his opening remarks in B.

This conflation of two sources has created considerable awkwardness and lack of logical sequence in story C. As we have already seen in v. 7, this author has a certain tendency to invert the order of the material he borrows, as for instance in the two phrases taken from 12:18-19. But in the second half he inverts the accusation and reply with rather serious consequences; after Isaac has stated his defense Abimelech begins his accusation over again with the question "why." The logical order in story B is thereby completely destroyed. This is evidence of literary borrowing and a clear indication of the direction of that borrowing.[37]

The command of the king in 26:11 is the author's way of summing up the episode. In form it is similar to apodictic law (cf. Exod. 21:12, 15-17), but it has been changed from general law to a quite specific case, "this man or this woman." The form has affinities with the divine injunction placed upon Abimelech in 20:7, which ends in a very similar threat, "you shall surely die." But more important, there is an interesting use of the verb ng^c since for a man it means "to inflict bodily injury," but for a woman it means "to approach sexually." In story B, 20:6, it has the latter meaning while in A, 12:17, it has to do with bodily harm in the sense of the divine plague. This rather ingenious double entendre provides the conclusion of the episode for this author.[38]

Let us now turn to the theophany in vv. 2-5. The first basic question that must be answered is: does the theophany belong to the story? The fact that one can go directly from v. 1 to v. 6 without any

---

37. Another instance in which an author has combined two sources by means of dividing a speech into two parts may be seen in Num. 20:14-21. For a discussion of this passage see Van Seters, "The Conquest of Sihon's Kingdom: A Literary Examination," *JBL* 91 (1972): 190-91.

38. Another instance of word play within the story is *yiṣḥāq mᵉṣaḥēq* (v. 8), with no serious etiological intention behind it.

difficulty does not immediately answer the question. We have already seen that narrative structure plays a very weak role in the story as a whole. Although there is a theophany in story B, it has an entirely different dramatic and theological function, so this too can scarcely answer the question. There is in Gen. 12:1ff. a theophany to Abraham prior to his descent into Egypt, which, while not original to story A, was known at least in part by the author of story B, as seen in 20:13. Since story C has already been shown to be dependent on both stories A and B, there is no reason to suppose that the author did not also know this framework for story A and, following the lead of story B, make some direct use of it. Consequently, story C very likely included the theophany to Isaac.

The second question is whether the theophany must be reduced to a certain bare minimum with the rest being considered as redactional additions, or whether the whole is a unity. The only argument which has any literary integrity, it seems to me, is to show that part of the theophany has a certain dramatic function that is vitiated by the supposed additions. But it has already been shown at the outset that a theophany in any form is a serious interruption of the story structure. It comes between the situation and the plan and has no dramatic function. Isaac is already in Gerar and does not need to be told to go there. God gives him great promises of prosperity and protection but he immediately resorts to the self-protection of lying. Yet nothing is made of this lack of faith. The theophany plays no role whatever in the rest of the story. Consequently there is no reason to see only part of it as original and the rest as the work of a redactor.[39] It is all part of the work of this author-redactor who created story C.

If the theophany has no function within the story, it can only have a thematic function in terms of a much larger whole. The content of this theophany is easily recognized as the themes of promise, both of land and prosperity, which run through the Abraham stories and are here extended to Isaac. I will not take up a separate treatment of these themes until a later point in this study. But it is enough to observe here that the author of story C is also the author of this thematic framework for the basic pre-priestly narrative source, the so-called Yahwist.

39. The only criterion used for ascribing vv. 2–5 and similar passages to a late redactor is its Deuteronomistic or late prophetic affinities (see Kilian, *Abrahamsüberlieferungen*, pp. 204–06).

To summarize the study thus far, I have tried to show that the account in 12:10–20 (A), is the oldest story, appearing very much in its primitive folktale form. It was originally quite independent and unrelated to the immediate context in which it is now found. However it is very likely that the first narrator to record the story in written form also set it in some framework that at least included the reference to Abraham's call in 12:1 along with some itinerary.

The second account in chap. 20 (B) gives a fairly consistent revision of the first story, by means of a changed setting, for the purpose of dealing with certain moral and theological issues. This is a literary compositional variant directly dependent on the earlier story, as indicated by the many "blind motives" but especially by the way in which it takes for granted the whole setting and early development of the plot with the greatest economy of words. It also assumes a broader context of the call and wanderings of Abraham.

The third account in 26:1–11 (C) is yet another composition variant—this time a literary conflation of both the other stories. It appears to have no interest in the storytelling aspect, nor is it a theological revision. The intention of the author is suggested instead in the opening remarks in which he directly parallels Isaac's life with that of Abraham. It seems to be an artificial literary tradition about Isaac based directly on the traditions of Abraham.

The implications thus far for literary criticism, form-criticism, and tradition-history are considerable, and these will have to be tested in the study of subsequent pericopes. For literary criticism there appears to be an early "Yahwistic" source, a subsequent "Elohistic" source, and finally a late "Yahwistic" source. Each later writer is directly dependent upon the earlier level of the tradition. For form-criticism it appears that while there are some folkloristic pericopes, the variants may be only literary compositional variants. In the area of tradition-history we have discovered serious problems with Noth's view of the priority of the Isaac tradition, which demands considerable revision.

The Covenants Between Abimelech and the Patriarchs

The stories about the patriarch's beautiful wife in a foreign land should not be treated in isolation from other episodes connected with the same dramatis personae. The reason for many doing so in the past is the presupposition that the stories in Genesis are virtually all based directly on specific folktales and were put into their present form by narrators working quite independently of each other. Since such a presupposition has been rejected in this study there is every reason why they should be treated together.

Many scholars from Gunkel on have suggested that 21:22–34 is not a unity,[40] although this opinion is far from unanimous.[41] Nor have the particular proposals for the division into sources been entirely satisfactory. There are three points of obvious tension in the passage. Firstly, in v. 24 Abraham agrees to enter into a covenant with Abimelech, but in v. 25 he brings a serious complaint against him. Secondly, in v. 27 the two men enter into a covenant, but in v. 28 Abraham is still proceeding to a resolution of his complaint. In v. 31 there are two explanations for the naming of Beersheba. These points of tension make it fairly easy to separate the two sources. The one source, vv. 25–26, 28–31a, has to do only with the problem of Abraham's complaint and its resolution.[42] It may be rendered as follows:

> Then Abraham made a complaint against Abimelech concerning a well of water which the servants of Abimelech had seized. Abimelech answered, "I don't know who has done this deed. You yourself had not informed me, nor had I heard anything at all until today." So Abraham set apart seven ewe lambs by themselves. Then Abimelech asked Abraham, "Why is it these seven ewe lambs have been set apart by themselves?" He replied, "The seven lambs you are to take from me, that you may become my witness that I dug this well." Therefore they called that place "Well of Seven" (Beersheba).

This episode, according to the last line, represents an etiology of the place name, Beersheba.[43] But this does not necessarily lead to

---

40. Gunkel, *Genesis*, pp. 233–34; Skinner, *Genesis*, p. 325; and recently D. J. McCarthy, "Three Covenants in Genesis," *CBQ* 26 (1964): 179–189.

41. Cf. Noth, *Pentateuchal Traditions*, p. 35, n. 131; von Rad, *Genesis*, pp. 230–31; Kilian, *Abrahamsüberlieferungen*, pp. 257–62; Mowinckel, *Pentateuch Quellenfrage*, pp. 100–01. It is difficult for me to accept the view of these scholars that the obvious discontinuities in the text are the result of combining oral traditions prior to the literary work of the Elohist. The criteria for making source-critical judgments have been totally discarded at this point.

42. Cf. works in n. 40, in which a different division is suggested.

43. This reconstruction fits completely with "form II" of Fichtner's and Long's etiological categories; see Long, *Etiological Narrative*, pp. 6ff. Consequently, I cannot agree with Long's division of the two sources, pp. 18–20, in which he violates his own form-critical principles.

the conclusion that an old tradition is preserved here. The brief episode hardly constitutes a real story or conforms to any basic genre of legend. One can speak here of nothing more than a folklore motif; but of course such *aitia* were very common as literary devices in the ancient world and were especially well-known in classical literature.[44] So the presence of etiology says very little about the unit's form.

The unit certainly has a logical, straightforward movement and comes to a satisfactory conclusion. But its beginning is defective because it assumes the complete knowledge of Abraham's relationship to Abimelech, the identity of Abimelech, and the general locale in which the events take place. The clearest solution to this problem is to place the episode directly after 20:17(18). As soon as this is done the new context gives to the unit an entirely different significance. In this position Abraham's charge of a stolen well is made to counterbalance the previous charge that Abimelech made against Abraham. And the clear implication in Abimelech's reply to the charge of not having been informed about it previously is that this act of violence had occurred *before* the confrontation scene of 20:9ff., so that Abraham had further right to act in the cautious way that he did. Since the well is Beersheba the implication is that it happened before Abraham's sojourn in Gerar and some distance from it. Furthermore, just as the previous dispute was settled by a legal act of vindication in which Abimelech paid Sarah, so in this instance there is another legal transaction that is meant to bind Abimelech as a witness to the legitimate ownership of this well. And here it is Abraham who gives to Abimelech the payment of sheep.

This means that story B is a longer literary unit than previously suggested, and that there is even less reason to view it as an oral variant of story A. The story also incorporates an etiological motif which, while it is useful as a device for developing the final episode, is hardly basic for the story as a whole. If, for convenience, we may refer to the author of chap. 20 as the "Elohist," then we must also regard 21:25–26 and 28–31a as part of the "Elohistic" source.

If the unit discussed above is removed from 21:22–34 we are left with vv. 22–24, 27, 31b–34. Many scholars have preferred to ascribe these verses (or most of them) to the "Elohist;" that is, to the same

---

44. See the article on etymology in *The Oxford Classical Dictionary* (Oxford: Clarendon Press, 1949), pp. 341–42.

source as in chap. 20. The only reason for this is the use of Elohim as the term for deity. But such a criterion for source analysis is not adequate by itself. If instead, this unit is compared with the source in chap. 26, the result is an impressive similarity in terminology. Firstly, Abimelech is viewed as king of the Philistines and is accompanied by one or more officers, vv. 22,32, cf. 26:1, 14–15, 26. In story B Abimelech is known only as the king of Gerar, 20:2, and those about him are called his "servants," 20:8; 21:25. Secondly, Abimelech's request for a covenant is almost identical in 21:22–24 and 26:28–29. The notion of a covenant is not at all suggested in the earlier account. Thirdly, the name Beersheba is explained by "oath" in both 21:31b and 26:31–33, but with "seven" in story B, 21:30–31a. Fourthly, the phrase "to call on the name of Yahweh" at a holy place occurs in both 21:33 and 26:25. Consequently, I would allocate vv. 22–24, 27, and 31b–34 to the same source as chap. 26, i.e., the Yahwist.[45]

The second important problem is the relationship between the two units in 21:22–34. The general tendency has been to suggest that two independent accounts have been spliced together by a redactor. This is possible only if one assigns vv. 31b–32a to the redactor as a connective passage. The reference to Beersheba in v. 33, however, presumes that the locale has been named previously in the story, and that the reason for planting a tamarisk tree at this particular spot is self-evident. Thus vv. 31b–32a can hardly belong to a subsequent redactor, but must be from the Yahwist's hand.

It is also not possible to speak of the Yahwist's account as a self-contained unit. The opening phrase "at that time" demands a connection with something previous, and it is assumed that the dramatis personae are known, so a knowledge of chap. 20 is taken for granted. However, there is no motivation for Abimelech's action in that chapter. The response of Abraham is quite colourless and passive, and the unit gains nothing by any connection with chap. 20.

One must conclude from this that vv. 22–24, 27, and 31b–34 are a secondary supplement to the earlier account. It was never an independent story at any time, but was meant to reshape the existing episode in a particular way. The point of departure from the older account was the legal agreement with its witness element. The later

---

45. Cf. McCarthy, *CBQ* 26:179.

writer endeavoured to broaden the limited legal act into something like an international treaty. So he gave the occasion an appropriate preamble in vv. 22–24 and made the witness procedure part of the convenant ceremony by putting v. 28 after v. 27. He also shifted the story's etiology from "seven" to "oath," which meant covenant.

What could have been the purpose of supplementing the earlier account in this way? The answer to this question is much more obvious in the parallel, 26:26–31. Here Abimelech's desire to enter into a treaty is clearly connected with a prior series of events that go back to vv. 12–23. Isaac has become a powerful household because Yahweh has blessed him. But his power and prosperity become a threat to the Philistines, who ask him to leave. Yet a period of territorial disputes continues until it is resolved by the treaty in vv. 30–31. In proposing the treaty Abimelech specifically acknowledges that Yahweh is with Isaac and has blessed him, and this is the same motivation that occurs in 21:22.

For this author the patriarchs are not just small nomadic families but represent the later nation of Israel, and it is only as other nations acknowledge Israel's destiny and the fact that Yahweh is with Israel, that the nations can hope, through a covenant of peace, to obtain a blessing from Israel. This is part of the whole thematic structure of the Yahwist's work, and he wished by his supplementing of the earlier story in chap. 21 to make this perspective primary in this story as well.

The series of events in 26:12–33 is more complex than that of 21:22–34 and must now be considered in greater detail. It has been suggested by Noth and frequently repeated since that the unit 26:12–33[46] is made up of originally unconnected elements of tradition about Isaac, which were artificially strung together by the Yahwist. The only concrete basis for this judgment must lie in the frequent use of etiology in these verses. But there is certainly no etiological *legend* here, and it is difficult to see how any of the etiological statements could have formed the basis for one.[47] Once it is recognized that etiology need not reflect any oral tradition at all, but can be a useful literary technique as well the whole discussion of this chapter takes on quite a different perspective. Let us now proceed to test these alternatives.

46. Noth, *Pentateuchal Traditions*, pp. 106–07; von Rad, *Genesis*, pp. 266–67.
47. Cf. Long, *Etiological Narrative*, pp. 22–23.

The unit 26:12–33 is a continuation of 26:1–11 just as the unit 21:22–34 was intended to continue the story of chap. 20. The first episode in the series, vv. 12–16, seeks to deal with a particular theme from the stories about the "jeopardy of the ancestress" in 12:10–20 and chap. 20. It tells of how Isaac became very wealthy and powerful, but does so in a way quite different from the other two stories. In story A Abraham becomes wealthy through direct gifts from Pharaoh when Sarah is taken into the royal household. In story B the king gives Abraham his wealth *after* the confrontation as a gesture of goodwill. This modifies considerably the morally questionable fact that Abraham received his wealth by trickery. However, in 26:12–16 the king is not at all responsible for Isaac's wealth, and this is consistent with the Yahwist's negative attitude toward this Philistine. It is God alone who prospers the patriarch and to such a remarkable degree that the king and his people are envious of his bounty and threatened by his might, for he is more powerful than the Philistines (v. 16). The notion that God blesses (*brk*) and makes great (*gdl*) the patriarchs and their offspring is, of course, the basic theme of the Yahwist. It is found in 12:2–3 in the promises of blessing prior to the episode relating the trip to Egypt. It is repeated in much the same form to Isaac in 26:3–5, and these promises are now made good in vv. 12–16. The promises to Abraham were regarded as having their first basic fulfillment in the Isaac story.

There is still one problem in this pericope that is not yet explained, and that is how Isaac, a sojourner, was permitted to practice agriculture in the region of Gerar (v. 12). This difficulty is not answered by speaking of the possibility of semi-nomads doing some limited agricultural activity.[48] This was, after all, the land belonging to Gerar and, as we saw above, Isaac is hardly being described as a nomad. Given the feeling of hostility that was aroused between Isaac and the Philistines, it is strange that he could carry on agriculture and become wealthy and powerful at the Philistines' expense on land that he does not own.

The solution to this problem must lie in the fact that the narrator is assuming for Isaac the privilege granted by Abimelech to Abraham in the earlier story (B), in which the king says (20:15) "See, my land is before you; dwell wherever you please." Either it is a case of a "blind motive" or the author wants us to assume Isaac had this

---

48. Noth, *Pentateuchal Traditions*, p. 104.

privilege but does not want to say so explicitly because he does not want to make Isaac dependent on the king in any way for his prosperity. It is entirely the result of God's blessing.

The conclusion of this episode, v. 16, presents the expulsion of Isaac from Gerar, and here again there is a motif which corresponds to Abraham's expulsion from Egypt (12:20). Yet the motive for the expulsion is entirely different in both cases. In the first case Abraham leaves under rebuke by the king and as a punishment for his deceit. In 26:16, however, Isaac is requested to leave because he has become too powerful—a very significant shift in orientation. Every aspect of this tradition in vv. 12–16 (except v. 15) is tied into the previous stories and their present contexts, and the tradition's development is strictly along the thematic lines of J. There is no need to conjecture any primitive tradition behind it whatever.

The next section, the dispute over the wells, vv. 17–22, follows directly from v. 16, "So Isaac went from there and camped in the valley of Gerar ...," and the subsequent verses indicate that his withdrawal from Gerar is only by stages. Now this pericope is tied to the preceding one in the closest fashion by v. 15, about Abraham's digging wells, and the repetition of this in v. 8. These verses, however, have generally been viewed as redactional, and it is true that vv. 17 and 19–22 provide a unified narrative without them. But the important question is: are we thereby left with an old self-contained unit of tradition?

If we go back to story A we find that immediately following it is a story about conflict between two groups of herdsmen, $rô^cîm$, those of Abraham and Lot. This story has no direct connection with the preceding at all. But in chap. 26 Isaac, following his expulsion from Gerar, is involved in a controversy between his herdsmen and those of Gerar in the Valley of Gerar. Furthermore, in story B the final scene pertains to a dispute over a well, although here there is no mention of "herdsmen," but only of "servants," v. 25. In chap. 26 the dispute between the herdsmen is over a group of wells, although it is the "servants" of Isaac who dig the wells. Now it cannot be fortuitous that in this account various motifs and elements are present from both the previous episodes in the life of Abraham *in the same sequence of events* and with a closer literary unity than exists between story A and chap. 13. It is difficult to imagine, despite the prevailing opinion, how the Isaac tradition could have developed into the diversity of the Abraham tradition. Consequently, 26:17 and 19–22 represent a literary conflation of themes from the two Abraham stories into a new episode in the life of Isaac.

But this means that there can be no objection to vv. 15 and 18 belonging to this same literary process. They simply make the borrowing from the Abraham tradition more obvious. More important, they provide a reason for the repetition of events from the time of Abraham in the life of Isaac. There are, however, references to events in Abraham's life that are not, in fact, recorded there. In chap. 21 there is nothing about a series of wells, only Beersheba, which is not included here, and there is no suggestion about a continuous difficulty after this one well dispute is settled. Yet in J's additions to story B a careful allowance has been made for such events by stating that "Abraham sojourned in the land of the Philistines a long time." This period he now fills in retrospect (26:15 and 18).

It was stated above that the naming of the series of wells does not really constitute a number of etiologies, but a literary technique. The etiologies have the function here of claiming legitimate possession by Israel of territory in Philistia but also show that such claims, because of the ancestor's generosity, were not being pressed. Isaac simply withdrew to Rehoboth, some distance away (v. 22). All of this is meant to suggest that Israel was "historically" magnanimous toward its neighbors even in the face of hostility—which is good political propaganda.[49]

Mention is made in 26:24 of a theophany to Isaac. Its contents are simply a shortened version of the earlier one in vv. 2–5. Here it becomes one of a number of events connected with the last well story, that of Beersheba. In the parallel Beersheba story in chap. 21 no such theophany occurs. But in chap. 13, following the settlement of the dispute between Abraham and Lot (Moab and Ammon) through the magnanimity of the patriarch, there is a theophany containing the theme of promise. The same thematic pattern is carefully being maintained for Isaac, even though motifs and elements are incorporated from other stories as well.

In chap. 21 the well story is made up of two separate sources with the well episode and etiology actually originating in the earlier source. But here the story about the well of Beersheba cannot be

---

49. The propaganda function of such stories in Greek literature is very well described in the work by Nilsson, *Cults, Myths, Oracles and Politics*, pp. 12ff.

isolated as a separate entity. It is used as a framework for both the theophany and the covenant-making episode. The building of the altar (v. 25; cf. 21:33) is more logically tied to the theophany, while the naming of the well is linked with the swearing of an oath between the Philistines and Isaac. The author concludes by pointing to the "city" of that name as evidence in his day that such important events once took place.[50] The fact that almost identical events happened in the days of Abraham even to the point of naming the same well is accounted for by the author in v. 18, in which he says that Isaac merely redug the wells and renamed them with the same names. This also allows him to freely identify Beersheba (vv. 23 and 25) before Isaac has named it.

The conclusion to be drawn thus far is that the process that was evident in the case of the first three parallel stories has been confirmed. In the case of 21:22-34 two sources were combined, not by a separate redactor, but by the work of J himself. In the case of chap. 26, the whole Isaac tradition is a complex literary composition worked out entirely by J and using as his sources not old oral traditions, but elements and motifs from the Abraham tradition. There is no evidence whatever of an oral base, nor is it possible to suggest a process by which the Isaac tradition could have been the origin for the Abraham stories. There is also no need for any *Grundlage* to account for similarity—it is a matter of direct literary dependence of one source on another. There is no need for redactors because the process was supplementary and the later authors were the redactors of the earlier material as well. This is the literary theory that I shall attempt to apply and confirm in the examination that follows.

A note must be added at this point on the designation of literary sources. Instead of using the sigla J_1, E, and J_2 to represent the three literary levels of Gen. 12:10-20; chap. 20; and 26:1-11 respectively, I will refer only to the third source as the "Yahwist," and to the other two as "pre-Yahwistic" authors. The term "Elohist" for the second source (Gen. 20:1-17; 21:25-26 and 28-31a) would be quite misleading. It usually stands for a comprehensive pentateuchal source, parallel to that of the Yahwist and subsequent to it in date. Since this is called into question here the term Elohist (E), except as it is used by other scholars, will be avoided.

50. For a discussion of this witness element in historical narratives see B. S. Childs, "A Study of the Formula 'Until this Day,'" *JBL* 82 (1963): 290-92.

CHAPTER 9

The Birth of Ishmael and Isaac

Another doublet that is used as the basis for literary criticism in the Abraham tradition is the story about the birth of Ishmael to Hagar (chap. 16) and the expulsion of Hagar and her son (chap. 21:8–21). Once again, however, we are confronted with the problem of whether or not this constitutes the true limits of the discussion. Reasons will be presented below to show that the birth story of Isaac, in 18:1–15; and 21:1–7, must also be taken into consideration. The same basic principles that were used in the previous investigation of doublets will be employed in this case as well.

The Birth of Ishmael, Genesis 16

Chapter 16 presents a considerable form-critical problem because there are indications within it of "redactional" additions, so that the limits of the earliest story are not clear. This constitutes an immediate difficulty in the recognition of the form of the story. Yet it is precisely *form* that gives the best control over literary criticism; that is, what is redactional or additional and what is not. Fortunately, there are enough resemblances in the story's structure with that of 12:10–20 to suggest that its form is that of an anecdotal folktale of the same kind. If this is correct, then it would suggest the following structure and content according to the model previously given for such stories. First, the situation of need is that Sarah has no children. Second, the plan to deal with this need is to follow the custom of the times by Sarah providing a maid for her husband so that she may regard the maid's children as her own. Abraham agrees to this, and the plan is executed but certain complications arise. When Hagar, the maid-slave becomes pregnant she adopts a haughty manner toward her mistress and makes life intolerable for Sarah. The latter therefore receives permission from Abraham to discipline her. Yet this corrective measure leads in turn to the flight of the slavegirl. At this point it would seem that Sarah's plan has completely failed. But now there is an unexpected intervention by a divine messenger, who encourages Hagar to return to her mistress and to submit to her. Yet the story ends with an ironic twist because the slavegirl is given the knowledge that the son to be born to her will have a destiny that will be anything but submissive and his defiance will be her ultimate vindication. In this way all the tensions are resolved, and the story has a firm conclusion in v. 12.

This judgment about the final part of the story excludes some previous alternative suggestions concerning its form. One of these is to say that the purpose of the story is etiological; to explain the name and holiness of the well, Lahai-roi.[1] But the well is scarcely nothing more than a piece of scenery in the story, a place where strangers meet in the desert. The indication of its location (v. 7b) represents an awkward repetition which is almost certainly secondary in order to establish a link in the story with the statement in v. 14. This means that vv. 13–14 cannot be a fitting conclusion to the story and must be additional.

The form is also not a theophany story intended to give special sanctity to the meeting place. It is quite possible to have a story that includes the encounter between a human and a divine being without any special significance being attached to the place of the encounter. There are no indications in the story itself that the encounter was considered extraordinary or created a holiness at that place. The encounter functions only to communicate to the slavegirl the destiny of her offspring. So again vv. 13–14 are additional and unnecessary for the story itself.

Once the form of the story is recognized as a folktale, this has important implications for literary criticism. For instance, v. 1a is regularly ascribed to P but this half-verse is vital to the basic form of the story; it sets the situation of need.[2] Similarly, the whole of v. 3 is also given to P. But in v. 2 Sarah states her plan and in v. 3 she carries it through, the same pattern that occurs in 12:10–20. There is no good reason to exclude the whole of v. 3 from the story. It is likely, however, that the chronological statement that interrupts

1. See Gunkel, *Genesis*, pp. 190–92; Skinner, *Genesis*, pp. 284–85; cf. Long, *The Problem of Etiological Narrative*, p. 9.
2. If v. 1a is removed there is no antecedent for *lāh* in v. 1b, and this would create an impossible literary introduction. One must then resort to supplying what isn't there.

the middle of the verse belongs to P.[3] This conclusion would suggest that there is no basis to suppose there was a separate P version of the story that was combined by a redactor. On the contrary, it points instead to the fact that P was himself responsible for the "redactional" chronological addition.

There are also some literary problems with the latter part of the story, vv. 8ff. The fact that there is a repetition three times of the phrase: "the angel of Yahweh said to her..." (vv. 9–11) without a change of speaker is a good indication of this. One solution is to regard v. 9 as an insertion to create a link with the story in 21:8ff.[4] But this is most unlikely since v. 9 fits very well in the context, and without it the question posed in v. 8 would be rather meaningless. In v. 9b there is also a reference back to the situation in the earlier part of the story, v. 6, but there is no such "oppression" in 21:8ff. Since Hagar is not in any particular danger there can be only one other reason for this divine appearance, and that is to have the slavegirl return to her mistress.

The real problem lies with v. 10. It is quite incompatible with v. 11 for it talks about Hagar's offspring before mentioning the birth of the child and the whole perspective is quite different from what follows in vv. 11–12. In fact it is a reiteration of the theme of numerous progeny to an eponymous ancestor, which is part of the J framework of the patriarchal stories.

But what are we to make of vv. 11–12? Here the text suddenly shifts to a prophetic oracle. The form of this oracle, according to the recent study of Robert Neff,[5] is the "Announcement of Birth, Nature, and Destiny (ABND)," by a divine messenger or prophet, of a child who is to become a king or hero. Other examples of this genre in the Old Testament are: Gen. 17:19, Judg. 13:5,7; 1 Kings 13:2; 1 Chron. 22:9–10; Isa. 7:14–17. The basic elements of this form are: a) the announcement of birth with a *hinnēh* clause, usually to the father or the mother; b) the designation of the child's name;

---

3. This is not entirely certain and may belong to the earliest collector (J) of these stories. In this case P would be dependent upon this source for constructing his chronological framework.

4. Gunkel, *Genesis*, p. 184; Skinner, *Genesis*, p. 285; Kilian, *Abrahamsüberlieferungen*, pp. 76–78.

5. This is discussed at length in R. Neff's thesis, "The Announcement in Old Testament Birth Stories," (Ph.D diss., Yale University, 1969). See also idem, "The Birth and Election of Isaac in the Priestly Tradition," *Biblical Research* 15 (1970): 5–18.

and c) the nature and destiny of the child. The first and second items may resemble rather closely an etiological formula for the naming of a child, but there is a basic difference in temporal orientation. The etiology is in narrative past and the explanation of the name generally relates to an accompanying past event. The ABND is future, and if there is an explanation of the name it is generally tied to the future nature or destiny of the child (cf. 1 Chron. 22:9–10). In this regard, therefore, the explanation of the name in v. 11c seems to correspond to the etiological model and may rightly be suspect as an addition. This is further strengthened by the fact that Hagar has not complained to God about her "oppression," and in v. 9 the messenger has already told her to submit to it. Yet even if v. 11c is regarded as "redactional" there must still be a strict accounting for it.

Neff, however, argues that the whole of the ABND, vv. 11–12, is a secondary literary addition to the story.[6] He does so largely on the basis of certain literary and traditio-historical presuppositions that are here very much under question. He also suggests the argument that since Hagar is pregnant a birth announcement is redundant. But this is not entirely the case. If the emphasis is on the *destiny* of the child, one way to express this is by the use of a set formula that may include one item that was not necessary.[7] Furthermore, while the ABND form can occur as a self-contained oracle, this need not be the case. It can also be linked to a previous divine command as the reason or explanation for it (see Judg. 13:4–5, 7; 1 Chron. 22:9–10; and Isa. 7:3–14). In 16:9 the command to return to servitude would fit very well with the assurance in the ABND that Hagar's offspring would have a notable destiny.[8]

If these observations on form are correct then additional folkloristic characteristics become evident on the basis of Olrik's laws. The principle of scenic dualism is consistently carried through the story. But there is also the triad involving the two women and Abraham, with Abraham playing a purely passive role. The focal

---

6. Neff, "Announcement," p. 108. Neff considers that v. 10 is original!
7. Cf. Judg. 13:2ff., in which the angel also tells the woman something she already knows.
8. The last line of the *ABND*, v. 12c, may look anticlimactic, and it could be interpreted as having the larger perspective of the Abraham traditions in view (25:18). But the plural ʾeḥāyw does not allude to Isaac specifically and may simply refer to the destiny of the nomadic Ishmaelites not in servitude to anyone.

concentration is on the struggle between the two women and the ironic interplay between their status and their natural or hidden advantages. The primary figures are introduced in v. 1, and the contest between them is not resolved until the final speech of the divine messenger. There is a clear structure to the story with a singleness of direction. The miraculous is not used, in spite of the appearance of the divine messenger, and the action proceeds largely according to the logic of the natural.

In many respects 16:1–12 resemble 12:10–20, and there is no reason why it could not stem from the same basic source.[9] Even the characterization of Hagar as an Egyptian makes this plausible. Yet this question must await the literary analysis of the other pericopes in this group.

The Expulsion of Hagar

Before a proper evaluation of chap. 21:8–21 as a variant of chap. 16:1–12 can be made, some rather basic questions about it have to be answered. The first question is whether or not this pericope is a self-contained unit. It is apparent in v. 8 with its opening reference to "the child" (*hayyeled*) instead of naming Isaac immediately, and with its reference to his growing up and being weaned, that there is a strong connection with the preceding episode about Isaac's birth in vv. 1–7. But v. 8 also sets the scene for the episode that follows, so that while it forms a bridge between the two stories it remains an integral part of the second one. In any storytelling genre, particularly in the oral form, the introduction is so important to the whole that it cannot be treated as insignificant. Yet an appropriate beginning to the story that would make it an independent unit cannot be constructed out of what is extant in vv. 8–9.

Another question has to do with the significance of the phrase "the son of Hagar, the Egyptian, which she bore to Abraham." Contrary to most commentaries, this is not a statement about the boy's status. This only becomes obvious when "slavegirl" (*'āmāh*) is used as a parallel for Hagar in the next verse (v. 10). The statement of the child's identity in v. 9 can only be construed as an allusion to a prior episode that is taken for granted as known. Likewise, Hagar's status is only revealed through a parallelism of use that

---

9. See also Gunkel, *Genesis*, p. 184; Skinner, *Genesis*, p. 285.

assumes this knowledge instead of providing it very explicitly, as in the case of 16:1. According to Olrik, the practice of assuming prior knowledge of this kind is quite contrary to oral storytelling. It does not occur in the other variant, chap. 16.

Furthermore, the story situation demands even more knowledge than this. The son of an ordinary slavegirl could never challenge the inheritance rights of the son of the principal wife.[10] It is only in the special circumstances such as portrayed in chap. 16 that Hagar's son can acquire the full status of a son and heir. One can hardly escape the conclusion that a full knowledge of precisely the episode in chap. 16 is taken for granted in the portrayal of chap. 21:8ff. This is a case of a literary composition variant of the earlier story with direct knowledge and dependence on it. It may be argued against this that Hagar is not regarded as Sarah's maid in this story. However, Sarah's use of "this slavegirl" is simply contemptuous, and the fact that Hagar was given to Abraham does make her in some sense his. Sarah no longer has complete control over her. And, as stated previously, an ordinary concubine could not give to her son the rights of inheritance suggested here.

If the story lacks certain basic prerequisites for considering it an independent tradition unit it is likely that other features of Olrik's epic laws are also missing. There is, for instance, the matter of focal concentration. The opening passage, v. 8, highlights Isaac, and this remains true down to the end of v. 10 since he is the only child named. Yet by v. 11 the interest has clearly shifted to Ishmael, and Isaac completely disappears from view. Yet while Ishmael is the central character in much of the story he is not once named in the whole account.[11] It could also be argued that Hagar is equally prominent, but she does not come on stage, so to speak, until the second act. The focal concentration has become confused, indicating that the dramatic concern is not the primary one.

This is also brought out by the story's motivating situation of conflict or need. In the first half one can hardly speak of conflict between Isaac and Ishmael or even between Sarah and Hagar. The only tension seems to be between Sarah and Abraham over the

---

10. See DMBL 1:332–33; Gen. 25:1ff.
11. It is true that some Greek manuscripts include the name Ishmael at the end of v. 11, but even if it is original, in comparison with the frequency of the other names this hardly changes the picture much.

demanded expulsion of Ishmael, but this is fully resolved by Abraham's compliance in v. 14. Yet this act of Abraham leads to a new situation of need quite separate from the principals involved in the conflict of the first half. In many ways it is structurally an independent episode, though it is closely tied to the preceding by v. 14. Thus the expected skeletal outline, which would move from a situation of tension to one of resolution, is confused. The resolution comes in two separate theophanies (vv. 11–13, 17–18), in which the first is clearly anticlimactic for the second and the second does no more than reinforce one part of the first.

Olrik has also emphasized the importance, in oral tradition, of scenic duality and the presence of triads of persons, events, and other features. The trend of the two wives and the husband in chap. 16 is broken in chap. 21 by the presence of the two sons, however passive their role. The scenic duality is also obscured. Isaac and the unnamed Ishmael hardly constitute a contrasting pair. Sarah and Abraham may be regarded as such but the contrast is not a very clear one and not central to the whole story. The two wives, on the other hand, never share a scene. Even in the desert scene the divine messenger tells Hagar that he has heard the child's cry and responded to it, thus breaking the scenic dualism. The fact is that one cannot find in this pericope a single example of Olrik's epic laws of folklore.

In the past a number of arguments have been used to support the view that chap. 21:8–21 is an independent variant of chap. 16, so it is necessary at this point to give some consideration to these arguments.[12] First, it is emphasized that the persons involved are basically the same. While Isaac does not come into the former account, both stories recognize the priority of Ishmael. Yet this argument is very weak since true variants often tell the same story with considerable change of names and locality. On the other hand, there can always be a series of *different* stories about the same persons from the same or different authors. The fact that chap. 21:8–21 is specifically placed at a point of time much later than the episode in chap. 16, thus allowing for successive events, speaks against its being a variant.

In the second place, it is suggested that both stories answer the same etiological questions about the origin of the name Ishmael,

---

12. See Gunkel, *Genesis*, pp. 231–32; Skinner, *Genesis*, p. 324.

the way of life of the Ishmaelites, and the sacredness of the well in the region in which they live. The problem with this argument is that it presupposes the form-critical generalization that all of these stories in Genesis are etiological legends. However, the stories do not seem to be concerned about these etiological questions at all, and it is doubtful that they should be completely reconstructed to make them answer such questions. For instance, the explanation of Ishmael's name in 16:11c is probably not original and is irrelevant to the story. In chap. 21 Ishmael's name does not even occur. The characteristics of Ishmael are present to some extent in both stories, but they are not strictly etiological. In chap. 16 the story closes before the child is born and with the clear indication that he will be born in Abraham's household. The prediction about his nature and destiny is intended to contrast the son's future greatness and defiance with the mother's present humiliation. In chap. 21 one can hardly say that the account is pointing clearly to vv. 20–21. These verses are more in the nature of "supplementary anecdotes."[13] The real point of the story is to suggest that Ishmael, as a son of Abraham, will also become a "nation" (*gôy*) just as has already been promised to Isaac. Finally, the well in the first story functions only as a meeting place in the desert. The naming of the well, its location, and the deity associated with it (vv. 7b, 13–14) are all secondary. On the other hand in 21:19, in which the well is a significant and somewhat miraculous element, it is not named or located, so the story could hardly be used as an etiological cult legend.

A third argument used is that both accounts proceed in much the same fashion. Both are said to begin with a discourse between a jealous Sarah and Abraham in which Abraham complies with her request and in which Hagar leaves Abraham's household in the end and goes into the desert. Both describe Hagar in a state of need to which the deity responds. What is overlooked in this argument is the fact that while scenes and players are the same, the basic plot and outcome are different. In chap. 16 the story arises out of the rivalry between the barren mistress and her pregnant maidservant, who belittles the former. That is quite a different motive from the second story, which issues from conflict over inheritance. In the first story Hagar's "need" is for justice stemming from her treatment in scene one and not from her surroundings. In the second

13. Skinner, *Genesis*, p. 324.

story Hagar's need and that of her son are entirely physical and directly related to being in the desert. Consequently, in the two stories the situations are resolved in different ways: in the first by a return to Abraham's household, and in the second by remaining in the desert under divine providence.

In Olrik's discussion of epic laws, and especially with regard to the problem of variants, he emphasizes the great importance of the stability of introduction; that is, the setting forth of the situation, which gives basic direction to the whole plot, and the conclusion, the way in which the situation is ultimately resolved. The details of the movement between these two are the elements that tend to vary in the transmission of stories. But in our case the opposite is true. There has been a fundamental change of introduction, plot motivation, and conclusion while preserving a similarity of scenic details. And some of these details, such as the designation of Hagar as an Egyptian, would ordinarily be the ones most readily subject to variation. Since there are no elements of folklore in 21:8–21 or any indications of a real tradition variant, these facts can only point in one direction: 21:8–21 must be a literary composition drawing its material from chap. 16, but written for its own distinctive purpose and concern.

These conclusions mean that 21:8–21 does not correspond to any genre of narrative so that form-criticism cannot function in this case as a guide or control of literary criticism to clarify what the basic motivation is for the story and whether it has undergone any editorial changes. With regard to the latter there are no reasons on other grounds for seeing any significant redactional additions in the story, so that the pericope is a unity. But the question of literary motivation is not so easy to deal with.[14] If the motive is not to tell a story, since it takes for granted chap. 16, it must be elsewhere. The clue is in the two theophanies, which reinforce and complement each other.

There are two interrelated themes present in the pericope: Israel inheriting the land, and Abraham's offspring becoming great nations. These themes are easily recognized as the central concern of the Yahwist. In this story they receive rather special treatment.

---

14. One motive suggested for this story is to see it as a revision by E in order to excuse Abraham's behavior, as in chap. 20. But this does not work so well here. Cf. F. V. Winnett, *JBL* 84 (1965): 5–6; Mowinckel, *Pentateuch Quellenfrage*, p. 100.

First of all, Israel's inheritance (*yrš*) of the land is tied to the expulsion (*grš*) of non-Israelites. The theme of expulsion dominates the first scene, and the divine approval given to this action indicates its importance. This connection between inheritance and expulsion is not fortuitous. In J's treatment of the conquest theme he consistently speaks of God expelling (*grš*) the nations, and this is in contrast to Deuteronomy, which always speaks of annihilation, *ḥerem*.[15] Furthermore, Deuteronomy always refers to dispossessing the seven primeval nations, but here the expulsion includes a descendent of Abraham: Ishmael, father of the Arabs. Closely tied to this theme of inheritance is another, that of special divine election of the Isaac line, "through Isaac shall your offspring be designated," v. 12. This election of the forefather fully secures the claim to the land— the inheritance of Israel. It is so obviously theological in its concern, similar to Deutero-Isaiah (41:8f), that commentators have been puzzled by its presence here and have tried to secularize it or rationalize it away.[16] However, it can mean nothing else than the theological concept of election.

The second theme that is mentioned is that of Abraham's offspring becoming a great nation.[17] But here it applies not to Israel's line but to that of Ishmael as a modification of Israel's election. God's blessing and providence extends beyond Israel to also include those who are expelled. This is reiterated in both of the theophanies. This same theme occurs in 16:10, in the statement of the angel, but it was noted that this was an editorial addition. In the light of this theme in 21:8–21 it is very probable that the later author added this remark to the earlier story to make the two divine responses harmonize with each other.

If this last suggestion is correct it may be possible to see the author of the second story as responsible for other redactions in the first story. The remark in 16:11c that God heard the slavegirl's "affliction" does not fit well with the first story, but fits very well with the second. Furthermore, as stated above, the secondary conclusion focusing on the naming of the well and its location added to the first story does not fit with its place in that story. But the second

15. For a discussion of this thematic difference see Van Seters, *VT* 22:70.
16. Cf. Gunkel, *Genesis*, p. 229, in which he takes the passage to mean that only in Israel would the name of Abraham be preserved.
17. The MT of v. 13 simply has "a nation" but the Samaritan text with the versions all support a reading *lᵉgôy gādôl*, "a great nation," and this agrees with v. 18.

story provides a much more impressive motive for the honor paid to the well.

There is one further question of literary criticism that must be dealt with. The passage 21:8–21 has almost always been assigned by source analysis to E on the basis of the use of the designation ᵓelōhîm for deity.[18] It is also pointed out that in chap. 16 the term used for maid-servant is šiphah, whereas in chap. 21 it is ᵓāmāh. The criterion of the divine name has already been rejected, and the fact that the two terms for maid occur together in 30:1ff, where a source division is doubtful, does not make it a useful criterion either. What seems clear is that 21:8–21 is a different source from that of chap. 16, and that it actually made use of the latter story to construct its own narrative. The thematic concerns of 21:8–21 would strongly suggest that the author is, in fact, J.

The Birth of Isaac

The task before us is to establish the limits of the birth story within the texts 18:1–15 and 21:1–7. The unity of 18:1–15 has been questioned, first of all, on the basis of an alternation between the singular and plural in the references to Abraham's visitors. Yet this alternation does not function as a very effective criterion for a division of the text into two self-contained stories. This has resulted in various responses to it. One approach is to say that the original story had to do with the appearance of three deities, traveling incognito, to an elderly couple who offer them hospitality and are rewarded for it. This story was then presumably reworked by the Yahwist under the influence of monotheism to make it appear that the three really represent the one deity.[19] Yet there have been some attempts to divide the text into two early sources along the lines of the singular and plural, but this approach has been forced to take some liberties with respect to emending the text into its more "original" form, even changing the singular to plurals and vice versa in some instances.[20] Even resorting to such a questionable procedure clearly structured, self-contained units do not emerge. One must resort to the notion of considerable redactional "reworking," and it is by no means certain who is responsible for such editorial

---

18. See commentaries.
19. Gunkel, *Genesis*, pp. 193–201; Skinner, *Genesis*, pp. 299–303; von Rad, *Genesis*, pp. 199–204.
20. See Kilian, *Abrahamsüberlieferungen*, pp. 96–189.

work or what his or their purposes were. Such a method of approach is completely rejected here.

There are a number of factors that must be considered in any solution of the literary problem of 18:1–15. The alternation of singular and plural is only one of these. There is also, for instance, the occurrence of two distinctive themes or folk motifs. One theme has to do with the divine promise of a son to an elderly couple, and this theme does not continue on in the present context past v. 15. So one would expect one of the sources to be limited to this pericope as well. A second motif is that of gods (or divine beings) visiting men incognito to scrutinize their behavior in order to bring appropriate punishment on the wicked and reward to the righteous. This motif invariably also involves the offering of hospitality to the gods (strangers) by the old or the poor, who are then spared from judgment.[21] It is quite clear that this theme begins in vv. 1–15 but carries on throughout the rest of chaps. 18 and 19. Any attempt at division of the text must help to clarify these two motifs.

Another factor involved in any decision about the unity or sources of 18:1–15 has to do with the reconstruction of the defective introduction and conclusion of this unit. Attempts to do this must be controlled by literary and form-critical considerations. Tradition-criticism cannot function as such a control because it is the *object* of the whole endeavor. Conjectured additions intended to yield the "original" tradition are no more than wishful thinking. If they cannot be controlled they simply create a complete circle in the reconstruction of the tradition-history.[22]

The problem with the introduction is that in 18:1 Abraham's name is not mentioned, and there is no clear antecedent for the pronominal suffix in ʾēlāyw, "to him." Gunkel proposed that 18:1ff. was a continuation of 13:18 but there has been considerable reluctance by him and others toward seeing this connection as part of the original story.[23] This reluctance is based largely on the question of how and why this verse should have become separated from the rest and how it happens that so much material now intervenes between the two, a question that certainly needs to be answered. But if one accepts the connection between 13:18 and 18:1, it means

---

21. See Gunkel, *Genesis*, pp. 193–94, for the many references to parallels in other literature.
22. This is my basic criticism of Kilian, *Abrahamsüberlieferungen*, pp. 96ff.
23. Gunkel, *Genesis*, p. 193.

that the story begins by establishing Mamre as a sacred place. It was in response to Abraham's building an altar that God appeared to him.

The conclusion in 18:15 is very abrupt and, from the viewpoint of narrative structure, not very satisfactory. The story does have a natural continuation in 21:1–2, 6–7, but scholars have been reluctant to make a connection because most of these verses have been assigned to E. The basis for this source analysis is that 21:8–21 is considered E's parallel to the J account in chap. 16, and 21:8–21 is closely tied to the preceding story of the birth of Isaac. Also, the divine designation Elohim is used in vv. 2–6. However, since I have argued earlier against the assigning of 21:8–21 to E, as well as the use of the divine name as a source criterion, the relationship of 21:1ff. to 18:1–15 must remain open.[24]

Perhaps some control over the question of the relationship between 18:1–15 and 21:1ff. can be established by a consideration of form. In his study of birth stories Neff has been able to identify the form in 18:10ff. as a healing narrative, involving the healing of infertility.[25] There is another instance of such a form in the Old Testament, and this is found in 2 Kings 4:8–17. In this story a woman who has no children is rewarded for her hospitality to the prophet by the gift of a son. The latter part of the story (vv. 14–17), which contains the form in question, is most significant for Gen. 18:10ff. and may be set down in parallel columns, as follows:

Gen. 18:10–14; 21:2	2 Kings 4:14–17
	14. He said, "What is to be done for her?" Gehazi answered, "Only that she has no son and her husband is old."
10. He said, "I am going to return to you in a year's time and then Sarah your wife will have a son. (Now Sarah was listening at the door of the tent and she was behind him).[26]	15. He said, "Call her." So he called her and she stood in the doorway.

---

24. It may be noted that the Greek uses *kyrios* in both 21:2 and 6.
25. Neff, *Biblical Research*, 15:6–14.
26. This half-verse is awkward and somewhat redundant in view of the fact that Sarah laughs "to herself," $b^eqîrbāh$ (v. 12). It may simply be an addition intended to link this scene more closely to the preceding one with the three strangers.

THE BIRTH OF ISHMAEL AND ISAAC 205

11. Both Abraham and Sarah were old, in their advanced years, and Sarah was beyond the age of child-bearing.

12. Sarah mused to herself, "After I am worn out and my husband is old, will I have sexual pleasure?"

13. Then Yahweh said to Abraham, "Why is Sarah amused, saying, 'Shall I indeed bear children now that I am old?'

14. Is anything impossible for Yahweh? In due season in a year's time I will return to you and Sarah will have a son."

21:2. So Sarah became pregnant and gave birth to a son for Abraham in his old age in due season just as God had said to him.

16. He said, "In due season, in a year's time, you will embrace a son." But she said, "No my lord, O man of God, do not lie to your servant."

17. But the woman became pregnant and gave birth to a son in due season in a year's time just as Elisha had said to her.

The form basic to both of these stories is: a) the situation of infertility, b) the prediction of the childbirth in a set period, using the terms *lammôʿēd* and *kāʿēt ḥayyāh*,[27] c) some expression of doubt, and d) the fulfillment of the promise exactly as predicted. This same pattern with slight modification may be found in other prophetic healing stories as well.[28] Furthermore, in the cult of Asklepios at Epidauros there were records kept of healings, some of which included infertility, which describe how those wishing to be healed spent the night at the shrine.[29] The god appeared to them, announced their healing, and within a stated period, one year for childbirth, they were healed. One interesting feature of these accounts is the frequent expression of doubt before healing, just as we find it in the stories above.

What is most significant in this form-critical analysis, however, is

---

27. On the meaning of this phrase see O. Loreta, "*Kʿt ḥyh*-wie jetz ums Jahr. Gen. 18, 10," *Biblica* 43 (1962): 75–78. See also Neff, *BR*, 15:10.
28. See Neff, *BR*, 15:11.
29. Neff, *BR* 15:12-13; idem, "Announcement in Birth Stories," pp. 44ff.

that the fulfillment follows the prediction and is an integral part of the genre. This would seem to indicate that 21:2 follows directly on 18:14. This means that the story is not a "promise narrative,"[30] but a birth story with its conclusion outside of the chapter and separated from it as in the case of the introduction. This reconstruction of the story would also suggest that 18:15 and 21:1 are additional as well. It is difficult to see what function 18:15 could have, with its denial and rebuttal, in the birth story. The speech of Sarah to the deity does not fit very well because only Abraham was addressed and 21:2 continues to refer to the promise as one made to Abraham. Likewise 21:1 is rather redundant; it cannot serve as the conclusion, and its only purpose must be to provide a transition for the statement about Sarah's childbirth in its present context.

On the other hand, we need not immediately assume from this form that 21:2 is the end of the story. It is, I think, correct that vv. 3–5 are part of a P addition already anticipated in 17:21. But this still leaves vv. 6–7 with their extended word play on $ṣḥq$, "to laugh" as an allusion to the name of the famous child Isaac. There is an interesting balance in this word play, which has been overlooked by commentators because they make it part of a different source from 18:10–14. In 21:6a Sarah says that God has given her joy ($ṣḥq$) which is intended as a counterpart to her earlier question (18:12) "Can I have pleasure ($ʿednāh$)?" In 21:6b–7 Sarah states that everyone is going to laugh at her and ask questions expressing wonder, and this is the direct counterpart to Sarah's laughing at God and asking questions of doubt. This is an elaborate etymological word play interwoven into the other birth story form that is intended to make the identity of the child quite clear.

Another question that must be answered is whether or not any of 18:1b–9 belongs to the original birth story. One reason for associating v. 3 with vv. 10ff. is the use of the singular in place of the expected plural. But it is scarcely possible to remove this verse from its context, so attempts are made to assign it to both sources.[31] Such a procedure is unacceptable. In chap. 19:18–19 there is a similar shift from plural to singular exactly where the same formula occurs,

---

30. C. Westermann, "Arten der Erzählung in der Genesis," *Forschung am Alten Testament*, pp. 18–19. Westermann constructs a completely false category here.
31. See Kilian, *Abrahamsüberlieferungen*, pp. 98, 167–68. Note that the Samaritan text has the plural forms throughout.

"Your servant has found favor in your eyes . . ." (cf. 18:3). This passage also does not give any other indication of a different source. It may be argued, however, on the basis of 2 Kings 4:8ff., that hospitality is part of the basic motif of the story, and this can also be supported by examples from classical authors.[32] The problem with this argument is that the introduction to this story—the building of the altar and the clear statement of a theophany, that "Yahweh appeared" to Abraham—does not fit a story about gods traveling incognito. In the healing stories of the Asklepios cult it was through a theophany at the cult place that the promise was made. The theme of gods traveling incognito to examine the deeds of men in order to reward the righteous and hospitable and punish the wicked is much more common in this form. The theme of a gift of children may come into these stories as a reward for hospitality, which is clearly stated as such.[33] But in 18:10–14 there is no suggestion of any reward or of disclosure. The addition of v. 15 may have been made for the purpose of suggesting such a disclosure, but it is a rather weak attempt compared with other Old Testament examples.

The structure of the birth story (in 13:18; 18:1a, 10–14; 21:2, 6–7) is therefore fairly clear. Abraham builds an altar at Mamre, and Yahweh appears to him there. He announces the miraculous birth of a son to the aged couple. Sarah laughs in disbelief, but the promise is repeated. It turns out exactly as promised. While the son remains unnamed, it is obvious from the elaborate word play on the name that it is Isaac, and this etiological element is primary even though it does not fit very well one of the set types of etiology in the Old Testament.[34] The etiology is, therefore, not an independent genre or tradition but only a technique used in telling the story.

The question still remains whether or not the story as we have defined it above constitutes a self-contained unit of tradition. There are some indications that suggest that it does not. The introduction, for instance, makes the episode part of an itinerary, and thus points

---

32. See the often-quoted example in Ovid, *Fasti*, 5:495ff, in which three gods visit an old peasant, who shows them hospitality. After their meal they grant the widowed and childless man his wish of a son, who through a miracle is born to him after ten months.

33. So, for example, in the story of Hyrieus (ibid.). The child, however, is purely of divine origin. But in the story of the aged Philemon and Baucis (Ovid, *Metamorphoses*, 8:625ff.) there is no mention of children as a reward.

34. On these types see Fichtner, *VT* 6:372–396; also Long, *Problem of Etiological Narrative*.

to a larger context. Furthermore, the story mentions that Abraham and Sarah are old, but it does not tell us that they were childless. This knowledge is assumed from a previous episode, chap. 16. It would appear that there is a sequence of early stories: a) Abraham and Sarah in Egypt in their youth when Sarah is most beautiful, b) Abraham and Sarah after a few years of marriage dealing with the problem of childlessness through Hagar, the maid-servant, and c) Abraham and Sarah in their old age, when they receive their own child from Yahweh. The question of the framework for these stories must still be considered.

A number of questions from the above analysis of the birth story of Isaac still remain unanswered. There is the question of the second source in chap. 18, its extent and relationship to the first source, the birth story. There is also the question of how the first source became so divided and of what the relationship of its introduction to its conclusion is in their new contexts. These questions can only be clarified by consideration of the Lot-Sodom stories, to which we will now turn

CHAPTER 10

The Lot-Sodom Tradition

The logical order for a discussion of the traditions concerning Lot and Sodom would be to begin with the earliest references to them in chaps. 12 and 13 and then to proceed to chaps. 18 and 19, where the climax of the story is reached. But against our following this procedure here are the difficulties that are immediately encountered in trying to assess the various literary sources and levels of chaps. 12 and 13: a variety of plausible reconstructions of the literary growth and the tradition's development have been put forward, all lacking any convincing criteria. It is, therefore, necessary to work from the literary units that have already been clarified back to the more difficult problems. Consequently, we must begin with chap. 18 and that part of the tradition that has been combined with the story of the birth of Isaac.

The Destruction of Sodom

Once the story of the birth of Isaac has been restricted in this chapter to vv. 1a and 10-14, there remains alongside of it the theme of the "heavenly visitors." There are certain fairly constant elements to this theme that may be outlined as follows.[1] The divine visitors travel incognito and usually receive hospitality from the poor or elderly but only after many others have acted in the opposite fashion. The most usual number of such visitors is two, though there are instances of single deities or of three together. There is, in the course of the visit, a disclosure of the deities' true nature and then a reward is given for the hospitality. But upon the inhospitable and wicked a dire judgment falls, which may still be seen in certain landmarks of the region.

It needs to be emphasized that such a theme is not a literary genre that has a fixed form, *Sitz im Leben*, and tradition-history.

---

1. See Gunkel, *Genesis*, pp. 193-94 for references. Also the discussion in J. Rendel Harris, *The Cult of the Heavenly Twins* (Cambridge: Cambridge University Press, 1906).

The freedom with which this theme is used and adapted and its widespread appeal over many regions for a long period of time means that it cannot give much control over literary and traditio-historical questions. The idea that one can actually reconstruct *the* pre-Israelite history of this theme is wishful thinking.² It may well have circulated as a non-Israelite story in various forms without being pre-Israelite. There is no evidence to suggest that the theme was especially popular in the Late Bronze Age; all our examples are from a later period. The idea that the story must have been pre-Israelite and associated with a particular region stems from a general presupposition about the history of all the patriarchal traditions that has been rejected in this study. The alternative to this can be stated quite bluntly. An author in a highly literate period could have taken over such a non-Israelite motif, which spoke of the gods' visitation and subsequent destruction of a certain place, and used it to fill out a purely Israelite tradition about divine destruction of Sodom and Gomorrah. The fact is that the "divine visitors" theme is not reflected in any of the prophetic statements about the destruction of Sodom and Gomorrah, so there is no old or fixed association of the theme with any specific place.³ The only form of the tradition about divine visitation to Sodom is the artistic literary creation in the text of Genesis. Discussion of the tradition's history must take this literary form of the tradition seriously first of all.

There are several reasons for believing that the author who made use of the "heavenly visitors" theme did so with considerable freedom. This can be seen first in the way in which he combined the theme with the story of Isaac's birth. The account of the heavenly visitation begins with v. 1b. Yet it is not an independent introduction, but is built on to the earlier introduction, v. 1a, in the closest possible way.⁴ Similarly, v. 9 ends the plural reference to the visitors,

---

2. As attempted by Noth, *Pentateuchal Traditions*, pp. 151–154. See also recently, R. Kilian, "Zur Überlieferungsgeschichte Lots," *BZ* NF 14 (1970): 23–37.

3. It is very unlikely that any of the other references to Sodom and Gomorrah outside of Genesis are in any way dependent on the pentateuchal form of the tradition.

4. Kilian tries to solve this problem (*Abrahamsüberlieferungen*, pp. 97 and 187) by offering a reconstruction of the text. He suggests the reading ואברהם ישב for והוא ישב, which is not much of an improvement. It is doubtful whether any such episode would begin with a circumstantial clause (cf. 19:1). One can, of course, prove anything by such radical reconstructions.

but this is in no way a conclusion to the scene. It merely acts as a transition from the visitation scene to simple divine pronouncement (vv. 10ff.), which was contained in the older story.[5] It should be fairly clear that vv. 1b–9 do not have any independent story purpose. They simply supplement the older story to make it into one about heavenly visitors. Yet a further addition was also needed. The older story, which simply stated that "Yahweh appeared to Abraham and said . . .," did not have any disclosure scene, and this was very much a part of the heavenly visitors theme. For this reason the second author suggested a moment of recognition by the addition in v. 15 of Sarah's denial, followed by the remark "for she was afraid." This addition is, from the literary viewpoint, still very weak.[6] It forces Abraham into a completely secondary and passive role and does not explain at all how *he* recognized the deity. Yet in what follows Abraham is fully aware that it is Yahweh with whom he is speaking, a recognition that is not adequately accounted for. Another difficulty that the second author faced in using the older story was its ending. The birth story of Isaac originally moved immediately from the prediction in 18:10–14 to fulfillment in 21:2 a year later. This, of course, would not do for the second author's purpose, so he placed the fulfillment some time later and inserted other events between. Such a method of handling older material should not be regarded as surprising, and it is a frequent literary device of this later author.

Another indication of the author's liberty toward the older forklore theme is the way he adapts any part of it to suit his own purpose. Rather basic to the "heavenly visitors" theme is the contrast between the lack of hospitality generally shown to the strangers and the warm welcome given by the elderly couple. Yet there is no hint in chap. 18 of any such contrast. This only occurs in chap. 19 and in a somewhat bizarre form. Furthermore, it is quite remarkable that the author presents two different versions of the theme; yet they are not variants, but only two scenes of the same story. The fact that he can vary the scenes so much only emphasizes the degree of liberty he felt in relating the material. Moreover, this freedom

---

5. Cf. Kilian, *Abrahamsüberlieferungen*, pp. 101–02, who divides v. 9a from the rest and ascribes the two parts of the verse to his two main sources: a "plural version" and a "singular stratum." That such a process results in two completely fragmented sources does not bother him.

6. Cf. the disclosure scene in Judg. 13:15–22.

was often at the expense of the story interest. For instance, Abraham's show of hospitality greatly weakens the contrast of Lot's welcome of the strangers with the behavior of his wicked neighbors.

Furthermore, in whatever form the author first encountered the theme, he felt entirely free to adapt it to his own Israelite perspective. This was done so thoroughly that attempts to remove these changes in order to reconstruct an "original" form are quite arbitrary. By making his additions about the heavenly visitors directly onto the older statement that Yahweh appeared to Abraham, the author leaves no doubt about the identity of the strangers despite their number. And as if to strengthen this identity, he has Abraham do obeisance to the visitors in a manner befitting only a king or deity. This is certainly more than a show of politeness. Abraham also begins by addressing them as if speaking to Yahweh alone (v. 3) and only subsequently includes the others as well. Later, in v. 22, the author makes a clear distinction between Yahweh and the other two, who are then identified as two accompanying "angels" (19:1). These beings are also appropriately acknowledged by Lot as more than human, v. 2, and from vv. 12ff. they become clearly identified as Yahweh's spokesmen and with his authority. This complete freedom in the author's use of the heavenly visitation theme points to the fact that there was no strong and fixed tradition about such a theme, and all the efforts to try to extract an "original" tradition from the present text are arbitrary and improbable.

The real thrust of the second author is in the dialogue between God and Abraham, vv. 16–33. This unit is comprised almost entirely of reflective theological discourse.[7] The long dialogue is tied to the larger narrative by only a few brief connectives. The transition from the first scene to the second is made in v. 16. The long dialogue is broken (v. 22) with a brief statement about the men going on to Sodom but Yahweh remaining, thus making the distinction between Yahweh and the two "angels" and anticipating the second story. Finally Yahweh's own departure (v. 33) ends the discourse, and Abraham also returns to his place, from which he set out with the strangers (v. 16).

The scene presented in vv. 17ff. is really akin to that of the heavenly council. There is admittedly a certain difficulty in the logic of this section. The scene of the divine council could precede

---

7. See especially the treatment by von Rad, *Genesis*, pp. 204–210.

the declaration of the need for a divine inspection tour and thus precede as well the heavenly visitation that has already begun by the previous scene. The heavenly council could also meet to deliberate on the judgment after the inspection tour had been made, and this would have to follow at least the early part of the scene in Sodom, 19:1–11, but before the judgment was pronounced. The present divine council scene is a combination of both, the declaration of an inspection as well as the anticipation of judgment, at the only point where it is possible to include Abraham in the deliberation. So in spite of the problem of logical movement it is a fairly skillful compromise.

If vv. 20–21 belong to the story of chap. 18 and reflect the divine council they virtually demand that vv. 17–19 precede them. For the whole point of the first visitation is to specifically include Abraham, the forefather of Israel, in the divine deliberations. And v. 19 in particular emphasizes the reason for Abraham's inclusion in the divine council. Sodom is to be a kind of object lesson of God's grace and judgment, which Abraham is to pass on to his offspring. There is, therefore, no literary justification for regarding vv. 17–19 or any part of them as redactional.[8] The appropriateness of the thematic statements within this unit to the larger thematic structure of the author will be dealt with later.

Abraham's response to God is preceded by a discreet silent interlude in which the two men proceed to Sodom. Then follows, in vv. 23–32, the dialogue between Abraham and Yahweh on how the fate of the "righteous" is related to that of the "wicked" in the corporate community. A number of scholars have felt that this theological discussion could not belong to the "ancient" level of the tradition, so they regard vv. 22b–32a as a redactional addition.[9] But how likely is this? If it is accepted that the divine speech of vv. 20–21 is made to Abraham, it is scarcely conceivable that no response to it would have been made. Why tell Abraham about

---

8. See Gunkel, *Genesis*, pp. 202–03; Skinner, *Genesis*, p. 303; von Rad, *Genesis*, pp. 204–05; Kilian, *Abrahamsüberlieferungen*, p. 106. These authors, and others, cite as the strongest argument the Deuteronomistic character of v. 19 as the reason for considering it additional. But since this study allows for the strong possibility of such a late dating of the Yahwist this argument loses all of its force.

9. Gunkel, *Genesis*, pp. 203–05; Skinner, *Genesis*, pp. 304–05; cf. Noth, *Pentateuchal Traditions*, pp. 238–39; von Rad, *Genesis*, pp. 206–10 who regard it as the work of J, but as J's own theological reflection, which he added on to a received folk-narrative.

Sodom, since he didn't live there? If it is because the story assumes that Lot, Abraham's kinsman, lives there how could Abraham possibly keep silent? Just because Abraham's response is not a direct appeal for Lot's life, but takes the form of a theological conundrum, this cannot be an argument against its genuineness in the story, since it still fulfills a very necessary dramatic function. It cannot be separated from the preceding verses, unless one invents a substitute response—which is an unacceptable alternative.

The emphasis in vv. 23–32 is on individual responsibility, which is certainly a dominant theme of the prophets, such as Ezekiel,[10] at the beginning of the exilic period. One must, of course, presuppose that vv. 23–32 have in mind the specific salvation of the righteous one, Lot, from Sodom. Even though this is not specifically stated, the larger context of chap. 19 leaves no room for doubt about this. Abraham begins his plea with the statement in v. 23 "Will you really sweep away (*tispeh*) the righteous with the guilty?" This is certainly unusual metaphorical language, but it is repeated again in v. 24. In 19:15 the angels urge Lot to leave the city quickly, "Lest you be swept away (*tissāpeh*) in the guilt of the city." The same verb (*sph*) is used as in 18:23–24, and it is repeated for emphasis in 19:17. The similarity is not fortuitous but is a very deliberate linking of the two scenes. Abraham's question is answered in the events that follow.

Nevertheless, von Rad is correct in pointing out that there is also in 18:23–32 the concern for the community beyond the salvation of the individual righteous.[11] He emphasizes that it is Sodom as a whole that is being considered. Yet this is not just the old collectivism, but a rather revolutionary formulation of it. For it is not now a question of whether the wicked in a community will bring about the destruction of the whole, good and evil alike, but of whether it is possible for a righteous minority—a holy remnant—to have a "vicarious preserving function" for the larger group. This, of course, can be recognized as an important theme of the exilic period. Von Rad states: "Actually, the section 18:20ff. jumps over many generations and links up with the prophetic utterances about the Servant of God who works salvation 'for the many' (Is. liii.5, 10)."[12] While

---

10. See Ezek. 14:1–20; 18:5ff.; also 2 Sam. 24:17—a late addition. For a discussion of these see von Rad, *Old Testament Theology*, 1:394–95.
11. Von Rad, *Old Testament Theology*, 1:394–5; also idem., *Genesis*, pp. 206–10.
12. Von Rad, *Old Testament Theology*, 1:395.

this is true, von Rad treats this theological discussion in 18:23–32 too much in isolation from its context as a special reflective passage. In 19:19ff. Lot makes a plea to be permitted to go to Zoar instead of to the mountains, the divine messenger gives assent (*nś'*) to this, and the city escapes final destruction on Lot's account, although the story emphasizes that the city was just a little one. Again the terminology used is reminiscent of the dialogue in 18:23–32, in which God says he will pardon (*nś'*) Sodom if fifty righteous are found in it, v. 26.

The strongly reflective character of the whole section (18:16–33) and its particular content as it relates directly to the theological concerns of the exile make it extremely likely that we are dealing with an author of this late period. But it is not a case of late redactional additions, as some scholars have assumed. This section is quite integral to the whole presentation of the second author in chaps. 18 and 19. His primary concern is not the preservation of some old traditions. Rather, he uses themes and motifs with considerable freedom to construct a tradition about the past as a means for articulating his own theological perspective.

A most important question for the whole theory of tradition-history has to do with the nature of the relationship between chaps. 18 and 19. For it has been suggested that the two chapters represent originally independent traditions that arose in separate regions and were only subsequently related to each other.[13] The only way that one can deal with this suggestion is to evaluate the degree of similarity between the two passages. The following chart will illustrate the vocabulary similarities.[14]

Gen. 18		Gen. 19	
והוא ישב פתח האהל	1)	ולוט ישב בשער סדם	1)
כחם היום	1)	בערב	1)
וירא וירץ לקראתם	2)	וירא לוט ויקם לקראתם	1)
וישתחו ארצה	2)	וישתחו אפים ארצה	1)
ויאמר אדני	3)	ויאמר הנה נא אדני	2)
אם נא מצאתי חן בעיניך	3)	הנה נא מצא עבדך חן בעיניך	19)
אל נא תעבר מעל עבדך	3)	סורו נא אל בית עבדכם	2)
ורחצו רגליכם	4)	ורחצו רגליכם	2)
והשענו	4)	ולינו	2)

13. See note 2 above.
14. Cf. the discussion of these similarities in Kilian, *Abrahamsüberlieferungen*, pp. 150–152.

(5	אחר תעברו	(2	והשכמתם והלכתם לדרככם
(5	כי על כן עברתם על עבדכם	(8	כי על כן באו בצל קרתי
(8	ויקח חמאה וחלב ובן הבקר אשר עשה ויתן לפניהם ויאכלו	(3	ויעש להם משתה ומצות אפה ויאכלו
(20	זעקת סדם ועמרה כי רבה	(13	כי גדלה צעקתם את פני יהוה
(21	ואראה הכצעקתה הבאה אלי		
(23	האף תספה צדיק עם רשע	(15	פן תספה בעון העיר
(24	האף תספה	(17	פן תספה
(28	לא אשחית[15]	(13	כי משחתים אנחנו ... וישלחנו יהוה לשחתה

The verbal similarity between the two chapters is so striking that the two episodes cannot be regarded as separate stories. Furthermore, even the differences point in the same direction. The first episode takes place at mid-day, the second in the evening, and this accounts for all the changes in detail from reclining in the shade of a tree to spending the night in the "shade" of Lot's house, as well as for the change in location from Abraham's tent encampment to Lot's home in the city of Sodom. There is also the change from the three strangers to the two messengers, since the two were sent on by Yahweh while he remained with Abraham. And there is the theme of potential destruction in the discourse between Abraham and Yahweh, which is actualized in the Lot story. The notion that these stories could gradually come together and develop such similar vocabulary and thematic dovetailing through a complex process of oral tradition is complete fantasy. All of these features are indications of deliberate literary composition.

The same point can be made from a consideration of the interrelation of the various motifs employed in chap. 19. The basic theme of this chapter is certainly the theme of the heavenly visitors, who bring about the destruction of the cities. This theme is carried through here much more fully than in chap. 18, especially in the contrast between Lot's hospitality and the behavior of his neighbors, and in the treatment of the ultimate catastrophe. Yet still absent, as in the case of chap. 18, is a clear recognition scene in which the strangers are revealed as divine beings. It is simply assumed that Lot understood who his visitors were (vv. 1, 18f.) and acted on their commands in much the same way that Abraham recognized in the three strangers a visitation from Yahweh (18:2–3).

15. Also in vv. 31 and 32 and perhaps to be restored for לא אעשה in vv. 29 and 30; cf. BH.

But there is also a number of secondary motifs that have been incorporated into the primary theme. These are the etiologies on the city of Zoar, the pillar of salt, and the ancestry of the Ammonites and Moabites—the last of these the so-called "cave story." It is a generally-accepted view that all of these motifs were at one time independent of the dominant theme and some effort has even been made to demonstrate this fact by literary analysis.[16] But is this really so? If they were independent motifs one would have expected rather loose connections, which would permit an easy separation of the secondary motifs from the main story. But this cannot be done without considerable emendations or reconstruction of the text.

Consider, for example, the Zoar etiology contained in vv. 17–22(23). Some have regarded this unit as a separate etymological etiology explaining the place name Zoar and only secondarily linked with the story.[17] The reason for this opinion is the concluding etiological statement in v. 22b, "Therefore one calls the name of the city Zoar." But there is something artificial about the use of this form. This is not the concluding remark about Zoar, for the narrative continues to mention it in vv. 23 and 30. In order to defend the integrity of the etiological form these later references are regularly eliminated as redactional connectives.[18] Yet the mention of Lot's arrival at Zoar certainly seems necessary in the light of the statement by the messenger in v. 22a, "I am not able to do the deed until you arrive there." Furthermore, the wordplay in v. 20 that explains the name of Zoar, "a little one" ($mis\bar{\ }^c\bar{a}r$), is separated from the concluding remark in v. 22b by the messenger's speech in vv. 21–22a. Yet, in my opinion, it does not make any sense to solve the problem by ascribing vv. 21–22a to another source.[19] In fact it is the etiological statement in v. 22b that causes the problem by interrupting the narrative flow, which would continue quite smoothly without it. Still, its connection with the word-play $mis^c\bar{a}r$ in v. 20 is unmistakable, so it cannot be secondary. Therefore, the real question that must be answered is why the author would sacrifice the logical

16. See especially Kilian, *Abrahamsüberlieferungen*, pp. 112–147. The present study is a criticism and rejection of Kilian's whole traditio-historical approach.
17. Gunkel, *Genesis*, p. 206; Skinner, *Genesis*, p. 309; Long, *Problem of Etiological Narrative*, pp. 20–21.
18. Gunkel, *Genesis*, p. 212; Kilian, *Abrahamsüberlieferungen*, pp. 123, 128.
19. Kilian, pp. 121–23.

narrative flow to include this etiological allusion to Zoar, and to this problem we will return.[20]

The beginning of the Zoar motif, likewise, does not have any independence from the larger context. It is clearly not possible to go from v. 16 to v. 24 without gratuitously supplying what would otherwise be lacking without vv. 17–22, namely Lot's safe escape.[21] Similarly, vv. 17–22 cannot stand by themselves, but take for granted the story that has gone before. There is a smooth transition between v. 16 and v. 17 and many connecting links between earlier and later statements. The remark in v. 17 "Lest you be swept away" is a repetition of the longer one in v. 15 "Lest you be swept away in the guilt of the city." The comment in v. 16 "because of the mercy of Yahweh on him" is again reflected in the words of Lot (v. 19) "Since you have shown mercy to your servant and have been very concerned to save my life...." In v. 21 the messenger states "I will not overthrow ($h\bar{a}pk\hat{\imath}$) the city which you mentioned," and this anticipates the report in v. 25 "He overthrew ($wayyah^ap\hat{o}k$) these cities." The time sequence is also carried further; v. 15 states "as soon as it was dawn," and v. 23 remarks "The sun arose over the earth." The conclusion from these observations is clear. There are no reasons for regarding the Zoar motif as a tradition or source independent from the rest of the main Lot story.

In the case of the pillar of salt motif it is likewise impossible to delimit a separate tradition. It is easy enough to say that v. 26 reflects an old story, but as it stands it is certainly not an independent statement.[22] The previous references to Lot's wife as one of those rescued from Sodom are found in vv. 15 and 16. But the warning for Lot not to look behind him, using precisely the wording of v. 26, is found in v. 17. This constitutes a very serious problem for those who want to make a source division between v. 16 and v. 17. All the essential elements, taken for granted in v. 26, are embedded in the previous narrative. Consequently, in spite of the etiological character that the incident suggests, there is no justification

---

20. Long's treatment (see note 18 above) is seriously weakened by the fact that he does not deal with the problem of the unit's context.

21. I fail to see how so many scholars (Gunkel, *Genesis*, p. 211; Skinner, *Genesis*, p. 308; Long, *Etiological Narrative*, p. 21) can see a continuity between v. 16 and vv. 23a and 24. Since the whole valley was destroyed, v. 17ff. is absolutely necessary.

22. Gunkel, *Genesis*, p. 213; Kilian, *Abrahamsüberlieferungen*, pp. 145–6.

in the present text for any conclusion that it represents a separate tradition.[23]

Concerning the story of Lot's daughters in vv. 30–38, however, it appears at first glance that one could argue here for an originally separate tradition. It is true that v. 30a contains a connection with what has gone before, but this link is regarded as secondary and v. 30b is then reconstructed to include Lot's name. This, so it is held, would yield an original etiological tradition.[24] But the matter is not so simple, for an introduction such as v. 30b is hardly adequate for the following episode. For one would certainly be left to wonder why Lot went to live in a cave, where the cave was, why he did not have a wife, and why the daughters had not previously married.

All of these questions are answered by the preceding narrative. The two virgin daughters are mentioned in v. 8. They were both betrothed, though not yet married, according to vv. 12 and 14.[25] But the future sons-in-law did not want to leave the city, so Lot took his daughters without their bridegrooms (vv. 15,16). Lot's wife also left Sodom with them, but she looked behind her and was turned into a pillar of salt. Lot could have stayed in Zoar but he was afraid to remain there, so he went into the nearby hills where the cave was situated. All of this in the preceding narrative is preparation for the episode of vv. 30–38, and many of these details have no function in the earlier story except as anticipation of the final episode. There is even a certain irony between the earlier part of the story and the last episode. Lot freely offers to sacrifice the chastity of his two virgin daughters to the crowd of Sodom men (v. 8), but later when there is no one else with whom to have sexual relations the daughters make use of their own father without his consent.

On the question of form, it has been noted that the episode is a

23. Kilian, *Abrahamsüberlieferungen*, pp. 145–46, circumvents the problem by suggesting that these interconnections were made at some point in the preliterary stage. As we have stated earlier, however, the whole notion of a complex redactional interweaving of folktales is complete nonsense and has no scientific support whatever.
24. Gunkel, *Genesis*, pp. 217–20; Skinner, *Genesis*, pp. 312–14; Kilian, *Abrahamsüberlieferungen*, pp. 136–43.
25. I am inclined to agree with Kilian (*Abrahamsüberlieferungen*, pp. 115–16) that חתן is original and that the following phrase, ובניך ובנתיך וכל אשר לך בעיר, is additional. Such a scribal gloss is quite understandable, but from the story viewpoint the focus is on possible bridegrooms of the two daughters, who may be rescued.

mixture of etiological types and formulae.[26] By itself it can hardly be called an etiological story just because it moves from a problem to a solution.[27] The unit of vv. 30–38 has few other marks basic to oral storytelling. It only functions as the concluding scene of a much longer literary unit and has dramatic interest because of this connection. Furthermore, the episode does not find its conclusion in the etymological explanation of the names, but in a wider interest in the origins of the Ammonites and Moabite peoples.[28]

The conclusion to be drawn from these observations is that the unit of vv. 30b–38 does not represent a separate source or tradition. Like the other two secondary motifs, it was interwoven by the author into the narrative as a whole and from whatever source he may have derived it, he did not hesitate to make it completely his own. It is, in my opinion, quite futile to try to isolate the secondary motifs as actual traditions as they might have existed prior to this present literary unity in chap. 19.[29]

A much more important question is why the author would have included etiologies, even when they created some problems for the logical movement of the narrative, as in vv. 22b and 26. The answer to this must be in his desire to present a number of "historical" evidences for the tradition that he is putting forward. The etiologies of the barren Dead Sea region, the survival of Zoar, and the salt rock formations are not included simply for antiquarian purposes, but as a kind of historiographic support for the author's more serious religious and political concerns. Such a witnessing element cannot be viewed here as a redactional addition by which a collector was giving his own confirmation to an ancient tradition, but is instead quite integral to the narrative as a whole. The one who has given shape to the whole story is also the one who seeks to give evidences that his tradition is true and reliable and must be taken seriously.[30]

26. Long, *Etiological Narrative*, pp. 51–53.
27. See Westermann, "Arten der Erzählung," p. 65.
28. Long, *Etiological Narrative*, pp. 52–53.
29. It is noteworthy that in von Rad's treatment (*Genesis*, pp. 211–20), while he concedes to Gunkel and Noth the idea of originally separate units of tradition, he nevertheless treats the whole Lot story as a carefully constituted unity.
30. See Childs, *JBL* 82:279–92. Childs regards the etiological formula as "secondarily added as a redactional commentary on existing traditions" (p. 290). However, in parallel extra-biblical material he notes that the etiological motifs have often been reworked in a literary form, where it has been considerably altered and adapted for literary purposes. Furthermore, the "personal witness" element may appear in stories that are otherwise

The last etiology, the cave motif, does not seem to function in this way, for the cave itself has a very vague locale and plays no part in the etiology itself. Likewise, the existence of the Ammonites and Moabites at a later date could hardly be proof for the "history" of the Lot-Sodom tradition. The primary focus of the etiology seems to be the linking of the Transjordanian peoples' origins with Lot. In the wider context of this author's work there is a very prominent concern for the nature of the relationship between Israel and its neighbors. In chap. 19 the accent is upon the status of the Ammonites and the Moabites vis à vis Israel. In chap. 13, another episode which includes Lot, the emphasis is on land possession. Gen. 13 belongs to the wider context of the author of chap. 19, and it is to this framework in chaps. 12 and 13 that we must now turn.

The Separation of Lot and Abraham

There is only one episode that involves Lot in chaps. 12 and 13, and that is the rivalry between the two groups of herdsmen, leading to the separation of the two forefathers in 13:7–12(13). It is scarcely possible that references to Lot would occur in any earlier source in these chapters, for certainly Lot's travelling with Abraham leads up to the moment of separation and is all a part of the same tradition (or a supplement to it). The account consists of the following basic elements. Abraham and Lot have been traveling together with their flocks and herds in Palestine when a dispute breaks out between the two groups of herdsmen. So they agree to separate, and Abraham allows Lot to take first choice of any region he wants to live in. Lot views from a height the very fertile valley of the Jordan and chooses this. He then leaves Abraham for this region, while the latter remains in the land of Canaan.

The first question to be answered is whether or not this is a self-contained story and therefore reflects an originally independent

---

regarded as basically etiological in character. See, for example, the Baucis and Philemon story in Ovid, *Metamorphoses* 8:612ff., which begins with a statement of personal witness by the storyteller of having seen the two trees and the swamp region that was once densely populated. In many instances the witness of the author has become completely incorporated into the story and becomes the chief point for telling it, so that it is pointless to call it redactional. See also the conclusions of Long, *Etiological Narrative*, pp. 87–94. While Long's study calls into question the folkloristic function of the "etiologies" in Genesis, he does not discuss how the etiological formulae function in their present literary mode.

tradition.³¹ The fact that the episode has a problem and a solution is trivial, and there would certainly be no storytelling interest in recounting a separation of two groups and no more. Clearly, the interest arises in a disclosure of the ultimate outcome of these choices, particularly Lot's first choice, as it unfolds in the events of chaps. 18–19. One certainly cannot argue here on the basis of form that a separate unit reflecting an old oral tradition is present here.³²

The usual arguments used to support the notion of a separate tradition for the above account are literary. It is commonly held that the obvious connections with the Sodom story found in vv. 10b, 12b, and 13 are all redactional and can easily be removed from the story.³³ Yet this judgment is not based on any form-critical or literary criteria, but on a general presupposition that all of the episodic units represent originally separate traditions. So this suggestion becomes completely circular for evaluating the unit's tradition-history. Furthermore, the argument is fundamentally weak for another reason. Verse 10a implies that Lot chose the "Plain of the Jordan" because it was well-watered and fertile. But the plain of the Jordan is not well-watered and fertile, and especially not at the southern end in the region closest to Moabite territory. With a few exceptions, like the oasis of Jericho, it is very arid and is poor agricultural land. Only with extensive irrigation can it be made otherwise. The statement in v. 10a, which any inhabitant of the land could contradict, is immediately qualified by stating that this is the way it was before the destruction of Sodom.³⁴ Any radical reconstruction or emendation that would have Lot originally choosing the Moabite plateau would make nonsense of the first choice, for it cannot be viewed as being an obvious preference over Palestine. Once it is admitted that v. 10a is necessary, there is no longer any reason to regard either v. 12b or v. 13 as additions, and the whole scene becomes a prelude to chaps. 18–19.

31. Cf. Kilian, *Abrahamsüberlieferungen*, pp. 16–35. This analysis is based on completely different methodological presuppositions.
32. Cf. Westermann, "Arten der Erzählung," pp. 66–67. He talks about a report of the resolution of a conflict between two groups preserved in tradition as the basis of 13:5–13. But this is hardly a serious form-critical evaluation and is of little value.
33. See Kilian, *Abrahamsüberlieferungen*, pp. 20–23.
34. Kilian's attempt (pp. 20–21) to distinguish between ככר הירדן in 13:10 and הככר in 19:17 and 25 is quite unconvincing. In fact, Deut. 34:3 (from the same source) clearly indicates that the "plain" extended from Jericho to Zoar, precisely the region here in question.

If the episode in vv. 7–13 belongs to the Sodom story, the rest of the references to Lot can be no older than this source, J, although some may be younger and belong to P. Put in this way the literary problem becomes a negative one. Is there any part of chaps. 12–13 that does not belong to the Lot-Abraham strand, which may be older? We have already concluded from our previous analysis that 12:10–20 is from an earlier source, and there are reasons for thinking that it had a larger context that included a divine call and an itinerary. This would mean that 12:1 at least belongs to this source. But vv. 2–3 may rightly be regarded as an expansion along the thematic lines of the later source, J, and break the continuity between vv. 1 and 4a, 6–7, all having to do with the theme of the land. In v. 4a Abraham obeys the divine command, but the remark that Lot went with him is an addition from the later source, J. All else in vv. 4b–5 is also additional and we will return to it below. The direct fulfillment of the divine promise in v. 1 is vv. 6–7. However, the remark in v. 6b about "the Canaanite being then in the land" is similar to one in the Lot story of 13:7 and therefore added by this later source.

There is a problem with vv. 8–9, because there is no immediate explanation of why Abraham would move from Shechem, where he has received the promise of land and built an altar, to the region of Bethel in order to do the same and then go on to the Negeb. Verse 8 undoubtedly has some connection with 13:3–4. These last verses, however, have often been considered a redactional addition to the Abraham-Lot story.[35] But vv. 3–4 are quite necessary, as they indicate from what place the Jordan valley was viewed. It would certainly make no sense to speak of viewing the Jordan valley from the Negeb.[36] It also provides a central location from which Abraham views the land in v. 14. It is best then to regard 12:8 as an anticipation of 13:3–4 and 12:9 as a further transition to 12:10–20.

This still leaves 13:1–2 to be considered. The only way to deal with the source question here would be to compare their suitability for both sources. Verse 1 does contain a reference to Lot, but it

---

35. Gunkel, *Genesis*, p. 174; Kilian, *Abrahamsüberlieferungen*, pp. 18–19.
36. Kilian (pp. 18–19), gets around this problem by making 12:8 come directly before the Lot-Abraham separation story. This means that 12:10–20 is a secondary addition that was later interpolated by a redactor. Our reasons for seeing this story as part of the first layer of the tradition make this impossible.

could have been added as it was in 12:4a. The description of Abraham's wealth in v. 2, however, is not as appropriate as that of Lot's possessions in v. 5 for what follows. On the other hand, if 16:1–12 once followed 12:10–20 rather closely, then 13:1 does make a good transition between an episode in Egypt and one that clearly took place in the south of Palestine. The fact that no geographic location is given in 16:1ff. until the flight of Hagar makes such an introduction all the more necessary. Furthermore, the remark in 13:2 fits very well with the opening statement in 16:1. Together they would read: "Abram was very rich in cattle, silver and gold. But Sarai, Abram's wife had borne him no children. . . ."[37] Consequently, I would assign 13:1–2, without the phrase "and Lot was with him," to the earliest source. Finally 13:18, which also belongs to this same early source, is a transition passage from the Hagar-Ishmael story of 16:1ff. to the story of the birth of Isaac, which begins in 18:1a.

If the framework of the earliest source has been correctly identified, a number of observations follow. First of all, the introduction in 12:1 is very abrupt and certainly not like any usual narrative model. It seems to approximate most closely a prophetic prose tradition form in which a divine command comes to a prophet, followed by the appropriate action, often followed again by a subsequent word from Yahweh.[38] The author apparently chose this model for his rather short introduction to the Abraham tradition. Second, the origin of Abraham is not specified, nor is the land that he has been given clearly named. But since he passes "through the land to its full extent"[39] and it is "this land" that is given to him, it cannot simply be the limited region of Shechem itself. Third, Abraham comes to "the sanctuary of Shechem" $m^eqôm\ š^ekem$, further identified by the terebinth of Moreh. This provides a rather striking parallel with the other important site in this source, "the terebinths of Mamre which are in Hebron." At both places Abraham builds an altar, and at both places he experiences a theophany, the one

---

37. The syntactical structure of these two sentences is of some interest. The first (13:2) is either a verbal sentence with a stative verb and inversion of subject and verb, or a nominal sentence. The second (16:1) is a verbal sentence with inversion of subject and verb. This suggests a contrast between the two statements, between Abraham's wealth and his wife's barrenness. This theme with similar comparison is taken up again in 15:1–3.
38. See Jonah 1:1–3; 3:3; Jer. 18:1–6; 13:1–11.
39. Reading לארכה after בארץ in v. 6 with the Greek.

granting him the land to his offspring and the other promising him a child. It seems highly likely that this author has deliberately chosen the sites of the two earliest capitals of the two kingdoms as the basis for his presentation of the Abraham tradition.

There is still one other task of literary analysis to complete in chaps. 12–13, and that is to decide what is later than the basic Abraham-Lot story, namely P. The first reference to Lot in the present text occurs in the Abraham genealogy of 11:26–32. This, in turn, is part of a long linear genealogy from the time of the flood to Abraham, ascribed to P, 11:10–26. Verses 28–30 are almost universally ascribed to "J," but this is done on very dubious grounds.[40] The reason is simply to create two independent parallel genealogies for Abraham. Such an attempt, however, is entirely forced. The opening remark in v. 28 "And Haran died prior to Terah his father" is hardly an adequate way to begin a genealogy for Abraham. It clearly presupposes the remarks in v. 27, which has all the marks of P. Consequently scholars speak of the earlier J material as being lost or suggest that v. 27 represents the reworking of J by a later priestly "redactor"—the favorite trick for solving any problem.[41] But v. 31 presupposes v. 28, because it speaks of Terah taking Lot the son of Haran with him, but it does not mention Haran himself because we know from v. 28 that he was already dead. All of these verses fit together in a unity. There is no sound reason for making any division in vv. 26–32; it all belongs to P. This makes it obvious from repetitions of the same material that 12:4b–5 also belongs to P. There is the same point of departure from Harran, the same designation of Lot as Abraham's nephew, and the use of much similar terminology. In 13:6 we again encounter P's terminology and repetitious style. Consequently, P supplemented the earlier tradition with an introductory genealogy, 11:26–32, additional remarks about Abraham's departure from Harran, 12:4b–5, and a statement about overcrowding as the reason for the separation, 13:6.

This conclusion has an important implication for the Lot story. Nowhere prior to P is Lot regarded as Abraham's nephew. At most Abraham and Lot are merely "kinsmen," $^{a}n\bar{a}\check{s}\hat{i}m$ $^{a}ah\hat{i}m$ (13:8), and

---

40. See Gunkel, *Genesis*, pp. 162–63; Skinner, *Genesis*, pp. 235–39; von Rad, *Genesis*, p. 154; Kilian, *Abrahamsüberlieferungen*, pp. 279–80.
41. So Kilian, ibid.

it is likely that they were regarded as more nearly equals. This calls into question Noth's whole elaborate tradition-history of the Lot tradition, in which he sees Haran as a primary figure behind much of the Lot tradition.[42] In fact, the whole elaborate relationship is simply contrived by the priestly erudition and has no relevance whatever to the problem of tradition-history.

One addition that the Yahwist wished to make by using the Lot story was to expand the land promise theme to include the forefather's relationship with the ancestor of the Transjordanian peoples. It was Abraham, the peacemaker, who magnanimously allowed Lot to make his choice of the best even though it did not entirely turn out that way. This is clearly political propaganda read back into the primitive age. However, it does seem, in the present account, that all the land east of the Jordan is conceded to Lot, the father of the Transjordanian peoples.

---

42. Noth, *Pentateuchal Traditions*, pp. 151–54; cf. Kilian, *BZ* 14: 35f.

CHAPTER 11

Abraham and Isaac

Besides the birth story of Isaac, which we have considered in another place, there are two stories that have to do with Abraham and Isaac as father and son. There is some advantage to considering them side by side, because they are usually assigned different authorships and regarded as having quite a different history of development. Since Noth's pentateuchal studies,[1] the opinion has become commonplace that the connection between Abraham and Isaac is quite secondary and a late stage in the tradition's development. Thus Genesis 22 is regarded as a tradition with a long history and whose association with Abraham is far older than with Isaac. Genesis 24, on the other hand, is viewed as a much more recent work composed largely as a bridge tradition to connect the two patriarchs. Kilian's recent study of the pre-priestly Abraham traditions[2] excludes Genesis 24 from consideration without comment or explanation. Yet in spite of this traditio-historical opinion, Genesis 22 is assigned a more recent authorship (E) than that usually given now to Genesis 24 (J). Our present study will approach these two chapters without either of these literary and traditio-historical prejudices.

The Sacrifice of Isaac—Genesis 22

The story of the "binding of Isaac"[3] in Gen. 22:1–19 points up the contrast between the two basic methods of approach used in the study of the patriarchal narratives that have been under review here, the "archaeological-historical" and the "traditio-historical" methods. Scholars of both groups have long felt that behind the present story lies an older tradition from a very early period in Israel's history or pre-history, but the two approaches differ widely as to the

---

1. Noth, *Pentateuchal Traditions*, pp. 102–09.
2. Kilian, *Abrahamsüberlieferungen*.
3. The *akedah* or "binding" of Isaac has become a traditional way of referring to this story, based on the use of the verb ᶜ*qd*, "to bind," in v. 9.

nature of this tradition. One view holds that the oldest tradition contains a memory of a change in cult practice during the early nomadic period of Israel's history; that is, in the so-called Patriarchal Age. This view is expressed by G. Ernest Wright:[4]

> Abraham's sacrifice of Isaac (Ch. 22) ... is concerned in its present form to portray Abraham's faithful obedience as the true response which God desires. Yet at one stage it must once have been concerned with the abolition of child sacrifice.

This view fits in well with the "historical" orientation that sees in various customs in the patriarchal stories reflections of an earlier era, and in this particular story a memory of an actual event from an earlier period of history.

The other view regards the point of the story not as event but as explanation and hence ascribes to it an etiological character.[5] The explanation may have to do with a change in cult practice, but it is especially seen in the etiological formula in v. 14 for the naming of the sacred place. The story is then viewed as a cult-legend tied to a specific sanctuary and not to a specific people. In fact, it is generally regarded as having been originally Canaanite and only secondarily taken over by Israel after their settling in the land. This approach fits very well with a theory of tradition-history that views the growth and development of the patriarchal traditions as suggested by Gunkel and expanded by Alt and Noth.

These two opposing positions are now represented in two recent monographs by H. G. Reventlow and R. Kilian.[6] Reventlow is quite impressed by the supposed evidence for a patriarchal age, so it is not surprising that he follows a view similar to that expressed by

---

4. Wright, "Modern Issues in Biblical Studies: History and the Patriarchs," *Ex. Times*, 71 (1959–60): 293.

5. See von Rad, "History and the Patriarchs," *Ex. Times*, 72 (1960–61): 213–16. Wright's article (note above, pp. 292–96) was a protest against this line of approach, to which von Rad then made a reply. Von Rad argues quite correctly that both methods are concerned with the tradition behind the text; they just have different ways of evaluating it. Yet it should be noted that von Rad is very cautious about what can be said about the *Vorlage* of Genesis 22, and his own commentary concentrates most heavily on the form in the present text (see *Genesis*, pp. 233–40). Such a caution is not shared by the works cited in n. 6 below.

6. H. G. Reventlow, *Opfere deinen Sohn, Ein Auslegung von Genesis 22*, Biblische Studien 53 (Neukirchen-Vluyn: Neukirchener Verlage des Erziehungsvereins, 1968); Kilian, *Isaaks Opferung, Zur Überlieferungsgeschichte von Gen. 22* SBS 44 (Stuttgart: Verlag Katholisches Bibelwerk, 1970).

Wright that the story behind the written source is an old non-etiological folk tradition that goes back to the people in their earlier prehistorical period.[7] Like Wright, he is critical of literary and form critics who do not appreciate the depth behind the text[8]—the "historical kernel" that reflects life in a semi-nomadic tribe in the early second millennium B.C. Kilian, on the other hand, is committed fully to Gunkel's traditio-historical approach and argues strongly for a cult-legend that in origin is non-Israelite and belonged to a local sanctuary.[9] Only at a rather late stage in the process of oral tradition was the patriarch given a connection with the story. The story says nothing about an event as such but is completely etiological in its preliterary form. Since Reventlow and Kilian present the two sides of this debate in a rather detailed discussion of Genesis 22 it will be best to give special attention to these recent studies. Yet it would be wrong to assume that these are the only alternatives. As I hope to show, there are certain weaknesses with both positions and a quite different course must ultimately be pursued.

The Source

There is widespread agreement on the source analysis of Gen. 22:1–19.[10] Apart from vv. 15–18, which are usually regarded as a later addition, most of the remainder (vv. 1–14, 19) is ascribed to E. The arguments used to identify this source are: 1) the use of Elohim, vv. 1,3,8,9,12; 2) the Angel calling from heaven, v. 11; 3) the reference to Beersheba as the primary abode of Abraham, v. 19. The problem with the first criterion is that the name Yahweh appears in v. 11 and twice in v. 14. One solution is to suggest that the divine name Yahweh belongs to a previous level of the tradition. Another is to say that the designation Elohim has been changed to Yahweh by a post-Elohistic redactor.[11] In both cases the solutions

---

7. See Reventlow, chap. 1 and his statement on p. 61.
8. Ibid., p. 32.
9. Kilian, *Isaaks Opferung*, pp. 62ff. See also Kilian's earlier treatment in *Abrahamsüberlieferungen*, pp. 263–78, esp. 272ff. Reventlow's work is in strong disagreement with this earlier study of Kilian, while Kilian's later monograph is an answer to Reventlow's book.
10. See the commentaries. Cf. Speiser, *Genesis*, p. 166. Speiser attributes the chapter, largely on the basis of style, to J. Cf. Reventlow, *Opfere deinen Sohn*, pp. 21–31; Kilian, *Isaaks Opferung*, pp. 27–47.
11. On the basis of the use of Yahweh in v. 14 Speiser regards the references to Elohim as redactional!

seem arbitrary and only weaken the divine name criterion. The other two criteria only have significance if the previous episodes in 21:8ff. also belong to E. However, we have given reasons above for considering 21:8–21 as part of J's work, so the "angel from heaven" would be a distinctive characteristic of this source. Furthermore, a reference to Beersheba occurs in both sources in the unit 21:30–32, but it is J in particular who emphasizes Abraham's stay at Beersheba for an extended period of time, v. 34.

Other marks of vocabulary and phraseology are not so easy to assess because the source analysis of the comparative passages is also under question. There is, for instance, the introductory formula "after these things ...," *way^{e}hî ʾaḥar hadd^{e}bārîm hāʾēlleh*, which occurs also in 15:1 and 22:20, two passages that also belong to the Yahwist. But more specific is the remark in v. 2 "upon one of the mountains which I will designate to you," *ʿal ʾaḥad hehārîm ʾ^{a}šer ʾōmar ʾēleykā*, and this is repeated in v. 3, "he went to the place which God designated to him," *wayyēlek ʾel hammāqôm ʾ^{a}šer ʾāmar lô hāʾ^{e}lōhîm*. This corresponds very closely to the divine injunction in 26:2, "dwell in the land which I designate to you," *š^{e}kōn bāʾāreṣ ʾ^{a}šer ʾōmar ʾēleykā*. These factors taken all together would suggest that the author of 22:1–14, 19 is not E but J.

The real difficulty, however, has been in the relationship of vv. 15–18 to the rest of the story. The device of having the angel appear from heaven *a second time* looks like a convenient way of making an addition to the story and it has been rather widely interpreted in this way. Yet all the problems of source analysis are not immediately solved by this proposal. The content of this addition is very similar to that of many so-called J passages emphasizing the blessing of the patriarch. But since J is dated considerably before E it is suggested that the addition is, instead, the work of a redactor adding to E in the style and outlook of J, perhaps as much as three hundred years after J![12] This whole notion seems to me a rather lame rationalization of the old source analysis.

Yet as we have seen, the themes present in vv. 15–18 are those that are characteristic of J as well. The only question this raises is whether or not these verses must be regarded as an addition to an otherwise self-contained unit. The fact that such a notion of an addition is very plausible is not enough to conclude that this is

---

12. See, for example, Wolff, *Interpretation*, 20 (1966): 148–49.

actually the case. The question cannot be answered immediately, but must await a consideration of the form and structure of the story itself.

The Form:

Part of the problem of literary analysis of this story has to do with whether or not there was a preliterary *Vorlage* to it and what form such a story would have taken. Much of the decision about form is based upon an evaluation of v. 14 and its relationship to the rest of the story. So a preliminary consideration of this verse will be helpful before reviewing any theories about the history of the text. The text states as follows: "So Abraham called the name of that place, 'Yahweh Provides' as it is said today, 'On (this) mountain Yahweh appears/provides.'"[13] In spite of the difficulties and ambiguities in the meaning of this verse, the form is fairly clear; it contains elements that reflect an etymological etiology. There are two basic types of such etiologies.[14] The first type, form I, usually has to do with the naming of a child and consists of the following elements:

1) a narrated event or report
2) the act of naming by a principal figure in the story using the regular narrative past tense, *wayyiqrāʾ ʾet šemô* PN
3) the etymological explanation introduced by a *kî* clause with the verb also in the narrative past tense, the same as the preceding naming clause and usually with the same subject.

The second type, form II, is often associated with the explanation of a place name. It consists of recounting an event that takes place in a specific location and then of drawing an inference from the event to the meaning of the name of the place. The basic mark of this form is the concluding statement, "Therefore its name is called...," *ʿal kēn qārāʾ šemāh*, often modified by a reference to the time of the narrator, "To this day," *ʿad hayyôm hazzeh*.

---

13. MT as it stands is rather difficult with no subject or clear antecedent for the implied subject of the final verb. Consequently, the translation here follows the Greek text in regarding *har* in the absolute state and probably also qualified by the demonstrative adjective *hazzeh* as in the Greek. This would make *yhwh* the subject of the final verb. One would also expect both instances of *yrʾh* to be vocalized in the same voice and not mixed as in MT.

14. The classification system is that of J. Fichtner, "Die etymologische Ätiologie in den Namengebungen der geschichtlichen Bücher des Alten Testaments," *VT* 6 (1956): 372–96. See further Long, *The Problem of Etiological Narrative*, pp. 1–8.

If we apply the above form-critical analysis to the story of Isaac's sacrifice, it is apparent that there is some mixture or confusion of form.[15] The narrative itself resembles form II, since it begins by placing considerable emphasis on the location of the place and the particular event that happened there. It would have been most appropriate to have a form II conclusion with a reference to a well-known place name in it. But instead v. 14a is clearly of the form I type. The name of the place is not a real name at all but a purely fictitious one, and this must be the reason for the shift to the narrative past.[16] By so doing there is no need for the place to be identifiable. On the other hand, in v. 14b, instead of an explanation introduced by *kî* and referring back to the historic past as in form I, there is another shift to the passive imperfect, "as it is said," and a temporal modifier ("today," *hayyôm*), which now moves to the time of the narrator, so that v. 14b is similar to form II. Yet the focus is not on the name of the place but on the nature of the event, which has now become recurrent and timeless. Furthermore, it has nothing to do with the institution of a cultic act but speaks only of the divine response. The result is a very subtle, artificial, and highly unusual etiology. There is no easy emendation that can make out of this a standard form such as one might expect of an old tradition. Consequently, all proposals about the *Vorlage* of chap. 22 must take serious account of the character of v. 14.[17] It is to such proposals in Reventlow and Kilian that we now turn.

Kilian has tried to defend the notion that behind the written source (E) lies a cult etiology that was intended to explain the origin of a certain cult practice of substitutionary animal sacrifice.[18] He formulates the etiological question that the story is intended to answer thus: How is it that one offers an animal sacrifice and not a child sacrifice at the holy place, ʾ*el yirʾeh*, as it was usually done there earlier? This question is no longer suggested by the introduction because according to Kilian the original introduction was lost when

---

15. Cf. Long, ibid., pp. 28–29, who classifies it under form I but then states that "the form has been broken."

16. Gunkel's attempt (in *Genesis*, p. 241) to reconstruct an original name *yrwʾl/yryʾl* is far from convincing.

17. This was certainly the primary point of departure for discussion of the preliterary *Gattung* in Gunkel, *Genesis*, pp. 240ff. See also von Rad, *Genesis*, p. 238; idem, *Ex. Times* 72:213f.

18. *Isaaks Opferung*, pp. 99ff.

it was replaced by the later writer's introduction, vv. 1–2. There is no longer any hint of it in v. 14a (which is all that Kilian retains of this verse) even though he has emended *yhwh yirʾeh* to *ʾel yirʾeh* in order to find a possible place name. As we saw above it is still the wrong form because it is still historical past without any suggestion of a continuity into the narrator's time of either name or cult practice. So there is only the nature of the episode itself that seems to Kilian to demand such an etiological question. But is this really necessary? There is, in Euripides' works, a version of the sacrifice of Iphigenia, in which the goddess Artemis miraculously substitutes a hind for the girl, who is thus rescued from death.[19] It seems perfectly clear from the many versions of the story in which the girl is actually sacrificed that Euripides' alteration does not reflect any etiology about a change in the cult of Artemis or at the site of Aulis. The ability to formulate an etiological question that a story might answer does not mean that such a story actually came into being as an answer to one's question. In fact, the great popularity of this motif of the hero who is forced to sacrifice his own son or daughter, usually full-grown, may account for the origin of this theme more readily than etiology.[20]

Kilian is also confronted with the fact that there is more than one cultic element in the preliterary material, as he defines it. He notes the theme of pilgrimage in the three-day journey to the holy place. He also notes as distinctive the naming of the sacred place. Consequently, he suggests that the preliterary *Vorlage* was actually composed of at least two or three motifs that were worked together into the one etiological story.[21] But this division into yet earlier stages of tradition leads to such utterly formless trivial fragments that it is hard to see what advantage such a suggestion might have. Furthermore, the process of conflation of tradition sources suggests rather serious confusion about the whole process of oral tradition. It has become the fashion to attribute any kind of transformation of the tradition to the oral level without having to account for how it could happen. But experts in the field of oral tradition as a living phenom-

19. See Euripides, *Iphigenia in Aulis*: 1578ff.; idem, *Iphigenia in Taurica*: 26ff., but cf. idem, *Electra*: 1000ff., where the more usual form of the story is given, in which the girl is actually slain.
20. For further examples of parallels see Gunkel, *Genesis*, pp. 241ff.
21. Cf. *Abrahamsüberlieferungen*, pp. 272ff., where he suggests that it was the Elohist who combined these two major motifs.

enon are very wary about making any such judgments without rather strict controls over the whole process. In fact, such conflation of fragmentary elements, motifs, and the like is much more normal for written composition, which suggests instead the activity of the last writer and nothing earlier. There seems to me to be very little in Kilian's treatment that clarifies the question of the preliterary form.

Reventlow, on the other hand, takes quite a different approach to the question of the form of the preliterary *Vorlage*. He disagrees with Kilian that even on this level there is any real etiological form to the story.[22] Consequently, he regards v. 14 as merely an "etiological motif" used as a play on words for the sake of enjoyment. The story in general has quite a different *Gattung*, which he describes as a "folkloristic story."[23] In this respect it is quite secular in character and not a cult legend or religious story. The angel of Yahweh in v. 12a is only a *deus ex machina* who effects a crucial rescue. This judgment is made, of course, on the understanding that vv. 1 and 12b are not a part of the original but were only introduced by the final author (*Entverfasser*). Reventlow further proposes that this story belongs to a type that Westermann has characterized as "family stories" and regards it as part of a larger group of such traditional stories in Genesis.

It must be observed at this point that this is hardly acceptable form-criticism. Firstly, the description "folkloristic story" implies nothing specific about the actual form or structure of the episode, either on the oral or written level. It is purposely vague so as to include anything. Secondly, Reventlow is entirely unconvincing about the "secular" character of the story. All the acts of the primary figure are religious acts, and the notion of entertainment is completely lacking (cf. Gen. 12:10–20). Thirdly, Reventlow's dependence upon Westermann's treatment of "family stories" needs little comment, since we have seen above that this is an entirely erroneous basis for discussion of oral tradition in Genesis. Fourthly, Reventlow cannot dismiss v. 14 as merely a motif if he includes it in the oral tradition level of the story. Is it possible that such an important oral story form could degenerate into a mere secondary motif on the oral level of the story? Such a unique and artificial use of this etiological for-

---

22. *Opfere deinen Sohn*, pp. 34–40.
23. "Volkstümliche Erzählung," ibid., p. 55. See pp. 53–61 for his discussion of this supposed *Gattung*.

mula could hardly reflect the stock forms of oral storytelling. It is entirely on the literary level that such etiological elements develop the primary function of subtle word play rather than explanation. In the end, neither Reventlow nor Kilian can delineate any specific form or *Gattung* to which their preliterary stories belong, nor can they describe the function that such an oral tradition might have had in preliterate Israelite (or non-Israelite) society.

Regarding the actual content of the *Vorlage*, both Reventlow and Kilian begin with the presupposition that there was an oral form of the story that the later writer took up and modified for his own purpose.[24] So whatever belongs to the final writer's theme and perspective must be eliminated, and in this way the *Vorlage* itself will be clarified. Thus both scholars agree that vv. 1a and 12b are the work of the later writer, but beyond this the two reconstructions of the "original" are entirely different.[25] The reason for this difference is obvious. They have quite different ideas about what the end product should look like. *There is really no other criterion that controls the retention, elimination, or radical alteration of the text as it stands.* But these completely contradictory results should be the clearest warning that this traditio-historical method is faulty and unreliable.

Reventlow makes some effort to bolster his version of the *Vorlage* by appealing to Olrik's laws of folk literature.[26] Yet it is clear that if some of them work for his *Vorlage* they also work equally well for the final version of the story. At one point he tries to show that the final author altered the basic folkloristic structure. He states that the writer has made Abraham the principal figure of the story, whereas according to the laws of folklore it is the weaker, less obvious one who is the principal figure, and therefore the son is more important than

---

24. Kilian, *Isaaks Opferung*, pp. 9–10; Reventlow, *Opfere deinen Sohn*, p. 32. Reventlow speaks about the dangers of literary critics and form critics not appreciating the depth behind the text. However, to my mind there is much greater danger in the completely speculative assumption that any such "depth" exists and, if it does, that anything can ever be known about it.

25. Reventlow's reconstruction (pp. 52–53) consists primarily of vv. 1b, 2–4, 6–12a, 13, and 14. He eliminates "Moriah" from v. 2 and removes all reference to Isaac. He also reconstructs v. 3 as follows: "Then Abraham arose early in the morning and saddled his ass, took *his son* and went to the holy place" (emphasis mine). Kilian's reconstruction (pp. 88–89) contains vv. 3*–5, 9–10, 12a, 13, 14a, and 19a. However, he emends v. 3 to read: "Then Abraham arose early in the morning and saddled his ass, took *his two servants* and went to the [holy] place" (emphasis mine). He changes v. 11 to read simply: "Then El called to him" and alters the place name in v. 14a to ʾel jirae.

26. *Opfere deinen Sohn*, pp. 55ff.

the father.[27] But this judgment is quite forced. The focal concentration is entirely on Abraham, and how would it be possible for the principal figure, the son, to remain nameless while the secondary foil, the father, is named throughout?

Two serious difficulties with Reventlow's *Vorlage* are the introduction and conclusion. The story begins without any setting and a quite unmotivated divine command, which is hardly likely in an independent folklore unit, so he must concede that something has been lost. But he assumes that the conclusion is complete. The etiology of v. 14 does not really sum up the action or intent of the story as Reventlow conceives it but is an appended motif. Yet this treatment of a conclusion is quite contrary to folklore style.

Completely fatal to Reventlow's attempted reconstruction is the fact that with the elimination of vv. 1a and 12b the story itself is destroyed. Without the element of the divine test there is no way of structuring the movement in the story to a climax. How can there be any point to Abraham's reply to his son in v. 8 without it? How else can the reader or hearer understand the original command or the reason why the command was suddenly contradicted without explanation? The structure and clarity so strongly emphasized by Olrik are completely lost.[28]

Kilian is more sensitive to the significance and impact of the opening statement in v. 1a and therefore eliminates the whole of the divine speech in vv. 1b and 2, as well as the episode in vv. 6–8, in order to get back to the *Vorlage*.[29] But for this very reason his "story" completely lacks any clear skeletal structure, plot, or dramatic movement, and he must assume that even more of the original has been lost. But what is "lost" is all the crucial evidence that there ever was such a *Vorlage*. For the rest, most of the criticisms of Reventlow's approach apply equally to Kilian.[30] If one does not accept the presupposition that there *must* be an oral *Vorlage* behind the written

27. Ibid., p. 57; so also Kilian, *Isaaks Opferung*, p. 98.
28. Reventlow often uses Olrik's laws to reconstruct and interpret the "original" story. Thus, for instance, he eliminates the two servants (vv. 5 and 19) in order to have scenic duality (p. 56). But this use of Olrik's laws is hardly legitimate and creates a complete circularity of argument. Cf. Kilian, *Isaaks Opferung*, pp. 90ff.
29. Kilian, *Isaaks Opferung*, pp. 89ff.
30. Ibid., pp. 96ff., in which Kilian invokes Olrik's laws to show that they work as well for his story as they do for Reventlow's original story, even though he admits that on the whole they do not fit very well. But the real issue is whether they clarify his *Vorlage* or fit equally well the final written version, and the answer here must be quite negative.

form of Gen. 22:1–19, there is no need to be concerned with such fragmentary "sources" as Kilian has proposed.

The only *story* that we have is the written one. Whatever "sources" were used, such as popular folklore motifs, etiological models, or the like, there is every indication that the writer exercised considerable freedom in the use of them so that the present account is in every meaningful sense his own. Without further specific and concrete evidence there is no way of moving behind this level in the tradition to any other "historical" or sociological reality. Those who believe that they can, do so on faith that they call the "archaeological-historical" or "traditio-historical" method. As illustrated by the works of Reventlow and Kilian, this allows for a very wide scope of possibilities but very little that is certain or even probable. Since there is no form of control from inside or outside the text, there is no way of disputing their claims or any number of other possibilities that may arise in the future.

The Themes

The only real alternative to the approaches we have reviewed is to regard the story as a literary work and to analyze it from this basic perspective. Every element in the story is consciously and carefully taken up and used for a specific purpose and effect. The remarkable thing about the story is that for all its simplicity and economy of detail it weaves together three themes that are now completely interrelated. These are: 1) the testing of God, which moves from command (vv. 1–2) to obedience (v. 3, 9–12), 2) the testing that calls forth the faith of Abraham in the providence of God (v. 1, 6–8), which in turn is answered by the act of God's providence (vv. 13–14), and his promise of blessing (vv. 15–18), and 3) the sacred place that is the place of Abraham's obedience and of God's provision (vv. 2–5, 9, 14).

The first theme provides the broad framework for the whole story, even though it cannot account for all its parts. The second theme is not necessary to the earlier one in any formal sense, but it gives to the testing its great subjective depth. The third theme is also not necessary to the presentation of the first. Yet by giving the general location of the main events in the initial command and the naming in the final statement of the drama (v. 14), the whole somewhat resembles the model of a place etiology. But there are some unusual features about the place theme. First of all, the two names "land of Moriah" (ʾereṣ hammōrîyāh) and "Yahweh Sees/Provides" (yhwh yirʾeh) are not actual names but fictitious creations.[31] The meaning of the second name is clear, but the first one must mean something like "land of the fear of Yah(weh)" (mōrāʾ + yh).[32] Such names give to the whole account a highly symbolic and paradigmatic character. The place by the first name is tied to the theme of Abraham's obedience, and the second name stresses the theme of divine providence. But another feature of the place theme is the constant reiteration of the remark, "[the place] which God said to him" (vv. 2,3,9). This is more than just a unifying repetition. It clearly points to divine election of a cult place, just as in 26:2 (also J) it signifies the divine choice of Palestine as the promised land. It must certainly be the counterpart of the Deuteronomic "Place which Yahweh your God will choose ...." Are we to suppose, then, that the writer really had Jerusalem in mind? I hardly think so, for then he would have used specific rather than symbolic names. Instead, one may speak here of a "demythologizing" of the concept of the sacred place. This is a radical break, by means of the Abraham tradition, with the election of Zion. The holy place is the place of the fear of God (vv. 2), the place where one goes to pray (v. 5), the place where the providence of God is seen (v. 14).

It is also in the broader context that one must consider the other themes. A concern in a number of the J stories is the theme of the providence of God. Note, for instance, in the previous story of 21:8ff. that God *heard* the cries of Hagar and the lad and provided the well for their thirst in a most natural way. In this story God *looked out* for Abraham and the boy Isaac and also provided the ram in an apparently natural way. Included *within* the Hagar story is the larger providential promise of Ishmael becoming a nation, made in the single speech by the angel from heaven. It can hardly be regarded there as secondary. In chap. 22, however, the providential promises are more numerous and would make the first speech too large, delaying the action of v. 13. So it is placed in a second speech from heaven, even though from the viewpoint of the story structure it is an

---

31. Note all the attempts in the commentaries to find some geographical significance for these names.
32. Conflation of a quiescent aleph in internal position in a proper name is not uncommon.

appendix. The theological concern has become more important at this point than the story's structure.[33]

However, it is the theme of "testing" and of obedient response to that testing that is most basic to the whole story structure as we now have it. It seems easy enough to see the connection between the statement of the test in v. 1 and the obedience that results in the rescue of the child in vv. 13–14. But if this were the end of the story, as so many propose, the whole purpose of testing would have no real consequence. Nothing would be changed. It is only with the inclusion, in the second speech, of the divine confirmation of the patriarchal promises, vv. 15–18, that the ultimate aim of the testing becomes clear. Because of Abraham's obedience his children will be blessed.

The significance of this theme must be seen in its larger biblical context.[34] It is worth noting how strongly Deuteronomy stresses the divine testing of the fathers in the wilderness to see if they would obey the divine commands, trust in the providence of God, and so receive the good land and all its divine blessing (Deut. 8). The Deuteronomic history also makes clear how these fathers and successive generations failed this test. But here is a transfer of the theme of testing from the fathers of the exodus to the fathers of the "preexodus" period. Abraham, the original father, was obedient to the command and had faith in the providence of God; thus, he became both the ultimate paradigm of obedience and the guarantor of the promises for all Israel (cf. Gen. 26:3–5). The full significance of this thematic development will be discussed below.

In summary, we have seen that there are no firm reasons for ascribing Gen. 22:1–19 to E. The literary and thematic affinities are all with the Yahwist. It is very doubtful that he used any ancient

---

33. Von Rad, in his Genesis commentary, also views the story in its wider context in spite of his opinion about the older tradition and the ascription of the story to E. Much of what he says about the story I can heartily agree with, even though I have not repeated his remarks here. Cf. also G. W. Coats, "Abraham's Sacrifice of Faith: A Form-Critical Study of Genesis 22," *Interpretation*, 27(1973): 389–400. This article appeared too late to be discussed above. Nevertheless, Coats anticipates and confirms a number of points made here, especially on the literary unity of the work. His structural analysis is perhaps too elaborate and detailed to be convincing.

34. See most recently L. Ruppert, "Das Motiv der Versuchung durch Gott in Vordeuteronomischen Tradition," *VT* 22 (1972): 55–63. The literary presuppositions of this study are debatable, and Ruppert's lack of any comparative treatment with Deuteronomy makes a new study necessary. See also von Rad, *Old Testament Theology* I, p. 174.

tradition in etiological form. The etiology here is entirely his own literary device, as it is elsewhere. If he used any other folkloristic motif or story theme as a base he did so with complete freedom, so that it is scarcely possible to reconstruct it or to derive any historical conclusions on that basis. It is a highly polished story with a number of theological themes carefully interwoven to yield the strongest possible impression with the greatest economy of words. Our exposition has certainly not exhausted the meaning of this text but has only suggested a somewhat different literary and historical context of the writer, which must be further explored.

The Matchmaking—Genesis 24

The Source

There is disagreement in the commentaries over the unity of Genesis 24. Some have argued for the presence of two sources within the story, while others have been equally adamant that the present account constitutes a unity in spite of a few minor irregularities. Those who do argue for a division of sources must presuppose a rather extreme case of the "scissors and paste" method of redactional splicing with two virtually identical variants. Nevertheless, it may be worthwhile to consider briefly some of the reasons that have given rise to proposals for a source division. Firstly, v. 23b refers to Rebekah's house as her "father's house," but in v. 28 as her "mother's house." However, the first phrase is put into the mouth of the servant as a question, which would be natural enough. On the other hand, it was customary for a daughter (v. 28) to speak of her home as her *mother's* house (Ruth 1:8; Song of Solomon 3:4; 8:2). Secondly, vv. 29b and 30b present two parallel references to Laban's trip to the well. But this problem is easily solved by transposing v. 29b after v. 30a, which produces a much better narrative flow.[35] Thirdly, some have seen a difference between v. 51, in which the family gives permission for Rebekah to go, and vv. 57f., in which Rebekah herself is asked if she is willing to go. But the first request has to do with the consent of marriage, which had to be obtained from mother and brother. The second request has to do with whether Rebekah will be willing to go immediately without prolonged

---

35. So BH. Also perhaps read לעיר for אל העין (v. 29), "to the man who was outside the city;" cf. v. 11.

leavetaking, to which she was entitled. There is no basic conflict between the two. Fourthly, a difficulty has also been noted in the mention of "nurse" (v. 59), but "maidens" (v. 61), as those who accompany Rebekah. But the reference to the "nurse" must certainly be suspect, for Rebekah scarcely has need of a wet nurse מנקה until she has infants. The Greek versions suggest reading מקנתה as "her property" instead of מנקתה "her nurse," and this would then fit very well with what follows. None of these difficulties, to my mind, indicates the need for proposing two sources in this chapter.

On the other hand, vv. 7 and 40 constitute a somewhat different problem. M. Noth, who otherwise holds to the unity of the chapter, states: "Vs. 7 and vs. 40b are presumably 'pious' additions in view of the question of doubt in vs. 5 and vs. 39."[36] A judgment of these two verses is very important to the evaluation of the whole chapter. First of all, it is quite possible to read the text without v. 7 and to go from the end of v. 6 directly to v. 8. Still, the repetition of v. 6b in v. 8b becomes awkward and without explanation. It is precisely in v. 7a that we are given the reason why Isaac is not to return to Abraham's homeland. It is because God took him from there to give, under oath, this new land to his offspring, and, therefore, for Isaac to return to his father's homeland would be a rejection of that promise. It is for this reason also that the command not to return Isaac is repeated in v. 8b.

Furthermore, in v. 7b the theme of divine guidance is stated, and this becomes the underlying theme of the whole chapter. It is not at all haphazard that it originates with Abraham, since it is the necessary complement to the statement in v. 7a. God, who called Abraham and promised him the new land, will overcome the problem created by his own call and promise. This theme of God sending his angel before the servant, הוא ישלח מלאכו לפניך, is directly reflected in the servant's prayer in v. 12, "Yahweh, God of my master Abraham, Let good fortune be mine today" (lit. "let it happen before me today"), הקרה לפני היום. The servant's appeal is based directly on Abraham's faith. The same theme of guidance is expressed again in v. 27 in the servant's thanksgiving, "While on the way Yahweh led me to the house of my master's kinsmen" (also v. 48).

Similarly with v. 40, it is possible to follow v. 40a with v. 41

36. Noth, *Pentateuchal Traditions*, p. 29, n. 90.

directly. But this does not immediately disqualify v. 40b as original. V. 40 uses the phrase, "He [the angel] will make your journey successful," והצליח דרכך. In the second version of the servant's prayer in v. 42 the same expression is repeated as "if you will make my journey successful," אם ישך נא מצליח דרכי (see also vv. 27 and 56). It is noteworthy, as von Rad has pointed out, that the context both before and after v. 40 does not talk about the command not to return Isaac to that land.[37] But precisely for this reason Abraham's remarks in v. 40 begin with a very general statement, "Yahweh before whom I live my life ...," יהוה אשר התהלכתי לפניו, instead of the very specific call and promise theme in v. 7a. All these evidences of very deliberate literary composition make it highly unlikely that vv. 7 and 40b may be dismissed as secondary. On the contrary, they are quite basic to the theme of the whole chapter.

The unity of this chapter has important implications for questions of oral tradition and the unit's tradition-history. First of all, if the chapter has a basic unity it cannot be used, as Gunkel did,[38] to illustrate the fidelity in the preservation of variant oral traditions behind the present text. We have evidence here for only one tradition. While Noth conceded this last point, he still regarded the story as belonging to the latest stage of oral tradition, functioning as a bridge narrative between the Abraham and Isaac tradition cycles, but before it was incorporated into the general thematic framework of the Yahwist.[39] But if vv. 7 and 40 are not secondary, this strongly argues against Noth's proposal. This is especially so also because the Isaac cycle, chap. 26, which he regards as based on primary oral tradition, has been shown above to be composed in a purely literary fashion based directly on the Abraham stories.

The Form

This raises the question of the story's form. For Gunkel there were no clear marks in the story of etiology or of other types of legend.[40] Instead, he spoke of it as containing an advanced discursive style that was rather distant from a folkloristic base. But the question of form remains somewhat ambiguous in his work. Noth accepted Gunkel's characterization of the story's style as discursive and regarded this as simply an indication of the latest stage in the growth of the oral

---

37. Von Rad, *Genesis*, p. 253.
38. Gunkel, *Legends*, p. 68; idem, *Genesis*, p. lxv.
39. Noth, *Pentateuchal Traditions*, p. 110.
40. Gunkel, *Genesis*, pp. 248–49.

tradition.[41] But the question of form is certainly not answered. In fact, the features of discursive style of which Gunkel speaks are marks of written composition, and the notion of a discursive oral tradition is self-contradictory.

It seems to me that the only way to evaluate the form of the unit is to apply the basic criteria of folk literature that we have used above; that is, if the story is derived from oral tradition, it would contain a clear narrative structure, movement, and unity, and it would have the features that correspond to Olrik's epic laws.

If one merely observes that the story moves from a problem (Isaac needs a wife) to the solution (Isaac obtains a wife), that scarcely justifies the judgment that the unit is a folktale.[42] A simple report could have exactly the same structure. Yet the dramatic structure of the unit, in spite of its length, could be summarized in the following way: Abraham sends his servant to Mesopotamia for a wife for Isaac, and the servant obtains a most suitable wife for him *without any difficulty*. The last point is, of course, the central point of the episode. Through God's hidden assistance the very first girl that the servant meets is the right one, and she and her family immediately agree that Rebekah should be Isaac's wife and leave home without delay. There are no hardships of any kind on the way. It is this lack of any difficulty that completely negates the dramatic storytelling interest of the whole episode. If Laban, for instance, had been presented as a real antagonist whose resistance had to be overcome by persuasion or otherwise, that would have created a dramatic encounter appropriate to a tale. But he is not, and there are no other obstacles, so for all its idyllic character the account has little dramatic quality. The whole structure of the episode centers in a confessional, theological concern—the hidden guidance of God—which will not tolerate interference by any dramatic element.

Furthermore, the chapter is not self-contained. Only with difficulty could one reconstruct from the scattered statements in vv. 1–8 the fact that Abraham had left his original homeland long before (where it was is not evident until later), and had gone to the land of Canaan *alone* and not as a larger family or tribal unit.[43] Nor could

41. Noth, *Pentateuchal Traditions*, pp. 104–110.
42. Cf. Westermann, "Arten der Erzählung," pp. 58ff.
43. This story represents a serious difficulty for anyone who sees in the patriarchs a form of tribal history, for such an episode denies the existence of a larger tribal unit. The story reflects the concern for ethnic purity such as arose in the exilic period.

one easily determine that this was the period when the indigenous population, the Canaanites, were in the land with which there was some antagonism, or that the destiny of Abraham's future offspring was closely bound up with this land. This background, indispensable to the unit as a whole, is not described but only alluded to as something previously well-known. Later in the servant's speech, vv. 34–36, there is a recapitulation of a number of episodes and themes from other parts of the Abraham story. Finally, at the end of the chapter, v. 67, there are allusions to events that are not clearly told in the story itself: the death of Sarah and possibly of Abraham.

Regarding the laws of folklore there are also considerable deficiencies in oral characteristics. Firstly, there is no consistent focal concentration on any principal character. Abraham begins the story, and it is Abraham's wish that dominates it. But he himself soon fades from view and in the end disappears without any explanation. Isaac takes his place as the new "master" in the closing scene.[44] The servant is certainly prominent throughout, but he remains nameless[45] and easily becomes a secondary figure in the final scene. Rebekah also is active at some points and passive in others; she does nothing from v. 28 to v. 57. The focal concentration is weak and unclear. Secondly, there is some use of scenic duality in the first two scenes, but it is certainly not carried through in the third and fourth scenes at all. There is no use whatever of dramatic contrast, nor are there any triads of characters or situations. Thirdly, a case can be made for seeing an instance of dramatic repetition between the prayer of the servant and the actions of the girl, and this is certainly the most interesting moment of the chapter. In contrast to this the long repetition in the servant's speech, from vv. 34–49, is certainly anticlimactic. The only possible movement in the story is perhaps psychological, persuading the hearers, although we cannot be sure that they needed it. This "psychological" interest Gunkel attributes to the discursive style, which is another way of stating that it is not a characteristic of oral folk literature or of any other oral genre.[46]

A recent "tradition-critical study" by Wolfgang Roth also calls

---

44. Many commentators have noted this fact and have wanted to fill out the story with "lost" elements on the presupposition that the account is a complete self-contained story.

45. There is certainly no justification for identifying him with "Eliezer" of 15:2. See von Rad, *Genesis*, p. 249.

46. Gunkel, *Legends*, pp. 85–86; idem, *Genesis*, p. lv.

for some comment here.⁴⁷ While he acknowledges that the unit is basically the work of the Yahwist in its present form he seeks to go behind this version to an earlier stage of composition, although not to the level of folklore. He asks: "What were the traditions which the Yahwist used in shaping Gen. 24? It is unlikely that *all* of Gen. 24 is the Yahwist's creation...."⁴⁸ He then goes on to answer.

> I would like to argue that the tradition employed and reshaped by the Yahwist in Gen. 24 was (and remained) an example story, illustrating the scope and limit of wise action of a trusted, senior steward as demonstrated in matters of marriage arrangement. To be sure, it is not possible to arrive at the exact wording of the underlying example story by way of a literary-critical procedure; the interpreting pen of the Yahwist reshaped considerably the example story precisely because J shared its basic outlook and was possibly at home in the circles where such example stories were told. The themes and motifs of the example story can however be discerned and isolated.⁴⁹

This quotation is a good illustration of the confusion that surrounds the term "tradition." Roth admits that all he can say about the "traditions which the Yahwist used" for Genesis 24 is that they are "themes and motifs" but not the actual form or structure of any tradition; nor can he see that they had any association with Abraham prior to the Yahwist's work. Since each theme or motif could have been independently familiar to the Yahwist by Roth's own admission, why can he not give the Yahwist credit for composing the story as it stands? It is very misleading to call themes and motifs of such a general character "traditions," as Roth does.

Furthermore, it is questionable to suggest that the "tradition" underlying the present story is a genre (which he calls "the example story") when no formal characteristics can be given to it apart from a vague didactic intention. If, for instance, one can include Prov. 6:6–11; 24:30–34; 7:1ff. within the category of example story,⁵⁰ the grouping has no form-critical value and should not be described

---

47. W. M. W. Roth, "The Wooing of Rebekah: A Tradition-Critical Study of Genesis 24," *CBQ* 34 (1972): 177–187.
48. Ibid., p. 179.
49. Ibid., pp. 180f.
50. Ibid., p. 180, n. 13.

as a genre. We are really left with a few motifs common to the book of Proverbs that have to do with servants, messengers, giving answers, the value of a good wife, etc.[51] But all of these rather commonplace themes are completely subservient to that of divine guidance and providence, which is, by Roth's admission, basic to the perspective of the Yahwist. So one can go no further back in the history of the tradition of this story than the text as it is in its present form.

We may draw from these observations the conclusion that chap. 24 is a deliberate literary composition, and that it is difficult to speak in terms of a precise genre just as it is for most of the literary units of the Abraham tradition. Instead, one must identify the chief point of concern, the kerygmatic theme, around which the author has created his traditional unit. This theme is the divine providence of God toward Abraham ("Yahweh blessed him in everything," v. 1), but especially as seen through the divine guidance in the acquiring of a wife for Isaac in order not to negate the promise. It is Abraham's faith primarily (v. 7) and the servant acting as the agent of that faith and in the name of the God of Abraham that allow this providential act of God to be carried forward. The family of Abraham in Aram Naharaim responds immediately and without possible resistance to the servant's witness to God's guidance (vv. 50f.) and so further God's providential activity. There is no action that is allowed to stand outside of that theme; hence the complete suppression of any opposition motif for dramatic effect. There is no objection, no delay, only strict compliance with the disclosure of the divine will. One cannot even describe this as a didactic story. Rather, it is the reporting of a spiritual event.

Such reporting of events with a dominant confessional interest we have come to recognize in this study as the work and perspective of the late Yahwist. Of course, he had before him the whole of the pre-priestly Abrahamic tradition, since he built on his predecessors, so it is not surprising if affinities are found with much of this corpus. The relationship of chap. 24 with this wider context is usually discussed in terms of identifying the author as J on the basis of similarity in vocabulary. One notes, for instance, the same treatment in the offering of hospitality in chap. 24 and chaps. 18–19. But the matter goes quite a bit deeper than this. The connections have to do much more with the fundamental theological orientation and the

---

51. Ibid., pp. 181–186.

author's basic skeleton of the Abraham "history." One such important theme is God's promise of blessing on Abraham, which comes to him at the time of his "call," 12:2–3. At the end of Abraham's life God has blessed him in everything (vv. 1,35), which results in his prosperity just as it also does for Isaac (26:12b–13). Of interest is the list of Abraham's goods in v. 35b, which combines those of 12:16 and 13:2. We earlier identified these as belonging to the pre-Yahwistic source. However, the use of these earlier lists is deliberate. In pre-J texts these goods seemed to be the result of Abraham's deceit in Egypt and the result of Pharaoh's generosity. But here they are viewed as given by God and as the direct result of his blessing, as also in the Isaac story, 26:12–13. It is also significant that even Abraham's servant is addressed as "Blessed of Yahweh," v. 31, just as Isaac is greeted in this way by Abimelech, 26:29.

One of the most striking features of the whole episode is the behavior of the servant—he prays by this busy profane city well! He does not have the use of oracle, holy man, or theophanic vision. He is not a forefather but only the servant of one, and he is in a foreign land. There is hardly anything comparable to this in the OT, except in the latest books. Furthermore, as has often been noted, the sign is a very natural one that combines with it a certain "worldly-wise calculation." When the prayer is answered by the immediate appearance of the right girl the servant prostrates himself and utters a prayer of thanksgiving, v. 26 (v. 48), as he does also when he receives the final answer from the family that Rebekah may go with him, v. 52. This act of prostration, וישתחו ליהוה, should not be ignored. It cannot be assumed that it is simply the posture of prayer, because there is no hint of it in v. 12 (42). We noted earlier that both Abraham and Lot prostrated themselves before the heavenly guests even though they were outwardly strangers and their divine presence was hidden. In this account the fulfillment of the sign, even though it is not miraculous or theophanic,[52] is nevertheless for the servant a disclosure of God's presence, which he immediately acknowledges in prostration and thanksgiving. This is a most remarkable, sophisticated, and thoughtful approach to non-cultic religious experience, especially for those in the exilic period who were on their own, living in foreign lands and devoid of the cult.

Perhaps this story also throws some light back on 22:13–14. For

---

52. Cf. Judg. 13:15–20 and the act of prostration after the theophany.

besides the angel's voice from heaven there just happened to be the divine provision of the ram caught in the thicket, and the enigmatic statement of v. 14 combines and identifies both God's provision and his appearance.

This episode also refers to a number of events in the life of Abraham, especially as it had to do with Isaac. The birth of Isaac is mentioned in a form that certainly depends upon 21:2. There is also a reference in the same verse to Isaac's inheritance, and this corresponds to the statement in 25:5. This would suggest that the unit 25:1-6 perhaps directly preceded chap. 24, perhaps as a part of the other genealogical unit in 22:20-24. This later genealogy provides the background for Rebekah's family, and this too is frequently repeated in 24:15, 24, and 47. It also seems likely that 25:11 followed chap. 24 as well, but this would be difficult to prove.

In summary, we have seen that chap. 24 is a unified literary work of the Yahwist with no indication of any dependence upon a folkloristic tradition of Isaac as a forefather of Israel. Like chap. 22, it deals with the theme of divine providence but emphasizes more strongly the hidden and natural guidance of God in the promises to Abraham in response to simple piety and faith. The specific historical circumstances to which this message was directed will be discussed in the next chapter.

CHAPTER 12

The Covenant of Abraham: Genesis 15

There is great diversity of opinion about the unity or disunity of Genesis 15 and about the antiquity of the traditions contained in the chapter.¹ It would seem to me to be helpful if some preliminary assessment were made of some of the problems involved and of the approaches used toward their solution.² A number of clues within the chapter have suggested a division into two or more sources. There is, first of all, a discrepancy in the time of day: v. 5 reflects a nighttime scene, whereas vv. 12 and 17 point to early evening. The subject matter of vv. 1–6, the gift of an heir and numerous offspring, is different from vv. 7–21, the promise of land guaranteed by covenant. There are parallel self-introductions by Yahweh in v. 1 and v. 7 and parallel responses by Abraham in vv. 2–3 and 8. Furthermore, in v. 6 Abraham expresses faith, but in v. 8 he appears to be in doubt again. These features would seem to support arguments for a division horizontally between vv. 1–6 and vv. 7–21. There are, however, some indications of doublets within these two units. The most obvious is the double reply of Abraham in vv. 2 and 3. Also the promise of numerous offspring in v. 5 is distinct from, and additional to, the promise of a single natural heir in v. 4. In the second

---

1. See the commentaries and general studies on the literary criticism of the Pentateuch. Some important recent literature may be listed here: J. Hoftijzer, *Die Verheissungen an die drei Erzväter* (Leiden: E. J. Brill, 1956); O. Kaiser, "Traditionsgeschichtliche Untersuchung von Genesis 15," *ZAW* 70 (1958): 107–126; L. A. Snijders, "Genesis xv: The Covenant with Abram," *OTS* 12 (1958): 261–79; A. Caquot, "L'alliance avec Abram (Genèse 15)," *Semitica* 12 (1962): 51–66; H. Cazelles, "Connexions et structure de Gen. xv," *RB* 69 (1962): 321–49; H. Seebass, "Zu Genesis 15," *Wort und Dienst* NF 7 (1963): 132–49; R. E. Clements, *Abraham and David: Genesis xv and its Meaning for Israelite Tradition*, SBT 2/5 (London: SCM Press, 1967); N. Lohfink, *Die Landverheissung als Eid, Eine Studie zu Gn. 15* SBS 28 (Stuttgart: Verlag Katholisches Bibelwerk, 1967). An important unpublished work that should also be mentioned here is W. M. Clark, "The Origin and Development of the Land Promise Theme in the Old Testament" (Ph.D. diss., Yale University, 1964).

2. See the surveys in Kaiser, *ZAW* 70:108, n. 4; Caquot, *Semitica* 12:51–56; Lohfink, *Landverheissung*, pp. 24–30.

unit the divine speech of vv. 13–16 is a doublet to the one in vv. 18–21 and seems to come too soon, before the theophany of v. 17. These "doublets" have led some to argue for a vertical division of sources through both parts of the chapter.

Discussions of source division in this chapter have been complicated by another factor. There seems to be little agreement as to whether we are concerned in this chapter with a basic core of material supplemented by a later redactor, or whether it is a case of two independent sources that have subsequently been combined. In the latter instance verses are assigned to the two classical sources, J and E, but the difficulty with this is that the divine name, Yahweh, is used throughout. Consequently, the divine name is emended in some instances to Elohim, which looks like a very arbitrary procedure, especially since any other signs of E are difficult to assess. There is also little agreement on whether J or E is the basic source and how the actual source division should be carried through but it has in mind the combination of two parallel variants. On the other hand some verses, such as vv. 3, 5, 6, 7, 13–16, and 18–21, are assigned to a redactor who would be merely supplementing the previous account. It is noteworthy that the same verses can often be ascribed by one author to a variant version, for example E, and by another to a redactor, even though two entirely different literary processes are involved. Yet a decision for regarding a verse as belonging to a redactor or a variant is not made on the basis of literary criteria, but on a vague feeling about dating or Deuteronomic influence or the like. This leaves one with the strong impression that the source division has usually been carried forward on a largely arbitrary basis.

Another complication that has entered into the discussion of Genesis 15 is that of tradition-history. Since Alt's study on the "God of the Fathers," it has been suggested that in this chapter lies the oldest pre-settlement level of the forefather's tradition, so efforts have been made, quite apart from the source designation, to see in either vv. 1–6 or vv. 7–21 the oldest tradition. Of course, when this completely speculative approach is added to the arbitrariness of source division, anything can happen because any seeming tension in the text that cannot be solved by source division can always be accounted for by the prior oral history of the traditions.

It is to Otto Kaiser's credit, it seems to me, that he introduced a very important control over the whole literary and traditio-historical discussion of Genesis 15 by means of his form-critical analysis.[3] He could on this basis, for instance, immediately call into question Alt's notion about the "Shield of Abraham" being a possible archaic reference to an ancient patriarchal deity. However, Kaiser seems to have limited his form-critical scrutiny to the first part of the chapter, vv. 1–6 as well as v. 7 of the second, all of which he regarded as quite late. But the nucleus of vv. 9ff. he still regarded as based on an old tradition that did not have to be shown form-critically. A rather retrograde step was subsequently taken by H. Cazelles,[4] who resisted the implications of Kaiser's approach toward a late date for part of the chapter and instead appealed to vague and sporadic second-millennium parallels without any appreciation of the form-critical method. Unfortunately, many scholars have simply invoked Cazelles' study to support their prejudice for an early date.

Claus Westermann attempted to carry forward the form-critical approach along somewhat different lines from the approach of Kaiser, though complementary to it.[5] He raised the question of the nature of the narratives in both parts of Genesis 15 in order to decide whether or not their form could provide a basis for old promise traditions in either part of the chapter. The question that he raised was a most appropriate one, even though there may be some misgivings about the criteria he used for answering it. In the end Westermann also succumbed to the seduction of the traditio-historical approach instead of trying to establish some control over it. He suggested that even if 15:7–21 does not correspond to an appropriate oral narrative form one must assume that it originally existed anyway and was lost through later "reworking."[6]

The recent study of Lohfink also takes seriously the question of form-critical control, especially as it has to do with the assumption of a narrative base for the chapter and the issue of disunity that follows from this. In this respect his form-criticism controls his

3. See work in n. 1 above.
4. See work in n. 1 above.
5. Westermann, "Arten der Erzählung," pp. 21–24.
6. Ibid., p. 29: "Mann kann dann annehmen, dass hinter Gen. 15:7–21 eine alte Erzählung von der Verheissung des Landes steht, die aber stark verandert und stark überarbeitet wurde." This is another way of saying that since the evidence he would like to find doesn't exist he will presuppose it anyway.

literary analysis.[7] He also emphasizes the additional control of structural analysis of the text that illuminates the nature of the compositional movement of the text.[8] Nevertheless, for Lohfink as for many others, there are apparently two dogmas over which form-critical judgments are not permitted to exercise any control. The first is that the basic literary source belongs to the tenth century. Forms that are attested only in late sources may be extended back several centuries or assigned to the work of the redactor. The basic text is always interpreted strictly in terms of the context of the Davidic-Solomonic "empire." The second dogma largely unaffected by form-criticism is that behind this chapter there must be an ancient tradition that has a historical continuity with the "Patriarchal Age" itself and is a key to one or more of the basic themes and functions of the whole forefathers' tradition. All other considerations are adjusted to these two tenets, however difficult such explanations may be.[9]

It seems to me that the only viable method of approach is to restrict one's analysis and interpretation of the chapter to what can be reasonably controlled and not to speculate beyond those limits. The form of control of both literary and traditio-historical questions is form-critical analysis, which gives the best indication of the smaller or larger unities in the text and the environment[10] out of which the text comes. The second control is a structural analysis of the whole literary unit. Structural analysis is useful, it seems to me, for two reasons. Firstly, it allows for form-critical comparison to be made with oral narrative forms that are thought to lie behind the text and thus to judge whether such reconstructions of an earlier level of the tradition are reasonably possible. Secondly, it may bring to the surface a compositional design and movement that might otherwise be lost through various attempts at source division and thus constitute a strong argument for the text's unity. The full

---

7. *Landverheissung*, pp. 31–34.
8. Ibid., pp. 45–49.
9. This is also the approach of Clements in *Abraham and David*, which is almost entirely lacking in any form-critical approach and is completely speculative in its reconstructions of its tradition history. Kilian also (in *Abrahamsüberlieferungen*) is criticized rightly by Lohfink in *Landverheissung*, p. 31, n. 1 for his lack of any form-critical evaluation.
10. I use the term "environment" for a writer rather than *Sitz-im-Leben*, which has a narrower sociological perspective and does not allow sufficiently for the secondary appropriation of a form or genre in a purely literary work.

implication of these controls, form-criticism and structural analysis, must be taken seriously in the final interpretation of the text.

Forms and Structure

The forms (*Gattungen*) of this chapter constitute an amazing variety. The opening words of v. 1, "After these things..." *ʾaḥar haddᵉbārîm hāʾēlleh* form a literary connective used elsewhere in Genesis and in some other prose works. This generally functions as a very indefinite temporal connection with no indication whatever that any specific prior events are related to what follows.[11] To describe it as "editorial" may be a little misleading if this suggests that it does not belong to the author of what follows. But it is certainly the mark of written prose style of an extended prose work.

This opening statement is followed by the remark "The word of Yahweh came to Abram." This phrase, *hāyāh dᵉbar yhwh,* or the variant nominal form in v. 4, is a *terminus technicus* for the report of a divine speech to a prophet.[12] It first occurs in prophetic works in Jeremiah and becomes very frequent in Ezekiel. It also occurs frequently throughout the Deuteronomistic history in narrative having to do with prophets and was undoubtedly a convention for reporting prophetic revelation, which came into vogue at the end of the monarchy period. It does not occur in works of prophets before the time of Jeremiah except as late superscriptions of these works.

The word of Yahweh is here spoken of as coming in a "vision," *maḥᵃzeh*. This seems to be a rather strange combination of two different modes of prophetic reception of revelation that are usually kept quite distinct. Such, for instance, is the case in Ezekiel, where both modes are referred to frequently. However there is a fairly close parallel in the Deuteronomist's treatment of the dynastic oracle of Nathan to David in 2 Sam. 7. It is stated, v. 4, that at night "the word of Yahweh came to Nathan...," and the report is concluded by the remark "In accordance with all these words and all this vision [*ḥizzāyôn*] Nathan spoke to David," v. 17. In Gen. 15:1 it is hard to decide whether the reference to a vision is meant

---

11. In Genesis see 22:1,20; 39:7; 40:1; 48:1. Outside of Genesis see Josh. 24:29; 1 Kings 17:17; 21:1; Ezra 7:1; Esther 2:1; 3:1.

12. Kaiser, *ZAW* 70:110.

to suggest a nocturnal experience and thus anticipate v. 5 or not. At any rate, the report form is not very clear, for what immediately follows in v. 1b indicates that Abraham is both the medium of the oracle and its ultimate recipient.

The first phrase of the divine speech, v. 1b, "Fear not Abram" (*ʾal-tîrāʾ ʾabrām*), is the familiar mark of the salvation oracle (*Heilsorakel*), followed by the divine self-predication "I am your shield" and a word of encouragement, "your reward will be very great." Kaiser has pointed out that this same genre of oracle with the same components may be found among the oracles of Esarhaddon and Ashurbanipal.[13] There can be no question, from an examination of these, that they are all a form of oracle given to the king before a military campaign as an assurance of victory. They appear to be in response to the king's prayer of lament about the threats of the enemy, and they demand trust in the deity's power to bring victory. The belief that the deity is a shield or protection to the king is also stated in these Assyrian inscriptions as well as in the royal psalms of Israel. The "reward" (*śākār*), likewise, comes from this same military context and has to do with payment derived from the spoils of war and given for military service.[14] Consequently, this genre of oracle belongs to the sphere of the royal court and in this specific form fits the time of the late monarchy and exilic period.

These forms in v. 1b raise a number of questions. Are we to think of Abraham as a king preparing for battle? Some have tried to circumvent this problem by associating chap. 15 with chap. 14.[15] However, quite apart from the literary difficulties involved this is most unlikely, for this would place the oracle after the battle and after the booty has been rejected. Another problem is that the oracle is unmotivated by any lament for divine assistance, and this difficulty is only heightened by the use of the vague connective "after

---

13. *ZAW* 70:111ff. See also *ANET*², pp. 449–50. See also H. M. Dion, "The Patriarchal Traditions and the Literary Form of the 'Oracle of Salvation,'" *CBQ* 29 (1967): 198–206; idem, "The 'Fear Not' Formula and Holy War," *CBQ* 32 (1970): 565–70. The evidence for a late date for this form seems clear enough, and Lohfink (*Landverheissung*, p. 49, n. 9) indulges in some special pleading to try to find an original Aramaic origin for the form, which he would then like to make much earlier.

14. Kaiser, *ZAW* 70:113ff.; Westermann, "Erzählung," pp. 22–23; Lohfink, *Landverheissung*, p. 57. Cf. Cazelles, *RB* 69:328; also M. Kessler, "The 'Shield' of Abraham?" *VT* 14 (1964): 494–97.

15. See Caquot, *Semitica* 12:63–66, followed by Lohfink, *Landverheissung*, pp. 84–88.

these things." These problems cannot be lightly dismissed by the excuse that the writer was unconsciously using the court language of his day. On the contrary, the use of such a form has the appearance of being a deliberate and conscious choice, and any solution to the interpretation of v. 1 must take seriously these problems raised by the forms of the text.

There is no difficulty with the genre of vv. 2–3, which are easily recognized as a lament.[16] But its literary unity is another matter. Many scholars have felt that v. 3 is either a doublet of v. 2 coming from another source or a later explanation given to clarify a rather enigmatic statement. The difficulty is v. 2b with its anomalous grammatical construction and the problematical phrase *ben mešeq*. As it stands, it is a nominal sentence with explanatory glosses: "And a *ben-mesheq* (is) in my house, that is Damascus, Eliezer."[17] The many explanations of this half-verse are not very convincing. It may contain a special allusion that entirely escapes us to circumstances in the time of the writer. At any rate, nothing can be built on it. Nor can it be assumed that v. 3b is a parallel to it, and even without v. 2b there is a clear progression from the issue of childlessness to the problem of inheritance. Furthermore, a certain repetitious restatement of a complaint is quite typical of the lament form, even though it is not set down here in very poetic form. As it stands v. 2a follows directly from v. 1b, and v. 3b leads into v. 4 with the theme of inheritance, *yrš*. But vv. 4 and 1 have the same form of introduction, so there seems to be no adequate reason to doubt the unity of the whole passage, vv. 1–4.

The real problem with the lament of vv. 2–3 is how to understand its form-critical relationship to the salvation oracle of v. 1b. One would expect the reverse of the order here present, a lament-salvation oracle, and would not anticipate the shift in theme from war to lack of offspring. Even if one admits that the lack of an heir is a most important concern for a king,[18] it is hardly an issue appropriate to the war language of v. 1b. This peculiar juxtaposition of

16. Westermann, "Erzählung," p. 22; Lohfink, *Landverheissung*, p. 45.
17. For this rendering and a general discussion of the various proposals see Caquot, *Semitica* 12:57–58. Cf. Cazelles, *RB* 69:330f.; Speiser, *Genesis*, pp. 111–12; Clements, *Abraham and David*, p. 18; Seebass, "Gen. 15, 2b," *ZAW* 75 (1963): 317–19; H. L. Ginsberg, "Abram's 'Damascene' Steward," *BASOR* 200 (1970): 31–32.
18. In this connection note the similarity of language between v. 4 and 2 Sam. 7:12, especially the phrase $^{\jmath a}$ šer yēṣēʾ mimmēʿeykā.

various themes means that the apparent report form of oracle and response is highly artificial, and that the combination must be for an entirely different purpose.

The first dramatic element of the chapter is contained in v. 5. Yet it hardly functions as an adequate setting for the first unit. We are told that God took Abraham outside to view the stars, but we are hardly prepared for this action unless the scene is suggested by the vague phrase "in a vision," v. 1. This action of God taking someone to a certain spot to view something is a feature more characteristic of late prophetic visionary reports, such as that developed in Ezekiel and the later exilic prophets.[19] But if the words "he brought me outside" introduce a visionary experience the time of day suggested by the appearance of the stars is not a true dramatic element or any indication of a narrative tradition. But it does link up with the prophetic report forms of vv. 1 and 4.

The connection between v. 4 and v. 5 is not regarded by some as "original" because vv. 2–4 deal with the theme of an heir, while v. 5 has to do with numerous offspring. This argument loses much of its weight from the fact that there is no consistent form or theme in vv. 1–4. Also, v. 4 by itself would be a rather weak ending with just a simple rejection of the lament in v. 3. It is common to have a divine promise confirmed by a sign (cf. 2 Kings 20:8ff.; Isa. 7:10–17), and v. 5 is intended to be such a sign. Furthermore, there is some hint of a dynastic promise form in v. 4, and with such a promise there is always the extension of that promise to include a lengthy dynasty (2 Sam. 7:12,16; Ps. 89:29ff.; 132:11–12; cf. Jer. 33:20ff.). So the combination of a natural heir and numerous progeny is not a real difficulty.

The first pericope is then concluded by an expression of confidence in v. 6a, "So he believed Yahweh...."[20] This is a most appropriate conclusion, form-critically, to a unit that contains a salvation oracle and lament and confirms the connection of vv. 5–6 with vv. 1–4.[21] But v. 6b immediately introduces us into quite a different sphere,

---

19. See especially Ezek. chaps. 8–11.

20. Although the Hebrew verb appears to be waw consecutive perfect, the following verb is in the narrative tense, waw consecutive imperfect, so the first verb $w^eheˀĕmīn$ ought to be rendered accordingly.

21. Cf. Clements, *Abraham and David*, p. 19. Kilian (*Abrahamsüberlieferungen*, p. 61) ascribes vv. 4a, 5–6 to E and then amends *yhwh* to *ˀĕlōhîm* in both vv. 4 and 6. Such an approach could scarcely be more arbitrary.

that of the cult. Von Rad has clarified the usage of the phrase "And he reckoned it to him as righteousness," *wayyaḥšebehā llô ṣedāqāh*, by showing that it was the responsibility of the priest to accept or reject the worshipper on the presentation of his sacrifice or in various other acts of cultic examination.[22] The same declaration of acceptance (righteousness) is found in the temple liturgies of Pss. 15 and 24 and in the moral declarations of Ezek. 18, which are built on these. That this cultic form has here been placed in a radically new and quite uncultic context is a matter that will have to be taken quite seriously in the interpretation of this passage. What is significant for our form-critical discussion is that a form from yet another *Sitz im Leben*—the cultic—has been brought into combination with royal and prophetic forms. How is one to account for this mélange of forms? While von Rad has emphasized the significance of the particular combination in v. 6, the historical horizon to which this statement along with the whole unit of vv. 1–6 belongs has yet to be explained.[23]

A new theme begins in v. 7, and this is emphasized by another self-introduction formula from the deity. However, the *Sitz im Leben* of this formula is not the royal court, as in v. 1, but the cult, as is clear from its occurrence in the Holiness Code and the Priestly Code as well as from its adaptation in the exilic prophets. Its reference to the past activity of God makes it strongly confessional in nature also.[24] But this opening verse to a new theme cannot be regarded on the literary level as an entirely new beginning, because both the subject and the indirect object of the opening verb have their antecedents in the previous unit. Nor is v. 7 simply a late redactional link because the response by Abraham in v. 8 demands some prior statement, and its connection with the land promise in v. 7 is obvious. The theme of inheritance in vv. 7–8 returns to that of vv. 3–4, but with a shift in interest from the question of an heir to the

---

22. "Faith Reckoned as Righteousness" (1951) in *The Problem of the Hexateuch and Other Essays*, trans. E. W. Trueman Dicken (Edinburgh and London: Oliver & Boyd, 1966), pp. 125–30; idem, *Old Testament Theology* 1: 377–79.
23. Cf. von Rad, "Faith," pp. 129–30 for rather vague statements about the historical horizon of the passage.
24. On the form see W. Zimmerli, "Ich bin Jahwe" (1953), in *Gottes Offenbarung, Gesammelte Aufsätze zum Alten Testament* TB 19 (Munich: Chr. Kaiser, 1963), pp. 11–40; K. Elliger, "Ich bin den Herr-euer Gott" (1954), in *Kleine Schriften zum Alten Testament* TB 32 (Munich: Chr. Kaiser, 1966), pp. 211–31.

question of the land. In v. 8 Abraham asks for a confirmation of the promise in v. 7. This is not a lament, as in vv. 2–3, but a prayer for a sign, which is quite appropriate in the context.[25]

The instruction and preparation for the covenant ritual are given in vv. 9–10. There is no need to repeat what was said earlier about the problem of its form. I am still inclined to see the example in Jer. 34:18 and similar mid-first millennium parallels as the most appropriate way of understanding the ritual as a form of oath or self-imprecation. Nevertheless, since in this special circumstance the deity himself is involved (and not just as the guarantor of the oath), there are certain modifications. It has been noted that the specific designation of the kinds of animals and the treatment of the birds resembles cultic regulations for sacrifice.[26] Yet it is clearly not a sacrifice, so that the special preparations are the result of a hybrid of ritualistic forms to symbolize a unique historic act. One cannot find entirely suitable analogies for it because by its very nature it was never intended to be repeated. Another modification in form has to do with the representation of the deity in the smoking oven and flaming torch. Undoubtedly these have some reference to the smoke and fire theophany of Sinai. But it is also possible that we have here an instance of cultic instruments being used as symbols for the presence of the deity in place of images in an imageless cult.[27]

One detail that seems totally unnecessary is the mention of birds of prey coming down on the carcasses, v. 11. Since there is such great economy of presentation, it is hardly possible that this is simply meant as a picturesque detail. It must, in fact, be a clue to an ill omen.[28] Furthermore, birds of prey were primary symbols for the Egyptian monarchy,[29] so we may well have a reference here to the omen contained in vv. 13–16. But this raises the further

---

25. See also Lohfink, *Landverheissung*, pp. 48–49.
26. See S. E. Loewenstamm, "Zur traditionsgeschichte des Bundes zwischen den Stücken," *VT* 18 (1968): 500–06; but see already Clark, "Land Promise Theme," p. 62.
27. The importance of cultic objects as non-representational symbols of the deity becomes of paramount importance in the Greco-Roman period. See E. R. Goodenough, *Jewish Symbols in the Greco-Roman Period*, 13 vols. (New York: Pantheon Books, 1953–68), especially vol. 4. Goodenough also suggests (vol. 4, p. 74) a connection between the burning bush of Exodus 3 and the menorah.
28. See Gunkel, *Genesis*, p. 182; Skinner, *Genesis*, p. 281.
29. Cazelles, *RB* 69:338.

question of whether vv. 13–16 belong to the original account. Most scholars regard it as secondary and late and therefore suggest that in the original text v. 12 directly preceded v. 17. But is this likely? Why would the final episode be introduced by two statements of time, one a little later than the other? The difficulty is also increased if the action of v. 17 is to be thought of as taking place during the trance of v. 12, which is governed by the first time period. The two temporal introductions only make sense if they set off two different events. Within the larger covenant ceremony there is the omen-prophecy event. It is introduced by the appearance of the birds of prey, after which Abraham falls into a deep and terrifying trance (v. 12), in which he receives the prophecy (vv. 13–16). Only subsequent to this event does the final covenant ratification take place. This setting of a scene-within-a-scene set off by temporal indicators is also found in the Lot-Sodom story (chaps. 18–19). I can see no literary or form-critical reasons for excluding vv. 13–16 from the larger account.

Since vv. 13–16 are usually considered additional, very little attention is paid to the question of their form. It is not a case here of a prediction of a single event sometime in the future. Rather, it is the outlining of a historical period containing a series of events and presented *vaticinium ex eventu*. Such forms of prediction are typical of late apocalyptic literature, but this form of prophecy is also known from a somewhat earlier period in Mesopotamia.[30] The function of the prediction here is as a confirming sign of the promise in v. 7. Abraham asks (v. 8) "How shall I know . . . ?" The answer in v. 13 is "Know for certain . . . ." In Deuteronomy and the late prophetic books fulfillment of prophecy becomes an important proof of the true word of God.

The terms of the covenant are given in vv. 18–21 in the form of a divine grant of land with its boundaries specified.[31] These limits and

---

30. See A. K. Grayson and W. G. Lambert, "Akkadian Prophecies," *JCS* 18 (1964): 7–30; W. W. Hallo "Akkadian Apocalypses," *IEJ* 16 (1966): 231–242; *ANET*², pp. 451–52.

31. M. Weinfeld, "The Covenant of Grant in the Old Testament and in the Ancient Near East," *JAOS* 90 (1970): 184–203 (especially pp. 196–99); S. E. Loewenstamm, "The Divine Grants of Land to the Patriarchs," *JAOS* 91 (1971): 509–10. However, Clark, in "Land Promise Theme," pp. 22–29, emphasizes a distinction between land grant and land promise and does not regard the legal concept of land transfer as adequate to explain the form of a *promise* of land.

the names of the indigenous inhabitants are known from the Deuteronomic sources, except that three names, the Kenites, the Kenizzites, and the Kadmonites, are additional.[32] Yet there is no form-critical reason for making any source division in vv. 18–21. Such decisions have been made on the basis of a theory of tradition-history and not on any controlled criterion. The text itself gives no warrant for any such reconstruction.

We may summarize our survey of the forms in chap. 15 by noting the great number and complexity of genres that have been combined in this chapter. They are drawn from the royal court, the cult, prophetic narrative conventions, and legal spheres. Yet in spite of this variety there is no reason form-critically why any particular verse should be separated from the basic account and considered as secondary or why there should be a general source division into more than one source. It still remains to present briefly a structural analysis of the whole chapter. This will give us an additional criterion by which to judge its unity and will clarify the question of whether or not there is a still older story-tradition form that is the chapter's ultimate origin and unity.

In his recent study Lohfink has given a discussion of the structure of this chapter.[33] It becomes immediately clear that the whole unit has been carefully composed of two balanced parts, vv. 1–5 and vv. 7–21, with v. 6 as a connecting link between the two halves. Both sections begin with divine self-introduction and make use of conventional formulae (vv. 1 and 7). In both cases Abraham replies with the invocation of the divine name and epithet, "O Lord, Yahweh," ᵓ*adōnāy yhwh*. In one case he uses a lament; in the other, a prayer for a sign, vv. 2–3 and 8. To both of these prayers Yahweh replies in a twofold manner. In the first instance Abraham is given a promise, v. 4, followed by a sign, which *extends* the content of the promise, v. 5. In the second part, since the promise is part of the opening word of Yahweh, the reply has to do only with the guarantee. But this itself is in two forms, the covenant (vv. 9–10, 17–21) and the omen-prophecy (vv. 11–16), which at the same time *qualifies* the immediate effectiveness of the covenantal promise. Both sections

---

32. On the development of the lists see Van Seters, "The Terms 'Amorite' and 'Hittite' in the Old Testament," *VT* 22 (1972): 67–72. There is no justification for Clements' (*Abraham and David*, p. 21) viewing these three names as the most original. To do so he must radically emend v. 18.

33. *Landverheissung*, pp. 45–49; cf. also Westermann, "Arten der Erzählung," p. 22.

also have some dramatic and temporal notations at about the same point in the structure, vv. 5, and 9–12, 17. Each section deals with a basic promise theme: the promise of offspring in vv. 1–5 and the promise of land in vv. 7–21. But they are closely tied together by the use of important catch words such as *yrš*, "to inherit", vv. 3,4,7, and 8; and *zeraᶜ*, "seed", vv. 3,5,13, and 18, which are basic to the theme of both parts. The balanced structuring of the whole as well as of the two parts and the interconnections between the two are such that they could not have resulted from a series of fortuitous additions and reworkings. The plan of the whole chapter is far too deliberate for that.

One other question must be considered here. It has frequently been suggested that behind Genesis 15, or part of it, lies an ancient story about theophany and promise to Abraham. If this is the case one might at least expect that the basic structure of such an account is still evident within the present text. There is a number of such theophany stories that still retain at least some of the essential dramatic structure of such accounts, and these can be used for purposes of comparison. They are: the call of Moses (Exodus 3), the call of Gideon (Judg. 6),[34] and the birth announcement to Manoah and his wife (Judg. 13). The structure of these episodes is as follows:

1) There is a general situation of distress for Israel, Exod. 2:23–25; Judg. 6:1–6; 13:1.
2) There is the appearance of the messenger of Yahweh at a specific time and place and in a dramatic form, Exod. 3:1–5; Judg. 6:11ff.; 13:2ff., 9.
3) The appearance of the messenger is in response to the situation of need, and its purpose is to commission a deliverer, Exod. 3:7–10; Judg. 6:12–14, or to announce his birth, Judg. 13:5.
4) This commissioning may be followed by a protest of weakness, calling forth a promise of the divine presence, Exod. 3:11–12; Judg. 6:15–16.

---

34. For these two episodes see W. Richter, *Die sogenannten vorprophetischen Berufungsberichte. Ein literaturwissenschaftliche Studie zur I Sam. 9, 1–10, 16, Ex. 3f. und Ri. 6, 11b–17* FRLANT 101 (Gottingen: Vandenhoeck and Ruprecht, 1970). However, Richter does a structural analysis of Exod. 3 only after he has divided it into two sources on the basis of rather dubious criteria. I can therefore accept little of his analysis.

5) Confirmation of the promised deliverance is by means of a sign or self-disclosure of the deity with an expression by the petitioner of fear, Exod. 3:12 (3:6, 13–15); Judg. 6:17–23 and 13:15–21.
6) This deliverance is carried out in the rest of the story, Exod. 5ff.; Judg. 7–8 and 14–16.

It appears that Exodus 3 contains the greatest modification of this pattern, in which the unusual form of the theophany has itself become the divine disclosure (v. 6) rather early in the pattern. But even here the self-identification is repeated in fuller form after the sign and in response to the question about the name (vv. 13–15, cf. Judg. 13:17ff.). This change, it seems to me, was for theological purposes and was not a reflection of the basic form. The sign also, in the form of a prediction about future worship at Sinai, is dramatically weak, since its fulfillment would come *after* the deliverance. Moses' protest takes on the character of resistance to a prophetic commissioning similar to Jeremiah's confessions, since there is a concern about Israel's lack of faith and his own inability to speak. For the purpose of our present discussion, what is most important to note, firstly, is that the theophanic episode cannot exist independent of the situation of crisis that precedes or of the resolution of the crisis that follows. Its sole function is to indicate that the turning point in the events is by direct intervention from God. But this is not the case with Genesis 15, which has nothing corresponding to either the first or the last element of the above outline. It is a self-contained unit of reflection with the barest minimum of dramatic movement of any kind. How could it possibly reflect a theophanic legend without such essential elements present?

Secondly, it is possible to observe on the basis of Exodus 3 that even where the pattern of such a story is present its various components may be modified by influences from quite different aspects of Israel's cultic and religious life because the components had their counterparts in other genres. Note, for instance, how the divine disclosure motif, typical of legend, becomes in Exod. 3:6 and 13ff. various forms of liturgical and confessional self-predication formulae. There is no justification for thinking that such formulae actually originated in legendary traditions. In Gen. 15:1 and 7 this is all we have, unaccompanied by any dramatic elements whatever. So too with every other element in Genesis 15. We have seen that form-critically they all belong to various spheres of Israel's religious and national life, its cult and liturgy with scarcely a trace of any legendary motif present anywhere.[35]

It seems to me, therefore, quite illegitimate for Lohfink and Westermann to suggest, in the absence of any legendary form or motif, that an ancient legend has been reworked or modified by a later author.[36] As far as the traditions behind the chapter are concerned, we have previously suggested that in the earliest written source both the story of Isaac's birth and the promise of land were present in their simplest forms. It is perfectly reasonable to suppose that the treatment of the two themes in this source was built directly on this earlier written tradition, since literary dependence has already been demonstrated. No other hypothetical schemes or fanciful reconstructions are necessary.

The Meaning of Genesis 15

This brings us to the difficult task of discerning the author's meaning in the use of just these particular forms and themes. Admittedly, this is only possible if we have some clear indication of the period in which he lived and if the character and concerns of that period are known. The idea held by some scholars that one can reconstruct a multilayered history of the tradition into early preliterary levels, then guess correctly what the meaning and function of those various levels were, and go on to reconstruct certain historical aspects of those periods is surely a great delusion.[37] We will deal with this passage as a unit and as something immediately meaningful to the audience of its day, about whom we can have fairly direct knowledge.

It is best to start with the second part, and v. 7 in particular, because it contains a fairly precise date for the whole unit.[38] There

---

35. Lohfink's approach (*Landverheissung*, pp. 51–78), which seeks to find some element of antiquity behind the various formal elements misses the whole point of form-critical control of tradition-history.
36. Lohfink, ibid., p. 54; Westermann, "Arten der Erzählung," pp. 24, 29.
37. See especially the study of Clements, *Abraham and David*; and Kilian, *Abrahamsüberlieferungen*, pp. 54–73.
38. See Van Seters, "Confessional Reformulation in the Exilic Period," *VT* 22 (1972): 455f. Many of the observations made in this article were already anticipated by Clark in his study of the land promise theme (see n. 1 above). However, my article was written quite independent of this study, which I did not consult until the spring of 1973.

we have a reference to "Ur of the Chaldeans" and this can only have meaning in the Neo-Babylonian period, during the period of Chaldean dominance and the reign of Nabonidus in particular.[39] So the period from which the Abraham tradition is being viewed is the late exilic period, and it is to the exilic community that the words of this chapter are being addressed. Verse 7b states: "I am Yahweh who brought you from Ur of the Chaldeans to give you possession of this land." As discussed above, the form of the divine speech in this passage is the "self-introduction formula," which in the form expanded by a participial phrase regularly has reference to the exodus event as it does in the Decalogue (Exod. 20:2, Deut. 5:6) and in other preexilic and early exilic sources. A particularly close parallel to the one in Genesis comes from the Holiness Code, Lev. 25:38, which states: "I am Yahweh your God who brought you from the land of Egypt to give you the land of Canaan and to be your God." This liturgical statement is a declaration of Israel's election through the exodus as well as Israel's right to the land of Canaan.[40] In the form of paranesis this confession also dominates the book of Deuteronomy. Until the time of the exile Yahweh's most important predication or confession of identity was in terms of the exodus-election tradition.

In Gen. 15:7, however, the reference to Egypt has been changed to Ur of the Chaldeans, and with it there is a fundamental shift in the whole election-tradition. Yahweh is now the God of Abraham and his offspring. Just when this shift took place can be quite clearly traced in the biblical texts.[41] Jeremiah and Ezekiel, the last prophets of the monarchy and the early exilic period, still held to the theme of divine election through the exodus event and the promise of land to Israel *at that time* (Ezek. 20:5-6). Ezekiel, it is true, does mention Abraham once (33:24), and he is the first prophet to do so. But the claim to land based on the Abraham tradition is treated in rather disparaging terms.[42]

But with Deutero-Isaiah the situation has entirely changed.

---

39. Clark, in "Land Promise Theme," pp. 61-72, argues for an exilic date for 15:7-21.
40. Lohfink's treatment of this comparison (*Landverheissung*, p. 60f.), in which both references, Gen. 15:7 and Lev. 25:38, are vaguely suggested as belonging to old cultic formulae, completely misses the point at issue.
41. The shift is certainly complete by the time of the Chronicler. See Neh. 9:7-8, which is dependent upon both Genesis 15 and 17.
42. See more fully *VT* 22:448-451.

Isa. 41:8f. contains a clear reference to election through the forefathers. It states:

> You, Israel, my servant,
> Jacob, whom I have chosen,
> Offspring of Abraham, my friend
> whom I seized from the edge of the world
> and summoned from its farthest parts,
> And said to you, "You are my servant,
> I have chosen you and not rejected you."

Here God's election and call of Abraham from a distant land is viewed as Israel's election also. And the relevance of this for the exiles is that God can again bring them from these same distant regions to the promised land.

Likewise, of considerable importance in Gen. 15:7 is the connection between the election of Abraham and the land. I have recently tried to show that in the Deuteronomic tradition and in the prophets Jeremiah and Ezekiel, the land promise theme was closely tied to the exodus from Egypt and to the conditional covenant of the wilderness.[43] Disobedience to the law meant a curse upon the land, which could eventually result in forfeiture. The exile was proof that the covenantal relationship was broken, and with it the legitimate claim to the land. This was not only a crisis of faith but also a crisis of corporate identity. Only by establishing a new basis for a claim to the land that would supercede the older covenantal basis could this crisis be overcome. Such a basis was found by associating the promise of land not with the "fathers" of the exodus, but with the forefathers long before the exodus, a promise which was not conditional. It is in this light that one must view the question by Abraham in v. 8, "How can I be sure that I will inherit it?" This is the question of the exilic community concerning the land. They had become uncertain because the previous covenantal basis was no longer valid as any grounds for hope in a restoration. Consequently, in what follows (vv. 9–10 and 17–21), there is a "new" covenant in the form of the strongest possible oath. It is a promise that is entirely unconditional.

A word must be said here about the dimensions of the land. It is often asserted that this description in vv. 18–21 corresponds to the

---

43. Ibid., pp. 448–454. See also Clark, "Land Promise Theme," pp. 44–46.

Davidic-Solomonic empire, but there is no justification for such a claim.[44] The major part of Syria, the Phoenician coast, and Philistia were never a part of those kingdoms even though the Deuteronomistic account attempts to idealize their reigns as much as possible. These dimensions in Gen. 15:18–21 are known from Deuteronomic sources as the "land of the Amorites," in which the seven indigenous nations lived. The development of this idealized boundary was the product of the Assyrian domination of the West from the eighth century onward.[45] However, there are two important differences with the earlier Deuteronomic form. If we may trust the extant text, v. 18 speaks of the southern boundary being the "river of Egypt" *nᵉhar miṣraim* (the Nile) and not the "wadi of Egypt,' *naḥal miṣraim* (El Arish). This latter, more northern, boundary of Egypt was apparently valid for most of the Assyrian empire period but after the rise of the Neo-Babylonian power there is good reason to believe that the whole region from Gaza to the Eastern Delta was no longer under Egyptian control. Arab tribes now ruled this region and cooperated with the Babylonian and Persian authorities. So the change here might have been quite deliberate. In the same way one should interpret the three additions to the list of traditional peoples, the Kenites, Kenizzites and Kadmonites, as representing the Arab peoples in the immediate vicinity of, or within, the boundaries specified. Thus, it included not only the land of the settled peoples but the regions of the nomadic groups as well.

In light of this new election-covenant construction, the reason for the prediction in vv. 13–16 becomes clear. Its purpose is twofold. Firstly, it is able to incorporate the exodus tradition into the land-promise to the forefathers as a way of explaining historically the delay in the fulfillment until the conquest. Secondly, it is possible that the author was using the sojourn in Egypt as a model for the exile, since it is known from Deutero-Isaiah that such exodus typology was popular in the time of the exile.[46] There is the statement in v. 14 "But the nation which they will serve I am about to judge" (*dān ᵓānōkî*), as if the matter were fairly imminent. There is also the

---

44. See Clements, *Abraham and David*, pp. 21–22; Lohfink, *Landverheissung*, pp. 73ff. For the historical arguments see A. Malamat, "Aspects of the Foreign Policies of David and Solomon," *JNES* 22 (1963): 1–17.
45. See *VT* 22:6ff.; also Clark, "Land Promise Theme," pp. 65f.
46. B. W. Anderson, "Exodus Typology in Second Isaiah," *Israel's Prophetic Heritage*, ed. B. W. Anderson and W. Harrelson (New York: Harper & Bros., 1962), pp. 177–95.

apparent discrepancy between the four-hundred-year sojourn and the fourth generation returning "here." This problem cannot be resolved by mathematics or by proposing that two different historical periods are in view.[47] It is much easier to see in the "fourth generation" a prediction about the actual end of the exile. Finally, the last statement that "the guilt of the Amorites has not yet reached its limit" may be seen as a statement concerned about the delay of the return from exile.

This brings us to a consideration of 15:1–6. On the basis of what we have discovered above we can now suggest that v. 1 is really a prophetic word addressed to the exilic community. It may appear in the present context to come "out of the blue" without explanation, but for its hearers it had a very familiar ring. It is the same prophecy that becomes the theme of Deutero-Isaiah. The latter states in 40:9–10:

> Get up to a high mountain,
> Zion, herald of good tidings;
> Lift up your voice with strength,
> Jerusalem, herald of good tidings,
> Lift it up, don't be afraid; [$^{\flat}al\ t\hat{\imath}r\bar{a}^{\flat}\hat{\imath}$]
> Say to the cities of Judah,
> "Behold your God!"
> Behold, the Lord, Yahweh comes with might,
> And his arm rules for him;
> Behold his reward [$\acute{s}^ek\bar{a}r\hat{o}$] is with him,
> And his recompense before him.

Here we have together in the same short space of one saying several of the same ingredients that we find in Gen. 15:1. Even the designation for deity, $^{\flat a}d\bar{o}n\bar{a}y\ yhwh$, of 15:2 is found here. It was J. Begrich who pointed out that this prophet has developed the salvation-oracle (*Heilsorakel*) taken from the cult into a prominent form of prophetic speech for the exilic period.[48] But one can go beyond this, for we know that this form of salvation oracle originally had a quite specific royal context. So this prophet has democratized it and addresses it directly to the people to turn them toward a new hope in God's mighty promise of restoration. And by addressing

---

47. See Lohfink, *Landverheissung*, pp. 85–86.
48. J. Begrich, "Das priesterliche Heilsorakel," *ZAW* 52 (1934): 81–92.

such a royal form to Abraham in Gen. 15:1, our author there has done exactly the same thing. To my mind such a similarity cannot be fortuitous. Likewise, in Isa. 41:10, following the theme of election through Abraham, there is another salvation oracle: "Fear not, for I am with you . . . ," and this same form occurs in the theophany to Isaac, Gen. 26:24. Also, in both stories about Abimelech requesting a covenant treaty with the forefather, the foreign king acknowledges that "God/Yahweh is with you" (21:22; 26:28). All of these statements, according to our literary analysis, belong to the same Yahwistic source.[49]

Following the salvation oracle in Gen. 15:1, which states the divine word of promise to the exilic community, there is a lament by Abraham about his childlessness and a threat to the loss of his inheritance. One of the characteristic features of Deutero-Isaiah is the way in which his prophecy is interspersed with direct or indirect references to laments by the exilic community about the hopelessness of their plight. One passage in which the prophet seeks to encourage the despondent community, 54:1–3, is particularly instructive. The prophet depicts the survivors in Judah as a barren woman and promises her many children. He also speaks about enlarging the tent and lengthening the cords. This is not a reference to the mode of living in Judah at this time, but a direct allusion to the Abraham tradition. Furthermore, v. 3 directly connects the great increase in population with the expansion of territories and makes the statement "your offspring will inherit nations," $w^e zar^c \bar{e}k\ g \hat{o} y \hat{i}m\ y \hat{i}ra\check{s}$. This statement could also serve as a summary for Genesis 15 and for the final promise in vv. 18–21. But it is important to see that the themes of offspring (collective) to a barren individual, numerous progeny, inheritance of the land ($yr\check{s}$), and extensive territory, are all in close combination here. These themes in the rest of the Abraham story will be taken up again below.

This brings us to the remarkable statement of Gen. 15:6: "And he believed Yahweh, and he reckoned it to him as righteousness." It is remarkable, as von Rad points out in his form-critical study of it, because the reckoning of one as righteous has been extracted from its usual cultic and liturgical context and applied to the act of faith in the promise of God, specifically this promise of Abraham having numerous descendants who would inherit the

---

49. See also Gen. 21:17ff., where the salvation oracle occurs again in this same source.

promised land.⁵⁰ Von Rad did not attempt to find any historical context for such a "revolutionary formulation."⁵¹ He seems to suggest vaguely that it was the isolated reflection of one man (E) living sometime during the monarchy. Placing this text in the exilic period, however, makes its significance immediately clear. Cultic activity was at a minimum and it was, at any rate, entirely secondary to one completely overriding concern, namely, whether or not a particular Jew living in the exile really believed there was a future for Israel any longer. One cannot read through Deutero-Isaiah without being convinced that his fundamental concern is with faith in God's desire and ability to restore his people once more. In this exilic context the statement about faith being reckoned as righteousness becomes most appropriate and Abraham, the sojourner, becomes the ideal of the Jew who lived in this hope.

Of course, viewed in this light, there is nothing contradictory about a Jew who held to this promise and yet who wanted to know on what basis he could lay claim to the land, especially since the old covenant basis was broken. The explanation of this new basis is set forth in vv. 7–21 and includes a reorientation of Yahweh's confessional identity, a new land-promise covenant, and an accounting for the delay in the fulfillment. In this way the whole chapter became a very close-knit unit, fully intelligible to the Jew of the exile, telling him exactly where he stood and what his future was if he would exercise faith in this word of salvation from the God of Abraham.

The Promises to the Fathers

The two promise themes of numerous progeny and land that formed the basis of reflection in Genesis 15 must now be considered within the context of the larger Abraham tradition.⁵² Of course, these themes are not restricted to the Abraham tradition alone, but run throughout the rest of Genesis and are reiterated elsewhere in the Pentateuch. However, a comprehensive treatment will not be

50. See the works in n. 22 above.
51. Von Rad, *Theology* 1:329.
52. In addition to the works cited in n. 1 above, see J. Muilenberg, "Abraham and the Nations," *Interpretation* 19 (1965): 389–398; H. W. Wolff, "The Kerygma of the Yahwist," *Interpretation* 20 (1966): 131–58; G. von Rad, "The Promised Land and Yahweh's Land in the Hexateuch" (1943), in *The Problem of the Hexateuch and Other Essays*, pp. 79–93; J. Schreiner, "Segen für die Völker in der Verheissung an die Väter," *BZ* N.F. 6 (1962): 1–31.

undertaken here. The two themes as they relate to the forefathers are most dominant in the Abraham tradition, and we will therefore concentrate on a reevaluation of these.

In a study of the divine promises to the forefathers, J. Hoftijzer distinguished between two groups of promise passages in Genesis, those related to Genesis 15 and those by the author of Genesis 17.[53] This distinction was made on the basis of affinity in vocabulary, phraseology, and motifs within the two groups. The group associated with Genesis 17 is generally recognized by all the literary critics as the work of P, and we will consider this group together with a treatment of Genesis 17. Those of the other group, however, are often assigned to various sources, but their uniformity, as Hoftijzer has shown, speaks against this so I will also treat them here as a group.[54] On the other hand, I cannot follow Hoftijzer in his view that all the references to the promises outside of Genesis 15 are secondary, and in many instances we have seen that they are part of the primary source.

In a more recent treatment of the promise themes, Westermann approached the discussion in quite a different way.[55] He wanted to deal with the problem that had arisen in the traditio-historical studies on Abraham, as to which promise theme is the more original and how far these themes reflect a very early preliterary level of the tradition. In order to do this he attempted to classify the promise stories into various types, but his classification may be immediately disputed. For instance, he regarded both the accounts of 18:10ff. and 16:1–16 as belonging to his first type, that of stories about the promise of a son,[56] but this is hardly an accurate description of these episodes. The first, as we have seen, is part of the birth story of Isaac, and the second is a story of a quite different character ending originally with 16:12. It is hardly a promise story, since Hagar is already pregnant when the heavenly messenger appears to her. So there are still only the two basic promise themes, as we mentioned at the outset.

The opening statement of the Abraham tradition presents what

53. *Die Verheissungen an die drei Erzväter*, chap. 1.
54. The only exception to Hoftijzer's groupings is Gen. 12:7 which I have assigned above to the earliest source, the first pre-Yahwist. But even this reference was included in the Yahwistic source as the origin of his land promise theme.
55. "Arten der Erzählung," especially pp. 11–34.
56. Ibid., pp. 19–20.

many scholars feel is an important kerygmatic statement by the so-called Yahwist. The passage in 12:1-3 states:

> Yahweh said to Abram, "Go from your homeland, your birthplace and your father's household, to the land which I will reveal to you. And I will make you[57] into a great nation, and I will bless you and make your name great, so that you will be a means of blessing.[58] I will bless those who bless you but the one who curses you I shall curse. Through you will all the families of the earth obtain a blessing.[59]

I proposed earlier that on the older level of the written tradition the Abraham story opened with the land promise alone (12:1 and 6-7). Consequently, it is the later Yahwist who builds into this older theme the promise of numerous progeny. It is suggested in the opening statement of v. 2 that with the gift of the land God will also make Abraham into a great national state, and such a theme is repeated in 18:18 (cf. 21:13 and 18 re. Ishmael). Frequently we are told that this statement reflects the Davidic or Solomonic period and functioned as a legitimation of the empire.[60] But is this really the case? What this statement has in mind is a purely ethnic form of identity with no necessity for a monarchy whatever. Abraham is not the beginning of a royal line but of all the families in Israel. Now in the Davidic-Solomonic period there does not seem to be any such sense of unity, even between Israel and Judah, let alone all the other disparate elements.[61] The king was the fundamental and sole basis of unity, and there is not a hint anywhere of the monarchy being traced back to Abraham. So the significance of the statement must be otherwise.

---

57. There is some question about the significance of the cohortative after an imperative. Here it expresses more than simple futurity and probably signifies strong intention or promise; cf. Wolff, *Interpretation* 20:137, n. 28.

58. There is no need to emend the text to waw consecutive perfect third person singular. The imperative here expresses purpose and refers directly to Abraham. See Schreiner, *BZ* 6:4-5.

59. The niphal of the verb is used here and in 18:18 and 28:14, while the hithpael is used in Gen. 22:18; 26:4, and Jer. 4:2. Since the pual and the qal passive participle are not used here it is suggested that the meaning of the niphʿal and hiphʿil ought to be more reflexive. See Schreiner, ibid., p. 7; Wolff, *Interpretation* 20:137, n. 31.

60. Schreiner, *BZ* 6:29-30; Wolff, *Interpretation* 20:133-37; cf. Wagner, "Abraham and David?," pp. 12ff.

61. A. Alt, "The Formation of the Israelite State in Palestine," (1930) in *Essays on Old Testament History and Religion*, pp. 205ff.

The situation of the exile fits this promise much better. It was not enough for either the exiles or the remnant in Judah to have the promise of the land; they must also have people to fill it and to become strong and respected. This theme of great numbers is strongly emphasized by comparisons with the stars of heaven, the dust of the earth, or the sand by the seashore (13:16; 15:5; 22:17; 26:4; 28:14; 32:12). Deuteronomy has a great deal to say about Israel becoming a people (ʿam) of God, but it is not at all concerned about size or might; in fact, if anything the opposite is true.[62] Israel is not a great nation and must depend entirely on the strength and protection of Yahweh. The important thing is that it is a holy people separate from the nations and obedient to God.[63] As such they will live long on the land that God gives to them. The issue for Deuteronomy was not how many people there were but how loyal to God they were. Only with the threat of extinction in the exile does the divine promise of numbers become important.

The next term, "I will bless you" (waʾabārekekā), presents some difficulties. First of all, by itself it is ambiguous but from the other passages it is clear that it can refer to both human fertility (22:17) and material prosperity (24:35; 26:13). So it may have reference to both the theme of progeny and the blessing of the land. The more difficult problem is the form-critical one.[64] This term suggests the promise of blessing but not the blessing itself. The original *Sitz im Leben* of the divine blessing would certainly be in a cultic context in which the word of blessing is spoken directly (Num. 6:22–27). The cultic act of blessing would never project a blessing for a certain time in the future.[65]

But there is another sphere of blessing that may be more helpful.

---

62. Only in the late prologue, Deut. 1:10, is it suggested that by the end of the wilderness journey Israel had become as numerous as the stars.

63. On this theme see M. Weinfeld, *Deuteronomy and the Deuteronomic School* (Oxford: Clarendon Press, 1972), pp. 226ff.

64. For recent treatments of "blessing" in the OT see J. Scharbert, "'Fluchen' und 'Segnen' im Alten Testament," *Biblica* 39 (1958): 1–26; Schreiner (as cited in n. 52 above); W. Schottroff, *Der altisraelitische Fluchspruch* (Neukirchen-Vluyn: Neukirchener Verlag, 1969) especially pp. 163–198. This work contains an extensive bibliography on the subject.

65. Cf. Schottroff, *Fluchspruch*, pp. 170–72. I cannot agree with Schottroff that these blessing promises originated in the Salvation oracle, for he can offer no such examples. They are secondary in their development, whether in the first- or third-person form (Deut. 7:13; 15:10; 16:15).

THE COVENANT OF ABRAHAM

In Deuteronomy the notion of the curse as the result of breaking the law is very strong, and this has been carried over from the whole realm of Near Eastern law and treaty.[66] But alongside of this Deuteronomy places blessing for those who keep the law. Thus one is blessed, *bārûk*, or cursed, *ʾārûr*, according to his obedience or disobedience to the law, Deuteronomy 28 (cf. 11:26–28). This form is expressed by the use of a passive participle expressing an immediate and automatic consequence of a particular action. In another passage, 7:12–14, Deuteronomy projects into the future the blessing of fertility that will result from obedience to the law. Here it is expressed with an active finite verb and with God as subject.[67] But the direct relationship between law and blessing is maintained. In Gen. 12:2 the promise of blessing is made by the deity in the first person, and it is now viewed as the result of Abraham's one act of obedience. A similar act of obedience in chap. 22 results in a promise of blessing, vv. 16–18. In 26:5 these acts by Abraham are apparently interpreted as corresponding to the charges, commands, statutes, and laws of Deuteronomy. At this point the whole notion of a blessing associated with a specific set of laws or code has become abstracted to a very considerable degree. But what is even more remarkable about 26:3–5 (24) is that Abraham's past obedience effects a blessing for the following generations as well. This is certainly a concept of the "merits of the fathers" that insures the destiny of the people as a whole. While one may regard the phraseology of 26:5 as Deuteronomic it is quite a different conception of law and blessing. It suggests that in spite of Israel's sin, which brought about the exile, the promises of land and offspring made to Abraham are still good.

This raises the problem of how law is to be related to the Abraham tradition.[68] The answer is given in Gen. 18:19 in which Abraham is now the one who instructs his children and household "to keep the way of Yahweh by doing what is right and just," and he then becomes the example of piety for all his descendents. This is not just a Deuteronomic addition of little consequence, as is so often

---

66. See recently Weinfeld, *Deuteronomy*, pp. 116–157; Schottroff, ibid., pp. 152ff.
67. See also Deut. 15:10; 16:15.
68. This is an important question raised throughout Hoftijzer's book *Die Verheissungen an die drei Erzväter*. My basic disagreement with Hoftijzer is that he did not consider the possibility of his Genesis 15 group coming *after* Deuteronomy. This would solve a great many difficulties that arise from his treatment of the promises theme.

suggested, but a matter of great consequence. Since, on the basis of Deuteronomy, the Horeb-wilderness covenant was broken and invalid the whole realm of law was left in limbo. By associating the law with Abraham and constituting it as a family responsibility separate from any larger state authority it had a new validity (cf. Deut. 6:6–9). It is also suggested in 18:19 that the promises are at least partially conditional upon obedience of the children to the ways of God.

The question that immediately arises is how these two themes of obedience to the law and the merit of Abraham's obedience could be maintained together. The answer is found once again in the conception of the Israelite monarchy. The Deuteronomist continually points out that the kingdom of Judah, and specifically its king, was spared from ultimate judgment or disaster for David's sake, both because of God's election of David and also because of David's faithfulness to God's commandments (1 Kings 11:32, 34; 2 Kings 19:34; 20:6). Nevertheless this ultimate loyalty to the Davidic dynasty is qualified by the notion that breach of God's commandments could lead to disciplining and temporary suspension of the blessings (2 Sam. 7:14–16; cf. Pss. 132:12). It is this specifically dynastic principle that has been transferred by the Genesis writer to Abraham and hence to Israel as a whole.

The rest of the motifs in Gen. 12:2–3 properly belong to the royal court. It is the king whose name is made great (cf. 2 Sam. 7:9) and through whose name and person blessings come on the whole realm (Ps. 72). Such blessings also extend beyond the nation itself and have imperial dimensions (also 18:18; 22:18; 28:14) and this has its parallel in the coronation blessing, Ps. 72:17:

> May his name be blessed forever,
> As long as the sun may his name endure;
> So that all the families of the earth
> may be blessed by him,
> All nations regard him as blessed.[69]

The theme about blessing those who bless Israel and cursing the one who curses Israel also has its origin in the concept of an imperial monarchy. This is true of the related theme of Abraham's offspring possessing "the gates of their enemies" (22:18, 26:40). Such an

69. The text is restored on the basis of the Greek, which suggests the addition of מברך in 17aα and כל משפחות הארץ in 17bα. In 17aβ, ינין, which is a hapax legomenon and of uncertain meaning, is rendered in the Greek by *diamenei*, "may it remain."

imperial monarchy does not have in mind the Davidic-Solomonic period, which never had such effective dimensions.[70] It is, instead, an imitation of the great Assyrian and Babylonian empires of the eighth to sixth centuries.

Gen. 12:2–3 has deliberately and consciously taken over this royal form of expression and applied it to Abraham in the same way as in Gen. 15:1. That is to say, when Abraham is addressed in this way it can only mean the democratization of royal forms. Just such a process is also evident in Deutero-Isaiah, in which the Davidic covenant itself is reapplied to the whole people (Isa. 55:3–5).[71] In both Gen. 12:1–3 and Deutero-Isaiah there is a kind of beneficent imperialism toward the nations.[72] This is in contrast to Deuteronomy, whose attitude was one of antagonism toward other nations. Deuteronomy speaks of being "blessed more than all the peoples" (7:14), but not as a means of blessing to other peoples.

These promises of numerous increase and of becoming a "blessing" $b^e r\bar{a}k\bar{a}$ can only be properly understood against the background of hope in the exilic period. Jer. 30:19 contains the divine promise "I will multiply them, and they shall not be few; I will make them honored and they will not be small." The statement in Zech. 8:13 is also instructive, "As you have been a [word of] curse [$q^e l\bar{a}l\bar{a}$] among the nations, O house of Judah and house of Israel, so will I save you and you shall be a blessing [$b^e r\bar{a}k\bar{a}$]" (see also Mal. 3:12). But it is especially in Deutero-Isaiah that the closest affinities with Genesis are found. Isa. 51:1–2 states:

> Listen to me, you who pursue victory,
> you who seek Yahweh;
> Look to the rock from which you were hewn,
> And to the quarry from which you were dug.
> Look to Abraham your father,
> And to Sarah who gave you birth;
> For he was only one person when I called him,
> But I blessed him and made him many.[73]

---

70. Cf. Malamat, *JNES* 22:1–17. Malamat's reconstruction of a great empire is based on a series of hypothetical reconstructions that may be seriously questioned.
71. See O. Eissfeldt, "The Promises of Grace to David," in *The Heritage of the Hebrew Prophets*, pp. 196–207.
72. See P. Ackroyd, *Exile and Restoration* (London: SCM, 1968), pp. 136–37 and literature cited there.
73. Cf. P. A. H. deBoer, *Second Isaiah's Message*, OTS 11 (Leiden: E. J. Brill, 1956), pp. 58–67.

Just as in Gen. 12:1–3, the themes of blessing and numerous offspring are directly connected with Abraham's call, and this is used as a symbol of hope for the restoration. But the matter goes deeper than just a historical analogy. What is deliberately emphasized is Israel's origin in, and continuity with, Abraham and Sarah. The imagery is of God as a skilled craftsman who "carves" Israel from its origin in the forefather.

This emphasis on Israel's origin calls to mind a number of other passages that speak of God "forming" Israel, even forming from the womb (Isa. 44:2; cf. 43:1, 5–7; 44:21–22, 24; 45:9–11; 46:3–4; 49:1–6). This imagery is to be associated with dynastic election and is common in Assyrian and Babylonian royal inscriptions.[74] In Deutero-Isaiah the motif has again been democratized, but in the light of the emphasis upon the forefathers there is undoubtedly some suggestion here of a kind of dynastic election through Abraham.

We have already discussed above, in connection with Gen. 15:7ff., the significance of the land promise theme in the exile.[75] There remains a brief consideration of those passages in the larger thematic framework, which also deals with this subject. The promise of land is made to Abraham in 13:14–17 in its full extent after his separation from Lot. The land promise here is in the legal form of land grant.[76] This form is followed by even making the grant to Abraham as well as to his descendents in perpetuity and without condition (v. 15), even though Abraham himself never actually gains possession. There is also the symbolic claiming of the land by walking over its full extent.[77] The fact that this legal form duplicates to some extent the covenant of 15:7ff. does not indicate a different source.[78] The author uses as many legal forms as possible to emphasize the certainty of the promise. Some scholars have suggested that v. 16, dealing with numerous offspring, is an intrusion into the theme and form. But the point of its inclusion, I think, is to recognize the

74. See Shalom M. Paul, "Deutero-Isaiah and Cuneiform Royal Inscriptions," *JAOS* 88 (1968): 180–86, especially 184ff.
75. See also Clark, "Land Promise Theme," p. 72, n. 2, in which a connection with the exile is also made.
76. See Weinfeld, *JAOS* 90:196–200; idem, *Deuteronomy*, pp. 74–81; Loewenstamm, *JAOS* 91:509–10; cf. Clark, "Land Promise Theme," pp. 73–81. Clark regards this passage as the earliest and the only one original to J's Abraham tradition. But how would this fit any broader literary theory?
77. So D. Daube, *Studies in Biblical Law*, pp. 34–9.
78. This is the argument of Clark, "Land Promise Theme," pp. 61ff.

realities of the exilic period. Only with greatly increased numbers of people in the land of Palestine was there any hope of spreading out and inheriting all the land. Such a close combination of themes also occurs in 26:4 and 28:14. In this last instance it is clearly stated that the numerous progeny will result directly in their expansion in four directions similar to the statement in Isa. 54:3.[79]

There is another aspect of the land promise theme in the Yahwist that is noteworthy. We have previously argued that the pre-Yahwist call and land promise theme was contained in 12:1,4a,6a,7. Now added to this earlier narrative is the remark by the Yahwist in 12:6b (and repeated in 13:7) that the "Canaanites were then in the land." This statement hardly seems necessary to this context except perhaps to suggest the pre-Israelite period. Nevertheless, its real significance can only be seen in Gen. 24:2–8, in which the theme of the divine call and land promise is recapitulated. But here the focus is on the antagonism between the indigenous population and the patriarchs, at least on the question of intermarriage. The inference in 24:7 is that for the patriarchs (and Israel) to intermarry with the Canaanites would be a rejection of God's promise to give all the land of the Canaanites to them.

Here we come into touch with a Deuteronomic theme of non-intermarriage with the primeval nations, which would lead to apostasy and a breach of the covenant (Deut. 7:3–5). For Deuteronomy states that no covenants of any kind are to be made with these people; they are to be exterminated. This theme of non-intermarriage becomes important in the Deuteronomistic history (cf. Judg. 3:5–6), always in terms of the threat of apostasy and particularly in terms of the nation's rulers (cf. 1 Kings 11:1ff.). For the Yahwist the focus is quite different. He is not averse to covenants of peace with the local authorities (cf. Gen. 21:22–24; 26:26–31). Nor is it a question of apostasy. Now it is primarily a preservation of the people as descendants of Abraham—racial purity—so that the land promise, which has become *the* covenant between Israel and Yahweh

---

[79]. It is also worth noting in Gen. 28:15 that, after the promises of land and numerous offspring have been made to Jacob, a unique promise follows: "See, I will be with you and will keep you wherever you go and will return you to this land for I will not desert you until I have done what I promised you." The occasion is Jacob's flight to Mesopotamia, but this seems to be a clear allusion to the exile and a promise of restoration, with its strong emphasis on not deserting Israel in a foreign land, but completely restoring her fortunes.

through Abraham (15:7–21), can be upheld. This concern with ethnic descent and racial purity becomes increasingly important in the exilic and post-exilic periods because it goes hand-in-hand with the patriarchal promises.

The promises to the fathers, when viewed in terms of the history of their form and in a comparison with both the pre-exilic theology of Deuteronomy and the concerns of the exilic prophets, can best be understood as a response to the needs of the late exilic period. The whole orientation is similar to that of Deutero-Isaiah, and it was at this time that the Abraham tradition was taken up and given its present basic shape as the fundamental unifying identity for the people of "Israel," on the threshold of the restoration.

CHAPTER 13

The Priestly Traditions of Abraham

There are two stories in the Abraham tradition almost universally attributed to P, and these are the covenant of circumcision, Genesis 17, and the purchase of Sarah's burial place, Genesis 23. Yet even including the other brief elements of the P framework it is scarcely possible that these ever formed the basis of an independent P tradition. Much more likely is the view that they are additions dealing with special subjects of concern. The two chapters provide a striking contrast, in that one is a highly theological work while the other is quite profane in character. The reason for such a strong difference will, I hope, become evident in the analysis that follows.

The Covenant of Circumcision—Genesis 17.

While there is widespread agreement that Genesis 17 belongs to the priestly corpus (P) of the Pentateuch, many problems and disagreements regarding the analysis of this chapter remain.[1] Attempts

1. For general discussion of the priestly corpus see the introduction to OT by Eissfeldt and Fohrer and the works cited there. The classical Wellhausen view of P has long held that it was an independent and separate literary work of the exilic period, which was only combined with the other pentateuchal sources by a redactor in the post-exilic period. A challenge to its independent origin was made by Max Löhr, *Untersuchungen zum Hexateuchproblem I: Der Priesterkodex in der Genesis*, BZAW 38 (1924), who rejected any independent P narrative in Genesis but considered the work more in the nature of editorial additions. This opinion was supported by P. Volz, *Der Elohist als Erzähler: ein Irrweg der Pentateuchkritik? BZAW* 63 (1933): 135–142. In quite the opposite direction G. von Rad, in *Die Priesterschrift im Hexateuch literarisch untersucht und theologisch gewertet*, BWANT 65, (Stuttgart–Berlin, 1934), argued for two complete strands of P even in the narrative portions, including Genesis 17. This study was strongly criticized by P. Humbert, "Die literarische Zweiheit des Priester-Codex in der Genesis (Kritische Untersuchung der These von Rad)," *ZAW* 17 (1940–41): 30–57. This criticism was accepted by Noth, among others, in his *Pentateuchal Traditions*, pp. 8–19 (especially p. 10). He reverted to the older view of P as the work of one man who had a considerable amount of received material (but not those of the other pentateuchal sources) and who worked them into a unified whole. It is this rather vague literary view that is most commonly accepted today. Two recent studies that call for special mention are: J. G. Vink, *The Date and Origin of the Priestly Code in the Old Testament* OTS 15 (Leiden: E. J. Brill, 1969); Sean McEvenue,

279

have been made in the past to see various strands or stages of growth in P, and this division has been carried over into Genesis 17 as well. The present study cannot answer for the priestly corpus as a whole, but we must give some consideration to the character of P in Genesis 17. The principal criteria for division of the chapter into at least two strands or stages have been the presence of repetition, contradiction, and variety of themes. Yet the application of these criteria has been hotly debated.[2] Repetition is the most doubtful as a reason for source division because it can often have the opposite literary function of unifying diverse elements in the same work. It cannot be assumed that the presence of repetition always means the existence of a tradition doublet. Contradiction or serious discontinuity of thematic presentation is a much firmer criterion of sources. But those who have attempted to find contradictions in Genesis 17 have not been very convincing. The mere presence, for instance, of the promise of numerous progeny alongside of the promise of one heir is hardly reason to claim a contradiction. There is a style of logical development in this chapter and in the priestly writing generally that goes from the broad inclusive statement to the particular, so that appreciation of the author's logic of movement eliminates most arguments for contradiction. There is, of course, also the matter of the author's sources, which may create a slight sense of unevenness between two parts. Similarly for the criterion of thematic variation, this will only have weight depending upon an evaluation of the chapter's genre, its sources and its pattern of structural integration of the various parts. It is possible for more than one theme to be combined in a larger structural unity without indicating the presence of more than one source, as was the case in Genesis 15.

In contrast to the arguments for the disunity of Genesis 17 there is the strong consensus that only P and no other pentateuchal source is present in the chapter. This opinion is based on the fact that the same characteristic vocabulary and terminology associated with P are used throughout. Furthermore, the same thematic elements

---

The Narrative Style of the Priestly Writer, An. Bib. 50 (Rome: Biblical Institute Press, 1971). What is quite significant in McEvenue's study is that he does regard the previous pentateuchal sources as a most important part of P's source material. More will be said about this work below.

2. For recent criticism of the arguments for disunity see McEvenue, *Narrative Style*, pp. 145–48.

present in Genesis 17 are repeated elsewhere in the Pentateuch in the P corpus,[3] and it has long been recognized that this chapter is a most important pivotal text for the understanding of the whole work. Part of the scholarly ambivalence toward Genesis 17 results directly from a lack of clarity about the literary nature of this source and its relationship to the antecedent pentateuchal sources. Once scholars had adopted a set of dubious criteria for the division of pentateuchal sources in general and the principle that all the sources were originally independent, self-contained units put together by a series of redactors, it was inevitable that the P corpus itself would be treated this way with questionable results. From the beginning of this study, however, we have followed the rule of first evaluating the relationship of the later sources to their antecedents by a study of the parallels and on this basis have dealt with the problem of the overall literary process. Coupled with this has also been a consideration of form and structure as controls over the questions of unity, originality and, ultimately, the author's purpose. These will be the steps in our consideration of this chapter also.[4]

The sources for Genesis 17 are primarily those that were already present in the earlier pentateuchal material and that were known to P.[5] The promises of numerous progeny and of land, presented in 17:1–8, are found in many places in J, as we have seen, but correspond here most closely to the form in Genesis 15. The promise of a son, Isaac, in vv. 15–21 has its counterpart in 18:10–14. However, included in this unit as well (vv. 18 and 20) are allusions to the two stories about Ishmael. The only theme that is additional to those drawn from the earlier story of Abraham is the cultic institution of circumcision in vv. 9–14, 23–27, and this corresponds so completely with the whole style and orientation of the priestly code that

---

[3]. See especially Gen. 28:3–4; 35:9–13; 48:3; Exod. 6:2–8. Lists of characteristic P terminology may be found in Gunkel, *Genesis*, p. 264; Skinner, *Genesis*, p. 289. On the various themes throughout the priestly source see Hoftijzer, *Die Verheissungen an die drei Erzväter*, chaps. 1 and 2.

[4]. A detailed treatment of these issues is given by McEvenue, *Narrative Style*, especially chap. 4. This work represents an important new departure in the critical analysis of Genesis 17 by the applications of stylistic criticism. My own presentation of Genesis 17 is heavily indebted to this work, but I have not attempted to give a complete review of all its arguments. Nevertheless, I have strong reservations about McEvenue's comparisons between P and children's literature and efforts to make such connections in chap. 17 seem particularly forced. Other minor points of disagreement will be indicated below.

[5]. See McEvenue, ibid., pp. 149–55.

it certainly represents P's own contribution to the tradition corpus.⁶

But this general statement about P's sources does not yet give a very clear idea of the precise relationship of P to these earlier sources. We have every reason to believe that P had available to him all the preserved earlier literary sources of the Pentateuch. Yet the case for direct literary dependence can best be shown by a closer comparison of Genesis 17 with its sources. The following items occur in both Genesis 15 and 17:1–8:

1) A theophany with a divine promise stated in general terms, 15:1 and 17:1–2.
2) Abraham's reaction, in the one instance by an act of obeisance, 17:3, in the other by a complaint, 15:2–3.
3) The promise of an heir with numerous progeny, 15:4–5, or numerous progeny alone, 17:4–6.
4) The covenant (*bᵉrît*) with Abraham and his descendants, 15:7–18; and 17:4–8.
5) The promise of land to Abraham and his descendants, 15:7 and 18; and 17:8.

The similarity of sequence of these items is especially significant as an indication of dependence, since it does not rest on any narrative structure in either case and since these promise themes occur elsewhere in various forms, contexts, and sequences. In Genesis 15 the themes are distributed between two parallel panels⁷ in a freely composed literary composition with very few narrative elements. In chap. 17 there are also two main parallel panels with a slightly different distribution of themes but even more artificially composed with the same lack of narrative quality. Even when the language is different from chap. 15 it may be similar to the treatment of the same theme elsewhere in J. Thus, the reference to God's increasing Abraham greatly (with hiphil of *rbh*) is found in 16:10; 22:17; 26:4,24. The belief that Abraham will become "nations" reflects the repeated statement in J that Abraham will become "a great nation," 12:2; 18:18, and the plural may be deduced from the fact that it is

---

6. For this feature of command-fulfillment in P see C. Westermann, *The Genesis Accounts of Creation*, Facet Books, Biblical Series 7 (Philadelphia: Fortress Press, 1964), pp. 7–8; McEvenue, ibid., p. 17; idem, "Word and Fulfillment: A Stylistic Feature of the Priestly Writer," *Semitics* 1 (1970): 104–110.

7. On the stylistic feature of "panels" see McEvenue, *Narrative Style*, pp. 155, 158–59.

extended to both Ishmael, 21:13,18, and Isaac, 26:3–4. In the second part of the chapter (v. 16) P connects the promise of blessing (*brk*) with becoming "nations," and this terminology is also closely linked in J, 12:2; 22:17; 26:24. The expression "I will establish [*qwm*] my covenant," (17:7) corresponds to the use in J "I will establish [*qwm*] the oath [*šebuʿāh*]" (26:3), since oath and covenant are equivalent terms here. The form of the land promise in 15:18 only mentions the descendants, while in 17:8 both descendants and the forefather are mentioned. But in the land grant form in 13:14–17, which corresponds in its legal form more closely to 17:8, both the patriarch and his descendants are included.[8]

Yet even when there are differences between P and J these do not point to a different tradition *Vorlage*, but are indications of P's own freedom with his source material. This can be seen in his elimination of the theme of a single heir from the first promises, as in chap. 15, in order to give greater attention to the theme in the later section, vv. 15–21. P also mentions *berît* at the very beginning and thereby includes all the promises under this term, while chap. 15 used it only in connection with the land promise. But since J also spoke of the other promises as a divine oath (22:16; 26:3) this is not a basic theoretical change. The purpose of using *berît* throughout will be to focus on the act of circumcision in vv. 9–14 and 23–27. P also uses his own terminology, which then takes on larger thematic significance beyond the present unit. For instance, there is the special use of the divine name, El Shaddai (cf. 28:3; 35:11; 48:3; Exod. 6:2–3). The combination of the verbal pair *prh* and *rbh*, which perhaps is meant to represent a kind of divine liturgical blessing, is very common in P.[9] Even the notion of name change does not belong to a special Abraham tradition. It is repeated in connection with Sarah (v. 15), and Jacob (35:10). The notion very likely derives from the older story about Jacob's name change at Penuel (32:28).

One may also compare 17:15–21 with 18:10–14, in which the following correspondence occurs:

---

8. On the land grant see M. Weinfeld, "The Covenant of Grant in the Old Testament and in the Ancient Near East," *JAOS* 90 (1970): 184–203 (especially 199–200); idem, *Deuteronomy and the Deuteronomic School*, p. 78; cf. S. E. Loewenstamm, "The Divine Grants of Land to the Patriarchs," *JAOS* 71 (1971): 509–10, who emphasizes that the priestly phrase for the posterity *zarʿakā ʾaḥareka* is found in the 5th century B.C. Elephantine papyri but not in earlier Near Eastern documents.

9. Gen. 1:22,28; 9:1,7; 17:20; 28:3; 35:11; 47:27b; 48:4; Exod. 1:7.

1) God speaks to Abraham and promises him that Sarah will have a son within a year, 17:15–16 and 18:9–10.
2) In one instance Abraham laughs, 17:17, and in the other Sarah laughs, 18:12, and both reflect to themselves on the impossibility of Sarah's giving birth in her old age.
3) God reaffirms his promise in the face of their doubt that the son will arrive in a year's time, 17:19–21; 18:13–14.

The priestly account, 17:15–21, is a freely composed doublet of the earlier story that, in its present position, becomes completely anticlimactic for the subsequent episode. But the narrative element has been almost entirely eliminated. Because the whole chapter is an address by God to Abraham, Sarah is replaced, and it is Abraham who laughs. This may also reflect P's propensity to have the father and not the mother name the child.[10]

A form-critical analysis of 17:15–21 is most instructive at this point.[11] In our earlier analysis of 18:10–14 we recognized this story as a "healing-birth" story that had its original completion in 21:2.[12] The Yahwist, as we saw, broke this form by separating the birth ending from the promise part of the story and thereby created a story about the "promise of a son," which is certainly not an original genre. However, it is precisely this edited "promise" story that P uses, without the birth ending, for his unit in 17:15–21. It is therefore certain that he did not have a *Vorlage* other than the J account, because his version breaks off at the same point. In fact, the ending was too abrupt to suit him, so he added to it (v. 19) to make it into an announcement of birth, name, and denstiy (ABND),[13]

---

10. See also Gen. 16:15 and 21:3. It may be noted that Abraham's response to God in v. 18 does not have a parallel in 18:10–14 but does correspond to the complaint in 15:2–3 at this same point in the narrative and in connection with the single heir. At this point, therefore, P conflates his two sources, even though they represent entirely different moods.
11. See R. W. Neff, "The Birth and Election of Isaac in the Priestly Tradition," *BR* 15 (1970): 5–18. Neff's reconstruction of the form in Gen. 17:15–21 is based on the assumption that there is no direct literary dependence upon 18:10–14, but only a similarity of common form.
12. Cf. Humbert, *ZAW* 58:51, and Neff, ibid., p. 6, who point to similar terminology with P and so ascribe it to this later source. But the key term *lammôʿed* (21:2) occurs also in 18:14 (and v. 10?), and the term *lizqunāyw*, not found in ch. 17 is repeated in 21:7 and reflects the frequent use of the root *zqn*, "to be old," in 18:11,12,13. The only reason for prefering P is the reference in 21:2b to Elohim which criterion I have rejected above.
13. Cf. Neff, ibid., pp. 13–18. Neff regards v. 19 as a "secondary intrusion," but it is not very clear what he means by this, for he regards both the primary birth story and the secondary ABND as belonging to P. Neff's form-critical analysis does not seem to clarify the literary history of the text.

probably using the model in the Hagar story (16:11–12). He also included from 16:10 and 21:17–18 the theme of a blessing for Ishmael and thus produced a veritable conglomerate of forms. But this was the result of his direct literary borrowing. It is not possible to make such allusions to persons and episodes "out of the blue" without taking for granted an established corpus of the Abraham tradition in the form that is now extant in J.

There still remains the further question of whether P merely used the earlier corpus to create his own separate tradition, or whether he supplemented the tradition as it came down to him. Here one surely encounters the dogma of "separate sources" in its most absurd form.[14] For apart from chaps. 17 and 23 there are only a few scattered notations by P for the rest of the Abraham story (11:27–32; 12:4b–5; 13:6; 16:3a, 15–16; 19:29; 21:3–5; 25:7–10). These together cannot possibly be construed as an account of Abraham's life, even if P is regarded as "summarizing" in the extreme. Most of them are brief editorial additions containing chronology or suggesting minor "adjustment."[15] As far as I know there is no reason against drawing the most obvious conclusion, that P merely supplemented the older tradition as he received it in the written form of J.[16]

Once one accepts this origin for Genesis 17 the question of its unity is largely answered in the affirmative. The tension between the promise of the many and of the one, or the shift in themes, is all accounted for by the nature of the chapter as a complex combination of elements from the older sources, taken together with P's own special interests. Repetition is used very deliberately to create a sense of unity between all the separate elements. The chapter cannot be analyzed as if it were a narrative because it contains virtually no dramatic elements or interest whatever.[17] Its structure and logic are

14. This is my most serious disagreement with McEvenue, *Narrative Style*, pp. 151, 181 ff., who still regards P as a separate document. But once he admits dependence on JE there is no reason any longer to see it as a separate work.

15. It is puzzling to me how Noth (*Pentateuchal Traditions*, p. 12) can speak about the final form of the patriarchal stories as the work of a redactor who "made the P narrative the *basis* of his work and enriched it by suitably inserting here and there parts of the other narratives." The P source of the Abraham story could not possibly serve as a basis for a continuous tradition cycle.

16. No redactor Rp is necessary. For recent protests against the notion of numerous redactors, apart from the main sources themselves, see S. Sandmel, "The Haggada within Scripture," *JBL* 80 (1961): 105–122; F. V. Winnett, "Re-Examining the Foundations," *JBL* 84 (1965): 1–19.

17. McEvenue, *Narrative Style*, pp. 150–51.

of an entirely different character. As Sean McEvenue has recently shown,[18] the whole unit is framed by an introductory and concluding statement of chronology (vv. 1a and 24–25), as well as a statement about God appearing to Abraham (v. 1b) and God leaving Abraham (v. 22). Within this frame there are five divine speeches. The second and fifth speeches are marked off by Abraham's falling down before God (vv. 3,17), but there is no dialogue except for the sole reply by Abraham in v. 18. The speeches are arranged, instead, to produce a balance of themes. The first two speeches deal with the theme of numerous progeny (vv. 2–8), and the last two deal with the individual heir (vv. 15–21). The central speech is instruction—priestly torah—concerning circumcision, which links the divine establishment of the perpetual covenant through successive generations, *l^edōrōtām librît ^côlām* (v. 7), with the maintaining of that covenant by means of circumcision through successive generations, *l^edōrōtām* (v. 9).[19] This divine instruction in the third speech is then immediately carried out at the conclusion of the divine address with the circumcision of Abraham's household given in the style of a report (vv. 23–27), a characteristic of P's stylistic structuring.[20] The fact that the central speech is priestly torah heightens its significance for this source, and it becomes the focus by which the borrowed traditions of the other speeches are interpreted.

There are also other ways besides this balancing of units whereby the two parts of the chapter are tied together, and one of these is the use of repetition. For instance, both Abraham and Sarah are given name changes (vv. 5 and 15), even though this motif is not developed further in the case of Sarah. Furthermore, although the second unit emphasizes the gift of a son to Sarah in addition to Ishmael, it repeats in the language of the first unit the theme of numerous progeny for both of them, and with both Abraham (v. 7) and Isaac (vv. 18b,21a) God establishes his eternal covenant. There is also considerable interlocking by repetition between the first two speeches

18. Ibid., pp. 157–58. A much more detailed structural analysis is given here. An earlier attempt at a unified structuring of Genesis 17, based on the covenant-treaty model, was attempted by S. R. Külling, *Zur Datierung der "Genesis-P-Stücke" namentlich des Kapitels Genesis XVII*, (Kampen, Netherlands: J. H. Kok, 1964), pp. 242–49. This work is rightly criticized by McEvenue, ibid., pp. 256f., n. 21.

19. There is a certain ambiguity in the meaning of *dor*, which can also mean "assembly" and may have this sense in v. 11. See McEvenue, *Narrative Style*, p. 164, n. 33.

20. See n. 6 above.

and the third, as well as the connection of the last two speeches to the act of circumcision by drawing special attention to the fact that Ishmael was also circumcised (v. 23, 25–26). The connection between Sarah's promised son and circumcision is postponed until the notation by P in 21:3–5. All of this careful structuring, bridging and interweaving, in spite of P's fidelity to the sources he uses, make it impossible to view chap. 17 as anything but the literary work of one author.

The Themes of Genesis 17

The chapter begins with an introduction in which it is stated: "Yahweh appeared to Abram and said to him, 'I am El Shaddai.'" The divine speech itself is a type of self-introduction formula that is encountered frequently in the OT, usually in a specific cultic, liturgical, or confessional context.[21] But the name "El Shaddai" clearly indicates that the form is borrowed with certainly no liturgical usage in mind. Secondly, it should be noted that the priestly writer uses the divine name Yahweh instead of the usual Elohim to make it quite clear that it was Yahweh who appeared to Abraham and with whom the latter was in covenant, even though under the name of El Shaddai.[22] There is, fortunately, no question about this interpretation because it is clearly stated in Exod. 6:2–3. This is not only a syncretism between Yahweh and El Shaddai but also the explanation of this syncretism in terms of successive stages of revelation. It raises the question of whether there was any anticipation of this development in the received tradition.

It is most usual to point to Exod. 3:13ff. as a similar instance of such a notion by E, in which the God of the fathers is only identified with Yahweh in the time of the exodus. The presence of an E source in this chapter at all is very questionable, and in v. 15 it is as much a question of identifying the fathers Abraham, Isaac, and Jacob as it is the name of Yahweh.[23] The passage by itself is quite inconclusive. On the other hand, within J in the Abraham tradition itself all the elements are already present for P's theological construction. There is,

21. See W. Zimmerli, "Ich bin Jawhe," (1953) *Gottes Offenbarung*, pp. 11–40 (especially p. 18).
22. A full discussion of this name is not possible here. See recently M. Weippert, "Erwägungen zur Etymologie des Gottesnamens El Shadday," *ZDMG* 111 (1961): 42–62. There is no reason to believe that the name *in Israel* is particularly ancient or derives from Israel's prehistory.
23. See my article "Confessional Reformulation," *VT* 22:456–57.

firstly, the shift of Yahweh's distinctive self-revelation through the exodus back to the time of Abraham (15:7), creating a scheme of successive stages in God's saving history and revelation, even though J retained the same divine name for each of these stages. Yet J also suggested a syncretism between Yahweh and the various forms of El that were known to him. But this is especially evident in 16:13a, which states: "So she [Hagar] invoked the name of Yahweh who had spoken to her, 'O thou El Ro$^\jmath$i' [or 'El who sees']."[24] P merely took up these two lines of development and created a consistent scheme, whereby each successive stage of divine activity is represented by a different designation for the deity: Elohim for the period from Creation to Abraham, El Shaddai for the time of the patriarchs,[25] and Yahweh from Moses onward.

The form of the covenant, $b^e rît$, in chap. 17 follows J as a divine oath of promise rather than as the so-called treaty pattern of Deuteronomy. This oath is not conditioned by various stipulations, but is in the nature of a reward for Abraham's righteous living, v. 2. As such it becomes an irrevocable pledge, $b^e rît$ $^c ôlām$, to all Abraham's descendants. This notion of the Abrahamic covenant as a reward for his righteousness is suggested in chap. 15 by the fact that the covenant follows the statement about Abraham's righteousness in v. 6. But this is made quite explicit in other J passages, such as 22:16,18; and 26:5,24, where the promises of land and progeny are directly related to Abraham's obedience to God. In all the instances in J and P it is God's oath that he will make good. It does not contain law and the related notion of curse as a part of it.

This oath in Genesis 17 contains a threefold promise: numerous progeny, the land of Canaan, and the promise to be Israel's God. In the promise of progeny the emphasis has shifted from one nation to many nations and to Abraham becoming the father of kings. This cannot be interpreted narrowly as a reference only to the two kingdoms of Israel and Judah and to their monarchies.[26] It is quite clear, for instance, that Ishmael and his descendants are included, v. 20. The reference there to twelve "princes," $n^e śî^\jmath im$, refers to the eponymous sons whose names are not those of historical rulers but

---

24. See also 21:33. Note the remarks by Winnett, *JBL* 84:11, and N. Wagner, "A Literary Analysis of Genesis 12–36," p. 49.
25. See McEvenue, *Narrative Style*, p. 166.
26. Cf. Weinfeld, *JAOS* 90:202.

are primarily geographical terms (25:13–16), so the "kings" in 17:6,16 and 35:11 may also be thought of primarily as eponyms. It is true that the covenant model as a perpetual covenant, $b^e rît \ ^c ôlām$ (17:7,19), is a dynastic one, and this could explain to some extent its narrowing down to Isaac. But it is scarcely possible for this form of the covenant to serve as a legitimation of the Judean monarchy. On the contrary, since the limits of the covenant are defined by circumcision, this is another instance of a royal form being democratized.

The promise of the land in 17:8 is in the form of a legal land grant, which is made as a possession in perpetuity both to the recipient and to his descendants. This goes beyond the donation form in 15:18 but is similar to the legal style of 13:14ff. Since the language of 17:8 seems to approximate a specific legal form, one cannot regard the inclusion of Abraham himself as an anticipation of the land purchase in Genesis 23.[27] This would hardly square with the references in 28:4 and 35:12, which already suggest that the whole land was given to Abraham. This promise of land does not have as prominent a place in chap. 17 as it does in chap. 15, but one cannot conclude from this that P plays down the land promise theme. It receives quite equal weight in 28:4 and 35:12 and even special emphasis as the covenant and oath to the fathers in Exod. 6:4,8. However, since P is supplementing the earlier tradition he can take for granted the emphasis on the land promise in Gen. 15:7–21 and merely summarize it in 17:8 in his own way.

The third promise has to do with Yahweh becoming the God of Abraham and his descendants. This promise is repeated twice, once in connection with Israel becoming "nations," vv. 6–7, and the second time linked with the promise of the land, v. 8. The first connection, between people and God, occurs frequently in Deuteronomy in the statement about Israel becoming God's people through his election and redemption in the exodus event.[28] But it also speaks of the same relationship in reciprocal form in the context of entering into the covenant relationship with God. Thus Deut. 26:17–18 states:

> You declare this day that Yahweh is your God [$lihyôt \ l^e k\hat{a} \ l\bar{e}^{\,\flat}l\bar{o}h\hat{\imath}m$] and that you will walk in his ways, and keep his

---

27. Cf. McEvenue, *Narrative Style*, pp. 142–44, 153.
28. Deut. 4:20; 7:6; 14:2; 27:9.

statutes and his commandments ... and Yahweh declares this day that you are a people for his sole possession, as he has promised you ....[29]

In contrast to Genesis 17 it is the people who covenant to make Yahweh their God by obeying his laws, and it is Yahweh who in reciprocal action makes the people his own. In a later exilic addition to Deuteronomy (29:11), in a covenant renewal that is here spoken of as entering a sworn covenant of Yahweh, $le^c obr^ek\hat{a}\ bibr\hat{\imath}t\ yhwh \ldots ub e^{\jmath}\bar{a}l\bar{a}t\hat{o}$ (29:11), the following terms are laid down by God (v. 12): "that he might establish [qwm] you today as his people and that he might be your God [$yihyeh\ ll^ek\hat{a}\ l\bar{e}^{\jmath}l\bar{o}h\hat{\imath}m$] as he promised you and as he swore to your fathers, to Abraham, to Isaac, and to Jacob." There has been a most important shift here from the reciprocal agreement form to the double promise, in which God promises to be Israel's God. This double promise form becomes quite frequent in the exilic period in expressions about the restoration of Israel as a people.[30] But alongside of this there is a connection made between Yahweh becoming Israel's God again and his gift of the land. Thus Ezek. 36:28 states: "You shall dwell in the land which I gave to your fathers; and you shall be my people, and I will be your God" (cf. 37:25–27; Zech. 8:8). Evidently, this promise of becoming Israel's God developed two connections in the exilic period: the one, God-people, and the other God-land. Consequently, P inherited both of these forms and for this reason repeated the promise of Yahweh becoming the God of Abraham's offspring in both of its forms (17:7 and 8).[31]

A feature of P's understanding of the covenant is that it is not only the oath itself but also the "sign," $^{\jmath}\bar{o}t$, (v. 11)—a perpetual or permanent mark of recognition, which in this case is circumcision.[32]

---

29. For a full discussion of this form see N. Lohfink, "Dt 26, 17–19 und die 'Bundesformel,'" *ZKTh* 91 (1969): 517–553.
30. Exilic references that have in mind the exodus are: Lev. 26:12; Jer. 7:23; 11:4. Those that point to the restoration are Jer. 13:11; 24:7; 30:22,25; 31:32; 32:38; Ezek. 11:20; 14:11; 36:28; 37:23,27; and Zech. 8:8. In the Jeremiah and Ezekiel references there is still a strong association with obedience to God's law as a basis for the reciprocal relationship, similar to Deuteronomy. The *later* they are the more they become promise alone (Zech. 8:8).
31. Contra Weinfeld, *Deuteronomy*, p. 80 and *JAOS* 90:202, who suggests a development in the opposite direction.
32. See McEvenue, *Narrative Style*, p. 171; von Rad, *Genesis*, pp. 195–96.

Keeping the covenant means, for P, maintaining this mark of identity as an Israelite. There is a certain amount of ambiguity in the matter of who is included within this covenant. Since all the males in Abraham's household are circumcised, including Ishmael, who also receives a special "blessing" (v. 20), the covenant would seem to be wider than Israel. Yet it is specifically stated, in a kind of dynastic sense, that the covenant is with Isaac with an implied contrast to Ishmael (v. 21). This may imply that Israel has a special "royal" role among the larger group of nations. The problem of ambiguity may also result from the fact that the sign of the covenant —circumcision—was in fact practiced by the Arab peoples of the day as well, so that some recognition was given to them on this account. On the other hand, the limits of the covenant are also narrower than all the natural born Israelites, because those who do not circumcise their children cannot participate in it.

This last statement in the instructions (v. 14), which speaks about "excommunication from the community," is most interesting. In place of the older agreement form of covenant, with its laws and attendant curses, there is only this threat of excommunication. Grelot's recent study of this form points strongly to the post-exilic community for this development of religious law.[33] In this post-exilic context it is the conscious choice of the people to maintain their identity, which alone can perpetuate the covenant community.

Genesis 17 in its Historical Context

It is not possible, on the basis of Genesis 17 alone, to answer completely or authoritatively the question of what the priestly work meant for its own time, or to decide conclusively on its date. Yet some observations can be made from our study thus far; these at least point in the direction in which that answer must be given. One of the remarkable features about the priestly work is that, in spite of all the emphasis on the Sinai legislation and the wilderness period as the time of the institution of Israel's cultic and religious life, P gives no direct attention to a Sinai covenant. Instead we have a heavy stress made on the covenant with Abraham as the initial event for

---

33. P. Grelot, "La dernière étape de la rédaction sacerdotale," *VT* 6 (1956): 174–189 (especially 175–76). Grelot regards this reference to excommunication as a later addition, but there is little in the text to support this; cf. McEvenue, ibid., pp. 161f., n. 40; also Vink, *Priestly Code*, p. 91.

the relationship of Israel with Yahweh and their beginning as his people. W. Zimmerli has recently attempted to explain this feature of the P work by citing evidence for the fact that the exile brought about a crisis for the Sinai-Horeb covenant.[34] Since that covenant was proclaimed as broken, the people stood under its judgment and curse. One way out of the crisis, as reflected in the Holiness Code, Lev. 26:42ff., was to point to a covenant with the fathers prior to that of Sinai, which consisted only of promise. Consequently, according to Zimmerli, P followed this lead and emphasized the already existing "covenant of grace" to Abraham in the older sources, to the exclusion of the Sinai covenant.

As far as Zimmerli's interpretation of the place of Abraham in the exilic period is concerned, I heartily concur, but suggest that there is considerable additional evidence that he has not considered.[35] Yet it is not P, in the first instance, who has given the Abraham covenant this special significance in the exilic period, but the Yahwist. As we attempted to show above, Genesis 15 is a very conscious effort to substitute the election and covenant of Abraham for the exodus election and Sinai covenant, and this was done in the late exilic period and close to the time of Deutero-Isaiah. Like this exilic prophet, Genesis 15 is a response to a crisis of faith for the exilic period much more than is the case for Genesis 17.

This dating of J would put P after the period of restoration and very likely not long before the time of Ezra and his reform movement.[36] P is no longer concerned with the crisis of the exile and its temptation to abandon the faith. Its preoccupation is with the creation of a new sense of order and stability in the universe, in the world of nations and history, and in the cultic community of the new "Israel." The work is thoroughly programmatic.[37] This, of course, is fairly obvious when one is dealing with the cultic legislation, but becomes more debatable in the interpretation of the narrative passages.

I would suggest that the covenant of Abraham in Genesis 17 was not primarily viewed as a message of hope, as it was in J, but was accepted as a fixed datum of the sacred tradition and was thus

---

34. W. Zimmerli, "Sinaibund und Abrahambund," *ThZ* 16 (1960): 268–80 (same as *Gottes Offenbarung*, pp. 205–216). Cf. Vink, *Priestly Code*, p. 89.
35. See J. Van Seters, "Confessional Reformulation in the Exilic Period," *VT* 22:448–59.
36. Cf. Vink, *Priestly Code*, p. 63.
37. See Vink, ibid., pp. 12ff., on its programmatic character.

institutionalized by association with the custom of circumcision. Such a form of continuous covenant "renewal" emphasized the individual responsibility of every family unit to affirm their identity with the people of God—a most crucial need in the post-exilic period. Furthermore, J's concept of a "blessing" to the nations, which reflected his situation in the diaspora, is worked out in P in the form of a possible non-Israelite inclusion within the "household" of Abraham through the sign of circumcision. This "ecumenical spirit" may be found in many parts of the larger priestly work.[38] Needless to say, precisely this form of the Abraham covenant allowed for the possibility of proselytism among the diaspora. It seems to me, then, that Genesis 17 represents a movement toward reconstituting the religion of Israel for the condition and needs of the post-exilic period.

The Burial Place at Hebron—Genesis 23

There is little reason, to my mind, to dispute either the unity of Genesis 23 or the P authorship ascribed to it.[39] This judgment is based on characteristic features of P: 1) the chronological framework, 2) the designation of the inhabitants as "Hittites" and the ancient name of Hebron as Kiriath-arba, 3) the vocabulary, which has many terms distinctive of P, 4) the highly repetitious style. Furthermore, in the following P framework of the patriarchal narratives it is P who refers back to the grave site at Machpelah and makes it the common burial place of the patriarchs and their wives (25:9; 35:29; 49:30; 50:13). The story of the purchase also appears to interrupt the genealogy of Abraham's Aramean relatives in 22:20-24 and the subsequent story in chap. 24 about obtaining an Aramean wife for Isaac.

The question of the story's form is of considerable importance because it has often been noted that it does not seem to correspond to P's usual theological style.[40] There is also scarcely any reference to deity in the whole chapter.[41] For these reasons the chapter's form has often been regarded as reflecting an ancient traditional

---

38. See Vink, ibid., pp. 90-91.
39. See the commentaries. One scholar who rejected its connection with P was Volz, *Der Elohist*, pp. 139-40.
40. McEvenue, *Narrative Style*, p. 22.
41. The only exception is the reference in v. 6 to Abraham as a "prince of God," $n^e\acute{s}i^{\ni}$ $^{\ni}el\bar{o}h\hat{i}m$, which must be understood as a superlative meaning "exalted," or "mighty" (RSV).

source behind the written product. Noth suggested that the story originally had an etiological base explaining a "double cave" in the region of Hebron used as a burial place for a forefather and his wife.[42] But there is certainly nothing in the extant version that suggests either an etiology or this particular version, and such a conjecture must be viewed as very doubtful. Another approach has been to accept the proposals made by Lehmann and others that the references to "Hittites" and to the legal procedures are evidence for great antiquity.[43] But these proposals have been shown above to be quite misleading and inadequate.

In our earlier discussion of the legal conventions reflected in Genesis 23 it was pointed out that the account reflects very closely the "dialogue document" of sales agreements that are well known from the Neo-Babylonian and Persian periods. The episode is presented not as a story, but as a straightforward report of a sale transaction having to do with the formal transfer of a piece of property. Such a report form, based on customary procedures of the post-exilic period, cannot be used to give any indication of an early date. Even the reference to Hittites corresponds to the usage of this same period as a designation for the general population of Syria-Palestine. The form of the story, therefore, gives no warrant for the view that there was any ancient grave tradition associating the patriarchs with Hebron much before the post-exilic period of the P writer. It is always possible that an old tradition about patriarchal burials in the region of Hebron did exist, but if so we can say nothing about its form, content, or transmission from generation to generation. Whatever such a tradition might have contained, the priestly writer does not seem to have been bound by it in any way.

The purpose of the story is not at all clear, and it is beyond the scope of this study to deal with this question fully. Von Rad interprets the story as an initial fulfillment of the divine promise of land.[44] Though the patriarchs all lived in a "land of sojourning" ($^{\circ}ereṣ\ m^egurîm$, 17:8; 28:4; 36:7; 37:1; 47:9), they at least possessed their graves as their own. They did not have to rest in "Hittite earth." While this suggestion is quite plausible, it is also weakened by the fact that

---

42. Noth, *Pentateuchal Traditions*, pp. 113f., 195.
43. So Westermann, "Arten der Erzählung," pp. 70–71; Fohrer, *Introduction*, p. 182.
44. Von Rad, *Genesis*, p. 245; see also K. Elliger, "Sinn und Ursprung du priesterlichen Geschichtserzählung," *ZTK* 49 (1952): 121–143.

such a theological perspective is not supported by a single reference to deity. The concluding statement about Abraham's possession of the land does not make any reference to the divine promises theme. A somewhat different interpretation has recently been suggested by Vink.[45] Since he views the whole of the priestly code as a programmatic work, he sees in this story an appeal to the wealthy Jews of the diaspora to buy back the promised land from the Edomites, who in the post-exilic period were now in possession of it. But the purchase of a grave site (cf. Gen. 33:19f) does not by itself suggest very strongly such a programmatic scheme.

Nevertheless, the earlier interpretation by Gunkel still seems to represent the best approach to the problem.[46] He pointed out that the specific location of grave sites of ancestors and heros in the ancient world encouraged and supported a cult of the dead, or at least hero veneration. There are indications in the OT that ancestors and holy men often had their grave sites identified, and a cult of the dead existed in spite of religious opposition to it. It may be that the priestly writer, in presenting the purchase of the patriarchal grave site in a completely profane manner and including virtually all the ancestors and their wives in it, wanted to lessen this inclination to undue veneration. Certainly the tone of the whole piece, with its repeated statement by Abraham "that I may bury my dead out of my sight," is so strongly contrasted with the very careful treatment of everything cultic in P that it cannot but suggest the opposite in this case. There is not a single religious act associated with the burial. Yet if that was his purpose it may ironically have had the opposite effect.[47] The grave site in Hebron, thought to be that of Machpelah, was certainly highly venerated by Jews of the first century B.C. and received special honor from Herod the Great. That honor has continued at the same location, the Ḥaram el Ḫalil, to the present day.

---

45. Vink, *The Priestly Code*, p. 91.
46. Gunkel, *Genesis*, pp. 273-74; see also S. Mowinckel, *Erwägungen zur Pentateuch Quellenfrage*, p. 30; cf. McEvenue, *Narrative Style*, p. 142. On the hero cult in Greece see M. P. Nilsson, *A History of Greek Religion* (Oxford: Clarendon Press, 1949), p. 250.
47. Cf. the tradition about Moses' burial in Deut. 32:6, which denies any knowledge of his grave site.

CHAPTER 14

Victory over the Kings of the East—Genesis 14

It is not my intention to become involved in a detailed discussion of this much-debated chapter. This is neither possible nor desirable in the context of the present study, and the whole subject has recently received rather extensive review.[1] The focus here will be on the relationship of this rather unique chapter to the larger tradition. This will involve the investigation of the sources behind the story as well as the problem of its dating and function as a piece of tradition in the history of the Israelite community.

Presuppositions about the traditions behind this chapter have a great deal of influence on views regarding its unity and the sources upon which it drew. Thus, the decision about how one proceeds with the analysis is most important. The first issue is the story's unity or lack of it. If there were various phases in its growth it is necessary to uncover the first basic written account involving the figure of Abraham and the subsequent stages of growth. This procedure will have to be controlled by form-critical and structural analysis as well as by such literary criteria as internal consistency. Only after its *redactional* history is clear can the issue of the story's sources be dealt with and some assessment be made of the chapter's place in the larger tradition.

---

1. M. C. Astour, "Political and Cosmic Symbolism in Genesis 14 and in its Babylonian Sources," *Biblical Motifs*, pp. 65–112; J. A. Emerton, "Some False Clues in the Study of Genesis xiv," *VT* 21 (1971): 24–47; idem, "The Riddle of Genesis xiv," *VT* 21 (1971): 403–439. This last author's work contains a comprehensive review of previous positions with many judicious criticisms, which I see no need to duplicate. However, I cannot agree with his own solution to the interpretation of Genesis 14, so much of my own criticism will be directed at Emerton's study. A work that came to my attention too late for detailed consideration is W. Schatz, *Genesis 14, Eine Untersuchung* (Bern and Frankfurt: Herbert Land/Peter Lang, 1972). It contains a detailed consideration of all the basic questions raised to date, but it does not differ very much in its final conclusions from those of Emerton.

Form, Structure, and Unity

A number of proposals have been made about possible additions to an original version of the story, and it might be helpful to begin with these as a way of highlighting certain issues that subsequent form-critical and structural analysis will have to clarify. First of all, the story contains a number of explanatory phrases that are intended to identify supposedly ancient places by their more modern equivalents. These have often been construed as secondary glosses.[2] While such a decision is clearly possible it is not a necessary one and rests on a prior literary judgment. It assumes an archaic account as a *Vorlage* behind the present literary version, which had to introduce the present names to make the account intelligible. But it is also possible that explanatory phrases are used as a literary device in order to give an archaic sense to the whole account. Such a use is not uncommon elsewhere in the Pentateuch.[3] Furthermore, some of these equivalents are clearly artificial. Thus, for instance, the city of Bela is identified with Zoar. But Bela means "devoured," which is nonsense as a name. Yet if the author knew that the name Zoar was given to the city at a later date by Lot he would have had to create an older name for it, and he did so using the same style of name as he gave to the kings of the other cities. It is likely that all the equivalents are purely artificial creations. Consequently, a decision about the primary or secondary character of the explanatory phrases rests entirely upon a decision about the form and literary character of the whole.

The next problem has to do with v. 13b (or part of it) and v. 24 and the criterion of the story's internal consistency. The question these verses raise is whether Abraham acted alone or with the assistance of allies, since in vv. 14 and 15 Abraham and his own men appear to carry out the whole military operation alone.[4] If vv. 13b and 24 are regarded as original it is possible to regard the men as of inferior rank—vassal princes under his authority—such that they could be spoken of as his "servants" (v. 15). Admittedly, this interpretation is somewhat forced. Yet if vv. 13b and 24 were added one is faced perhaps with a more difficult problem of explaining why such

2. Emerton, *VT* 21:404–438.
3. Note, for instance, the glosses in Gen. 23:2,19.
4. Emerton, *VT* 21:404,438.

an addition would have been made.[5] Thus, a decision for or against the originality of vv. 13b and 24 cannot be made very easily. Yet it is only a minor aspect of the story, and its absence would not affect the total interpretation very much.

A more important question is whether or not the references to Lot in vv. 12,14, and 16 are original.[6] The argument that since v. 12 is largely repetitious of v. 11 it is secondary counts for very little. The repetition may be used for deliberate effect to emphasize the capture of Lot. The same order of vv. 11 and 12 is maintained in v. 16. The only real difficulty in v. 12 is with the phrase "the nephew of Abram," *ben ᵃḥî ʾabrām*. It is clearly out of place following "his property," *rᵉkušô*, and it mentions Abraham prematurely since he is formally introduced in v. 13 as "Abraham the Hebrew." It also conflicts with the subsequent characterization of Lot as Abraham's "brother," *ʾāḥiyw*, vv. 14 and 16. So this phrase, "the nephew of Abram," is probably a later addition to make the story fit the priestly view of the relationship between Abraham and Lot.

The fact that the references to Lot in vv. 12 and 16 could be removed without disturbing the immediate context is not decisive against their originality. The real crux of the matter is v. 14a. Here the reference to "his kinsman," is directly related to the other two mentions of Lot, and it is integral to the verse in which it stands. It provides the whole motivation for Abraham's subsequent action. If references to Lot are to be removed a radical emendation of the entire story—not just of this text—would be necessary. For instance, v. 11 only mentions that booty was taken, but vv. 22f. indicate that this could not have motivated Abraham since he shows disdain toward such goods. The vague suggestion that the original story was just an act of friendship toward the king of Sodom is hardly reflected in Abraham's curt rebuff of any friendly gesture.[7] The whole event

---

5. Emerton, ibid., regards the references to the three allies in vv. 13 and 24 as having been added by the same hand that added vv. 18–20. If it is possible to do so in this instance, it is possible to do so in vv. 14–16.

6. Emerton, ibid., pp. 406–07.

7. Emerton, ibid., p. 407, states that "its reference to Lot could be removed without difficulty." But what appears to be simple for him to understand is very difficult for me, since it involves the complete reconstruction of the story in which Abraham goes to the assistance of Sodom as a friendly act to rescue captives not previously mentioned. His whole interpretation of the story ultimately rests on this radical emendation. What one does with v. 14a becomes the key for everything else, and Emerton's easy dismissal of this difficulty is unacceptable.

focuses on Abraham's magnanimous rescue of Lot for no personal gain of his own. Consequently, in spite of the somewhat awkward style of this author it is hard to see how references to Lot can be viewed as secondary.[8] They must all be part of the original story.

The question of the Melchisedek episode (vv. 18–20) is quite different.[9] There seems to be no motivation within the story itself for the appearance of this priest-king or for his proffering provisions, which in view of all the booty, was quite unnecessary. There is also some tension with the notion of Abraham giving a "tithe of all," since he later claims none of the booty for himself. But the strongest reason for viewing vv. 18–20 as an interpolation is the obvious way in which they interrupt the action of the story and the final scene between the king of Sodom and Abraham. The former comes out to meet Abraham in v. 17, but does not speak until v. 21. The reference to "El Elyon, creator of heaven and earth" in v. 22, in addition to the name of Yahweh, can probably be regarded as a connective added by the same hand that added vv. 18–20. Consequently, the original *written* story did not have vv. 18–20, so one must deal first with the version that does not have it and then account for its addition. In no case should vv. 18–20, the addition, be used as a point of departure to explain the chapter as a whole.[10]

The next question to be dealt with is that of the forms, or genres, within the chapter.[11] This will clarify the literary nature of the components used in its composition, which has a bearing both on the question of unity and on the problem of whether any forms of pre-literary tradition were incorporated into the account. The first part, vv. 1–11, is primarily in the form of a military campaign report.[12] The best examples of such reports are the Assyrian and Babylonian

---

8. Emerton, ibid., p. 407, uses the criterion of awkward style as a clue to a foreign source in vv. 12 and 16, but in *VT* 21:34–36 he rejects this criterion as evidence for a foreign source in vv. 1–2. What is evident is that there is a rather difficult non-classical style of Hebrew throughout.

9. Emerton, ibid., pp. 407–12.

10. As did Emerton, ibid., pp. 412ff., and many other authors whom he reviews. I find it very strange that the author of the addition actually becomes the earliest author of a written version of the story, according to Emerton's view.

11. A major weakness of almost all the previous studies, including Emerton's is that this form-critical question is given so little attention. Only Astour, *Biblical Motifs*, pp. 70–71, deals with it at all.

12. Cf. my previous treatment of this subject in "The Conquest of Sihon's Kingdom: A Literary Examination," *JBL* 91 (1972): 187–89.

royal inscriptions. These usually contain the following basic components: 1) the motivation for military activity, such as news of a rebellion in part of the empire, 2) preparations for the campaign, 3) the campaign with details of the route and battles conducted, 4) the results in terms of devastation of cities, captives and booty taken, and tribute imposed. Such a report is usually given in the first person singular as the statement of the victorious king who quelled the rebellion. The purpose of such reports was clearly for the glory of the king and the deity in whose name the king fought. A rather late style of such reports is the Chronicle form, in which the events are reported in a rather objective fashion using the third person and without reference to the deity. The report in Gen. 14:1–11 is in the "chronicle" style, but with a still further development toward historical reporting achieved by putting the event in a larger context of affairs between the two regions involved. It is also presented from a third party viewpoint of an uninvolved region. Such a form has nothing in common with local or tribal oral tales and can only be the product of a late literary development.[13]

If the report in 14:1–11 could be accepted at face value, the origin would almost certainly have to be Mesopotamian, since the campaign initiated from this region and up to v. 11 had a successful conclusion. Such campaign reports were not created or preserved by uninvolved nations, and the suggestion that this report could be based on an ancient record preserved in Jerusalem is quite unreasonable. The whole area of Palestine was not involved. Even in the period of the monarchy almost no attention was paid to foreign invasion of neighboring states unless it directly affected Israel.[14] Yet in terms of the content of Gen. 14:1–11, as we have seen above, the whole report is so completely fanciful that we can only suppose it to be a completely artificial literary creation, using the campaign report in chronicle form as a model. As such, the account has no

---

13. Emerton states (*VT* 21:437) "The possibility that such records existed as early as the reign of David cannot be denied" and mentions "Canaanite historical records." But these must be flatly rejected. The only possible form of a "record" would have been a royal inscription boasting of the local king's conquests, which is not what we have, nor would they have been preserved by David if they ever existed. The third-person chronicle genre is a very late form—arising in the late Assyrian empire—and there is no reason to think it was in vogue in the West any earlier.

14. Exceptions to this are the oracles against the nations, but such a genre could hardly form the basis for the account here.

independent self-contained status, no possible function as a piece of folk tradition, and therefore it could not go back to any preliterary *Vorlage*.

It may be noted that v. 12, from the point of view of form, is really a continuation of the report. But Lot is not a political figure who might receive special mention in such a report. He is a story figure connected with the Abraham tradition. So the mention of Lot in v. 12 creates an effective transition from mere report to story and becomes the vital connection between the two halves of the chapter. This means that the whole report of vv. 1–11 functions only as an elaborate way of setting the scene for the story that follows.

The second half of the chapter also begins with a military campaign report, in vv. 13–16, with all the same basic features. But the motivation for the action by Abraham is the action of the earlier report and particularly the capture of Lot. The report certainly has no independence, and any effort to make it self-contained is forced to reconstruct a new setting for it. The fact that it follows the same type of literary convention of a reporting genre also speaks against any oral *Vorlage* and points to the same authorship as the preceding unit. The whole treatment of the episode in this brief objective style scarcely justifies the characterization of the second part as a "popular oral tradition."[15]

The story concludes with a dialogue between the king of Sodom and Abraham, vv. 17, 21–23(4). This is a return to the story form, since many stories reach their climax with a discourse or dialogue. The reference to the "king of Sodom" provides a connection with the first part in spite of the apparent reference to his destruction in v. 10.[16] It is clear, however, that v. 10 does not refer to the king personally but to his forces. Yet the story does not prepare us in any way for this confrontation between king and patriarch, so that it becomes hard to see it as a climax or the resolution of a situation of tension or need. At the most it is only a brief vignette that adds nothing of dramatic significance beyond the conclusion of v. 16. In fact, the ending in v. 23 (or 24) is very abrupt and most awkward for an actual story form.

The form of the addition in vv. 18–20 is dominated by the two poetic lines in vv. 19b–20a. The statement in v. 19a "He blessed

15. Emerton, *VT* 21:437.
16. See Emerton, ibid., pp. 27–28, in which he discusses this apparent contradiction.

him" would suggest that the form is a benediction, but in fact since it refers to past events and since v. 20a is directed at the deity, it is more in the nature of liturgical doxology.[17] In some instances it could function as a very formal greeting conferring honor and respect upon the person addressed. But it could also have some confessional and liturgical function, especially in the mouth of a priest. In this respect the tithe (v. 20b) must then be viewed as a formal cultic response to the confession implied in the previous statement.[18] The question, of course, arises as to what function such a genre could possibly have in its present context. In terms of its position in the present story it stands at the point where one would expect to find the climax, and there is little doubt that this was the intention of the one who added it. But its very weak connection with the story (v. 18), as we have noted already, proves that it was not original.

This form-critical discussion makes the analysis of the chapter's structure rather obvious. The story contains the following components:

1) The setting: the invasion by the eastern kings, vv. 1–12
   a) The first campaign report, vv. 1–11
   b) The transition to the story: the capture of Lot, v. 12
2) The core event: Abraham's victory, vv. 13–16
   a) The second campaign report, vv. 13–16a
   b) The climax (?): the freeing of Lot, v. 16b
3) The concluding dialogue, vv. 17, 21–23 (24) Confrontation between the defeated king of Sodom (pt. 1) and the victorious Abraham (pt. 2)
4) Addition: the liturgical doxology by Melchisedek, vv. 18–20.

According to the above form-critical and structural analysis, the development of this unit of tradition was in two stages and both of these on the written level of the tradition. All the proposals for a pre-literary stage are speculative and from every perspective of form and

17. On this form see W. S. Towner, "'Blessed Be YHWH' and 'Blessed Art Thou YHWH': The Modulation of a Biblical Formula," *CBQ* 30 (1968): 386–399 (especially 386–90). Towner does not actually discuss this passage, but it certainly fits the first form.
18. Note the parallel in Exod. 18:10–12, in which Jethro, the priest of Midian, comes out to meet Israel and uses this same form of blessing. This is followed by the statement that he "received" sacrifices (*wayyiqqaḥ*, çf. RSV "offered"). Finally, there is a common meal between Jethro and the representatives of Israel. Towner (ibid., p. 389, n. 5) places this instance in the category of noncultic blessings, but it seems to me to be quite cultic in character.

content quite unwarranted. Any discussion about the tradition's meaning and function must begin with the basic story (nos. 1–3 above), and only after this has been done can one deal with the significance of the addition in vv. 18–20.

We are now ready to consider how this story is related to the other pentateuchal sources. The obvious point of connection is with the Lot-Sodom cycle in the late Yahwistic source. If we regard the phrase "the nephew of Abram" in v. 12 as secondary, for reasons stated above, the way in which Lot enters the story presupposes a prior introduction of his association with Abraham and his subsequent separation. And this is reinforced by the statement that "he was living in Sodom." It is also assumed that the reader knows that Lot is Abraham's "kinsman," ʾaḥiyw (v. 14, cf. 13:8). On the other hand, it is quite unlikely that the source is actually J. This story adds the names of Admah and Zeboiim following Deut. 29:23, in which they are all grouped together. Only Sodom, Gomorrah, and Zoar are mentioned in J's story. The general region of these cities is here called the "Plain of Siddim" (v. 2), while in J it is always referred to as the "Kikkar of the Jordan." If v. 13b is original there is the reference to the "Terebinths of Mamre" from J's combined sources, but here Mamre is construed as a personal name, which is certainly not suggested in the other sources. It would appear that the author of Genesis 14 made use of the Abraham tradition as he knew it, at least in the version of the Yahwist.

There is also a number of affinities between this chapter and Deuteronomy or the Deuteronomic school, so that one recent study has suggested that the author is the Deuteronomist.[19] Some of the similarities have to do with the same chronistic style in the campaign reports as we have pointed out above. But this convention is clearly broader than its use by the Deuteronomist, although it is unlikely that it is any earlier. More important are the borrowings of specific materials from Deuteronomy 2 and 3, especially the names of the primordial peoples of Transjordan. As I have tried to show above, these names are not derived from an old Israelite tradition. The Deuteronomist regarded the mythical Rephaim as the ancient inhabitants of the whole of Transjordan, but he recognized that the Moabites preferred to call them Emim and the Ammonites Zamzumim. It was the author of Genesis 14 who borrowed all these

19. Astour, "Genesis 14," pp. 68–73. Cf. Emerton, VT 21:404–06.

names and restricted them to the particular regions corresponding to the political states of a later day. The direction of this borrowing could only go from Deuteronomy to Genesis 14 and not vice-versa. Another strong argument against the author of Genesis 14 being the Deuteronomist is the fact that he has no qualms about making Abraham a treaty partner to three Amorite chieftains of the Hebron region. All of this suggests that Genesis 14 is directly dependent upon Deuteronomy, but considerably later in time.

Some have argued that Genesis 14 is dependent upon P. It is fairly clear that the use of the divine name Yahweh by Abraham would not be appropriate for P himself. But there is a similarity in vocabulary between the two sources. For instance, there is the use of $r^ekuš$, "goods" (but cf. 15:14), $y^elîd\ bayit$, "household slave," and $nepeš$ in the sense of "person." The expression for taking an oath by "raising the hand" using the verb rwm in the hiphil $+ yd$ is a close synonym to P's usage with the verb $nś^{ɔ}+yd$ (also found in Deut. 32:40; Ezek. 20:23). However, it is noteworthy that such a late source as Dan. 12:7 uses the verb rwm, similar to Genesis 14, and not the verb $nś^{ɔ}$. The argument from vocabulary usage is not very strong, but it would point to a rather late period and possibly even later than P.[20] And this would make the addition, vv. 18–20, whose terminology is clearly not that of P even later.

The Meaning of Genesis 14

Almost invariably the point of departure for a discussion about the meaning of this chapter is the addition of vv. 18–20, so that any stage of the story's development prior to this is given very little consideration. One usually finds only vague statements about the remains of a "hero story" having to do with Abraham's exploits. Quite apart from the fact that there is no trace of such a popular view in the rest of the tradition, such an approach can only be maintained on the basis of quite different form-critical and literary conclusions. The second part, containing Abraham's victory, does not have a scene of personal combat so typical of the *Heldensage*. It is in the same genre as the previous part. The personal confrontation only begins in part three (vv. 17, 21–24), which is tied to both the previous campaign reports but in itself contains virtually no *dramatic*

20. Note the similar styles of introduction in 14:1 and Esther 1:1. See Emerton, *VT* 21:35.

character whatever. It is only a pietistic vignette. Consequently, the description of the earlier stage of the Abraham story as a hero story is very superficial and quite inadequate.[21]

This form of the story, in which one finds a mixture of quasi-historical reporting of events with an admixture of heroic and legendary elements, was recognized already by Gunkel as characteristic of Jewish popular stories in the Persian and Hellenistic periods.[22] Such episodes are found in the work of the Chronicler, but they are best exemplified by the book of Judith. The perspective of these works is the confrontation of a world empire by very few, the strong sense of individual piety, and the love of a certain archaism by its efforts to reconstruct an elaborate past historical setting.

There are, nevertheless, a number of specific clues to the story's dating. Since virtually all the names of places and countries are intended to be the archaic counterparts of later entities it is clear that Elam must really stand for Persia. The supposed Elamite empire is really the Persian domination of the West of a later day. Chedorlaomer is presented as the leader of the expeditionary force, and the Western states are his vassals. The fact that Babylon is an ally probably points to a period long after the animosity between Persia and Babylon when all the three "kingdoms" in league with Persia represent major satrapies of a later day. The perspective of the story is the late Persian empire. Another such clue is the change in attitude toward the "Amorites." They are viewed as being in close association with the Amalekites, living primarily in the northern Negeb, but also in friendly association with Abraham at Hebron. How can one account for this change in attitude? It appears that the term Amorite shifted in meaning in the Persian period from the indigenous population to the Arab peoples. So they could then be viewed as the nomadic and pastoral peoples of southern Judah including the region of Hebron. And in the late Persian period there was an increasing mixture and absorption of these peoples, who largely represented the same cultural milieu. Likewise, the use of the term Hebrew to describe Abraham is very similar to that of the Jonah story, which comes from this same general period.[23]

It is difficult to see any programmatic or legitimating function to

21. Cf. Emerton, ibid., pp. 431ff.
22. *Genesis*, pp. 189–90.
23. So also deVaux, *Histoire*, p. 203.

the story in this first stage. It can hardly be regarded as supporting a claim to the land of Palestine parallel to the conquest tradition, as Astour has suggested,[24] because the story does not suggest that Palestine was a part of Chedorlaomer's empire or was threatened by his invasion. Abraham, by his victory, does not win anything for himself or his posterity. The only point of the story according to the closing discourse is to teach the virtues of courage, loyalty, and piety by Abraham's example.

The addition, vv. 18–20, is quite a different matter, and here the interpretations are many.[25] It will be possible to consider only the most recent arguments for an early date and then to suggest an alternative in the late post-exilic period. The early dating of these verses rests primarily upon a prior hypothesis about the nature of the Judean monarchy and the pre-Israelite form of religion in Jerusalem. On the basis of Ps. 110:4 it is suggested that the Judean monarchy was also priestly and derived this function from the previous "Canaanite" form of the monarchy, whose "founder" was Melchisedek. Secondly, the deity of the pre-Israelite Jerusalem cult is said to have been El Elyon, so that with the establishment of the Davidic monarchy an identity was made between El and Yahweh.[26] All the theories that date Gen. 14:18–20 early interpret the passage as a form of legitimation of the monarchy (or the priesthood) and this religious syncretism. However the dating and interpretation of Ps. 110 are very problematic and there is no evidence whatever to view the Judean monarchy as an extension of the Jebusite dynasty. Nor is there any proof that El Elyon was the deity in Jerusalem before the rise of David, or that a program of syncretism was carried through at that time.[27]

Furthermore, the early dating of vv. 18–20 must see in either Abraham or Melchisedek the figure of David. But such an interpretation becomes forced because there is not the slightest resemblance to

---

24. Astour, "Genesis 14," p. 74.
25. See the review of these by Emerton, *VT* 21:412–38. See also W. Zimmerli, "Abraham und Melchisedek," *BZAW* 105 (1967): 255–64.
26. This theory is set forth extensively in R. E. Clements, *God and Temple* (Philadelphia: Fortress Press, 1965), chap. 4.
27. The whole reconstruction has become completely circular. Emerton's dating of Gen. 14:18–20 rests heavily upon it and yet Clements states (ibid., p. 43) "The most important clue for the discovery of the nature of the worship of pre-Israelite Jerusalem, and of the god, or gods, venerated there, is to be found in Gen. xiv 18–24."

David's monarchy in this story. If David is the warrior Abraham, he certainly did not fight foreign invaders from Mesopotamia or come to the aid of the Transjordanian peoples. On the contrary, he subjugated them and took booty for himself. He was allied with no other powers in Palestine, and the Amorites of chap. 14 cannot simply be identified with the "Canaanites" of David's kingdom.[28] On the other hand, it would be strange to think of Melchisedek as David, since he appears quite aloof from the military and political events of the day.[29] There is nothing in the story that corresponds in any way to the realities of the Davidic period as we know it from the OT.

I think scholars are correct in seeing in the addition of vv. 18–20 the purpose of legitimation, but for quite a different period. First of all, the deity named in the "blessing" is not just the god Elyon, who is known from Aramaic and Phoenician sources of the first millennium. Instead, the name represents a combination of ^{c}elyon and $^{\circ}$el qn $^{\circ}$rṣ, who are two distinct deities.[30] And in the case of the second deity the title has been expanded to include both heaven and earth. The result is one complex title for the deity. This is then taken one step further in v. 22 by the attributing of this title to Yahweh, so that out of the divine names is created a complex epithet. Such a process was begun by J and carried forward by P in their identifying forms of El with Yahweh, and it reaches its culmination in Genesis 14.

The addition in vv. 18–20 is concerned with the legitimation of this form of syncretism. The clue to this interpretation is in the fact that a set liturgical form that regularly uses the name Yahweh

---

28. On the basis of our discussion of "Canaanites" above, it remains extremely doubtful whether there was such a people as "Canaanites" in David's kingdom. This term would imply a strong sense of unity among all the non-Israelite inhabitants of Palestine, but the existence of such a unity is very doubtful. It is also scarcely possible for the term Amorite to have been used in this way in the time of David.

29. Emerton's suggestion (*VT* 21:421ff.) that David is to be seen in both Abraham and Melchisedek is too farfetched. He completely blurs the differences between David and Abraham, which are considerable. Abraham did not defend anyone against an attack, although he conceivably had lots of time to join the coalition against the invaders. He did nothing until the damage was done because he had a concern only for Lot his kinsman. There was no foreign attack on Canaan, and his encounter with the foreign kings was beyond Israel's traditional borders. The whole theory is quite unconvincing.

30. Clements, *God and Temple*, pp. 44–47, weighs against the evidence of epigraphic data that El and Elyon were separate deities in the first millennium the theoretic possibility that in Jerusalem Elyon was only a title applied to El. Theories built on such conjectures can carry little weight.

("Blessed be Yahweh") is here modified to "Blessed be El Elyon."[31] This form of doxology was often used to express kerygmatically Yahweh's creative power and saving acts, but here the same is attributed to El Elyon. The fact that Abraham pays a tithe to this deity and then swears by him is further demonstration of the titles legitimation.

The crucial question is: when is the most likely period for such a syncretistic movement to have taken place? It is significant that although Melchisedek is called "priest of El Elyon" such a title is not used throughout the whole history of the priesthood recorded in the OT. It is only in the Maccabean period that the Hasmoneans used the title of "high priests of God most high."[32] It is unlikely that they simply borrowed the title from this passage or that the title originated with them. It is more probable that it belongs to the late Persian or early Hellenistic period, when such syncretism became common throughout the Near East, and even the Jerusalem religious community was caught up in it. By the time of the Hasmoneans it was probably a fixed title whose origins were no longer known.

Melchisedek, then, represents the priesthood of the second temple. It may be objected that the royal claims of the priesthood only became explicit with the Hasmoneans. But there is considerable evidence to indicate that such claims were very clearly implicit in the previous period, and that only the political situation prevented them from becoming clearly stated.[33] It is even possible that the dual role was actually inherited from the monarchy, but this is not entirely clear.

The dating and general historical situation to which Genesis 14 and the addition in vv. 18–20 speak must remain unclear since the history of the whole period from Ezra to the Maccabees is still obscure. Yet all the evidence of form and content would seem to point to this period, at the close of the fourth century B.C., as the time when the biblical tradition of Abraham received its final chapter.

---

31. See Towner, n. 17 above. This is similar to P's modification of the formula "I am Yahweh" to "I am El Shaddai."
32. See Skinner, *Genesis*, pp. 270–71.
33. On the royal aspects of the post-exilic priesthood see deVaux, *Ancient Israel*, pp. 400–01.

CHAPTER 15

Conclusion

The conclusions to this study regarding the Abraham tradition lie in two principal areas: the dating of the tradition, and the nature of its literary development. I have argued from the beginning that these two questions are interrelated to such a degree that any reconsideration of the one demands a review of the other as well. On the matter of dating I have tried to show that there is no unambiguous evidence that points to a great antiquity for this tradition. Arguments based on reconstructing the patriarch's nomadic way of life, the personal names in Genesis, the social customs reflected in the stories, and correlation of the traditions of Genesis with the archaeological data of the Middle Bronze age have all been found, in Part One above, to be quite defective in demonstrating an origin for the Abraham tradition in the second millennium B.C. Consequently, without any such effective historical controls on the tradition one cannot use any part of it in an attempt to reconstruct the primitive period of Israelite history. Furthermore, a vague presupposition about the antiquity of the tradition based upon a consensus approval of such arguments should no longer be used as a warrant for proposing a history of the tradition related to early premonarchic times.

Likewise, one cannot argue from the form of the tradition back to a preliterate stage for the tradition as a whole, the way that Noth has done. The degree to which the stories reflect any oral tradition may be explained entirely by the use of folkloristic forms and motifs that were accessible to Israelite culture throughout its history and not primarily by the deposit of a preliterate period. There is virtually no way of deciding when oral narrative forms or motifs became associated with a particular person such as Abraham, and it could well have happened in every case when the story was first put in written form. The results of the literary examination of the Abraham tradition, in Part Two, would suggest that oral forms and motifs are confined to a rather small part of the tradition, certainly much less than

Gunkel originally proposed. The notion, so frequently expressed and most strongly by Noth, that a long and complex tradition-history on the preliterate level lies behind the whole of the present literary form is regarded by this study as completely unfounded.

A date for the first literary formation of the tradition, by the Yahwist, to the time of the United Monarchy has also been rejected in this study. Such a date is so widely accepted because it serves as a convenient complement to the theory about the tradition's history in a preliterate period. The Yahwist is then viewed as the one who fixed in a written form the development of the oral tradition at that point with very little contribution of his own. However, specific arguments for a setting in the early monarchy are extremely sparse and become quite inadequate if one cannot accept the proposals regarding the preliterate development of the tradition.

The present study has argued that the Yahwistic version of the tradition dates to the exilic period. The Priestly version, which is viewed here as a direct literary supplement to the earlier work, must be later and post-exilic in date. This dating of the Yahwist is based on the fact that while he consciously portrays a primitive age without the political structures of a later day he still gives frequent clues to his own time. His use of various designations for the indigenous inhabitants is quite unhistorical and reflects the development of such archaisms in the late period of the monarchy. The prominence that he gives to the Arameans of the region around Harran (but not Syria) and the Arabs of north Arabia and the Negeb reflect a late date. The references to Ur of the Chaldeans and its close connections with Harran and the West point most clearly to the late Neo-Babylonian period. Even the portrayal of the nomadic element in the story, with camels and tents, points to a time when such bedouin were most prominent—in the mid-first millennium B.C.

The literary analysis of the Abraham tradition likewise confirms this late dating. The Yahwist sometimes employs cultic and prophetic forms that may be judged by comparative study to be quite late. At other points, as I have argued, he seems to make use of royal and cultic forms of the pre-exilic period and to reapply them to the new situation of the exile when the monarchy was ended and the formal practice of the cult was minimal. But above all the Yahwist must be viewed in the light of the history of Israel's sacred traditions of election. In this regard the tradition of Abraham as a means of corporate identity for Israel only came to the fore in the exilic period. Here the whole perspective of the Yahwist stands in a very close relationship to that of Deutero-Isaiah in contrast to Deuteronomy and the prophets Jeremiah and Ezekiel. It is to the despairing community of the exile that the unbreakable promises of the patriarchs are addressed, and Abraham becomes the focus of corporate identity and the lifeline of their hope and destiny.

Alongside of the matter of dating the tradition is the question of its literary form and development. Here I have taken issue with the current method of pentateuchal criticism as it has to do primarily with the Abraham tradition. On the basis of a study of the doublets, I have concluded that the literary sources are not independent developments of the tradition, which were only combined by a series of later redactors. Instead, each succeeding source is directly dependent upon, and supplements, the earlier tradition. The Yahwist, usually regarded as the earliest source, was in fact preceded by an earlier written level of the tradition, which included the stories of Abraham in Egypt (Gen. 12:10–20), Hagar's flight (16:1–12), and the birth of Isaac (18:1a, 10–14; 21:2, 6–7). It also included the first supplement to the Abraham story, the episode of Abraham at Abimelech's court (20:1–17; 21:25–26, 28–31a). This story is usually associated with a larger pentateuchal source, the Elohist (E), which is dated after the Yahwist. However, apart from this one episode I can find no further evidence of it in the Abraham tradition, and here it comes before the Yahwist. The whole existence of an extensive E source in the Pentateuch has been questioned by this study. What the Yahwist received in a written form he rearranged and supplemented to express in it his own concerns. He also added further stories and episodes of his own. The Priestly writer subsequently added to the Yahwist's tradition his own version of the Abrahamic covenant (chap. 17), which was strongly dependent upon the earlier source, as well as the burial of Sarah (chap. 23), which was an independent story. The last addition to the whole was the story of the defeat of the eastern kings (Genesis 14).

This reconstruction of the literary history of the Abraham tradition has important implications for the discussion of oral tradition. Oral tradition does not need to be used to explain why independent sources are similar, since the degree and character of that similarity point to literary dependency. The positing of any oral tradition behind the written version must be based entirely upon characteristics of form and structure belonging to preliterary genre such as enumerated in Olrik's epic laws. With the meager evidence of oral tradition that can be found in this way one can hardly reconstruct a form of society or social setting in a preliterate period in which such elements of the tradition had any special function.

The present study also proposes that form-criticism and structural analysis precede any attempt at source division in order to serve as a control over it. Failure to do so has resulted in a proliferation of source division using other more questionable criteria. The application of form-criticism in this study as a control of literary criticism has resulted in disputing the value of such long established criteria as the use of the divine name to separate a J and E source, the use of repetition within a story unit, the use of special vocabulary, etc. Form-criticism must also serve as a control over tradition-history and not vice versa. It is not legitimate to prejudge what the form and function of a unit of tradition may have been based on a preconceived history of the tradition, especially oral tradition. It appears to me at the present time that one can say little about any oral tradition. What must be clarified first and foremost is the place of the tradition in Israel's literature and history as reflected in the Old Testament texts. This has been the task of my study.

Appendix: The Literary Sources of the Abraham Tradition of Genesis

The following represent the various stages of growth, as argued in the foregoing study:

I. Pre-Yahwistic first stage: 12:1, 4a*, 6a, 7, 10–20; 13:1*–2; 16:1–3a, 4–9, 11ab, 12; 13:18; 18:1a, 10–14; 21:2, 6–7.
(* except the references to Lot). These references represent a small unified work with three episodes and a brief framework.

II. Pre-Yahwistic second stage ("E"): 20:1–17; 21:25–26, 28–31a. This represents one unified story that originally came after the adventure in Egypt (13:1), to which it was added. It was subsequently transposed to its present position by the Yahwist, who added 20:1a ("From there ... Negeb") as a transition.

III. Yahwist:
 A. brief secondary additions to previous works: 12:2–3, 6b, 8–9; 16:7b, 10, 11c, 13–14; 20:1aα; 21:1.
 B. larger episodic units: 13:3–5, 7–17; chap. 15; 18:1b–9, 15–19:38; 21:8–24, 27, 31b–34; chap. 22; chap. 24; 25:1–6, 11; (chap. 26). All of these were skillfully incorporated into the older literary work with some new arrangement of the materials.

IV. Priestly:
 A. Secondary genealogical and chronological additions: 11:26–32; 12:4b–5; 13:6; 16:3b, 15–16; 21:3–5; 25:7–10.
 B. Larger episodic units: chaps. 17 and 23.

V. Post-Priestly: chap. 14 (of which vv. 18–20 are secondary).

Indexes

AUTHORS

Ackroyd, P., 275n
Aharoni, Y., 42n, 47n, 105n, 111n
Albright, W. F., 7–8, 8, 11, 14nn, 23n, 32n, 33n, 39n, 40n, 41nn, 42nn, 45n, 47n, 53n, 59nn, 60nn, 61nn, 85, 86n, 87n, 98n, 105–06, 107, 107nn, 112n, 113n, 114n, 115, 131n, 132n
Alt, A., 9n, 110n, 132, 139–42, 146, 147, 148, 150n, 152, 228, 250, 251, 271n
Aly, W., 138n
Anderson, B. W., 266n
Anderson, T. A., 136n, 137n
Astour, M. C., 47nn, 61n, 112n, 113nn, 114n, 116–17, 116n, 118, 118n, 119–20, 296n, 303n, 306n
Augapfel, J., 66n, 97n
Avi-Yonah, M., 47n

Barnett, R. D., 53n
Beckerath, J. von, 109n
Begrich, J., 267
Besters, A., 130n
Beyerlin, W., 143n
Bietak, M., 22n
Blenkinsopp, J., 151n
Boer, P. A. H. de, 275n
Bottéro, J., 20n, 26n, 61n
Bowmann, R. A., 29n, 33n, 58n
Boyer, G., 90n
Branden, A. van den, 61n
Brekelmans, C., 130n
Bright, J., 9, 11, 23n, 39n, 40n, 59n, 65n, 71n, 98n, 104n, 110n, 112n, 133n
Brink, H. van den, 98n, 99n
Brinkman, J. A., 15n, 25n, 31n
Broome, E. C., 64n
Bruggemann, W., 151n
Buccellati, G., 40n
Burrows, M., 72n, 74n, 78n, 81n, 82nn, 84

Caloz, M., 130n
Caquot, A., 249n, 254n, 255n

Cardascia, G., 19n, 66n, 97n
Cassin, E. M., 66n, 89n, 93n
Cazelles, H., 12, 87n, 125n, 249n, 251, 255n, 258n
Chadwick, H. M. and N. K., 131n
Chiera, E., 66n
Childs, B., 133, 133nn, 143, 143n, 144, 147n, 191n, 220n
Clark, W. M., 249n, 258n, 259n, 263n, 264n, 265n, 276nn
Clements, R. E., 149n, 151n, 152, 249n, 252n, 255n, 256n, 260n, 263n, 266n, 306nn, 307n
Coats, G. W., 143n, 239n
Cowley, A., 67n
Cross, F. M., Jr., 141n
Culley, R. C., 157n, 158n, 159n

Daube, D., 174, 276n
Delcor, M., 53n
Dentan, R. C., 130n
Dever, W. G., 21nn, 51n, 106, 106nn, 107nn
Dhorme, E., 12
Dietrich, M., 66n
Dion, H. M., 254n
Donner, H., 40n, 41nn
Dossin, G., 20n, 22nn, 44n
Dostal, W., 17n
Dougherty, R. P., 36nn, 46n
Draffkorn, A. E., 93n, 102n
Driver, G. R., 65, 69n
Dumbrell, W. J., 35n, 36n, 62n, 64nn
Dupont-Sommer, A., 29n, 30nn

Ebeling, E., 26n
Edel, E., 31n
Edzard, D. O., 13n, 20nn, 30n, 44n
Eissfeldt, O., 9n, 12, 125n, 275, 279n
Elliger, K., 257n, 294n
Ellis, P. F., 149n

315

Emerton, J. A., 116nn, 118n, 119, 120n, 296n, 297nn, 298nn, 299nn, 300n, 301nn, 303n, 304n, 305n, 306nn, 307n
Engnell, I., 125n, 158n
Ephal, I., 37n, 60n
Engnell, I., 125n, 158n
Ephal, I., 37n, 60n
Erlenmeyer, H., and M. L., 53n

Falk, Z. W., 87n
Feigin, S., 79n
Fichtner, J., 133n, 184n, 207n, 231n
Filippi, W. de, 162n
Finkelstein, J. J., 33n, 58n, 59n, 90n, 95–97, 96nn, 98n
Finnegan, R., 158n, 159nn
Fitzmyer, J. A., 103n
Fohrer, G., 9nn, 125n, 127n, 128, 129, 129n, 143n, 145n, 148n, 279n, 294n
Földes, L., 13n
Frankena, R., 96n
Frazer, J. G., 100–01
Freedman, D. N., 75n
Fuss, W., 130n

Gabrieli, F., 13n
Gadd, C. J., 20n, 24n, 66n, 73n, 84n, 89n, 93n
Gardiner, A. H., 48n, 50nn, 52n, 70n, 81n
Gauthier, H., 50n
Gelb, I. J., 20n
Gibson, J. C. L., 33n, 43n, 45n, 47nn
Ginsberg, H. L., 86, 255n
Giveon, R., 27n, 56n, 63n
Glueck, N., 8, 11, 27n, 105–06, 105nn, 115
Goetze, A., 45n
Goodenough, E. R., 258n
Gordon, C. H., 9, 11, 66, 68n, 69n, 72n, 79, 81, 81n, 87n, 93nn, 98n
Grayson, A. K., 120n, 259n
Greenberg, M., 26n, 56n, 65n, 93–94
Greenfield, J. C., 53n
Greengus, S., 75n
Grelot, P., 291n
Grollenberg, L. H., 15n
Gröndahl, F., 40n, 41nn
Gunkel, H., 110n, 112n, 131–34, 135, 137, 138, 139, 141, 142, 144, 148, 160, 167, 168, 170, 171, 173n, 176, 184, 193n, 194n, 196n, 198, 201n, 202n, 203, 203nn,

209n, 213nn, 217nn, 218nn, 219n, 220n, 223n, 225n, 228, 229, 233n, 242–43, 244, 258n, 281n, 295, 305
Gurney, O. R., 32n, 45nn, 110n

Haase, R., 65n
Haldar, A., 44n
Hallo, W. W., 46n, 259n
Hand, W. D., 131n, 138n
Harding, G. L., 40n, 42n, 63n
Harland, J. P., 117n
Harris, J. R., 209n
Helck, W., 26n, 27
Henninger, J., 13nn, 14nn, 87n, 91n, 101n
Heusler, A., 134, 136
Hinz, W., 113n
Hoftijzer, J., 249n, 270, 273n, 281n
Holt, J. M., 10n
Hommel, F., 40
Horn, S. H., 62n
Huffmon, H. B., 40n, 41n
Humbert, P., 279n, 284n

Jeffery, A., 32n, 35n, 37, 60n, 61n
Jolles, A., 134, 135, 136, 137, 137n, 138

Kahle, P., 168n
Kaiser, O., 249nn, 250–51, 253n, 254, 254n
Kaufmann, Y., 125n
Keller, C. A., 167n, 174n
Kenyon, K. M., 47n, 106, 106nn, 107n, 108n
Kilian, R., 148n, 167n, 168n, 170n, 171nn, 177n, 178n, 179n, 180n, 182n, 184n, 194n, 202n, 203n, 206n, 210nn, 211n, 213n, 215n, 217nn, 218n, 219nn, 222nn, 223nn, 225nn, 227, 228–29, 229n, 233–37, 236nn, 252n, 256n, 263n
Kitchen, K. A., 17n, 27n
Klengel, H., 14n
Koch, K., 26n, 55n, 129n, 133n, 134, 137–38, 137n, 154n, 157n, 167n, 168n, 170n, 171n, 172nn, 173nn, 174n, 176, 176nn, 177n, 180n
Kohler, J., 66n, 83nn, 91n, 93n, 97n
Koschaker, P., 71n, 72, 72nn, 73n
Kraeling, E. G., 67n
Kramer, S. N., 113n
Kraus, F. R., 95n

Krohn, K., 160n
Külling, S. R., 286n
Kupper, J.-R., 13n, 14n, 15n, 20n, 23n, 24n, 30n, 44n

Lacheman, E. R., 66n
Lambert, W. G., 96n, 259n
Landes, G. M., 28n
Lapp, P., 106
Leach, E. R., 157n
Leclant, J., 22n
Lehmann, M. R., 98–99
Levine, L. D., 162n
Levi-Strauss, C., 157n
Lewy, J., 24n, 37n, 42n, 63n, 69n, 84n
Loewenstamm, S. E., 101, 102, 258n, 259n, 276n, 283n
Lohfink, N., 130n, 249nn, 251–52, 254nn, 255n, 258n, 260, 263, 263nn, 264n, 267n, 290n
Lohr, M., 279n
Long, B., 133, 133nn, 184n, 187n, 193n, 207n, 218nn, 220nn, 221n, 231n
Lord, A. B., 163n
Loreta, O., 66n, 205n
Luckenbill, D. D., 33n, 44n, 46n, 119n
Luddeckens, E., 75n, 76n

McCarthy, D. J., 101n, 102n, 103n, 184n
McEvenue, S., 279n, 280nn, 281nn, 282nn, 285nn, 286, 286nn, 288n, 289n, 290n, 291n, 293n, 295n
Maisler, B. See Mazar, B.
Malamat, A., 14n, 17n, 51n, 59nn, 108n, 152n, 275n
Mayer, W., 66n
Mazar, B., 32n, 33n, 41n, 47n, 48n, 62n
Meek, T. J., 12, 69n
Meissner, B., 67n
Mendelsohn, I., 18n, 19n
Mendenhall, G. E., 15n, 151n
Miles, J. C., 65, 69n
Mitchell, T. C., 53n
Montgomery, J. A., 35n, 60n
Moore, E. W., 66n, 93n
Moran, W. L., 76n
Moritz, B., 59n
Moscati, S., 20nn, 29n, 30, 35n,
Mowinckel, S., 125n, 127n, 133n, 148n, 172n, 173nn, 184n, 200n, 295n

Muilenberg, J., 269n

Neff, R., 194–95, 204, 205nn, 284nn
Neufeld, E., 78n
Nielsen, E., 158n
Nilsson, M. P., 29n, 148n, 190n, 295n
Noth, M., 9n, 12, 33n, 39nn, 40nn, 41nn, 42nn, 43n, 90, 90nn, 92, 105n, 110n, 114n, 126, 127, 128–29, 130n, 132, 133, 134, 134n, 135n, 143–48, 149, 152, 159n, 168, 170, 173n, 176, 180n, 183, 184n, 187, 188n, 210n, 213n, 220n, 226, 227n, 228, 241, 242–43, 279n, 285n, 294n, 309–10

Olrik, A., 132, 133, 137, 138, 160–61, 165, 169, 170, 171, 195, 197–98, 200, 235, 236, 243
Oppenheim, A. L., 159n

Parker, B., 70n
Parker, R. A., 50n
Parpola, S., 35n, 44n, 45n, 59n, 63n
Parrot, A., 12
Paul, S. M., 276n
Petschow, H., 67n, 74n, 77n, 84nn, 91n, 97nn, 99n, 100n
Petzoldt, L., 135n, 138n
Peuchert, W. E., 137n
Pfeiffer, R. H., 66n
Ploeg, J. P. M. van der, 18n
Porter, B., 67n
Posener, G., 21nn
Praag, A. van, 72n, 77n, 82nn
Pritchard, J. B., 10, 65

Rabinowitz, J. J., 67n, 76n, 99n
Rad, G. von, 19n, 132, 134, 142–43, 144, 146, 148, 149, 151n, 168n, 170nn, 180n, 184n, 187n, 202n, 212n, 213nn, 214–15, 214nn, 220n, 225n, 228n, 239nn, 242, 244n, 257, 257nn, 268–69, 269n, 279n, 290n, 294
Rainey, A. F., 36nn, 64n
Redford, D. B., 50n, 54n, 55n, 68
Reed, W. L., 61n, 63nn, 64n
Reventlow, H. G., 228–29, 229nn, 234–37, 236nn
Richter, W., 154n, 156nn, 157n, 261n
Rohrich, L., 137nn, 138n

Röllig, W., 40n, 41nn
Rosmarin, T. W., 35n
Ross, J. F., 110n
Roth, W., 244–46
Roux. G., 25nn, 31n
Rowley, H. H., 12
Rudolf, W., 126n
Ruppert, L., 239n
Ryckmans, G., 35n, 42n, 63n

Saggs, H. W. F., 25n
Sandmel, S., 285n
San Nicolò, M., 66n, 74n, 77n, 81n, 84nn, 91nn, 93nn
Scharbert, J., 130n, 272n
Schatz, W., 112n, 296n
Schmidt, H., 168n
Schmitt, G., 167n
Schorr, M., 69n, 74n
Schottroff, W., 272nn, 273n
Schreiner, J., 269n, 271nn, 272n
Seebass, H., 147n, 249n, 255n
Seeligmann, I. L., 133n
Shaffer, A., 51n
Sievers, E., 132n
Simons, J., 33n, 58n, 59n, 60nn, 63n, 117n
Skaist, A., 72n, 74n
Skinner, J., 42n, 60nn, 116n, 167n, 170nn, 184n, 193n, 194n, 196n, 198n, 199n, 202n, 213nn, 218n, 219n, 225n, 258n, 281n, 308n
Smith, M., 10n, 66n, 67n
Smith, S., 48n
Smith, W. R., 9n, 101
Snijders, L. A., 249n
Speiser, A., 11, 66, 66n, 68n, 69nn, 71, 72nn, 73, 74, 74n, 76–77, 82n, 84, 86n, 89n, 90n, 93n, 94, 94n, 95n, 112n, 113nn, 115, 116n, 229nn, 255n
Staerk, W., 127n, 129
Stamm, J. J., 39n, 40n, 42nn
Stark, J. K., 40n
Steindorff, G., 48n
Sveinsson, E. O., 136nn, 162n, 163nn
Sydow, C. W. von, 131n, 135n, 136n

Thompson, J. A., 17n
Tigay, J. H., 79n
Tournay, R.-J., 66n
Towner, W. S., 302n, 308n

Tucker, G. M., 65n, 99nn, 100nn

Ungnad, A., 40n, 66n, 81n, 83nn, 84nn, 91nn, 93nn, 97n

Van Seters, J., 22n, 23n, 43nn, 44n, 45n, 49n, 51n, 65n, 68n, 70nn, 79n, 80n, 107n, 108n, 109n, 111n, 118n, 120n, 178n, 181n, 201n, 260n, 263n, 287n, 292n, 299n
Vansina, J., 145, 153n, 158nn
Vaux, R. de, 10n, 12, 13n, 14n, 15n, 17nn, 18n, 19n, 20n, 23n, 24n, 26nn, 29n, 30n, 33n, 39n, 40nn, 41nn, 42n, 43n, 46n, 47nn, 48–49, 48nn, 49n, 51nn, 52n, 53n, 54nn, 55n, 56–57, 56n, 57nn, 59nn, 65n, 67n, 71n, 82n, 87n, 93n, 96n, 145n, 305n, 308n
Vink, J. G., 125n, 279n, 291n, 292nn, 293n, 295n
Volz, P., 126, 127n, 128, 129–30, 173n, 279n, 293n

Wagner, N. E., 127n, 128n, 130n, 148, 149, 149nn, 152n, 153, 271n, 288n
Ward, W. A., 21n
Weidmann, H., 141n
Weinfeld, M., 102–03, 102nn, 259n, 272n, 273n, 276n, 283n, 288n, 290n
Weippert, M., 13n, 14nn, 15n, 17n, 26nn, 27n, 31n, 50n, 56n, 57nn, 287n
Weir, C. J. Mullo, 66n, 75n
Wellhausen, J., 3, 7, 149, 279n
Westermann, C., 134, 135, 137, 148, 206n, 220n, 222n, 234, 243n, 251, 255nn, 260n, 263, 270, 282n, 294n
Whybray, R. N., 151n
Widengren, G., 162nn
Wilson, R. R., 152n
Winnett, F. V., 60n, 61nn, 62n, 63nn, 64n, 127n, 130nn, 148n, 200n, 285n
Wiseman, D. J., 46n, 102, 102nn
Wolff, H. W., 149nn, 230n, 269n, 271nn
Wright, G. E., 8, 9, 11, 104n, 107, 108nn, 109–11, 228–29, 228nn
Würthwein, E., 161n

Yaron, R., 67n, 74n, 82n, 84n
Yeivin, S., 108n, 112n, 114n

Zimmerli, W., 257n, 287n, 292, 306n

BIBLICAL REFERENCES

Genesis	Page no	13:1ff	170
1:22, 28	283n	1–2	170, 223, 224
9:1, 7	283n	1–13	165
10:7, 26	61n	2	18n, 224, 224n, 247
15f	45	3–4	223
15–19	43, 46, 51	5–8	18n
11–50	7	5–13	222n
11:10–26	225	6	225, 285
21–22	59	7	46n, 277
22–32	58–59	7–12 (13)	221–23
26–32	225	8	225, 303
27–32	285	10	222n
28–30	225	14ff	289
32ff	33	14–17	276, 283
12	172, 209, 221	16	272
12–13	221–26	18	203, 207, 224
12–25	1	14	18, 54, 105, 107, 108,
12:1	172, 183, 224		112–20, 166, 254,
1ff	182		296–308, 311
1–3	271, 275, 276	14:1–11	300
1, 4a, 6a, 7	277	5–7	117
1, 6–7	271	6	52
2	273, 282, 283	7	119
2–3	18, 188, 247, 274, 275	7, 13	43
4a	224	10	119
4b–5	225, 285	13	45, 54
5, 16	18n	14	18n
6–7	110	15	140, 141, 146, 151,
6	46n		153, 154, 166, 249–78,
6b	277		280, 282, 283, 288,
7	270n		289, 292
8	223, 223n	15:1	230, 267–68, 282
9	170, 223	1–3	224n
10	16n	1–6	267
10–20	71–76, 128, 154, 164,	2	244n
	167–71, 183, 187,	2–3	85–87, 282, 284n
	191, 192, 193, 196,	3	18–19, 18n
	223, 223n, 224,	4–5	282
	234, 311	5	272
11	179	6	268
13, 16	171n	7	264–65, 288
15	180	7–18	282
16	247	7–21	269, 289
17	76, 173, 181	7–22	100–03
18–19	180, 181	9	103n
20	189	13	16n
13	188, 190, 209, 221	13–16	152
13:1	224	14	304

15:16	43	18:20ff	214
18	44, 283, 289	23–24	214
20	45	23–32	214–15
20–21	43n	19	203, 209, 211, 214, 215–21
16	18n, 68–70, 154, 165, 192–96, 197–200, 202, 204, 208	19:1	210n, 212
		1–11	213
16:1	197, 224, 224n	9	16n
1ff	224	15	214
1–12	196, 224, 285, 311	17	214, 222n
1–16	270	18, 19	206–07
2	70	19ff	215
16:3a, 15–16	285	25	222n
9	195	29	285
10	282, 285	20	71–76, 154, 155, 165, 167, 170, 171–75, 178n, 183, 185, 186, 187, 188, 191, 200n
11c	199		
12	18, 37, 62, 64, 270		
13a	288	20:1	16n
15	284n	1–17	191, 311
17	126, 154, 166, 264n, 270, 279–93, 311	5	181
		6	181
17:1–8	282	7	181
4–6, 16, 20	18	8	186
6, 16	289	9	76
7, 19	289	9, 11	180
8	16n, 283, 289, 294	9ff	185
12–13, 23, 27	18n	11	181
15–21	283–84	11, 13	179
19	194	12	75–76, 181
20	283n	13	182
21	206	14	18n
25	155	15	19, 188
18	155, 203, 208, 209–16	17 (18)	185
18–19	222, 246, 259	21	155, 190
18:1a	224, 311	21:1	206
1a, 10–14	207, 209, 311	1ff	204
1–15	165, 192, 202–08	1–2, 6–7	204
2–3	216	1–7	165, 192, 202
7	18n	1–21	172
10	284n	2	205, 206, 211, 248, 284nn
10ff	270		
10–14	204–05, 211, 283–84, 284nn	2, 6	204n
		2, 6–7	207, 311
11–13	284n	2b	284n
14	284n	3	284n
16–19:29	117	3–5	206, 285, 287
16–19:38	165	6a	206
16–33	215	6–7	206
18	18, 271n, 274, 282	6b–7	206
19	273, 274		

21:7	284n	25		155
8ff	230, 238	25:1ff		197
8–21	18n, 154, 155, 165, 192, 196–202, 204, 230	1–5		60–62
		1–6		248
		5		248
10	88	6		88
13, 18	18, 271, 283	7–10		285
17–18	285	9		45, 293
17ff	268n	11		248
20	37	13–16		62–64, 289
20–21	18, 64	16		18
22	268	18		64, 195
22–24	277	20		58
22–34	165, 172, 184–87, 188, 191	23		18
		29–34		88
23, 34	16n	26		3, 155, 186, 242
25ff	175	26:1ff		52
25–26, 28–31a	191, 311	1–11		71–76, 154, 165, 167–68, 170, 175–82, 183, 188, 191
30–32	230			
32	52			
33	191, 288n	1–12		128
34	230	1–14		167n
22	165, 227–240, 239n, 248	2		230, 238
		3		16n, 103, 283
22:1–19	227–40	3–4		283
1, 20	253n	3–5		188, 239
3f	18n	3–5 (24)		273
13–14	247	4		271n, 272, 277
16	103, 283	4, 24		282
16–18	273	5		273
16, 18	288	5, 24		288
17	272, 282, 283	9, 10		180
18	271n, 274	10		76
20	230	12–13		19, 247
20–24	59, 165, 248, 293	12–33		165, 187–91
23	45, 98–100, 98n, 99nn, 126, 166, 279, 285, 289, 293–95, 311	12b–13		247
		13		18n, 272
		15ff		18n
23:2, 19	297n	24		268, 283
4	16n	25		19
24	17, 18n, 60n, 76–78, 127, 134, 165, 227, 240–48, 293	26–31		187, 277
		28		268
		29		247
24, 29–31	33	34		45
24–31	96n	40		274
24:2ff	18n	27		88
2–8	277	27:36		94–95
7	277	40		150, 151
10	58n	46		45
35	272	28		141

28:1ff	45	35:9–13	281n
2, 6, 7	58	10	283n
3	283, 283n	11	18, 283, 283n, 289
3–4	281n	12	289
4	16n, 289, 294	27	16n
14	271n, 272, 274, 277	29	293
15	277	36:2	45
29:13f	79	7	16n, 294
15–30	80	20–30	52
24, 29	84	37:1	16n, 294
30:1ff	202	39:7	253n
3	69	14, 17	54
9	69	40:1	253n
25	80	15	54
25–34	80	41:12	54
26	80	43:32	54
27–34	95–98	46:1–3	139
30	80	3	18
31ff	80	47:4, 9	16n
35	79	9	294
43	18n, 80	27b	283n
31	17	48	88
31:1	80	48:1	253n
1, 18	18n, 79, 82	3	281n, 283
2	82	4	283n
4ff	80	5–6	92
6ff	80	7	58
13, 18	80	19	18
14–16	81–84	49:3–4	89
15b	81n	5–7	89
27–32	80	8	89
38f	95n	10	153
38–40	95–98	29ff	45
38–42	80	30	293
39	96	50:13	293
41	80		
43	79	**Exodus**	
47ff	34	1–14	130n
51–54	84	1:7	283n
53	139	2:23–25	261
32:5	16n	3	156nn, 258n, 261
5ff	18n	3–4	261–62
12	272	3–17	130n
28	283	3:1–5	261
33:18–20	110	6, 13–15	262
19f	295	7–10	261
24	264	8, 17	43n
34	51, 150	11–12	261
34:2	46n, 51	12	262
30	46n	13ff	287

3:14	139	7:13	272n
5ff	262	14	275
6:2–3	283, 287	8	239
2–8	281n	11:26–28	273
4, 8	289	14:2	289n
13:3–14	130n	15:10	272n, 273n
18:10–12	302n	12–17	55
20:2	264	16:15	272n, 273n
21:2–6	55	20:17	43n
12, 15–17	181	21:15–17	92
23:23, 28	43n	23:5	58n
34:6	130n	26:5	33
6f	130n	5ff	147n
34:11	43n	5–9	142–43
36:28	290	17–18	289–90
37:25–27	290	17–19	290n
		27:9	289n
Leviticus		28	273
25:38	264, 264n	29:11	290
26:12	290n	23	117, 303
42ff	292	32:6	295n
		40	103, 304
		34:3	222n
Numbers			
6:22–27	272	**Joshua**	
13:22	109	13:2ff	49
29	50	2–6	46
20:14–21	181n	24:2b–13	142,* 143n
21:21–35	156n	11	43n
24:17	153	29	253n
34:2–12	46		
34:24	60n	**Judges**	
		1:10	45
Deuteronomy		3:3	52
1:10	272	5–6	277
2–3	303	8	58n
2:10–12, 20–23	117–18	6–8	17n
12	52	6	261
26	64	6:1–6	261
3:9–13	117–18	11ff	261
4:20	289n	12–14	261
5–11	130n	15–16	261
5:6	264	17–23	262
6:6–9	274	7–8	262
20–24	142–43	13	261
7:1	43n	13:1	261
3–5	277	2ff	195n
6	289n	4–5, 7	195
12–14	273	5	261

13:5, 7	194	20:8ff		256
15–20	247n	**1 Chronicles**		
15–21	262	4:25		64
15–22	211n	5:1		92
14–16	262	1–2		88n
		10, 15ff		62
Ruth		5:19		64
1:8	240	19:6		58n
4:17b–22	152n	21:23		99
		22:9–10		194, 195
1 Samuel		27:17		60n
4:6ff	55			
9:1–10, 16	261n	**Ezra**		
13:3ff	55	7:1		253n
14:11, 21	55	9:1		43n
25	18			
29:13	55	**Nehemiah**		
		9:6ff		143n
2 Samuel		7–8		264n
7	151, 253			
7:9	274	**Esther**		
12	255n, 256	1:1		304n
14–16	274	2:1		253n
8	150	3:1		253n
9–20	151			
11:2ff	151n	**Job**		
16:1–4	87	1:13ff		64n
19:12f	79	2:11		64n
29	87	6:19		64n
24:17	214n	32:2, 6		64n
22–23a	99			
		Psalms		
1 Kings		15		257
1–2	151	21		117n
11:1ff	277	24		257
14ff	151	60:2		58n
32, 34	274	72		95n, 274
13:2	194	72:17		274
17:17	253n	83:7		62
21:1	253n	8		62
		89:29ff		256
2 Kings		110:4		306
4:8ff	207	132:11–12		256
8–17	204–05	12		274
14–17	204–05	136		143n
8:20–22	151			
14:7	151	**Proverbs**		
16:6	151	6:6–11		245
19:34	274	7:1ff		245
20:6	274			

17:2	87	34:9, 14	55
24:30–34	245	18	103n, 258
		18–20	101, 103
Song of Solomon		49:7–8, 28–30	64n
3:4	240		
8:2	240	**Ezekiel**	
		8–11	256n
Isaiah		11:20	290n
7:3–14	195	14:1–20	214n
10–17	256	11	290n
14–17	194	16:3	51
11:1	152	18	257
15:3–5	275	5ff	214n
21:1–17	64n	20:5–6	264
40:9–10	267	23	304
41:8f	201, 265	22:11	174
10	268	25:13	64n
42:11	18	27:20–22	64n
43:1, 5–7	276	36:28	290n
44:2	276	37:23, 27	290n
21–22, 24	276	38:13	64n
45:9–11	276	47:15–20	46, 49
46:3–4	276		
49:1–6	276	**Daniel**	
51:1–2	275	12:7	304
53:5, 10	214		
54:1–3	268	**Hosea**	
3	277	11:8	117
60:6	61	12:12 [13]	58
6–7	64n		
		Amos	
Jeremiah		7:9, 16	39
2:10	64n	9:7	52
4:2	271n		
6:20	64n	**Jonah**	
7:23	290n	1:1–3	224n
11:4	290n	9	55
13:1–11	224n	3:3	224n
11	290n		
18:1–6	224n	**Zechariah**	
22:5	103	8:8	290, 290n
24:7	290n	13	275
25:23	64n	13:8	92
30:19	275		
22, 25	290n	**Malachi**	
31:32	290n	3:12	275
32:8–12	100n		
38	290n		
33:20ff	256		

FOREIGN WORDS AND PHRASES

Hebrew

ʾab	116
ʾadōnāy yhwh	260, 267
ʾaḥar haddᵉbārîm hāʾēlleh	230, 253
ʾaḥaṭṭennāh	96–97
ʾaḥîtennāh	97
ʾāḥiyw	298, 303
ʾkl	81n
ʾal-tîraʾ ʾabrām	254
ʾāmāh	196, 202
ʾanāsîm ʾaḥîm	225
ʾānōkî ʾaḥaṭṭennāh	96n
ʾanšêy hammāqôm	179
ʾarammî ʾōbēd	33
ʾārûr	273
ʾāšām	180
ʾašer yēṣē mimmēʿeykā	255n
ʾeḥāyw	195n
ʾēlāyw	203
ʾelōhîm	202, 256n
ʾel qn ʾrṣ	307
ʾel yirʾeh	233
ʾereṣ hammōrîyāh	238
ʾereṣ mᵉgurîm	294
ʾōt	290
ʿad hayyôm hazzeh	231
ʿal ʾaḥad hehārîm ʾašer ʾōmar ʾēleykā	230
ʿal kēn qārāʾ šᵉmāh	231
ʿam	272
ʿednāh	206
ʿelyôn	307
ʿibrî	54, 55, 57–58
ʿqd	227n
bārûk	273
bᵉkôrāh	87
ben ʾaḥî ʾabrām	298
ben bayt, bn byt	18–19, 86
ben mešeq	285
ben mešeq bêtî	86
bᵉqirbāh	204n
bᵉrākā	275
bᵉrît	283, 288
bᵉrît ʿôlām	288, 289
bᵉtām lᵉbābî ubᵉniqyôn kappay	174
bn byt	18–19
brk	188, 283
dōr	286n
gdl	188
gēr	16
gēr wᵉtôsāb	98
gôy	17, 199
gōyîm	113–14
grš	201
gzrm	103
hāpkî	218
har	231n
hāyāh dᵉbar yhwh	253
hayyeled	196
hazzeh	231n
hûʾ dammeśeq ʾelîʿezer	86
ḥaṭāʾāh gᵉdōlāh	180
ḥerem	201
ḥᵉšērîm	18
ḥizzāyôn	253
ḥṭʾ	96–97
kāʿēt ḥayyāh	205
kî	231
lāh	193n
lammôʿēd	205, 284n
lᵉʿābrᵉkā bibrît yhwh...ubᵉʾālātô	290
lᵉdōrōtām	286
lᵉdōrōtām librît ʿôlām	286
lᵉgôy gādôl	201n
lihyôt lᵉka lēʾlōhîm	289
lizqunāyw	284n
maḥᵃzeh	253
māqôm	179
maṣṣēbôth	110
mᵉqôm šᵉkem	224n
miṣʿār	217
miššām	172
miyyadi tᵉbaqšennāh	96n
mkr	84
mōhar	77, 84
nepeš	304
nᵉśîʾîm	288
nᵉśîʾ ʾelōhîm	293n
ngʿ	174, 181
nśʾ	215, 304
pî šᵉnayim	92
prh	283
qᵉlālā	275
qᵉṭôret	60
qwm	283, 290
rāʾîtā	178n
rbh	282, 283

$r^ekuš$	304	**Akkadian**	
$r^ekušô$	298	abam-rama/aba-rama	40
$rô^cîm$	189	aḫatūtu	71–75, 76, 78
rwm	304	akālu	81n
$s^eranîm$	53	ana aḫati	74
seren	53	ana aḫatūti	72, 74
sph	214	ana kallūti	73
ṣaddîq	174	eqlêti aramima	30–31
ṣḥq	206	errebu	78, 79, 85
śākār	254	gāyum/gāwum	18
$š^edē$-Aram	58	ḫapiru/SA.GAZ	55–57
$śn^{\ni}$	116	ḫaṣarum	18
$š^ebu^cāh$	283	ḫaṭū	96
$š^ekōn\ bā^{\ni}āreṣ\ ^{\ni a}šer\ ^{\ni}ōmar\ ^{\ni}ēleykā$	230	ḫâṭu	97
šipḥah	202	ḥiṭum	95, 96
$šm^c$	99	iḫīṭma iddaššu	99
šōse/šosim	57n	ikkal	73
tispeh	214	ilāni	93, 93n
tissāpeh	214	ilku	98
wa $^abārek^ekā$	272	išme	99
$wayyah^apôk$	218	mār bīti/bītāti	18–19, 87
$wayyaḥṣ^ebehā\ llô\ ṣ^edāqāh$	257	maryannu	52
wayyiqqaḥ	302n	māt kaldu	31
$wayyiqrā^{\ni}\ ^{\ni}et\ š^emô\ P.N$	231	nadānu	97
$w^ehe^{\ni}\ ^emîn$	256n	nadītu	69
$w^ezar^cēk\ gôyîm\ yîraš$	268	nudunnū	81n, 83, 84
yd	304	piṣāti u ṣalmāti	98
$y^elîd\ bayit$	304	qadištum	69n
yhwh	231n, 256n	qištum	86
$yhwh\ yir^{\ni}eh$	233, 238	riḫtu	71
$yihyeh\ ll^ekā\ lē^{\ni}lōhîm$	290	sinnišu ina zittu	89
$yiṣḥaq\ m^eṣaḥēq$	181n	$Sumu^{\ni}il$	63
$yr^{\ni}h$	231	šalšu	91
yrš	201, 255, 261, 268	šittīn	90, 90n
$zar^cakā\ ^{\ni}aḥ^arekā$	283n	[šum] Istar ušêli	102
$zera^c$	261	terḫatu	77, 83
zqn	284n	tupiš P.N ina libbi X šiklu kaspi…talqi	83n
		ṭuppi aḫati	74
Aramaic		ṭuppi aḫatūti	71
$^cgl^{\ni}$	103n	ṭuppi riksi	73
gzr	103	ušêli	102, 102n
mhr	82	zittu	81n
		2-ta qātē	91

SUBJECT INDEX

Abba-el, 102
Abida, 61
Abimelech, 52, 54, 155, 165, 172–74, 177–88, 247, 311

Abiram, 41
Abishai, 41
ABND (Announcement of birth, nature, and destiny), 194, 195

Abner, 41
Abraham, Abram: relation to Amorites, 23–26, 43; etymology of name, 40–42; victory of, 112–20, 296–308; God of, 140, 269; relation to David, 152; as prophet, 174; call of, 183, 247, 265, 276; testing of, 237–39; faith of, 237, 241, 246; "Shield of," 251
Abraham's covenant: with God (J), 100–03, 151–52, 154, 249–69, 311; of circumcision (P), 166, 279–93; with Abimelech, 183–91
Abraham tradition: dating of, 1–4, 148–53; as corporate identity, 2, 276, 310f. *See also* Promises, Blessings
Absolom, 41
Aburahana (ʾbwrhnʾ), 42
Acco, 48
Adbeel, 63
Admah (Adamah), 117, 303
Adoption, 69–74, 78–91
Adumu (*Adumatu*, Al Jauf), 25, 36, 64
Ahaz, 151
Aḥiram, 41
Aḫlamu, 30
Ai, 177
Akkad, 20, 30
Alalaḫ, 8, 10, 23, 44, 48, 56, 57, 90, 102, 111
Aleppo, 32, 45
Amalekites, 43, 150, 305
Amarna Age, 23, 52, 119
Amarna letters, 26, 29, 48, 56, 58
Amaziah, 151
Amenophis III, 31
Ammia, 48
Ammon, 36, 190
Ammonites, 26–29, 150, 217, 220–22, 303
Amor, 50
Amorites (*Amurru*), 20–26, 33–34, 36, 43–45, 49, 50, 56, 106, 118, 178, 266, 267, 304, 305, 307
Amraphel, 113
Anakim, 118
Apparu, 61
Aqaba, Gulf of, 61
Arabah, 62
Arabia, 15, 17, 25, 32, 34, 36, 37, 310
Arabs, 20, 28, 35–37, 60–64, 121, 201, 266, 291, 305, 310

Aramaic language, 32
Arameans, 24, 25, 28, 29–34, 57, 58–60, 121, 150, 293, 310
Aramean sources, 307
Aram Naharaim, 33, 37, 58, 246
Arauna, 99
Archaeological data/evidence, 7–8, 104–12, 309
Arioch, 114
Armenia, 51
Arrapha, 66, 89
Arriwuk, 114
Artemis, 233
Arvad, 45
Ashdod, 45, 53
Ashkelon, 45, 53
Ashurbanipal, 25n, 254
Ashurnasirpal II, 31
Ashurnirari V, 101
Asia Minor, 30, 45
Asklepios, 205, 207
Assyria, 24, 32, 35, 114
Assyrian empire, 24–26, 31, 34, 37, 38, 254, 266, 274, 300n
Assyrian inscriptions, 29–30, 162, 276
Aulis, 233

Baal, 111
Babylon, 8, 25, 36, 40, 114, 115, 305
Babylonia, 24, 31, 32, 34, 113
Babylonian inscriptions, 162, 276
Badᶜ, 61
Balih, 22, 34, 59
Bashan, 117
Batna, 59
Bazu (Buz), 60
Beersheba, 107, 111–12, 121, 140, 141, 168, 184–86, 190, 191, 229–30
Bela, 116
Benjaminites, 15, 19, 22
Beqa Valley, 48
Bera, 116
Beth Ammon, 45. *See* Ammon
Bethel, 112, 117, 140, 141, 223
Bethuel, 77
Bilhah, 69
Birsha, 116
Birth announcement, 261
Birth of Isaac, 192, 202–08, 224, 227, 248, 270, 311

Birth of Ishmael, 192–96
Bishri, Mount, 20
Bit-Adini, 24, 32
Bit-Agushi, 32
Bit-Amukani, 31
Bit-Bahiani, 32
Bit-Dakkuri, 31
Bit-Jakin, 31
Bit-Rehob, 31
Blessing: of nations, 187, 293; by God of patriarchs, 188, 189, 272–76, 283; promise of, 188, 237, 239, 247, 273, 283; of land, 272; of fertility, 273; and obedience, 273–74; and cursing, 274; and king, 274; of Ishmael, 285, 291; as doxology, 302n
Blind motive, 163, 180, 183, 188
Bogazkoi, 8
Burial of Sarah, 279, 293–95, 311
Byblos, 45, 48, 106

Cambyses, 36
Camels, 13, 15, 16, 17, 20, 35, 38, 310
Canaan/Canaanites, 32, 43, 45, 46–51, 150, 151, 169, 178, 221, 223, 228, 243, 244, 264, 277, 288, 307
Canaanite historical records, 300n
Carchemish, 45
Chaldeans, 23, 25, 26, 31, 32, 38, 59–60, 264
Chedorlaomer, 113, 305, 306
Chesed, 59
Childless wives, 68–70
Chronicler, 62, 64, 264n, 305
Circumcision. *See* Covenant
Compositional variants, 162–64, 183. *See also* Doublets
Covenant: making of, 100–03, 191; treaty model, 143, 268; Abrahamic, 151–52, 154; Davidic, 151–52, 153; of circumcision (P), 166, 279–93; with Abimelech, 183–91; as oath, 186, 288; of land (J), 249–69; Horeb-wilderness, 265; "new," 265; breach of, 277; of peace, 277; dynastic, 289–91; of grace, 292
Credo: confessional formula, 142, 143
Crete, 52
Cult legend, 142, 143, 229, 232, 234
Cyrus the Great, 36

Damascus, 31, 46, 48, 255
David, 54, 99, 119, 150–52, 253, 274, 300n, 306, 307
Davidic-Solomonic period/empire, 150–51, 252, 266, 271, 275, 306, 307
Dead Sea, 113, 116, 117, 220
Decalogue, 264
Dedan, 61
Democratization: of royal forms, 289
Demythologizing the sacred, 238
Deutero-Isaiah, 201, 264, 266–69, 275, 276, 278, 311
Deuteronomic corpus/redactor (Dtr), 125, 129–31, 143, 182, 238, 239, 250, 253, 260, 265, 266, 273, 277, 303, 304
Deuteronomy (D), 201, 239, 259, 264, 272–75, 277, 278, 289–90, 303, 304, 311
Dialogue documents, 97–100, 294
Diaspora, 293, 295
Dibon, 27
Didactic story, 246
Dimensions: of the land, 265f
Discursive style, 133, 242–44
Divine guidance, 241, 243, 246, 248
Divine names. *See* Source Analysis
Divine providence, 237–38, 246
Diyala River, 30
Documentary hypothesis, 125, 177
Doublets (variants), 126–28, 133, 134, 162–67, 169–202, 170, 249, 250, 280, 284, 311
Dumah, 64. *See* Adumu
Dynastic oracle, 253
Dynastic promise, 256

Eastern Delta, 266
Edom/Edomites, 27, 28, 35, 37, 45, 52, 62, 88, 118, 150, 151, 295
Edom: settlement of, 26–29
Egypt/Egyptian, 21–23, 25–27, 29, 31, 33, 35, 36, 105, 108, 146, 169, 172, 177, 182, 188, 189, 196, 200, 208, 224, 247, 264–66, 311, 313
Ekron, 45, 53
El, 111, 140, 147, 235n, 288, 306, 307
El Arish, 266
El Elyon, 299, 306–08
El Roi, 288
El Shaddai, 283, 287, 288, 308n
El ʿUla Oasis, 61

Elam/Elamites, 20, 113–16, 119, 305
Elamite empire, 305
Elda ͨah, 61
Election: of Isaac, 201; of Israel, 264–65; of Abraham, 265; of David, 274; in exodus, 289, 292
Elephantine, 66, 74, 82, 84
Eliezer, 244n, 255
Elim numina, 139, 140, 147
Elisha, 205
Ellasar, 114
Elohist, 125–30, 149, 170, 173, 178, 183, 184n, 185, 191, 202, 204, 227, 230, 239, 250, 269, 287, 311, 312, 313
Emim, 117, 303
Entertainment motive: for story, 168, 234
Ephah, 61
Epher, 61
Ephraim, 92
Ephron, 98–99
Epic laws (Olrik's), 132, 133, 137, 138, 160–61, 165, 168–74, 176, 195–98, 200, 235–36, 243–44, 312
Epidauros, 205
Eponyms, 39, 148
Esarhaddon, 45, 254
Esau, 37, 45, 88, 93, 95
Etiological motif, 185, 195, 207, 217–21, 234
Etiology, 1–3, 132, 133, 148, 181n, 184, 185, 187, 190, 193, 195, 199, 207, 217–21, 229, 231–33, 236–37, 240, 294
Euphrates: 20, 32, 44, 46, 58; Upper, 22, 25, 30, 31, 32, 34; Middle, 22, 31
Euripides, 233
Example story, 245
Excommunication, 291
Execration texts, 21, 42, 108
Exile: of prophets, 256–57, 278, 292; community, 264–65, 267–68, 272
Exilic period, 150, 214, 215, 243n, 247, 254, 264–69, 272, 275–78, 290, 292, 310–11
Exodus: tradition, 26, 143, 146, 147, 264, 265, 266, 289, 292; typology, 266
Expulsion: of Hagar, 192–202; of non-Israelites, 201
Ezekiel, 214, 253, 256, 264, 265, 290n, 311
Ezra, 292, 308

Family stories/sagas, 134–37
Feast of Weeks, 143
Feudal service (*ilkum*), 98–99
Fidelity: of oral transmission, 139
First-born: right of, 87–95
Focal concentration, 161, 170, 173n, 174, 176, 195f, 197, 236, 244
Folklore. *See* Oral tradition
Folklorists, 135, 158–59
Folktale, 158, 159, 167–71, 173, 175, 176, 177, 180, 183, 234, 243
Fulfillment: of promise, 205, 206; of prophecy, 259

Galilee: 42; Sea of, 48
Gath, 53
Gaza, 36, 45, 48, 53, 266
Gebal, 62
Gehazi, 204
Geistesbeschäftigung of legend, 137–38
Genealogy, 152, 153, 248, 293
Genesis Apocryphon, 116
Gerar, 52, 54, 75, 107, 108, 115, 147, 150, 165, 171, 172, 177, 179, 182, 185, 186, 188, 189
Geshur, 31
Ghwafah, 61
Gideon, 261
Gilead, 34
Gilgal, 143
Gindibu, 35
God: of the Fathers, 139, 140, 141, 142, 146, 147, 250, 269, 289; of Abraham, 140, 269; of Isaac, 140; of Jacob, 140; of PN, 147
Gods: traveling incognito, 203, 207, 209–12, 213, 216. *See also* Heavenly visitors
Gomorrah, 105, 107, 116, 117, 210, 303. *See also* Sodom
Grant: of land, 225, 259. *See also* Land grant
Grave of the ancestors, 295
Greece, 29, 148

Habur, 22, 34, 58
Hadad, 64, 151
Hagar/Hagrites: as ancestors of Arabs, 36, 60–64, 88; flight of, 68, 70, 154, 165, 192–96, 224, 270, 285, 288, 311;

Hagar/Hagrites (*cont.*)
  expulsion of, 154, 155, 165, 196–202, 238; and Sarah, 192–202, 208
Ḫagaranu, 62f
Haiappa, 61
Hamath, 21, 31, 45, 46, 51
Hammurapi: 113; law code of, 67, 69, 78, 89, 94, 95
Hamor, 51
Hanakiya, 61
Haneans, 22
Hanoch, 61
Ḫapiru/ʿapiru, 26–29, 55–58
Ḥaram el Ḫalil, 295
Haran, 225, 226
Haremhab, 27
Harran, 16, 23–26, 33, 34, 37, 38, 58, 59, 121, 225, 310
Hasmoneans, 308
Ḫatti. *See* Hittites
Hattusas, 8
Hazazon, 43
Hazo/Hazu, 60
Hazor, 44, 48
Healing narratives, 204, 284
Heavenly visitors, 209–12, 247
Hebrews: etymology, 54; used of Abraham, 54, 298, 305; relation to Ḫapiru, 57–58
Hebron/Mamre, 43, 45, 54, 98–99, 107, 108, 112, 117, 140, 151, 204, 207, 293–95, 303, 304, 305
Hejaz, 25, 35, 61
Hellenistic period, 305, 308
Hero legends (*Heldensagen*), 135, 304, 305
Herod the Great, 295
Heth, 45, 51. *See also* Hittites
Hexateuch, 142, 143
Hinzuri, 72
Ḥiram, 41
Historical narratives, 158–59
Historiographic use: of etiology, 220
Hittites (*Ḫatti*), 23, 31, 32, 43, 45–46, 50, 98–100, 113–15, 118, 293–94
Hivites, 43, 51, 111
Holiness Code, 257, 264, 292
Horeb, 274, 292. *See also* Sinai
Horites, 51–52, 118
Hurrians: 51–52; customs of, 71–72, 74
Ḫuru: land of, 27, 48, 50, 52

Hyksos, 22, 107, 108
Hyrieus, 207n

Ibadidi, 61
Iceland, 136
Icelandic sagas, 134–37, 145, 162, 163n
Idea-criticism, 138, 142
Idibaʾili, 63
Idrimi, 48, 56, 57
Imageless cult, 258
Images, 258
Inheritance of land: Israel's, 200, 201, 268, 269
Inheritance rights, 78, 80–82, 86, 87, 197, 248, 255, 257
Iphigenia, 233
Iron Age, 105, 111, 141
Irridi, 102
Isaac: parallel to Abraham, 3, 191; and nomadism, 19; as eponym, 39; treaty with Abimelech, 54, 187–91; death-bed blessing of, 94–95; birth of, 155, 165, 202–08, 224, 263, 270, 281, 311; at Gerar, 155, 176–83; theophany to, 168, 180–82, 190f; election of, 201, 289; sacrifice (binding) of, 227–40
Isaiah, 152
Ishbak, 61
Ishmael: as ancestor of Arabs, 36–37, 62–63; birth of, 155, 192–96, 270; expulsion of, 196–202; promise to, 238, 283, 285, 288; in P tradition, 281–86, 288, 291
Ishmaelites, 18, 28, 36, 37, 62–63, 64, 121, 195n, 199
Ishtar, 102
Itureans, 62, 64

J. *See* Yahwist
Jabbok River, 117, 303
Jacob, 3, 16, 29, 33, 34, 38, 39, 68, 70, 78–84, 88, 92–98, 139, 140, 146, 147, 277n, 283, 287
Jebusite dynasty, 306
Jeremiah, 253, 262, 264, 265, 290n, 311
Jericho, 222
Jerusalem, 108, 119, 153, 238, 300, 306, 308
Jesse, 152
Jether. *See* Itureans
Jethro, 302n

332 INDEXES

Jews, 269, 295
Jokshan, 61
Joktan, 61
Jonah, 271n, 305
Joram, 151
Jordan, 221–23
Joseph, 16, 54, 68
Joshua: Book of, 125, 148, 171n
Judges, 141, 145

Kadesh, 118
Kadmonites, 260, 266
Kedar/Kedarites (Qidri), 36, 63, 64
Kedemah, 64
Kenites, 64
Kenizzites, 260, 266
Kerygmatic framework. See Thematic framework
Keturah, 60, 88
Kikkar of Jordan, 303
King's Highway, 25, 34
Kiriath-arba, 293. See also Hebron
Kumidi, 48

Laban, 33, 34, 42, 77, 78–84, 95–98, 139, 243
Labyu, 27
Lahai-roi, 193
Lament, 260. See also Prayer
Land grant: legal form of, 276, 283, 289
Land promise. See Promises
Land purchase, 289
Late Bronze (LB), 29, 105, 210
Laws: Assyrian, 77, 78, 82–83, 89. See also Epic laws; Hammurapi: law code of; Lipit-Ishtar; Social customs
Leah, 42, 69
Lebo-Hamath, 46, 51
Legend ("saga," Sage), 131–37, 142, 144, 145, 155, 159, 180, 185, 199, 262, 263
Legitimation: of the monarchy, 271, 289, 306
Levi, 89
Lipit-Ishtar: law code of, 89
Literary compositional variants, 183, 197
Literary conflation, 183, 190
Literary criticism: of the Pentateuch, 125–30, 134, 154, 166, 167, 176, 183, 192, 200, 311, 313. See also Source analysis

Literary device/technique, 177, 185, 187, 190
Literary histories (Samuel-Kings, Chronicles), 144
Lot: 42, 113, 117, 170, 190, 247, 276, 297–303, 307n, 313; wife of, 217–19; daughters of, 219;
separation from Abraham, 221–26
Lot-Sodom story, 165, 208, 209–21, 259
Lulahhu, 57

Maacah (Ma'akah), 31, 60
Maccabees/Maccabean, 308
Machpelah, 98, 293, 295
Mamre. See Hebron
Manasseh, 92
Manoah, 261
Marduk, 25
Mari, 7, 8, 10, 14, 15, 17–18, 19, 22, 23, 24, 44, 56, 59, 90, 91, 92, 108, 111, 114
Marriage: Assyro-Babylonian, 69–70, 73, 83, 91; Nuzi, 69, 72–74; Hurrian, 71; Egyptian, 75–76; errebu, 78–79, 85; purchase-marriage, 83–84; to half-sister, 174
Massa (Masai), 63
Mati'ilu, 101
Megiddo, 109
Melchisedek, 299, 301, 302, 306–08
Merits of the fathers, 273f
Merneptah, 27
Mesopotamia, 243, 259, 277n, 307
Mibsam, 64
Middle Bronze Age, 9, 21, 104–12, 309
Midian, 37, 60, 61, 302n
Milcah, 42, 59
Military campaign report, 299–301, 303
Mishma, 64
Mitanni, 52
Mixture: of forms, 232
Moab/Moabites, 26–29, 36, 45, 62, 64, 118, 150, 190, 217, 220–22, 303
Moreh, 224
Moriah, 235n
Mosaic-Sinai tradition, 139
Moses, 139, 261, 262, 288, 295n

Nabaioth (Nabatu/Nabaitu), 63
Nabal, 18
Nabataean: inscriptions, 140, 141; religion, 142

Nabataeans, 36, 63
Nabonidus, 24–25, 34, 35, 36, 38, 264
Naharaim, 33, 59
Nahor/Naḫuru, 33, 59
Naḫrima (*Nḫrn*), 58, 59
Name change: for Abraham and Sarah, 283, 286
Names: Amorite, 39; of Patriarchs, 40–42; of peoples and places, 43–64
Naphish, 64
Narrative structure, 170
Nathan, 253
National tradition, 153
Nebuchadrezzar, 36, 53
Negeb, 37, 62, 105, 106, 107, 117, 121, 170, 223, 310, 313
Neo-Babylonian period: 264, 266, 294, 310; empire, 266, 275
Neo-Hittites, 32, 45
Nephilim, 118
Nile, 22
Nimrud, 70
Nomads/nomadism: and Israelite origins, 9, 228; camel-, 13; definition of, 13–14; in MB I, 13–14, 106; donkey-, 13, 85–94; characteristics of, 14–16, 38; and tents, 14, 19, 20, 38; in patriarchal traditions, 16–19, 37–38, 105, 146, 266, 305, 309; migrations, 19; and agriculture, 19, 187
Norway, 136
Nuzi, 7, 8, 10, 56, 66–74, 86, 89, 90–94

Oath: in covenant making, 100–03, 283, 289
ʿOfr, 61
Omen, 258, 260
Oral tradition/folklore: nature and characteristics of, 1–2, 145, 153n, 158–64, 233–35, 252, 300, 312; and legends, 131–36, 138, 229; and etiology, 132–33, 187; transmission of, 134, 139, 148, 161–62, 164, 233, 294; and pre-literary form of the Pentateuch, 142–48, 242; reliability of, 159; and doublets, 165–79, 183, 311; and tradition-history, 231–37, 242–45, 309–12. *See also* Epic laws
Orontes, 21, 46
Ovid, 207n

P. *See* Priestly writer/code
Paddan-Aram, 33, 58
Palestine, 177, 221, 222, 224, 238, 277, 294, 300, 306, 307n
Palmyrene Oasis, 20
Panels: as compositional structure, 282
Patriarchal age: dating of, 1–3, 7–13, 39–40; as earliest period of Israelite history, 9, 252; as idealistic, 11; as nomadic, 13, 228
Patriarchal religion. *See* God of the Fathers
Pentateuch, 125, 127, 128, 142–44, 164, 270, 297. *See also* Literary criticism
Pentateuchal tradition: history of, 125–28, 143–44, 149, 164; themes of, 127–28, 143–46, 147, 149
Penuel, 140, 283
Perizzites, 43
Perpetual covenant (*bᵉrît ʿôlām*), 286, 289
Persia, 305
Persian Gulf, 32, 113
Persian period, 294, 305, 307, 308
Persian sources, 307
Pharaoh, 173, 174, 180, 188, 247
Philemon and Baucis, 207n
Philistia, Philistines, 19, 43, 48, 52–54, 121, 150, 177–79, 187–91, 266
Phoenicia, Phoenicians, 32, 44, 48, 49, 76, 266
Pillar-of-salt motif, 217–19
Plain of Siddim, 303
Post-exilic period, 164, 293–95
Post-exilic priesthood, 308n
Prayer: of lament/complaint, 254–56, 268; for a sign, 260
Pre-deuteronomic source, 130
Prediction: of childbirth, 205–06
Pre-literary stage: of the traditions, 134, 144, 147, 307–10, 312. *See also* Oral tradition
Priestesses, 69–70
Priestly torah, 286
Priestly writer/code (P): nature of, 125–26, 129–30, 311; in Abraham traditions, 193–94, 223–25, 279–95, 313; relationship to other sources, 194n, 206, 282–91; terminology of, 257, 280, 304, 308n; plurality of sources in, 280, 282; as programmatic work, 292; syncretism in, 307

Promises: to become a great nation, 18; of land, 100, 146, 151, 182, 223, 241, 242, 249, 257, 261, 263–65, 266, 269, 270–77, 281–83, 288, 289, 294; to the fathers, patriarchs, 143, 146, 152, 166, 238, 239, 248, 269–78, 311; of numerous progeny, 146, 151, 249, 256, 268, 269, 272–76, 280–82, 286, 288; of prosperity, 182; fulfilled in Isaac, 188; to Isaac, 199; to Ishmael, 199, 238; of a son, offspring, heir, 203, 225, 249, 256, 257, 261, 270, 280–84, 286; of restoration, 267; and obedience, 288; to be Israel's God, 288–90; of blessing. *see* Blessing
Prophetic oracle, 194
Prophetic reception: of revelation, 253
Prophetic visionary reports, 256
Proselytism, 293
Proto-Arameans, 33n
Proverbs: Book of, 246
Post-exilic period, 164, 293–95

Qarqar, 35
Qatna, 44
Qidri. *See* Kedar
Quasi-historical reporting, 305

Rachel, 42, 68, 93
Ramesses II, 27, 28, 48
Ramesses III, 27, 53
Ras Shamra / Ugarit, 8, 30, 41, 55, 56, 76, 86, 106
Rebekah: name of, 42; marriage to Isaac, 77, 134, 240–48; in Abimelech's court, 155, 176–79, 181
Reed Sea, 143
Rehoboth, 190
Religious syncretism, 287–88, 306–08
Repetition: literary use of, 156, 285, 286, 293, 298, 312
Rephaim, 117, 303
Restoration period, 278, 290, 292
Reuben, 88, 89, 92
Reumah, 60
Re$^{\circ}$u / Ru$^{\circ}$ua, 59

Sacrifice: and covenant, 101–03; of Isaac ("binding"), 227–40; archaeological-historical approach, 227–29, 237; traditio-historical approach, 227–29, 237

Saga, *Sage*. *See* Legend
Salvation oracle (*Heilsorakel*), 254–56, 267–68
Samḫuna, 42
Samsi (Arab Queen), 37
Samsimuruna, 45
Sarah / Sarai: name of, 42, 283, 286; and Hagar, 68, 70, 88, 192–202, 224; in wife-sister motif, 75; burial of, 98, 166, 279, 293–95; and Abraham, 169–75, 178, 179, 180, 185, 188; and birth of Isaac, 202–08, 284; with heavenly visitors, 211; death of, 244; as ancestress, 275f
Sarugi, 59
Saul, 54, 62
Scene-within-a-scene, 259
Scenic dualism, 160, 195, 198
Sea-Peoples, 28, 31, 53
Sefire I, 103
Seir, 27
Self-predication formula, 254, 260, 262, 264, 287
Semi-nomads, semi-nomadism, 13–14, 106, 188, 229
Semitic migrations, 20
Sennacherib, 16–17, 33n, 45, 63
Serug, 59
Seti I, 27
Shalmanezer III, 31, 35
Sharkalisharri, 20
Sheba, 61
Shechem, 29, 51, 107, 108, 109–12, 140, 223, 224
Shemeber, 116
Shiloh, 101
Shinab, 116
Shinar, 113
Shishak, 41
Shosu (*š3sw*), 27, 57
Shuah, 61
Sidon, 45, 51
Simeon, 64, 88, 89
Sin (god), 24, 25
Sinai, 36, 139, 143, 258, 262
Sinai covenant, 291–92
Skeletal outline, 198
Slave / slavery, 18–19, 69–70
Sobah, 31
Social customs: parallels in second millennium, 7–10, 65–67, 251; parallels

Social customs (*cont.*)
  in first millennium, 10, 66–67;
  marriage, 68–85, 89, 93, 94; adoption,
  69–74, 78–91; inheritance, 78, 80–82,
  86, 87; right of first-born, 87–95;
  herding contracts, 95–98; land
  purchase, 98–100; covenant-making,
  100–03
Sodom/Gommorrah, 105, 107, 112, 116,
  208–26, 298, 299, 302, 303
Solomon, 111, 117, 150, 151
Source analysis/criticism: division and
  identification, 125–31, 154–57, 165–66,
  183–84, 191, 202, 229–31, 240–42, 250,
  261n, 270, 280, 312; use of divine
  names in, 125, 129, 156, 283, 284n,
  287, 288, 304; conflation of sources,
  155; relationship of sources to each
  other, 157, 171–75, 186, 282–91
Stability: of introduction and conclusion,
  160, 172, 176, 200
Stages of revelation, 287, 288
Story-telling, 169–70, 174–75, 182, 183,
  196, 243
Structural analysis: method of, 157, 157n,
  165, 312; in Abrahamic traditions,
  168–69, 175, 192–93, 207, 238–39, 252,
  260–61, 282, 286f, 296, 302–03
Suhu, 61
Sumuʾil, 63. *See also* Ishmaelites
Sutu, 30, 57
Synoptic Gospels, 162

Table of Nations, 43, 51
Tamar, 43
Tanis, 109
Taylor prism, 33n
Tebah, 60
Teima/Tema, 25, 36, 63, 64
Tell ed Debᶜa, 22
Terah, 59, 225
Teraphim, 93, 95
Tetrateuch, 125, 143, 148
Thamud, 61
Thematic framework, 142, 146, 166, 182,
  183, 189, 242, 246, 271, 276
Theophany: to Abimelech, 173–74; to
  Isaac, 176, 181–82, 190–91; to Hagar,
  194, 198, 200; to Abraham, 198, 200,
  204, 207, 224, 238, 261–63, 282; to
  servant, 247. *See also* Heavenly visitors

Tidal/Tudḫaliaš, 113–14, 116
Tiglath-Pileser I, 30, 31
Tiglath-Pileser III, 25n, 31, 35
Tigris, 30, 56
Til Naḫiri, 59. *See also* Nahor
Til Turaḫi, 59
Tradents, 158
Tradition-history, 131, 134, 139–48, 149,
  152, 167, 168, 173n, 195, 203, 209, 215,
  217n, 222, 226, 235, 250–52, 260, 270,
  310, 312
Transjordan/Transjordanian peoples, 221,
  226, 303, 307
Transmission variants, 161–62, 164
Treaty, 187. *See* Covenant
Triad, 160, 195, 244
Tyre, 45

Ugarit. *See* Ras Shamra
Umman Manda, 113
Upi, 48
Ur, 8, 16, 20, 21, 23, 24, 25, 30, 34, 38,
  59, 121
Uz, 60

Variants, 161–64, 167, 170, 240, 250.
  See also Doublets
Vaticinium ex eventu, 259
Veneration of patriarchs, 295

Yahwist (J): source of Pentateuch,
  125–30; themes in, 146, 182, 189, 194,
  200, 201, 202, 230, 239, 245–46, 270n,
  271, 277, 287–88, 292, 293, 307; dating
  of, 148–53, 292; as redactor, 170, 176;
  in traditions of Abraham, 183, 186,
  190, 191, 204, 223–25, 227, 230, 250,
  276n, 284–85, 303, 311–13; relation to
  P, 281–83
Yamhad, 102
Yarimlim, 102
Yasbuq, 61

Zamzumim/Zuzim, 118, 303
Zeboiim, 117, 303
Ziba, 87
Zikipa, 72
Zilpah, 69
Zion, 238
Zoan, 109
Zoar, 116, 117, 215, 217, 218, 220, 222n,
  297, 303